Where Thomas Aquinas and Aristotle left off, Richard Thieme picks up, exploring crucial questions about the nature of existence in the technology age and offering cogent commentary about truth and meaning that is as relevant to hackers as it is to CEOs. Thieme is truly an oracle for the Matrix generation.—*Kim Zetter, Wired magazine*

Richard Thieme speaks to the heart. His words more than inspire, they teach us how to think. The reader is left reeling, dizzy with insight.—*Robin Roberts, former head of Information Security R&D, CIA*

These warm but penetrating essays use insights from hacker culture, science fiction movies, religion, military doctrine, psychology, Midwestern family life, literature and history to illuminate unorthodox but deeply profound ways of understanding ourselves and everything around us.—*Jennifer Stisa Granick, Esq., Executive Director, Center for Internet & Society, Cyberlaw Clinic, Stanford Law School*

Richard Thieme presents us with a rare gift. His words touch our hearts while challenging our most cherished constructs. He is both a poet and pragmatist navigating a new world with clarity, curiosity and boundless amazement.—*Kelly Hansen, CEO, Neohapsis*

Richard Thieme is an extraordinary person in every sense. Only someone who has lived different lives and could cope with what those had in stock for him, who sees with soft eyes while reflecting everything around him can express the meta layer of today's world and technology as the one thing it is.—*FX*

WOW! You eloquently express thoughts and ideas that I feel. You have helped me, not so much tear down barriers to communication, as to leverage these barriers into another structure with elevators and escalators.—*Chip Meadows, USAA e-Security Team*

So often your story is my story. I am seldom drawn from lurking on many lists but your recent column draws me to thank you for what can only be called your past oring. You are among my teachers, an actual presence here in this archipelago.—*Michael Joyce, Author of Afternoon, Vassar College*

Richard Thieme combines hi-tech, business savvy and social consciousness to create some of the most penetrating commentaries of our times. I am always eager to read his work. —*Peter Russell, author, "From Science to God"*

Richard Thieme has a knack for not just writing about technology, but exploring and breaking down the intersection between technology, politics, society, and humanity. A needed and unique voice from a unique perspective on the bridge between the techno-mainstream and its counterpart—the cutting edge. With Richard, there is no spoon." —*Simple Nomad (Mark Loveless, Bindview and NMRC)*

These reflections provide a veritable feast for the imagination, allowing us more fully to participate in Wonder. This book is an experience of loving Creation with our minds. —*Louie Crew, Member of Executive Council of The Episcopal Church, Emeritus Professor at Rutgers University*

The particular connections Richard Thieme makes between mind, heart, technology, and truth, lend us timely and useful insight on what it means to live in a technological era. Richard fills a unique and important niche in hacker society!—*Mick Bauer, Security Editor, Linux Journal*

Register for Free Membership to

solutions@syngress.com

Over the last few years, Syngress has published many best-selling and critically acclaimed books, including Tom Shinder's *Configuring ISA Server 2000*, Brian Caswell and Jay Beale's *Snort 2.0 Intrusion Detection*, and Angela Orebaugh and Gilbert Ramirez's *Ethereal Packet Sniffing*. One of the reasons for the success of these books has been our unique **solutions@syngress.com** program. Through this site, we've been able to provide readers a real time extension to the printed book.

As a registered owner of this book, you will qualify for free access to our members-only solutions@syngress.com program. Once you have registered, you will enjoy several benefits, including:

- Four downloadable e-booklets on topics related to the book. Each booklet is approximately 20-30 pages in Adobe PDF format. They have been selected by our editors from other best-selling Syngress books as providing topic coverage that is directly related to the coverage in this book.

- A comprehensive FAQ page that consolidates all of the key points of this book into an easy to search web page, providing you with the concise, easy to access data you need to perform your job.

- A "From the Author" Forum that allows the authors of this book to post timely updates links to related sites, or additional topic coverage that may have been requested by readers.

Just visit us at **www.syngress.com/solutions** and follow the simple registration process. You will need to have this book with you when you register.

Thank you for giving us the opportunity to serve your needs. And be sure to let us know if there is anything else we can do to make your job easier.

SYNGRESS®

Islands
IN THE Clickstream

REFLECTIONS ON LIFE IN A VIRTUAL WORLD

Richard Thieme
September 27, 2004

Richard Thieme

Foreword by Andrew Briney
Editor-in-Chief, Information Security Magazine

KEY	SERIAL NUMBER
001	IVCXZ43ZX6
002	PO5FGLLP94
003	829KM8NJH2
004	CVPLQ6WQ23
005	Q23BV7M3F7
006	65T5T5UUTR
007	63WD3EGH76
008	2TWMKVBVB9
009	62DJTCVB62
010	I95T6TCVY7

PUBLISHED BY
Syngress Publishing, Inc.
800 Hingham Street
Rockland, MA 02370

Richard Thieme's Islands in the Clickstream: Reflections on Life in a Virtual World

Printed in the United States of America
1 2 3 4 5 6 7 8 9 0
ISBN: 1-931836-22-1

Acquisitions Editor: Jaime Quigley   Cover Designer: Michael Kavish
Page Layout and Art: Patricia Lupien

Distributed by O'Reilly & Associates in the United States and Canada.

Acknowledgments

We would like to acknowledge the following people for their kindness and support in making this book possible.

Syngress books are now distributed in the United States and Canada by O'Reilly & Associates, Inc. The enthusiasm and work ethic at ORA is incredible and we would like to thank everyone there for their time and efforts to bring Syngress books to market: Tim O'Reilly, Laura Baldwin, Mark Brokering, Mike Leonard, Donna Selenko, Bonnie Sheehan, Cindy Davis, Grant Kikkert, Opol Matsutaro, Lynn Schwartz, Steve Hazelwood, Mark Wilson, Rick Brown, Leslie Becker, Jill Lothrop, Tim Hinton, Kyle Hart, Sara Winge, C. J. Rayhill, Peter Pardo, Leslie Crandell, Valerie Dow, Regina Aggio, Pascal Honscher, Preston Paull, Susan Thompson, Bruce Stewart, Laura Schmier, Sue Willing, Mark Jacobsen, Betsy Waliszewski, Dawn Mann, Kathryn Barrett, John Chodacki, and Rob Bullington.

The incredibly hard working team at Elsevier Science, including Jonathan Bunkell, Ian Seager, Duncan Enright, David Burton, Rosanna Ramacciotti, Robert Fairbrother, Miguel Sanchez, Klaus Beran, Emma Wyatt, Rosie Moss, Chris Hossack, and Krista Leppiko, for making certain that our vision remains worldwide in scope.

David Buckland, Daniel Loh, Marie Chieng, Lucy Chong, Leslie Lim, Audrey Gan, Pang Ai Hua, and Joseph Chan of STP Distributors for the enthusiasm with which they receive our books.

Kwon Sung June at Acorn Publishing for his support.

David Scott, Tricia Wilden, Marilla Burgess, Annette Scott, Geoff Ebbs, Hedley Partis, Bec Lowe, and Mark Langley of Woodslane for distributing our books throughout Australia, New Zealand, Papua New Guinea, Fiji Tonga, Solomon Islands, and the Cook Islands.

Winston Lim of Global Publishing for his help and support with distribution of Syngress books in the Philippines.

Preface

Like so many projects that wind up becoming meaningful, *Islands in the Clickstream* started by accident. A society of professional engineers asked me to write a monthly column about the Internet. Then I offered the column to friends, colleagues, and clients as an e-mail list. Then my web site, www.thiemeworks.com, was named a USA Today Site-of-the-Day (remember when the net was so small that 365 sites/year was a big selection?) and the list grew. *Islands* has been read by thousands of subscribers in more than sixty countries and many more on the web. It has been published in print in Hong Kong, Bangkok, Singapore, Toronto, Djakarta, Dublin, Capetown, and many other places.

From the beginning, the genre or literary form of these writings has been ambiguous. They integrate attributes of a number of prior forms — columns, essays, articles, opinion pieces, prose poems, sermons — but because they were distributed online, none of those genres really fit. Writing a column that elicits immediate reader response feels like preaching, which I did in Episcopal churches in Utah, Hawaii, and Wisconsin for sixteen years. But while interacting with online readers overlaps with the intellectual products of both oral and written cultures, really, it has created a new thing, a different thing, and we do not yet have a critical vocabulary with which to discuss it precisely.

Over seven years, then, a dynamic community gathered around these writings, focused on the larger questions of our lives related to how technology was changing us.

I left the Episcopal priesthood, feeling that I was suffocating in a thought-world that did not want to examine the profound changes in identity and human destiny resulting from technological transformation. Re-reading early *Islands*, I think I was mostly right. I was obviously trying to find words for a vision of transformation that could be articulated only through metaphor. While some *Islands* are therefore prose poems, they were electronic prose poems first, not printed text as you have here. Editing these into a printed book was translation from one medium to another, and another, and I encourage readers to be mindful that the originals showed up on a monitor, glowing in the middle of the night, and reader and writer alike often felt each other's presence through the spooky wires.

But these are sermons too, in the sense that sermons form and inform a community that chooses to gather to hear them. There is a moral center, articulated in unconventional images of hackers and hacking culture and the emergence of new life structures on the edges. Images of new kinds of human beings in new kinds of communities could not be forced back into the molds from which they burst forth. These Islands are not about saving the appearances, but transforming them.

So having taught English lit and writing in my twenties, and ministering in diverse cultures in my thirties and forties, I was fortunately able to transform myself once again in my fifties and learn from people a lot smarter than myself. My professional speaking, while always focused on the human dimensions of change due to technological transformation, gravitated toward information security and intelligence because those folks understood best our brave new world of nested simulations at all levels of the fractal. They built and manipulated that world and I learned from young hackers and old intel pros alike how they did their work. I am deeply grateful to all of them for their wisdom. They taught me that mathematics and mysticism, deception and deep devotion, irreverence and piety, are polysides of the same geometric shape.

Those colleagues, along with diverse readers, fellow writers and editors, friends and companions from around the world, formed a community of learning, but I must salute especially my pals from Def Con, Black Hat and the Galway Group. Among those who said or did the right thing at the right time to help me understand, I think of Jeff Moss and Ping Look, Simple Nomad, Hal McConnell, Marcus Ranum, Dan Geer, Peter Neumann, Becky Bace, Ken Olthoff, Robin Roberts, Clint Brooks, Brian Snow, Bruce Schneier, Jennifer Granick, Sol Tzvi, Terry Gauditus, and Dave Aitel. Then there were Weld and Mudge, Jericho and RFP, Carole and Jon, aestetix and Grep, FX and aj, dear lost krystalia and good old William Knowles, Dead Addict and the real Dr. Evil, Space Rogue, Conrad Constantine, and Ralph Logan, even se7en and Carolyn, unexpected allies who taught me to be more careful. Some I have never met in the flesh, like Kathleen Jacoby and Louie Crew, South Africans Jenny Marais, Marthinus Bester, Adrianne Arendse, and Peter Walsh, Sushma Sharma in Bombay, See Ming in Malaysia, and Sue Ashton-Davies in Sydney. Writers Joel Garreau, Michael Joyce, Lew Koch, Gary Webb, and Bill Scott helped me understand life in the Matrix, and there were generous folks like Edgar Mitchell who shared the larger vision of life he discovered coming home from the moon on Apollo 14. He and others helped me know, at the end, that we were not all crazy. Speaking buddies Susan RoAne, Ivy Naistadt, Fred Gosman and Eileen McDargh were always close at hand, and with more than words, Isabel Morel, Jean Maria Arrigo, Lia Nirgad, and Joe Carson taught me to recognize real courage. Thank you for your patience to my editor, Jaime Quigley, who always had an e-mail cookie ready at hand when it was needed, to Andy Briney of Information Security who trusted me, and to Dion

Black of South Africa Computer Magazine, who gave me a great run. Day-to-day support, of course, comes always from those we love first and last—my beloved wife and best friend Shirley, our splendid offspring Julie, Barnaby, Rachel, Aaron, Scot, Susan, and Jeff and their companions, and Art, my big brother still who shows me as he did when we were young how to maneuver through the rocky fields of life with dignity and grace.

—Richard Thieme

About the Author

Richard Thieme is one of the most visible commentators on technology and society, appearing often on CNN radio, TechTV, and various other national media outlets. He is also in great demand as a professional speaker, delivering his *Human Dimension of Technology* talk to over 50,000 live audience members each year. *Islands in the Clickstream* is a single volume "best of Richard Thieme." Richard is a business consultant, writer, and professional speaker focused on the impact of computer technology on organizations, societies, and one's own self. Richard's columns convey simple wisdoms in an otherwise complicated industry, exploring topics from innovation to evolution, modernization to love. *Islands in the Clickstream* portrays the intricate relationship between man and machine, drawing on Thieme's experiences as an Episcopalian priest, a father, a public speaker, a traveler, and a man to convey the message of "living on the edge."

Contents

Chapter 6 Mostly True Predictions 151

Chapter 7 The Psychology of Digital Life:
Identity and Destiny 181

Chapter 8 Political Implications 221

Chapter 9 The Dark Side of the Moon and Beyond . .287

Foreword

One of the perks of being a magazine editor is that book publishers send me free copies of their latest releases, hoping I'll publish a review. Since my magazine focuses on computer and Internet security—the hot topic of the day—there's no shortage of titles to choose from. As I write this foreword, there's at least 10 Syngress titles on my bookshelf, ranging from *Building DMZs for Enterprise Networks* to *Ethereal Packet Sniffing* to *Security Assessment: Case Studies for Implementing the NSA IAM*.

These are all fine books, mind you. Each is chock-full of important information that helps technology professionals do their jobs better. The problem is that you may see Syngress on the spine of this book and assume it belongs with the others.

This book will not help you improve your job performance. It will, however, improve your life performance.

On the surface, this book is a selection of Richard Thieme's "Islands in the Clickstream" essays, 144 in all, originally published on the Web between late 1996 and spring 2004. But that's only what this book *is*. It's not what this book is *about*.

This book is about the complex interrelationship between humans and technology: how you interact with computers, how the Internet influences how you learn and perceive reality, and how technology both helps and distracts you from knowing thyself.

This book is about power and knowledge, insight and inspiration, culture and experience, physics and metaphysics. Like space and time, there are multiple dimensions to this book. I'll wager you've never read anything quite like it.

The first essay in this book was written in December 1997. It's called "Ferg's Law," which simply states: "When everything can go right, it will, and at the best possible moment." This is more than an optimist's overhaul of Moore's Law. It's a prophecy fulfilled as the pages of the essay—and the book—unfold.

"Ferg's Law" is about a scuba diving trip Richard took off the coast of Maui, a dive that took him out far beyond the stability of land and its creature comforts. At one point in the dive, Richard swims past the edge of the coral reef, where the sea bottom drops off dramatically. As he floats in liquid nothingness, something unexpectedly moves near him, something large and dark and unknowable. It is there, at the edge of his perception, and then just as quickly it disappears into the blackness.

The experience is akin to Sartre's description of spiritual nausea, a feeling of existential angst. Only when Richard has retreated to the safety of the reef does he regain his sense of self.

In many ways, this story is a metaphor for the rest of the book. Richard is an edge-dweller. Throughout these essays, he carries us center-dwellers to the precipice and forces us to see what's there in the inscrutable darkness. What he reveals is a glimpse of the "unknown possibilities…the invitation of life itself." He then brings us back to safety, flush with insight into the wonders that lay beyond.

So you may ask, "What does this have to do with technology?" The answer is: everything. Technology is a medium that continually expands our notion of "limits." Richard once wrote an article for *Information Security* on the topic of "wearables." In this piece he suggested that our reliance on technology has become so pervasive that we'll soon be wearing clothing and eyeglasses and shoes all connected into one great computer network. In fact, it won't be long, he argued, before we all have surgically implanted computer chips guiding how we interact with the world: how we see and learn and shop and drive and experience…and exist.

In "Field of Subjectivity," Richard tells the story about a man who already embodies this futuristic reality, a quadriplegic with a brain implant that allows him to move a computer screen cursor with thought. In these and other stories in this book, "the network that is the computer is linked to the human network.…A complex pattern of energy and information, life blurs at the edges into its raw materials."

Carbon and silicon, inextricably entwined. The only difference is the interface.

Much of this book is about the relationship between content and context, which Richard argues is ultimately the same thing. Caveat lector: some of this content is heavy lifting, not because the text is inaccessible but because it pushes us into unfamiliar territory, forcing us to consider new realities and new ways of thinking.

I mention these things not to scare you away but to entice you further. During her lifetime, Emily Dickinson wrote more than 1,800 poems. Because she rarely ventured out of the confines of her small room in Amherst, MA, her poetry reads like a diary, an intense survey of the landscape of her mind. Many of the essays in this book have the same character and quality. Unlike Dickinson, Richard is a world traveler. But his writing is similarly personal and undeniably human in its exploration of inner space.

As for the context, that's where the action is: the point of departure between what Richard writes and what it ultimately means to you. I tell you this: If you approach this book like a miner—digging deep, taking your time—you will discover a wealth of gold. Nuggets of wisdom surface in every story, for Richard is a master at aphorisms. Here are a few of my favorites:

"Cyberspace is 'space' indeed, brimful of gods and goddesses, angels and demons waiting to become flesh. That's neither good nor bad, it's just what's so." –"The Voice of the Computer"

"The seed contains the tree. The seed knows from the moment of germination where it is headed. It may twist in response to drought or food, but [it] knows how to become the mature tree. And we know how to become who we already are." –"Detours"

"Identity is destiny. Our task is to name ourselves, and we will, once we know who we are.... We are who we think we are, but we can always—with a mere word—transform who we think we were into who we choose to be." –"A Model for Managing Multiple Selves"

"The older I get, the more obvious it is that those who think they have a clue do not have a clue, and those who know they do not have a clue have a shot at having a clue." –"A Miracle by Any Other Name"

"Technology has defined cultures and shaped behaviors forever. The technologies that evolved out of organic molecules, we call 'nature.' Those that we made, we call 'culture.' Both kinds are melting into a gray area we don't know how to define." –"The Simple Truth"

Richard also is a raconteur, and his all-too-infrequent yarns are the best parts of this book. Some stories are long, woven throughout the essay; others are short vignettes that punctuate an insight or observation. In all cases, Richard's narration provides glimpses of the grace and beauty of everyday experience.

There's the story about his days as an Episcopal priest, rallying his congregation to engage in a special event; about his interaction with young computer enthusiasts (a.k.a. hackers) at the DEF CON and Black Hat conferences; about stargazing at his uncle's farm in Indiana; about sipping latte in a coffee shop with his son, gazing out onto the darkening woods beyond the Milwaukee River.

These stories are "visionary"—vestiges of Richard's memory and past experience that, in the act of retelling, transport us into timeless moments of intense clarity. In this way, Richard's content becomes our context.

I'm not embarrassed to admit that two stories actually brought me to tears. Both concerned "near-misses" with Richard's family. The first, "The Simple Truth," is about his wife's diagnosis with breast cancer. The second, "A Miracle by Any Other Name," is about how his son survived a near-fatal motorcycle accident.

Exactly what happens in these stories I'll let you discover on your own. What I'm concerned about here is context. Richard writes with grace and humility in these stories; he is clearly awed by the way that life spontaneously gives, and then takes away, and then gives again.

The first time I read these stories, particularly "Miracle," I was enveloped in raw emotion. I ceased to be a "reader," a passive receptacle into which Richard poured his words. I was with him. I was a spiritual participant in his experience. If you read this book deeply and with an open mind, the same thing will happen to you.

One sentence from "Miracle" had particular significance for me. After reading it the first time, I scribbled it down on a piece of paper and taped it to my computer monitor, where it remains today:

"Even in normal, mundane life, compassion and generosity of spirit are the glue of the universe."

This is Ferg's Law, expressed not as a concept, but as an imperative. But for me, it's more than that. It's Thieme's Theme, a living symbol of "the human dimension of technology."

As I work, there it is, a simple scribble affixed to the edge of my computer, out of focus but never out of sight. I do believe it improves my life performance.

—Andrew Briney
Boston, May 2004

Andrew Briney is editor-in-chief of Information Security magazine.

Chapter 1

Introduction: This is the Way the Internet Works

Ferg's Law

December 16, 1997

This is how the Internet works:

Somebody in Kentucky finds one of my columns and asks to reprint it in a newsletter. Our e-mail exchange begins a dialogue—in this case, on Buddhism, on-line spirituality, and how the world works—and in one of her exchanges, my email pal says, "I have a friend, Jim Ferguson, and this is Ferg's Law:

When everything can go right, it will, and at the best possible moment."

If that's how computer networks work, that's how life works too. Too many bugs or breakdowns or glitches can obscure the bigger picture: that a vast complex network pretty much works most of the time.

We are pulled in different directions by conflicting evidence—jokes abound about differences between optimists and pessimists. But this is deeper than that. This is about the tentative conclusions on which we base the way we live our lives. If the evidence were simple, our decisions would be simple too.

This weekend I am in Iowa for a family funeral. It was funeral weather, overcast and cold. We walked through snow to a hole in the ground and stood shivering in the zero wind as final good-byes were said. I have attended dozens, no, hundreds of funerals, and always there is a desire for some sign from beyond the grave. And always there is silence; the answer to our questions is silence. And finally the silence becomes the question to which we must discover our own answers.

Do you ever get sick and tired of the negativity, the whining and complaining about the Internet, computer technology, and where the world is headed? Negativity is a mode of control, a way to try to make people, places, and things fit into a manageable box that we can sit on or manipulate.

I guess we need to live within safe boundaries.

I was diving once in an isolated bay on Maui, far beyond Kapalua, where tourists seldom venture. I was swimming out over the dark corrugated texture of the reef. Toward the mouth of the bay and the open ocean, curtains of blue and deeper blue shimmered in the distance. Suddenly the reef ended and the drop below me was hundreds of feet to a sand bottom. I felt the loss of safety represented by the reef but kept swimming. Then, beyond the curtains of deep blue, something moved. Something large and dark. I didn't know what it was, and the next moment it was gone.

I turned and swam back toward the reef. Once I was over the coral again, fear of that unknown dark form disappeared. The reef represented the safe harbor we are always seeking, while the open water, with its unknown possibilities, was the invitation of life itself.

It is time to leave our comfortable rooms, the poet Rilke wrote, every corner of which we know, and venture forth into eternity.

Web sites that work best lead us by easy stages from accessible text or images into the complexity of information patterned beyond our comprehension. Our thinking, too, leads by degrees of precision from simple manageable truths to the highest level of insight.

When the Buddha became concerned that his teaching was at a depth most people would miss, he began salting his stories with "sandbox stuff," the elementary truths we need to remember: Don't hit. Be gentle and respectful. Don't take other people's stuff.

Murphy's law is a true description of life at the lowest level of insight. Things that can go wrong usually do. The tendency to break down seems to be woven into the fabric of all of our projects, and woven as well in stars that explode and galaxies that disintegrate. The myth of heat death articulated by physicists, our current high priests of cosmology, turns the silence of the grave into the silence of the universe.

Standing at the grave, I remember a friend, an artist named Jim. He called me from the hospital to say he was dying, but before I could visit, he checked out for a final European trip with his mother and sister. In a tourist hotel in London he lay down and died. They shipped his body back home for burial.

The following week I was discussing plans for a memorial service with his companion. Now, Jim always had long wild hair, shoulder-length hair, in keeping with his artist image. As I spoke with his companion, there suddenly emerged, on the edge of my consciousness like a stained glass window brightening as the sun came out from behind a cloud, Jim's face. And it stayed there, unlike a memory, as the conversation continued. But for whatever reason, his hair was very short.

Then he faded, and moments later, his friend mentioned that, to please his mother's conventional sensibility, he had cut off all his hair before leaving on that trip.

We can explain that event at any level of precision, but whatever our interpretation, something emerged in my consciousness that told a more precise truth than we usually know how to tell.

Negativity is a way to build a dark familiar reef under our swimming selves. The ultimate source of negativity is a lack of courage and a need to make the darkness safe, rather than risk the open water.

At the graveside—and we are always at the graveside—the powerful compression of grief tunes our awareness to what matters most. We surrender to the truth that is always there, but buried—our deep longing for forgiveness and mutual forbearance, our desire to surrender the need to be rigid or right. The readiness is everything, and during those moments of exquisite timing—tolled by a clock that ticks to a different rhythm—we know that when everything can go right, it will, at the best possible moment. We weep, and we embrace one another. The universe is gregarious and welcoming. We are built to live in space that is gateless, unbounded, free.

Chapter 2

Computer-Mediated Living: The Digital Filter

Games Engineers Play

Our societies teach us the skills we need through games. Playing games is how we explore possibilities, identify talents and interests, learn values.

Computer games are exploratory toys for investigating the digital world, but more than that, computers themselves are toys. The games—how they are built, how they change us when we play them—are a catalyst in the evolution of new ways of framing reality.

This summer at DefCon IV, the hackers' convention, I met a hacker who was twenty years old, an "old man" of hacking who had retired to mentor younger hackers.

He had been programming computers since he was six, when he programmed Pong on a computer that had no long-term memory. He remembers the sense of loss when, after weeks of Pong-playing, he turned it off and lost his beloved binary companion.

That young man is in the vanguard of a new variety of human being. I call them homo sapiens hackii.

Culture is a human simulation of genetic evolution. Our cultural symbols transmit what we learn to new generations. But we are changed by the structures of our cultural forms as well. The structure of our information systems determines how we think, how we frame reality. Our symbolic structures engineer our psyches in their own image and determine how we hold ourselves as possibilities for action in the world.

That hacker and his generation are trained from infancy to understand the world in ways dictated by computers. From one point of view, human beings are transitory forms for organizing and disseminating information, and the form of that organization is determined by our symbiotic relationship with our symbol-manipulating technologies, in this case, computers.

Thirteen years ago I bought an Apple II+ computer. I began playing with LOGO, a child's version of LISP. I learned about recursion working with LOGO and I learned how to write a program to substitute verbs and pronouns for the ones typed by a user.

Joseph Weizenbaum at MIT had just used LISP to write ELIZA. ELIZA is a simple substitution program, a natural language parser, that enables a computer to simulate the responses of a Rogerian therapist. Such therapists repeat back to the client what they think they have heard, thus returning responsibility for their own thoughts and feelings to the client.

People playing with ELIZA, however, responded as if they were engaged in an intimate conversation with a real person. Weizenbaum was upset and wrote one of the first "dire warning" books about the future of computers. The power of the computer to elicit projections was so strong that he felt we were in danger of losing our souls to the new machine.

Games like ELIZA taught us to project a gestalt or complete personality onto a machine that mimicked the response of a human being. Playing with ELIZA taught us how to relate to GUIs, expert systems, and smart agents. We were learning to relate to our projections as if they were external to us in order to interact easily and effectively with complex computer applications. We were learning a technique for manipulating symbols that tamed the power of the machine and made it manageable. This is analogous to playing word games as we learn to read and think in text.

A natural language parser, exchanging words and seeming to respond intelligently, generated a new genre of interactive fiction. The classic text games of Infocom stand out as the best.

One day my son and I were playing Hitchhiker's Guide to the Galaxy. I had written fiction and taught English literature, so I understood how text worked. Symbolic textual narratives disclose horizons of possibility far into the distance, toward the horizon of the text.

Playing that Infocom game disclosed a different kind of horizon, a different set of possibilities. The structure of the game itself, determined by computer programs using recursion, changed me as I played it. The game created a new way of framing myself. I learned to imagine my psyche—and my life—more as a recursive fractal landscape than a straight line.

Of course, a single game did not do all that at once. But playing computer games and experiences like that did disclose new possibilities for being human. The structure of that game is identical to the structure of the Internet. Networks, like fractals, are self-similar at all levels. Networks of networks look like networks. Interacting with networks changes how we think.

Newer games using movies and 3D-VR do the same for visual space. One of my recent favorites is The Pandora Directive, an interactive mystery. One of the "game spaces" is a virtual board room with beautiful indoor trees. As I watched the screen, my hand rolling the mouse across the pad, I noted the smooth glide of the trees past a large window. I turned and looked back at the green leaves and the gleaming wood of the conference table. Then I rolled out into the hall.

The following week I walked into a boardroom in a bank building that had similar trees, a similar table, a similar window. I felt myself rolling through the real room. The perceptual framework through which I experienced the real room was an image of the virtual world.

These days, reality often imitates a simulation, rather than vice versa. Playing games like The Pandora Directive creates the psychic space through which we subsequently filter our experience. The computer program programs us.

So look to electronic games for signs of what's coming next. Children play Doom while their parents guide smart bombs to bunkers in Iraq. Adolescents build robots while their parents use remote vehicles and telepresence to explore radioactive "hot spots."

On ESPNet SportZone, there's a virtual world of sports. Web surfers use data from the site to create fantasy teams. They channel aggression into fantasy football or baseball, a harmless pastime that helps bleed excess energy from a civilization with too much time on its hands. They do this by substituting images and symbols for the real thing.

But then, what else is civilization, but the weaving of a web of images and symbols which we mistake for reality? The first spoken and written words did the same. The game has not changed, but computers take the game to a higher level.

Dreams Engineers Have   *January 1, 1997*

I confess: I'm a right-brain guy in a left-brain world. Images and visions are more real to me than abstractions; I see the future more easily than things that are right in front of my face.

That's why I started writing fiction and sold my first story at seventeen. "Pleasant Journey" was published in *Analog Science Fiction*. It concerned a man selling a virtual reality machine to carnivals. Attach the electrodes and off you went into your own dream world. The carnival owner tried it out and didn't want to come home. He wanted to stay in that virtual world forever.

I studied liberal arts. We were taught that art and literature mattered most; the loss of an art object or literary work was a tragedy. I remember a professor weeping for the lost plays of Aeschylus.

No one grieved, however, for the streetlights of Cordoba or the sewers of ancient Rome. Engineers were practical people. Their plans and drawings were seldom the subject of scholarship, and I don't recall a single course in the art of engineers and how their dreams made real the infrastructure of our civilization.

In part, that was because plans and drawings were never intended to last. Once pencils were invented, plans were sketched in a way that smacked of impermanence, like something you'd draw on a napkin over lunch.

Leonardo da Vinci filled his notebooks with plans and sketches. Those notebooks, detailing his dreams, nearly disappeared after his death. He never published their contents, and more than thirty volumes were left to his friend Francisco Melzi with instructions for printing. Instead, they were ignored for fifty years. When the contents were finally published in 1880, most of Leonardo's inventions were obsolete.

Bill Gates paid a small fortune for those notebooks. He knows that they're works of art worth owning—the dreams that prefigure our civilization.

It was no accident that my first short story was science fiction and concerned technology enabling us to transform our lives. That's the story of our century. The invention of electronic media, including the Internet, is the infrastructure that enables dreamers and thinkers to be creative in new ways. The medium is so much the message that we're writing stories about the technology rather than the life it enables us to live. That will change, though. The technology, the new media through which we express ourselves, will fade into the background and become as transparent as contact lenses.

Henry Petroski's magnificent study of "The Pencil" begins with an anecdote about Henry David Thoreau. Thoreau made a list of everything he needed to take to his life in the woods but neglected to mention his pencil. Yet his pencil was always in his pocket, and the Thoreau family business was ... making pencils.

Science fiction is the way men and women in the twentieth century have dreamed of the future. I like to joke that people who call me a "futurist" are mistaken. I describe the present to the ninety-five percent of the population that hasn't arrived at it yet. That's why it sounds like the future. It's the same with science fiction, which depicts what is right in front of our faces, coming around the corner at the speed of light. It sounds like the future only if you aren't noticing what's happening.

I recently did an article on biometric identifiers—retina and iris scans, finger-scans, voice prints, and the like—the use of part of us to stand for all of us. Those digital artifacts don't merely stand for us, however, they become us in the social, economic, and political worlds to which they allow or deny access.

Our word will not be believed when a retina scan refuses to allow us into a secure area, just as we used to say "photographs don't lie," believing the photo rather than the person in the photograph. Now that photos and all forms of information can be digitized, we know that photos do lie. A photo is no longer worth a thousand words, when both words and images are subject to digital manipulation.

What will it be like in the virtual world in which digital bits "pass" for ourselves? Let's go further. What will it be like when the information that IS ourselves—i.e. our DNA code, the drawing or blueprint that is expressed as our bodies, our minds, our lives—can be uploaded and stored?

Teleportation used to be a sci-fi subject. Two years ago, an international group of six scientists confirmed that perfect teleportation is possible—but only if the original is destroyed.

That theoretical work changes teleportation from a sci-fi scenario into an engineering problem. If the information that constitutes our pattern or code can be transmitted and replicated, and the original is destroyed in the process—who arrives? Who is left behind?

In a similar way, we used to think the hard copy was the "real" document and photocopies were secondary. Now we think the virtual copy stored in digital memory is the "real" document and hard copies are mere images of the real one.

The network is the computer, and Marvin Minksy reminds us in "The Society of Mind" that turning over a multiplicity of representations in our collective mind instead of getting stuck in one way of seeing things is what we mean by thinking. The network does the thinking. We are merely cells in a single body, and a human being alone—like a stand-alone computer—is a brain in a bottle.

A Zen monk held up a cup and asked what was most important about it. One pupil said the handle, another the bowl, but the monk shook his head. "The most important thing about the cup," he said, "is the space it creates."

The Internet is "space" brimful of possibility and potential, but by virtue of its structure it organizes the form of our thinking and dreaming. Engineers who build the infrastructure of the world create the space in which we live and move and have our being, and we don't even notice. It's as transparent as Thoreau's pencil. We don't even know who's dreaming any more—the individual or the collective mind—and what is science fiction or science fact. We DO know that engineers dream up our space and, like God in creation, are everywhere present in our lives but nowhere visible.

That's the cost of making sketches with pencils. That's the cost of using materials that decay. But then, everything decays, and digital images are more transitory than drawings. Art and artifact converge, and those who build the infrastructure that informs how we dream are at least as creative as Aeschylus, as practical as Leonardo, and as holy as that Zen monk.

Fractals, Hammers, and Other Tools   *May 1, 1997*

"Fractint" was one of the first computer programs I encountered that blew my mind. (It's still out there on the Internet. Download one if you want to try it.)

Fractint generates fractals. Fractals are mathematical formulae that express complex realities with elegant simplicity. Before computers, you had to have a mathematician's mind to grasp the relationships expressed by fractals. Computers enabled those relationships to be represented pictorially. Fractint lets you generate images of fractals, then cycle through them in thousands of colors. The vision of a fractal in action is stunning.

Fractals often resemble natural objects. Simple formulae using recursion generate images that look like branching trees, clouds, coastlines, or fern leaves. Seeing those images on a computer changed how I saw the natural world. The computer generated a different framework for looking at and comprehending the "real" world.

Fractals are self-similar at all scales. If you magnify a section of a fractal, then magnify a section of the section, each one looks similar, like nested wooden dolls. You can keep magnifying smaller and smaller pieces until the image on your monitor is part of something so big that, if you spread it out, it would stretch from the sun to the orbit of Jupiter.

My wife, who is not a geek, looks up now as we walk through a forest or watch clouds move through the sky and says, "Fractals."

This brave new tool, the computer, is programming us to see things in its own image, teaching our minds as well as our mouse-clicking hands how to use it.

Fractint also taught me that intellectual property, as we have known it, is over.

The concept of an "author" who owned "a work" was invented by the printing press. The printing press fixed words in text and created an illusion of permanence, of something solid "out there." Students are still surprised to learn that Shakespeare did not care to preserve his plays for future generations. "Writing for future generations" was a conceit thinkable only after we had fully internalized the world of text and thought of books as artifacts that would last.

Fractint was built by "the Stone Soup Group," programmers who worked collaboratively online. Some of their names are known, but many are anonymous. A collective wrote the program, just as monasteries in the middle ages created illuminated manuscripts without a thought for the name of an "author" or owner of the "intellectual property."

Cultural artifacts like laws (copyrights, patents) are tools, too. The shape of those tools is determined by our information systems. After we use them a while, we forget that, and they become part of the background noise of our lives.

Fractals are a metaphor not only for what I see "out there" but also for what I observe within myself. Every decade or so, I discover myself in transition to another developmental stage. Each stage includes and transcends everything that came before. My psyche is self-similar at all scales, just like a fractal.

Civilizations too go through developmental transitions, and they too include and transcend everything that came before.

Back to tools.

It is said in the consulting business that "to the person with only a hammer, every problem looks like a nail." Our tools structure our perception and frame our possibilities for action.

I asked a number of engineers what tools they commonly use. All but one said "computer" first. Some added T-square, or architect's rule, or drafting board. Only one said pencils, although everybody uses them. Nobody said "words."

We only notice the new tools in our kit, like computers. Those we were given by prior generations disappear into the background. I notice that most people mean by the word "technology" the technology that has been invented since they were children.

The evolution of tools and the hands that hold them or the minds that think them is a cultural process. It's a chicken-and-egg kind of thing. Did we build more complex bridges and buildings because we had better tools, or did tools evolve that enabled us to build better bridges and buildings?

Computers simulate what we call "reality" but that "reality" in fact consists of nested levels of symbols. If it were a mathematical formula, it would look like this:

```
Digital images => printed texts => writing => spoken words.
```

They are all artifacts, nested in levels of abstraction that are self-similar at all scales.

Before human beings spoke, the artifacts or tools generated by language did not exist. We call those tools ideas, concepts, mental models. They are the building blocks of our maps of reality. Because they are modular, we can connect words and ideas in an infinite number of ways and build more ideas, more elaborate frameworks or architectures that enable us to build everything from bridges to religions.

Like speech, writing, and print, the computer is a tool that shapes our perceptions into forms the computer can use. If we are to bring our ideas to the computer, they must be expressed in language the computer understands.

To the person with a hammer, everything looks like a nail. To human beings who use speech, the only ideas we can think are ideas we can express in words. In a civilization transformed by interaction through networked computers, we will think only thoughts that can be simulated or manipulated by the worldwide network that mediates communication and the flow of information.

The world looks to me like fractals because Fractint taught me to perceive the world as fractals. Engineers will build the kind of infrastructure that networked computers teach and enable them to see and think. The physical structures of civilization will be determined by how computers think.

Everything is a flowing, the Greek philosopher Heraclitus said. If only he'd had a PC and a program like Fractint! Then he could have seen that flowing in thousands of colors, fractals of unimaginable simplicity and complexity, self-similar at all scales.

I bet it would have blown his mind.

Not a Book   *February 14, 1998*

The way things are when we are very young becomes the standard against which all of our subsequent experience is measured. Our parents are the measure of all men and women. Our city is the measure of all cities. And the process by which we receive information is the model of what "feels real."

I grew up in the world of printed text. Television soon intruded, but not at the very beginning of my time. So television has always been secondary to the world of print. Every significant shift in how I understood the world came through books. My undergraduate education, with its focus on literature and philosophy, was internalized as a complex matrix of cross-referenced meanings into which everything after somehow had to fit.

That experience was reinforced during graduate work in preparation for sixteen years of Episcopal priesthood. Although there was plenty of experiential learning during that intense time, the formal part included the application of literary analysis to religious texts. That illuminated in a deeper way how ultimate meanings are mediated symbolically in and through the text, how literary genres embody meaning even before the text is examined. A short story or written letter, for example, can not mean the same thing as a history or mean it in the same way.

Then came a kind of epiphany. Playing interactive text games with my oldest son on an Apple II+ in the early eighties, I realized that interactive fiction mediated meaning differently than books. But more than that, I realized that the experience of interacting with software on a computer changed me too. And the genre of the application or program embodied meaning even before the program ran.

Our way of thinking about ourselves and reality, how we hold or structure ourselves and reality as possibilities for action, is recreated in the form of the information technologies with which we interact. Networking with networked computers morphs print-text-people into digital people.

And print-text cultures into digital cultures. In addition to the transformation of our social, economic and political structures, the computer revolution is transforming religious structures as well. Images of ultimate possibility that had once been spoken, then written, then printed, are becoming digital, and so are we, inside. Everything is connected to everything else. Everything goes through the looking-glass together.

So a new generation is rising in a digital world, or more precisely, inside its internalized representations. Spacetime and causality inhabit that world in a different way. We are riding that wave at the edge of the curl, where emergent realities, like Michaelangelo's unfinished marble sculptures, are struggling to free themselves from the medium which is both their liberation and necessary constraint.

Someone asked recently, was I writing a book about all this? Which is also a way of saying, yes, you may be communicating through email lists on-line, but will it be published in print?

We don't have the language yet with which to describe what we're doing here. It's as if we are learning to scuba dive and move in several dimensions at once. But we still talk like walkers.

Compare it with speaking, for example. A speaker is aware of the energy ebbing and flowing between themselves and the audience. They ride the intensity, or cognitive dissonance, or laughter home to its source in the heart of the collective created by their speaking. The transaction transcends the individuals involved, making a momentary community. Speech is alive as long as speech endures. A tape of the presentation is a fading memory in a dead medium.

Writing, before electronics, used to be aimed at an audience, too. But the audience was an anticipatory echo in the writer's head. The best writers created an audience by naming realities just as they emerged so the writer's words became the normative thoughts of a person or culture. Then middle-ground writers rode the hump of the bell-curve, telling an audience what it already knew, reinforcing the consensus reality of the crowd. Then tail-end writers described what had already passed, or was passing, to a grieving audience clinging to a corpse.

"Writing" in this medium, however, is speaking as much as writing. These words glow only when the monitor is on, a window against which both noses are pressed. We can print the digital text onto paper, but that doesn't turn these words into "print." That is more like taping a speech than book-publishing of old.

We can feel but not see one another out there. The thoughtful nuanced responses of "readers"—almost in real time—co-creates bonds of real community. Our words are reciprocal, echoing in one another's minds. The residue of real conversation.

I flash back to those biblical studies. Jesus disdained writing. A man of an oral culture, he wrote only once in the scriptures, mocking the scribes and their newfangled ways. Yet Christianity happened because he was turned into his own image in textual form. The horizons of possibility that can be disclosed only in writing happened not only for Christians but for Buddhists, Taoists, and all the others connected to beings who emerged in human history during that narrowest band of time that coincided with the emergence of writing itself. But the representations in writing would not have felt real to the real Jesus. For people in an oral culture, writing felt artificial, once removed, the way voices sounded on the telephone when it was first invented.

Electronic interactivity is real, as real as speaking or writing books. But it may not feel real for a while. A generation is rising that will experience this way of framing reality as foundational. Speech won't disappear, nor will writing. The Internet will not "replace" books. Interactive electronic media redefine the relationship of symbolic content to itself and to the human symbol-user, redefining how we use other media.

And we, songbirds in our digital cage, will be both liberated and imprisoned by our pixilated glyphs.

Darling ... Are You Real? *March 7, 1998*

It is not news that sex sells. Nor that new media often contains sexual images. The first books, the first photographs. The initial demand for VCRs in the home, creating a critical mass that enabled Hollywood to sell films. And, of course, the Internet and other digital media.

Because pornographers routinely shoot scenes from various angles to meet the needs of diverse markets, their works are a natural for Digital Video Discs. Users can click on a scene from as many as sixteen angles and zoom in and out. It's an interesting mix on the user's part of a need for control and a need for the person or image they manipulate to be or seem to be real.

A "cyberbabe" sits in a cubicle responding to typewritten commands from people paying four dollars/minute to interact with her image in a small square on their monitors. Writing for *Wired*, Frank Rose wondered what request the women received most. It was not an explicit sexual act but ... "Would you please ... wave?"

Users need to know that the tiny image of the dancing digital doll ... is real. They want her really to be there ... and to be there just for them.

The mind boggles. The human soul is so hungry for self-deception that it will swallow a pig whole.

Those who manufacture pornography are not known for originality. Quite the contrary. Their clients do not want innovation or creativity, they want predictability, and as a genre, pornography is nothing if not predictable. Scenes follow a formula— A x B x C x D x E—the letters corresponding to increasingly explicit scenes, the Xs corresponding to filler that lets the user inhale before the next escalation. That's why, for example, Vladamir Nabokov could argue that Lolita was not pornographic.

The requests that flow to those booths are easily anticipated. Like children who never tire of hearing the same story read the same way, and who, in fact, will object if a single detail is different. Clients want the reassurance of the same scenario played out the same way again and again, the comforting touch of a mother as much as a lover.

It ought to be simple then, for programmers to set up a database of video clips indexed to specific requests, the variations linked to a natural language interface. When the client types, "wave your hand," the clip of a lady waving will respond. A hundred and fifty waves with each hand ought to handle the most suspicious client.

The next step, of course, is not to have an actor in the box at all. Just as session musicians who counted on studio work for their livelihood have lost jobs to synthesizers, a digital cyberbabe can be constructed, pixels of light substituting for an image of a real person. It isn't the pixels but the pattern, after all, that makes an image a symbol, and it's a symbol that clients of a digital interface—any digital interface— need.

Come to think of it, we used to call them "movies" ... images of shadow and light simulating the appearance of real people so well that we had to keep saying to ourselves, "it's only a movie" when we grew afraid or developed a crush on a leading man or woman—someone who wasn't there, never had been there, someone who hired a staff to pretend to be them when we wrote to confess our love.

People used to think characters in novels were real too. The Dickens character, Little Nell, was followed by serial readers the way soap operas are watched on television. A crowd burst into tears when the captain of the ship, bringing the latest installment to New York, told them that Little Nell was dead.

The film noir masterpiece *Body Heat* depicts a lawyer deceived by the words of the women he loves. He says at the end—speaking perhaps for all of us— "experience shows that I can be convinced of anything." We have to pinch ourselves to remember that there's no there there, that Mattie Walker is only a digital image of someone pretending to use speech to deceive.

The best "hacking" is done by people working on people, not computers. It isn't data that's relevant but patterns constellated by data, the intentions of a person in a particular context revealed by the way the data seems to connect. "Social engineering" is the art and craft of eliciting information by pretending to be someone you're not, acting a role that blends with its surroundings so seamlessly it seems real.

Which is one reason why businesses have replaced countries in the post-Cold War global free market; why intelligence and counterintelligence, information and disinformation, are axiomatic to remaining viable in a knowledge economy. The local head of the FBI just joined an accounting firm to work on fraud. A well-known hacker joined a big six firm as head of their Tiger Team. Business, intelligence, and hacking are in many ways indistinguishable.

It must have started with speech. One can imagine the shock when speech emerged in human culture and people realized that someone could know their thoughts merely by speaking with them, asking questions. Speech must have become a means of hiding in the same instant it became a means of self-disclosure. Truth and lies are Siamese twins, joined at the lips.

So the difficulty of knowing—"darling, are you real?"—is not new to the digital era. Nor the celluloid era of Meg Ryan as Sally in that restaurant scene. Our experience does show that we are capable of believing anything, that our primitive brains take appearance at face value. Betrayal and self-deception as a cause of human tragedy are as old as story and song.

And so ... I want you to know that I am here, I am real, I am saying good-bye ... and waving my hand toward the monitor as I fade into the distance ...

Sneaking Up On Ourselves   *March 14, 1998*

It's pretty tricky, sneaking around a corner which is really the surface of a sphere until we are looking at the backs of our eyeballs with our own eyes. That's what happens, though, when we see ourselves seeing ourselves.

That's a metaphor, of course, and metaphors are horses we can ride only to the limits of out-thinking. Then they dissolve into thin air, and we ride on, horseless, like cartoon roadrunners racing off cliffs into the middle of the air.

That may sound philosophical or even religious, but we really have to think like this at the dawn of genetic engineering. The practical applications are immense. We are beginning to engineer our very selves, to see our subjective ways of framing reality and being in the world as modular objects to be manufactured and enhanced. In the next century, it's going to be bootstrapping big time for the human species as we see ourselves as an image in our own collective mind, an image to be designed and executed. Not exactly a computer program, but something like it.

Subjectivity is hardwired into our brains. That's a way of saying that reality is an illusion, that even thinking we can slip outside the limitations of our minds—an experience that Zen adepts call enlightenment—and see what we are and what we are not; that is, see ourselves from a point of view outside ourselves. Maybe that's an illusion, too.

But think about this. A patient with a brain disorder was being probed with electric needles. Doctors were hoping to locate areas of the brain that were the source of her seizures. When the tip of the needle touched a particular area, the patient began laughing; laughing not at the needle or in response to it, but laughing enthusiastically and spontaneously because … well, because they were all so funny.

"Funny?" asked the doctor. "What's funny?"

"Well," she laughed, looking at them with sparkling eyes, "the way you're all just … standing around … is … so funny!"

I remembered a friend experimenting with hallucinogens. The drug induced a chemical change that enabled him to clearly see that everything in the world was … show business! He couldn't stop laughing at the spectacle of role-playing human beings acting as if their social masks were real. Whatever anybody said, he cried out, "That's show business!" and dissolved into laughter once again.

Another time he saw the earth as a marble, like the photograph of our planet from the moon or the world seen as a walnut in the hand of her Lord by Julian of Norwich in her anchorite's cell. He saw the earth as a sphere from the center of which a million lines radiated to the surface, at the end of which walked tiny ant-like humans crying, "Mine! It's mine!" Again, he laughed hysterically. And who can blame him? Humans, part of creation, acting as if they owned abstractions like "land" … acting as if their consensual hallucinations were reality instead of a game they agreed to play.

Stephen Hawking gave a lecture last week at the White House. Through the "wonders of modern technology," a RealAudio/Video feed played on my desktop as I worked late into the night. His electronic voice said that, unlike *Star Trek* or *Star Wars*, in which contemporary humans are projected pretty much as we are into the distant future, he believed we would recreate ourselves through genetic engineering in ways we can not even imagine. People think of obvious things—greater strength, longer lives, faster reactions—extensions of how we are today that make us more and better, but not significantly different. The real differences will be created and discovered as we learn how laughter and sadness happen, how we construct reality, how we use mood-altering experiences like religion, therapy, entertainment, other kinds of cultural play, how we mean and be.

Some religious sentiments—like wonder and awe—have been linked to particular genes, just as parts of the brain, altered by the use of spiritual tools, ingestion of chemicals, or electric probes, spontaneously generate visions that are ... so funny! Visions of human beings acting as if we are gods on a planet from the oceans and mud of which we have only recently crawled. This civilization is a phase, not a conclusion, and this earth is just one of the millions of planets teeming with life that will teach us how we have evolved and maybe even why.

Zen masters disdain the use of chemicals or electricity to induce enlightenment. They prefer traditions handed down for generations. That perspective may soon seem quaint and archaic. Genetic engineering will enable us to say at a particular level of description—a level appropriate to biochemistry and biomechanics—what happens when we experience that which emerges in our subjectivity as awesome, wonderful, or funny. We will create emotional states of being that do not yet have names. The beings that feel, think, and experience those states—our intentional progeny—will embody that unimaginable next step for the species of which Hawking was speaking.

Ethical reflection never anticipates the breakthroughs that make us sit up straight, nor do legal niceties. What will we do when our mistakes exhibit behaviors we don't want? Put them in reservations or safari parks, use insect-like cameras to scuttle among them, amusing ourselves with their wacky antics?

Will they vote? Will anyone? And will it matter?

Self-transcendence is an emergent behavior, perhaps the beginning of a rising spiral of possibilities—the ability to see ourselves from a meta-perspective, sneaking up behind ourselves and watching ourselves think thoughts like these. The ability to experience the disappearance of what we call our "minds" as we realize that "no-mind" simply describes what's so. The ability to decide what's funny or whether to include humor at all in our genetic program ... some of our progeny roaring with laughter at the mere thought while others stare, uncomprehendingly, wondering what's so blanking funny.

The Air We Breathe   *March 21, 1998*

Nothing is harder to see than what we believe so deeply—we don't know we believe it. That's why a frontal assault on our core beliefs is always doomed. Our minds think they themselves are under assault, rather than the beliefs they have adopted. Defenses go into gear to rationalize, minimize, or deny what they're hearing. Or else the anomalous data creates so much cognitive dissonance that our minds just plain shut down.

The degree to which technologies of communication, surveillance and control have insinuated themselves into our everyday lives is striking. Here, in Wisconsin, a bill just sailed through the legislature that expanded the state's authority to collect health care information. The bill allows the Office of Health Care Information to collect and publish financial and other data from doctors and health care providers, in addition to data gathered from hospitals and ambulatory surgery centers.

Remarkable to those concerned about "function creep" was the lack of concern on the part of the public. Everyone pretty much lined up on behalf of "efficiency and safety," the two horsemen of the apocalypse of privacy rights. The legislative committee was "stacked" on behalf of the measure and the public was informed after the fact, the bill having been called suddenly the night before the vote was scheduled.

This is a holographic slice of a bigger picture. The technologies of linkage and the power of those who profit from using them are the true weapons of information warfare. That war is fought not with lasers and satellites patrolling the "high ground" of earth orbit, but in the trenches of our daily lives. Because the consequences of ubiquitous linkage are often invisible, the average person—with limited time and mental resources—is unaware that the hidden infrastructure of a global political economy is being built out of the mundane data of their lives.

When I recently pressed a career officer in the intelligence community about practices that alarmed me, he maintained that those practices were illegal, hence nonexistent. After a few drinks, however, he acknowledged that many intelligence agents find it easier to ask forgiveness than permission and act accordingly. That all-too-human reality is why we will pay in the future for every time we refuse to speak or act in the present on behalf of the privacy that secures our freedoms. Without secure boundaries, there are no individuals … and no individual rights. The primacy of the collective, a by-product of the transforming power of information technology, is paradoxically entering mainstream thinking as a priority through the political action of those who believe they are supporting a conservative, business-friendly agenda.

It's as if the entire world is joining NATO, justifying Cold War behaviors by invoking the Evil Enemy. But unlike the Cold War, when there was at least another camp, the "other side" now means people anywhere who oppose the converging self-interested policies of the military-industrial-information complex.

And now for something completely different.

Children's toys are often an early warning system in which the future first becomes visible.

"Sound Bites" is the name of a new technology recently introduced at the annual Toy Fair in New York. A person inserts a lollipop in a Sound Bites holder, and when they bite into it, sound vibrations travel through their teeth to the inner ear where they are heard as normal sounds. This magical effect lets snackers hear music (guitars, drums, or sax), special effects, or voices.

The notion of slipping advertisements, propaganda, or suggestions into our meals is so outrageous I expect it to be adopted without a murmur. One imagines voices coming into our heads from every artifact. Deserts in the company cafeteria, basketballs as we dribble down the court, even sex toys will all have something to say. Everything will be a means for communication … as indeed, everything already is, but today those messages are still mostly implicit, while these songs and jingles will be as explicit and close to our noses as bumper stickers.

And now for something even more different.

A hobby in which I have indulged myself for years is the investigation of UFO phenomena. It's an interesting puzzle, requiring cross-referencing texts in the public record with the confidences of mostly plain people, as well as intelligence agents, air force officers, and airline pilots. Like most amateur investigators, I find that ninety per cent plus of what I read or hear can be explained or discarded, but, again, like most, the remaining accounts are pretty compelling.

Yet what interests me as much as the data is the widespread ridicule that greets even the most reasonable statements about the phenomena, e.g. it is worthy of investigation, if only as a psychological or sociological phenomena. One hesitates even to mention this interest because of that predictable response.

Such ridicule apparently became official policy around 1953. Before that, for five years (1947-1952), UFO phenomena was taken seriously by governments in public and private. An early head of Project Blue Book stated that behind the Pentagon's closed doors, the argument was not about the reality of the phenomenon, but whether its origins were Russian or extraterrestrial. A widespread wave of sightings in 1952 became the point of departure for a policy of debunking. Air force fighter pilots and commercial airline pilots alike have told me how they and their colleagues learned quickly not to risk their careers or reputations by making a report or going public with details of an encounter.

Indifference to the erosion of privacy rights … candy that sings to our brains … a policy of public ridicule that discredits innocent people.

It is easier than ever to engage in sleight-of-hand, manufacture a consensus, and manipulate dissent. Yet the truth, too, is boosted by technology. Truth too sings to our brains, and the linkage technologies that magnify the fictions we seem to need to sleep easily in our beds will disseminate as well the truths that fuel our hunger for knowledge and our passion to be free.

Voyagers   *April 4, 1998*

When we come to a new place or enter a new environment, the landscape looks all of a piece, and we have to learn how to see it in depth and detail. Our interaction with new cultures teach us over time how to understand them.

When I moved to Maui in the eighties, I lived about thirty feet from the ocean. From the sea wall, when I looked out at the channel that defined the "pond" among our islands, all I could see was ... water. Nothing but water. Of course I could see the other islands and waves breaking over the reef, but the ocean itself looked like nothing but undifferentiated water.

Last week I returned to Hawaii to speak about spirituality and technology. During the week, two canoe builders from the Marshall Islands made a public presentation and shared some of their lore, long believed to be lost. "Some of our navigators are trained to detect six different swells by the feel of the canoe," one said. Others specialized in navigating by the stars or weather. Despite the repression of their culture (and the explosion of dozens of nuclear bombs on their islands), they had somehow kept alive the knowledge of their ancestors.

They used tangled knots to map the night skies and learned to discern the subtle interacting patterns of the swells by crouching in canoes on what looked to a "mainland haole" like a perfectly calm sea. When they looked out at the ocean, they saw a lot more than just water.

After a few years on the island, I could see at a glance the direction of the wind and the complex pattern of the currents. That told me what I was likely to encounter when I went diving or spear fishing. I knew where the fish would be feeding, how to co-exist with morays and reef sharks, how to use the surge of the sea to slide without effort toward prey. The angle of the sun under the water, the length of the seaweed, the Kona wind, all correlated with the feeding habits of the fish on the reef. The sea resolved itself into a complex, richly detailed environment.

What I learned was child's play compared to the intimacy with which islanders know the ocean. Someone who lives on the mainland might look at the water and

see only a barrier, whereas islanders see an open invitation, a whole world waiting to
be explored, both highway and home.

The journey into ourselves and the journey into the symbolic landscape that
defines our culture—of which the Internet is an emblem—are the same journey.

When we first turn inward, the landscape may seem opaque, but as we explore
through meditation, prayer, and other disciplines, we too discover both a highway
and a home.

It's as if someone who spent his or her entire life on land hears for the first time
about the ocean. The word calls forth an image and a desire, and that is the beginning of the journey. We make our way to the water's edge and look out at the singular immensity of it. Some plunge in; others take scuba lessons, letting others coach
them. When we first snorkel or dive on a tropical reef, we are amazed at the beauty
and variety of living forms. That beauty can be a trap. If we're not careful, we stay at
that depth instead of learning to go deeper. If we do go deeper, new worlds are disclosed, new possibilities for communion with ourselves, others, and the universe of
which we could not have dreamed.

Over time, we become as comfortable under water as on land, and our framework expands to include the sea and what is under the sea as well as the narrower
life lived in the air. We move back and forth between them easily. Air and water
become dimensions of a single reality.

The first explosive photos taken by the Hubble telescope showed the richness
and complexity of space, a technology disclosing new possibilities for action. As
those possibilities percolate into our consciousness, what it means to be a human
being is transformed.

That's how it felt too when I downloaded my first browser and tumbled like
Alice into cyberspace, emerging from underground eight hours later, oblivious to the
passage of time.

The Internet is a vast sea of possibilities, a symbolic representation of our collective consciousness and our collective unconscious. When we explore the Net, we are
exploring ourselves. The Net is a swirl of invisible currents. We learn to surf swells of
meaning that surge back and forth like the sea. We learn to follow currents of information, feeling the swells interact in subtle and complex ways. We become voyagers
in the sea of information in which we are immersed, plunging through high seas in
outrigger canoes. We make our own tangled starmaps that represent and remember
for us how to find our way home.

There is ultimately only ourselves to know. When we try to understand everything, we do not understand anything at all, observed Shunryu Suzuki. But when we
understand ourselves, we understand everything.

The Internet is not so much a set of skills as it is a culture. Guided by mentors,
learning like wolves to hunt together, we learn how to hang in the medium. The

images on our monitors are icons, windows disclosing possibilities far beyond our home planet. Inner and outer space alike are explored by tele-robotic sensory extensions, revealing the medium in which we have always been swimming.

Consciousness is the sea, and the sea is all around us. The secrets that we think are lost are simply waiting to be found: supra-rational modes of knowing. Connection and community of such depth and complexity, we grow giddy with delight. A network in which we are both nurtured and fulfilled, each node of the web a reflecting facet—like one of Indra's jewels—reflecting each of the others and the totality of the whole.

Densities   *April 11, 1998*

Steven Hawking noted in a netcast from the White House that the next generation of humans will live inside a common sense world of quantum physics the way we have lived inside a Newtonian landscape. "Common sense" is simply what we're taught to see, he said, which is why new truths always appear at the edges of our thinking.

Or, as George Bernard Shaw put it, "All great truth begins as blasphemy."

Is it any wonder we are all beset by "cognitive dissonance" and see our reality-frames flickering the way clairvoyants (excuse me, "remote viewers") see images of distant sites? One moment we are living happily inside Newtonian space, walking down a straight sidewalk toward a right-angled corner when ... poof! ... with a puff of smoke, we experience ourselves bent along a trajectory like light pulled by an immense gravitational tug. Then we remember that how light bends *is* gravity and what we thought was a "pull" is simply the topography of energy wrinkling and sliding into whorls of various densities.

In a museum the other day I watched a marble spiraling down a funnel of smooth wood, circling towards the vortex. I thought of light travelling along the curves and bumps of space-time ("the universe is shaped like a potato," Einstein said, "finite but unbounded.") I thought of gravitational lenses, created when galaxies that are closer to us magnify and distort more distant galaxies.

Einstein predicted sixty years ago that a massive object would bend and intensify light, generating multiple images or stretching an image into an arc. When everything lines up just right, the distortion becomes a perfect circle, like the galaxy pictured last week in Science News (Vol. 153, No. 114).

That's the long view. Turn the telescope around to see what's happening right here in our own digital neighborhood.

Web sites are best characterized not by size but by density. A map of cyberspace would look like millions of galaxies and a map of the traffic between sites would look like a photo of electromagnetic energy across the entire spectrum.

A browser is a knowledge engine that organizes information in flux so it appears momentarily frozen. A site such as Yahoo that links links is a kind of gravitational lens that boosts distant clusters into the foreground. If we could see ourselves inter-acting in cyberspace, we too would look like energy pouring through our monitors and moving at the speed of light toward densities around which our interests coa-lesce. Our monitors, like worm holes, let us bypass the long way around.

Organizational structures, including web sites, are dissipative structures like whirlpools that retain their shape while exchanging energy and information. Humans, too, are modular structures of energy and information that interface over the Internet. That map of the energies of cyberspace is really a map of our mind.

Not quite common sense yet, is it? Words slip, slide, decay with imprecision, T. S. Eliot said of his efforts to fix, in poetic form, the world he discerned. In the world of printed text, the illusion that words and meanings are fixed is magnified. The same words in pixels are obviously transitory. Our media, too, function like gravitational lenses, magnifying meanings intrinsic to their nature. The digital world builds a "common sense reality" congruent with the quantum world, communicating by its very nature that words, meanings, and all things slip, slide away.

We build this island for ourselves in the always sea and comfort ourselves with the illusion that we are on dry land.

The trajectories of the energies of our lives—how they are organized, aimed, and spent—are determined by our deepest intentionality. How we intend to live our lives is how we wind up living them.

Cyberspace is a training ground for learning to live and move at the speed of our minds, the speed of light, to inhabit a landscape that morphs or changes shape according to our will, intention, and ultimate purpose.

The "sites" in our minds grow denser when our intentions coalesce like millions of marbles rolling simultaneously toward a single vortex. Space, time and causality may be woven into the very fabric of our minds, as Kant said, but in a quantum landscape, causality is a very different animal. An effect can precede its own cause.

Which is exactly how our minds operate.

Consciousness is always consciousness for or toward some end, always an arrow aimed toward a potentiality or possibility. As a mental construct, the image comes first. The effect precedes the cause and causes the effect to come into being. That's why some think consciousness is the origin as well as the goal of evolution.

A recent reflection on maps, filters, and belief systems brought from a reader an account of the moment he realized how much the Mercator projection exaggerated the size of the European community. He recalled the first time he looked at

Buckminster Fuller's Dymaxion map that looks at the world from the North Pole rather than the equator. From that point of view, the world is seen as a single unified landmass. The world has never looked the same to him since.

Consciousness manifests itself in a visible medium like the Internet so we can see it. We can never see the thing itself, because there is no thing there. Nothing. But we can see some of the infinite ways it manifests itself. Working and playing on the Internet is one way to practice handling ourselves in a quantum world that is fluid, modular, and interactive, a trans-planetary world, a trans-galactic world emerging on the edge of the grid in which we have been living. That grid contained reality in nice neat boxes. But the grid is flexing, morphing like an animation even as we look at it, turning into another of its many possibilities. Seen, of course—it's only common sense, isn't it?—from just one of its infinitely many points of view.

Waiting for the Bard Group   *April 18, 1998*

A mother stood behind her young son in the computer store, her mouth hanging open. The bloody carnage on the screen was taking its toll. I guess she had never blasted her way through Quake, wiped out the wounded in Postal, or just plain kicked digital ass in Doom. Maybe it was the way the gore spurted or the bodies burst apart that got to her. She looked worse than her son's digital victims.

The kid, meanwhile, oblivious to her concern, used every weapon he could to shoot, chop, grind and puree his way to the next level.

"What do you think?" I said.

"I can't believe it! It's disgusting."

"Mom!" the kid said, distracted for a moment. "Come on!"

Shaking her head, she walked toward a quieter aisle, muttering about violence and video games.

I don't think of video games as spanning a spectrum from less to more violent but from simple to more complex. Video games are new literary genres, representations of reality rendered in an interactive medium. We're waiting for a Shakespeare to take that mayhem and use it to transcend the form.

Maybe that kid is the one who will do it.

Start counting bodies in the great Shakespearean tragedies and you quickly run out of fingers and toes. Sword fights poking holes in people as if they're pincushions, death by poison, people gouging out their own eyes, husbands and wives murdered, suicide by drowning—how quickly the body count mounts. Add the history plays, with their vivid depictions of war and assassination, the murder of children, all that torture, and the blood runs deep.

Because Shakespeare wrote plays so relatively close to the invention of the printing press, the idea of plagiarism, with its attendant beliefs that an "author" owned his "work," something fixed in print, as tangible as a rock or bottle—that idea had not yet evolved. Shakespeare wrote when western civilization was becoming something else. Not every artist is blessed with living in such a rich transitional time, when everything is obviously morphing. But we are.

Shakespeare used stories that everybody knew. There were no lawsuits when plays were based on the same sources. They worked up the histories, myths and tales in different ways. Shakespeare simply used the material to create works of such complexity and depth that the meanings never cease. Each generation finds more to explore.

Motivation in a Shakespeare play is never just one thing. When someone acts, there are always multiple reasons. The Bard tried to do justice to a reality that is multi-valent, heterogeneous, complex.

I thought about that while reading of the commercial failure of a recent movie, "Primary Colors." There were lots of reasons for the thinly disguised story of our oversexed American President to fall flat, but among them was the simple fact that the movie was too intelligent. It depicts the best and the worst of American politics. It may be good filmmaking, said the Wall Street Journal, "but some in Hollywood believe that it may have made the protagonist too nuanced for a broad movie-going public."

Added director Alan Pakula, "Hamlet has never done across-the-board big business in small towns, that I know of."

But Shakespeare did make plenty of money in his day. He gave the groundlings in the cheap seats what they wanted—lots of violence, bawdy stories and sexual innuendo, jokes that would get you hauled into court these days—but he gave minds that thrived on richness and insight something too.

Shakespeare was no Puritan. He told us what he thought of Puritans in Twelfth Night, when Sir Toby Belch told the hypocrite Malvolio, "Dost thou think because thou art virtuous there shall be no more cakes and ale?" The Bard took his murderers and drunks as he found them, interlacing their words and actions in so many ways and on so many levels that those who liked action had plenty to relish, while those who loved to explore more deeply never reached the end.

I talked to that kid after he racked up a big score. He loves Doom and Quake, but he also plays games like Ultima and Diablo, simulations like Civilization, space operas like Wing Commander, sci-fi noir like Blade Runner and Pandora's Box. He also liked You Don't Know Jack, the clever Jellyvision game that uses words the way the great Infocom games did, to create multi-dimensional worlds in which we quickly find ourselves immersed.

The forms and genres, the archetypal myths and quests are already there. It's not the violence that makes most video games something less than excellent art, but that the depth and complexity of character and conflict implicit in the genres has not yet been mined. The questing heroes of familiar narratives, adventuring into caves or forests or interplanetary space, have not yet morphed into Hamlets or Lears.

Chaucer too used stories that everybody knew but had the Canterbury pilgrims tell them, changing what and how they meant. Then he interlaced both stories and pilgrims in a new way, cross-referencing images in an intricately layered texture. Re-contextualization. That's the name of the game. Genius sees what everybody sees but sees it more deeply, in a different context. When we—playgoers and readers of old or game players of today—are drawn into the vision, the context of our own lives and understanding is transformed.

The enemy is not simulated violence. The enemy is a mentality that says art or entertainment—plays, films or video games—must be dumbed down to the lowest level. Give the groundlings their violence and sex (and admit that we're all groundlings to a degree) but let the games evolve in the hands of masters into interactive digital experience brimful of meaning and mystery. Let the genius-team bring insight and wit to the virtual gardens waiting to be watered with more than blood so they can bloom with thousands of imaginary flowers.

Humanity Morphing   *May 2, 1998*

A funny thing happened on the way to the grave: It disappeared.

But first, as they say, a word from our sponsor.

The primitive brain that has helped us survive does not easily release its grip. As much as we like to think that we live in the outer domain of our brains, we snap back into the reptile stem whenever we think we're threatened. Then we react to things that look or sound like other things as if they *are* those other things. I guess looking silly when you run from a car backfiring is better than dying the one time in a hundred the bang is really a gunshot.

After a threat, it takes most brains a few hours to get back up to "flow" level and lose themselves again in the pleasures of creativity and selflessness. Reality has a way of interfering with our higher pursuits, and the brain thinks it knows which things to put first.

Labeling or categorizing is one of those things. Labeling must have great survival value, must save time and energy, must not cost us much in the long run.

After years of confronting black-and-white thinking, now I feel it's often a waste of time to suggest a more subtle interpretation. I used to think education would change all that, but sometimes I think education just makes our prejudices more subtle. The experience of living in the digital world will probably not percolate soon to that deeper reptilian brain that has, after all, our best interests at heart, even when we disagree with its conclusions.

Life in the digital world is interactive, fluid, modular. When I first used the word "morph" in speeches, I asked who knew what it meant. A few hands went up, then more and more. Now most folks seem to know that images can change from one thing into another. But they change through stages, and that's important. As a metaphor of how individuals and organizations adapt to changing conditions, it's critical to know that we move from phase to phase, not all at once. Grandmother does not turn willy-nilly into a wolf. Grandmother turns into a gray grandmother, than a gray hairy grandmother, then a gray hairy grandmother with fearsome teeth, then a wolf.

A young man from an evangelical Christian seminary asked to interview me for a project. His task was to talk to "others" so he knew how they thought. He had logged a Unitarian, a rabbi, and a Jew-for-Jesus when he came to me. He was genuinely interested in how I had morphed through careers and different religions. "What should I call you?" he said. "What are you now?"

"I guess, as the Buddhists say, I am 'not this, not that.' I'm in process. I like to think of myself as open to possibilities."

His pen halted on the pad and his consternation showed. Without a label, what was he to do? And what are we to do with reality itself, particularly when our interaction with the digital world (we are embedded in our time, after all, our historical context is the matrix of meanings with which we must wrestle) teaches us that life is fluid, interactive, and modular? Ultimately there is only the light of our monitors momentarily illuminating pixels that we gestalt into symbols that seem so real.

A friend recently criticized evolution, which for all its flaws as a Theory of Everything still seems to have some useful insights. A creationist, she spoke about species as if they were real things, rather than categories we invented. Taxonomy is an addiction, like the classification of knowledge itself. We need a map, but we know the map is not the territory. We know the territory intuitively by the immediacy with which it presses against us as we walk, alive and responsive and aware.

Hard to maintain our moorings, when everything is going through the looking-glass. Intellectual property, a category invented in the past few hundred years, is as blurred as a headline in the rain. The "protean" self celebrated by some and described ruefully by others is morphing along: we can choose careers and grow into others, we can choose partners and grow into others, we can choose identities and grow into others, and even our illusory self can watch with amusement or anxiety as it creates and discovers various personae as vehicles for being in the world.

Hemingway disdained adjectives because they diluted the aesthetic experience he intended to create. These days, we might be more in tune with Jorge Luis Borges who wrote about a culture that used verbs and adverbs to describe its perceptual world. Everything moved, nothing stayed slotted, and the world was a blur of temporary states.

It is not news that this is how it is, but it is news that we can't withdraw easily as we did in the past into a consensus that the fixed and rigid categories of our minds, from religion to science to metaphysics, are "real." They're a way our primitive brains need to know, a modality good for survival. Oversimplification gets our feet (and our mouths) moving fast when there's danger or perceived danger, but we use the word "flow" to denote that most highly prized state in which we lose ourselves and all illusory attachments to which that self is anchored. The energies of love, creativity and generosity flow outward into a world that accepts our contribution without comment, other than the reflexive joy we feel at knowing that our contribution and participation is a privilege and a gift.

In a network or web, we exercise power by contributing and participating. Life, whatever it may be, looks in these digital days more like a network or web than anything else. There, in that web, we allow ourselves to be woven into something we don't have to know or control. And even the grave, as I said when I started, vanishes into thin air whenever we flow in that direction.

Necessary Fictions *May 30, 1998*

Many religious and philosophical traditions assert that the "self," as a thing separate from everything else, is an illusion.

The Buddhist doctrine of no-mind, derived from the experience of enlightenment, is a way of saying that when the floodgates of perception are opened, the illusion of a separate self vanishes. When we have that experience, it's as if the mind—the mind we think ourselves to be—disappears. We experience a field of consciousness that is self-luminous, unabstracted, boundless. We see the illusory self as an emergent reality. During that experience, there is no consciousness of time or space, and yet … the next moment, we are back in our minds, within the world of here and now, creating of the experience a symbolic artifact that the mind can manipulate, which is exactly what I am doing now as I write these words.

I frequently invoke the movie Bladerunner because it captured so well the madness that was Phillip K. Dick's particular gift; a madness that was really a kind of sanity. Dick wrote the story, "Do Androids Dream of Electric Sheep?" on which the film was based. The world he imagined is here, now. Genetic engineering, ubiquitous electronic connectivity, and the outward migration of human beings into the cosmos is a single reality.

Like all organisms and organizations, we humans are systems of energy and information. We can manipulate that information at various levels to alter the particular forms in which energy and information coalesces at other levels. How we define ourselves is determined by the level at which we choose to view the system. The system is a system of systems, all nested and connected, fractal-like.

Like the bladerunner Deckard, we too are coming to question whether we are replicant or human, born or made. Deckard learned that the "cushion of memories" serving as the field of subjectivity that calls itself a self can be manufactured, as our societal system at a higher level manufactures illusory collective memories through mass media. It is a question of degree, not kind. When a woman makes a trip to the sperm bank and requests, as a friend did, some "intelligent brunette doctor sperm," she is making a more primitive use of technology than the person who will make that choice in the lab before the sperm is produced.

The subjectivity we take for granted as our field of identity is more than fragile. It can be shaped like clay; like earth itself. We catch ourselves watching ourselves watching ourselves watching ourselves in an infinite regression of reflexive self-conscious selves trying to grasp their origin or source. Did life spontaneously manifest itself on our planet in this particular form? Did alien races seed the process of evolution as we manipulate seed corn, something the corn itself will never know? Or was everything created by that which we call "God," which some think is the projection of a collective Self unable to bear the anxiety of being without knowing?

Many twentieth century Christians speak of "God" as a Being with which an "individual" can have a "personal relationship." That way of thinking is culturally relative and very recent. The collective Self of humanity used to be taken for granted. People derived their identity from the community in and through which they related to God and everything else. Hebrews did not think of themselves as "individuals." The notion of an "individual" with "rights," like the notion of intellectual property as "works" that exist independently, emerged after the invention of the printing press. Electronic connectivity is mediating the deconstruction of the notion of an "individual." Paradoxically, the liberation of individual energies by electronic connectivity changes how individuals define themselves as their experience of themselves changes.

Throughout the business world, for example, work space is becoming communal space, as if every business is a skunkworks in which no one works more than fifteen feet from the project. Organizations that are not virtual are virtualized. At a higher level, the Internet is a geodesic in which infinite strands of cross talk shrink the world to the size of a space station. The boundaries between individuals, like those between nation states, are increasingly permeable. Yet the necessity of the illusion of separate individuals is more critical than ever to the social order, as is the momentary necessity for "believing in" nation states. Commerce still depends on that illusion, and that is changing and will change—as Hemingway said of the way a person goes bankrupt—gradually, then suddenly.

The metaphor of humankind as a body consisting of interdependent cells is not new, but the realities of our world—from the consequences of global pollution to the spread of nuclear weapons—make the truth of it unavoidable. Human beings are slow learners. Insights can emerge in our collective awareness thousands of years before they become operative in our lives.

The exploration of telepathy, clairvoyance, and other modes of spontaneous knowing leads to an interesting paradox. Those modalities of knowing, as they are discovered to be real, erase the names we gave them as useful distinctions. When information and energy can be exchanged among all the cells of a body, what does it mean for one cell to say, "I know that?" The body knows it, not the cell. The Self knows it, not the self. Reincarnation begs the question of what to call the Self that persists when someone claims that "I" lived before. Who lived before? Whoever answers that question is not the Self that persists.

Consciousness is a field of possibility, a way the wrinkles in a diaphanous fabric invite self-definition. When we know how to shape the way self-consciousness emerges as a field, grasping the origins of our collective Self even as we radiate in all directions from our home planet, then we will see that to limit our thinking to what we saw through the cultural lenses of a dying time is to cling to broken toys.

The fabric is torn. We see through the tear more than we know how to say. It is time, as Rilke wrote, to leave our little room, every corner of which we know, and venture forth into eternity.

Building the Matrix   *June 6, 1998*

Those of us who are called "sir" by people we consider peers recognize sooner or later that the escalator has been moving up for a while now, that generations do come in dog years these days, and that the challenges of life at the forefront of our consciousness are linked to developmental stages.

The younger fellow in the coffee line this morning was mourning a mistake he had just made. He had accidentally erased a video tape of significant moments in the first ten months of his son's life. It was little consolation to know that the medium like all media (including ourselves) is dead or dying, that the image would decay in a few years, and that soon his son would be bigger than he was. He mentioned that he spent more time with his son than he did working, and all I could do was encourage him not to stop. I don't regret a single missed meeting or incomplete project, but I do regret whatever time was missed with any of my children as they grew.

Their adulthood is lived in a different matrix, framed as much by how they grew up as mine or that of my parents, whose depression-era prudence seemed so foolish in the abundance of the post war years that were all I knew.

Someone recently asked me to characterize the attributes of Generation X. The danger of being a speaker is that people take you at your words. What do I know about Generation X? I turned to a template in my brain that I often use: how had computer technology back-engineered that generation to think differently than I did?

Life and work in the networked world is interactive, modular, and fluid, so that's what I said was true of Gen X. Authority in virtual and virtualized organizations resembles the mobiles that turned above my children's cribs more than boxes arranged in permanent relationship in a hierarchical chart.

An IT guy speaking before me this week for a local organization tried to use a chart like that. He used a laptop computer and slides and—surprise!—something went wrong. The print in his hierarchical boxes was so faint that no one could read it. He gamely pointed to the empty boxes as he spoke and everyone in the audience pretended to see what he said was there.

Welcome to life in the digital world.

Welcome to life that is modular, more like a space station than a castle, in which leadership means naming the hubs at which people dock, creating links between them from nothing, and managing the flux. Welcome to life that demands mutuality because no one can know as much as they must so we have to work together, which means good communication and frequent feedback. Welcome to life in which real leadership is exercised less by virtue of structural authority than by virtue of knowing how to empower a group to do its job.

Older folks often live in castles in their heads, internalized blueprints that generate outdated behaviors. The tall walls and secure moats that were once called organizational structures offer an illusion of security and power, but the kaleidoscope has continued to turn, and alas! they simply don't exist. Like the bank that a colleague said was the challenge to her leadership, not the bank "out there" but the bank in the heads of the VPs who hid out in the tall office tower.

Alan Kay said perspective is worth fifty points of IQ. Middle-agers are a long way from finished; we just have to know what we have of value. And know that the willingness to contribute what we can to enhance the real power of others, to nurture their ability to grow in wisdom and inner strength, to communicate our faith that it's better to use ourselves up in the process of living than hold ourselves back … that is the gift we can give.

I recently congratulated a young producer at Jellyvision, the clever group that produced "You Don't Know Jack," on taking the interactive text of the old Infocom games to the next level. He was speaking about the simulated matrix they had created using sound effects, text, and imagination, which threw me back to the old days of playing Hitchhiker's Guide to the Galaxy. "Infocom?" he said. "What's that?"

The history of the social and literary dimensions of computer programs had better be transferred to electronic documents or paper before it disappears from our heads. Yet the unknown future is as much a haze as the unknown past. Our small island of awareness is bounded by a mist of both forgetfulness and unknowing.

I mentioned to a young woman in her late twenties that our fastest airplanes would look like covered wagons when she was old. She laughed, "Not in my lifetime!" But what is her lifetime? If she lives seventy more years in a society that is stable and making medical advances daily, she'll easily tack on enough years to live to 130. That's a hundred years from now. One hundred years ago, it was trains and steam engines, not jet planes and rockets to Mars.

The web sites we surf keep turning in a kaleidoscope: interactive modular and fluid. So do the passing events of our lives and the people we cherish. The mobile turns in the chill wind. The English we speak may be dead in a few centuries, our names will have been forgotten, our civilization will have morphed into something unimaginable. The best we can hope to know is that we share a leaky boat for a short ride. We are woven in a singular matrix of meaning and possibility. The best of humanity happens when we forbear, love, and have compassion. Yes, tasks must be done, crises must be managed, and war must be aborted. But today, we are here and we have one another, companions along the digital way, and that is our consolation and strength.

History and Myth   *August 29, 1998*

The way the world works when we are ten years old is the way we think the world will work forever.

Once upon a time, I read Mark Twain's "Tom Sawyer." That imaginative world became part of my foundation. I didn't think about it, it just happened. I absorbed his images with unconscious innocence.

A decade later, the memory of Twain's world somehow slid sideways suddenly. I saw it as a kind of three-dimensional pop-up instead of the flat background of my life. I saw that Twain had created a myth in his books that formed a cultural lens. Something happened that enabled me to see that lens, and that meant I could see something else, something beyond it, a matrix of understanding or possibility that had focused those images.

Another decade passed and I found myself in Hannibal, Missouri at the site of the house where the girl who became Becky Thatcher in "Tom Sawyer" had lived. I saw not only the house, but the signs and narrative that defined the house as "touristic space," teaching people to see a real white house through an overlay of interpretation derived in turn from the myth created by the book. It was like an experience of parallax, opening and closing now one eye and now the other, seeing how myths we believe become part of our history.

As we grow, the developmental stages of our lives strip us of illusions, leaving the bare skeletal bones of the scaffolding we had climbed inside our own minds. The images we once innocently believed peel like some ancient ad for a long-ago circus from a billboard in the rain.

One of this column's readers, Douglas Wright, wrote of a training film he had seen in the eighties that showed how we form our basic understanding of the world as children. Around ten years old, we wake up, look around and adopt an attitude toward life based on what we see.

Even then, Wright said, kids who had only video games viewed the world differently than those who had early computers who in turn viewed the world differently from those with fancier multimedia machines. The length of a generation was already contracting.

Wright was fascinated with how supervisors used that film. Employees raised during the Depression experienced it as punishment to have unpaid time off, while a boomer felt that mandatory overtime was a punishment. The Depression-era worker would have experienced this as a reward.

Their histories had generated different myths.

A myth is a fundamental construction of reality, a way of framing meanings and possibilities that are so fused with images—images of ideas, images of things we think actually happened—that we are offended when someone calls our belief system a "myth." In fact, a myth expresses our deepest beliefs. A myth is what we think is true.

In the past few hundred years, what we call "history" replaced other myths as a way of framing our experiences in a meaningful shared narrative.

When we share a myth with others, it feels like reality. That's why the challenge to our myths—from political myths to religious myths—feels like an assault on ourselves. That's why those who have never experienced the contextual shift that enabled them to see their myths in a bigger context are willing to slaughter those whose construction of reality feels like an attack on their very being. They don't know that their core self includes and transcends whatever myths they were given by their cultures, the way the myth of Tom Sawyer snapped in modular fashion into the world I was building as a child.

It is not a foregone conclusion that we will all choose the same myth as the organizing principle of an inter-planetary twenty-first century culture.

It is ironic that religious extremists resemble one another more than they resemble the open thinkers in their own traditions. They share a terror of the breakdown of the rigid structure that props up their fragile selves, a structure that quakes with fear rather than the certainty they express.

My insights have been influenced by my experience of computing. People who don't connect with people or systems that compute don't think that way. More than ever, we do not share a single history. When generations lasted a few decades, there was sufficient continuity in our myths to provide a platform for discourse. These days it feels like generations are about three years long. The great gulf fixed between those who learned "history" from books and those who learned it from television, computer games, and Hollywood movies can only be bridged from a point of view that includes and transcends both the text on a page and the flickering images on a screen.

The world of ubiquitous chips is developing its own myths. Myths so close to the hearts and minds of those inside that they can not see how they are molded by the information infrastructure that teaches them how to see and think. In the long run, there is no going back to thought worlds that have vanished, any more than we can live inside a ghetto of self-imposed isolation from a global economy. In the short run, however, frightened people, societies, and cultures sure can try.

What a spectacle we humans are! As a species, we're a million years old, with the wisdom of earthly life in our genes. In five thousand short years, we have tried on maybe thirty civilizations. The foundational myths of those civilizations seemed as real as Tom Sawyer whitewashing a fence on a summer afternoon. The kaleidoscope turns. The modular fluid world of computing teaches us that images morph faster than we can think, but—bless our hearts—we try to hold on to those images the way a Hollywood stunt man hangs onto a speeding car, his body horizontal, his legs in the air—if he ever existed, that is. Beyond that digital image. Beyond the hallucinatory fever of our brimming brains.

Modules and Metaphors   *September 26, 1998*

As the pace of reorganization has accelerated, the modular construction of reality has become the norm. Businesses, governments, and individuals have shortened the horizon of planning and hold "long range planning" lightly, knowing that the variables that will interact to create the future are too many to be factored. In our personal lives, we identify "developmental stages" and imagine the trajectory of our lives as a long swim from island to island.

When the experience of our lives is congruent with our descriptions of them, it feels like we know what we're talking about. The metaphors we have adopted become mistaken for literal descriptions of the landscape, protecting us from "the shocks and changes that keep us sane." Our beliefs work as a filter until they don't.

When I look at my current assumptions about modular life, I see that many of them derive from my interaction with the digital world. There (or here) I experience nested levels of modular reality that mediate the unthinkable complexity of our civilization.

"Civilization" is a name for the way we mediate energy and information. Information is retained in storage media appropriate to the task, but all media are dead or dying, including ourselves. Once organic media like dinosaurs or Neanderthals are no longer viable, they disappear. The evidence indicates that all storage devices are temporary, modular pieces that snap together in serial time as well as horizontally in space. Long before humans worried about killing off other species, thousands of organic media disappeared along with their unique ways of filtering data.

Many of the tidbits of information that find their way to my desktop computer concern genetic engineering and the splicing of humans and computers into new symbiotic configurations.

Sheep ranchers in Australia, for example, are injecting Bioclip, a naturally occurring protein, into sheep to cause fleeces to drop out. That saves money on shearing. But sheep shearers have a romantic image of themselves—as well as a union. They will fight to save the structure of their lives and the self-image with which it is fused, but it's only a holding action. It's more likely that they'll adapt, die, or save "Sheep Shearing Land" as a simulated touristic environment for children to visit like a "Living Farm."

Clearly evolution was served by a conservative stance toward memory storage and knowledge modification. Tribes and cultures that resisted change survived … for a while. But our environment is changing rapidly, so how do we change modules in a gradual way while still changing them as fast as necessary to stay connected to the changing environment? And when those environments are themselves symbolic modules, the simulated life we call "life" consists of a mental game, maintaining equilibrium among nested levels of symbolic reality that exist at different levels of complexity. Just like a computer game. Which is exactly what, for many of us, life has become.

Life inside a simulated civilization rewards those who are detached from their bodies until it doesn't. Until the cost of living inside simulated images butts heads with the "givens" of our lives—the way our bodies regulate themselves automatically, the way life on earth has evolved to deal with this planet at this point in time.

Because I studied literature in my formative years and then worked as an Episcopal priest for sixteen years, I learned how the modular symbols that make the most sense of our lives are constitutive of our self-image both as individuals and societies. In any religion, the "conversion process" involves the reconstruction of reality, substituting modular images that disclose life-giving possibilities for those that are dead-ends. Religious communities maintain those symbols at the center of their affirmations.

When we think those images are identical with reality, we think we are them and they are us. That those images might change threatens who we think we are. But the evidence is that we are not and never have been who we think we are. All of it – businesses, individuals, religions, societies—are always morphing.

The symbols of our dominant religions evolved when the medium of writing enabled human experience to be reconstructed in written images. Now that our images are digital—that is, interactive, modular, and fluid—our communities, our global economy, our religions are reconstructing themselves in ways aligned not only with those images but with how those images are generated. Our experience is back-engineered from our interaction with our technologies of information and communication.

Businesses see this or, to their peril, do not see it, and disappear. The reorganization of work, the manufacture and distribution of goods, services, and images, is driven by a technological revolution. Because organized religions are part of the world, they too are being reinvented. And because religions are predicated on a particular definition of self, as that sense of self is altered by the digital world, religious structures will have to morph to connect with our intuitive grasp of experience, our "common sense," which is simply what we have been taught to perceive or believe.

Genetic engineering is a way of altering the information storage and delivery of complex systems. So are computer networks. So are we. We are a medium of exchange between "organic" systems and "inorganic." But those names are already obsolete. The difference between a pacemaker and a chip in our heads is one of degree, not kind, and so are the distinctions we create and then believe that describe both "body" and "soul"—another dichotomy stretched to the breaking point. The simple truth is, we are inventing ourselves. But maybe—from the point of view of the single system that is the universe—we always have. It's just that "we" are so much bigger than we knew. We thought that our "species," one of many modular conscious molecular clusters, was unique. Instead, it looks as if life is singular, the universe gregarious, and what it will all look like in a hundred years to whoever calls themselves human is beyond our capacity to imagine.

Beyond Belief   *March 11, 2000*

In the human potential movement, we often hear words like, "As you believe, so you can achieve," that imply that everything in our lives is a function of belief. Of course, anyone who has had a flower pot fall on their head from a window ledge knows there's more to it than that. Our lives are bound by real constraints that have nothing to do with what we believe.

Those constraints exist in a domain of "objective reality" beyond our control. Sometimes we try to manipulate that domain through ritual, prayer or incantation, and who can blame us? Our little lives look like fireflies in the vast eye of night and thinking we can make the universe heel can be tempting. That's why the best-selling spiritualities in the religious marketplace pretend to give us control over what we can't control. They reference the Ego rather than the Self as the locus of our identity. When we move with the deeper currents of the Self, we surrender control to the flow rather than seize it and discover our real Selves in the process.

Still ... when I look back at the significant breakthroughs in my life, they have often involved stepping out of a belief system that had limited what I thought possible. Beliefs define parameters of possibility and when we break through limiting beliefs, we see options we never knew we had. It really can feel miraculous when that happens. The distance to the horizon is not exactly limitless, but compared to how it had looked, it can seem like it. Obstacles seem to vanish. Perhaps we can be forgiven a little excess when we say, "As we believe, so we can achieve."

Inside the realm of human subjectivity—the domain defined by language and culture—our beliefs do determine the scope and scale of our lives. How we imagine ourselves living is the outer limit of how we can live. When the questions we are capable of asking are pre-determined by our beliefs, the answers are already part of the script.

Computer programmers who work in only one language, like people who speak only one language, really speak no language, as Goethe said. A language shapes our framework of perception in ways we can't see. Inside the skin of a single language or culture, we're like people wearing glasses who are running around looking for their glasses. When we learn a second language, we see other ways of framing reality. Then we can make choices.

No distinctions, no choices.

We live inside perceptual frameworks like ants inside a balloon. But now the balloon is expanding and the stars on its skin are defining a different horizon.

In a civilization that thinks in and through its computer network, programming languages frame what is possible to think. The network extends the subjective domain in which belief and intention determine what's real. Because computers are symbol-manipulating machines, the symbols and syntax that determines how we construct reality literally define what is humanly possible.

To the degree that computer programmers are conscious of the implicit assumptions of all the levels of their languages, they really are masters of the Universe, aware of recursive levels of nested symbolic constructions of reality from the code to the top of our minds. The hardware behaves as the software says, which is why the number of computer applications seems limitless. The Network seems to extend our field of subjectivity beyond any known horizon.

Of course, it's messier than that. The "gray areas" where the field of human subjectivity intersects with the "objective world" is also expanding. When atoms were imagined as billiard balls rolling around in an "objective reality," the boundaries between humans and the Universe were clearer. When atoms are states of probability in a quantum Universe, human intentions have greater power to transform the energy and information that define the universe. Then "objective reality" does become more subject to what we believe. As this process of transformation evolves, consciousness might become synonymous with "objective reality" itself which it will wear as a jellyfish wears its cilia, gathering the raw data of itself. The window and the world through the window just one thing.

We are currently in a process of transformation into a trans-planetary cyborg-humanity, our genetic heritage enhanced and our hive mind augmented by sensory extensions. We are the ghost in that living machine.

But let's drop back inside a familiar landscape.

When our belief system is negative—which is a form of hunkering down into control mode—then unanticipated events that are genuinely wonderful can be a challenge. We can minimize or deny them or we can risk opening ourselves to the fact that the Universe in its better moments is capable of astonishing surprises. Then we must make a choice: will we remain huddled in our winter burrow or be cajoled upward by the heavenly scent of a spring breeze?

Neither humans nor the universe will ever write bug-free code. All code is buggy. Evolution moves through accidents toward surprising configurations that disclose new structures, enabling life to experience itself in new ways. Maybe bugs are feedback loops compelling us to remain present to the project of our lives. Maybe breakdowns are opportunities to sharpen the only tools we have—our-selves—and calibrate our behaviors with our best intentions so what we achieve is what we believe in those moments of astonishment. By definition, surprises are unpredictable, even if they seem somehow connected to our deepest beliefs. Maybe beliefs and breakdowns alike can take the shape of portals through which we pass on the way to discovering new ways of being ourselves.

Listening to the sweet-talk of that spring breeze.

The Crazy
Lady on the Treadmill   *September 19, 2002*

We've all had the experience by now. Someone next to us—in this case, the lady on the treadmill at the fitness center—suddenly starts laughing. She didn't snicker as if she had just thought of something funny. No. She laughed loudly for a long long time.

Laughter is a social event. When someone is laughing, we want to laugh too. Laugh and the world laughs with you, as they say. I turned without thinking to see what was so funny.

Of course, I couldn't tell because she was inside her own bubble. She was wearing headphones and staring at the small television screen mounted on the tread-mill, striding in one of those Monty Python power walks, going nowhere fast and staring at the miniature people on the screen.

The first time it happened was in a coffee shop at the condiment counter. I was stirring my caramel non-fat latte and getting ready to lick the foam from the wooden stick when the woman beside me suddenly began talking. She spoke in a conversational tone except there was no one there but herself. I assumed for a moment she was like the people we pass on the street engaged in animated conver-sations not exactly with themselves but with ghosts, imaginary companions or antag-onists inside the bubble of their heads. Then I saw the spongy ears of the barely noticeable headset and the tiny mic that indicated she was having a telephone con-versation.

I like to look at the eyes now of people inside those bubbles and see where they're fixed. In the case of the coffee shop conversation, they were aimed at a point about half way to the vanishing point. I am sure some social scientist is writing a thesis even as we speak—excuse me, even as I type—about the reconstruction of the ratios of social space we inhabit as a result of these bubbles. I know people are saying how irritating it is when someone in a restaurant speaks too loudly on their cell phone because the edges of the social space presumed to be part of our table have been broken and allow that intrusive conversation to cross the line.

I found myself wondering how different it was, really, having one of those electronically enhanced conversations and carrying on with people who aren't there. The blurred margins of the two kinds of experience make a cellphone conversation next to us feel strange because we thought that proximity meant we inhabited the same social space. It's like we're still living on a two-dimensional grid which is suddenly intersected by a portal or node in the abstract four-dimensional spacetime of electronic communication.

Maybe the difference is that someone out there in televisionland as we used to call cyberspace or in a wireless conversation is creating a virtual world self-consciously whereas the ranter is caught in a loop like a stuck record.

But I don't know about that. I often compose things I am writing or practice speeches in my head as I walk in my quiet neighborhood and I find myself gesturing, saying words aloud like someone in headphones singing along. I lose myself in the process and am pulled abruptly from that "rain man space" when I realize that someone is looking at me the way I looked at the crazy lady on the treadmill. I am not really talking to myself but to an audience I am recreating virtually, the one I imagine out there, as I am in this moment as I write. On radio programs I do that too, sitting in a studio with only a producer or in my office doing an interview over the telephone; I imagine a listener and speak to them directly.

Appearances can be deceiving. Back in my preaching days, I recall getting ready for an early church service when a church member whispered conspiratorially that someone had come in that I hadn't met. "You need to connect with her," she said. "She's incredibly rich and often gives large gifts to projects that catch her attention."

I went out to see who she meant. There was a new couple and a new single. The couple were well dressed and greeted me with warm smiles. The solo wore a stained sweatshirt, her dirty hair went in all directions,. and she looked around with a distracted rhythm that made it difficult to connect. You know, of course, that I guessed wrong, that the one who looked like a wandering homeless was in fact the one who was filthy rich. I realized then that the only difference between a street person and an eccentric was a trust fund.

Insanity, like wisdom is contextual. Someone said that the difference between a hallucination and a vision is that no one shares the hallucination. So what then is this dialogue between us? A portal in a new kind of spacetime or a closed loop back into myself? If our hallucination is consensual, as Gibson defined cyberspace, where is the emphasis? On the hallucination or the fact that it is consensual? Communities, societies and I guess planetary civilizations can all go crazy, but no one knows it inside the bubble unless someone external to the madness says so. Maybe everything is inside a bubble, one we create by pretending to have a conversation. Or maybe the boundaries between us don't really exist except as abstractions like broken lines indicating states on a map. Maybe we're all cells in a single brain having a single dream. Maybe the entire universe is like that; the universe itself becoming conscious through the various apertures which we call evolving organisms, each finding itself looking at the rest in a different way, trying to say what they think they see. Maybe the universe is just a crazy lady on a treadmill, going nowhere fast in a wild Monty Python walk, having one hell of a good time, laughing like a madman.

Chapter 3

Doing Business Digitally

Failing into Success

March 1, 1997

I wish I could say that I have always succeeded at everything I did. That every project I began was a win, but I can't. Some roads led into cul-de-sacs or dead-ends. I do know, however, that I'm not alone.

These crazy times of accelerated change make it hard for anyone to feel like an unmitigated success. Many of the people I meet are not even sure any more what success looks like.

Success during changing times is not the same as success during quieter, more stable times.

General Electric just had a record-breaking year. GE is the most profitable company in the United States. Success has many mothers, as they say, but success at GE stems in part from the courage and vision of Jack Welch. When he inherited the mantle of leadership in 1981, he threw cold water on institutionalized complacency by declaring that if GE continued on its current course, it would run right off a cliff.

Had Welch outlined his vision thirty years earlier in 1951, he would have been declared certifiably insane. Wisdom, under conditions of relative stability, called for a hierarchical structure and a different style of leadership.

Wisdom, like insanity, is contextual. What is wise under one set of conditions may be insane under others.

When I deliver a speech, for example, I am animated and passionate; I behave in a way that makes sense. But an hour later, when the audience has left and the room is empty, if I still behave the same way—talking away, gesturing for emphasis—I look a bit odd.

What looked like success a few years ago may not make for success today. Those who are complacent about their success may actually be failing. Those who feel as if they are failing may in fact be on the cutting edge of life that is outgrowing its organizational boundaries and its old ways of framing reality.

Robert Galvin, the grand patriarch of Motorola, says that "every significant decision that changes the direction of a company is a minority decision. Whatever is the intuitive presumption—where everyone agrees, "Yeah, that's right"—will almost surely be wrong."

His company has succeeded by fostering an environment in which creativity thrives. Motorola has built in an openness to heresy because the company knows that wisdom is always arriving at the edge of things, on the horizons of our lives, and when it first shows up—like a comet on the distant edges of the solar system—it is faint and seen by only a few. But those few know where to look.

Allen Hynek, an astronomer connected with the Air Force investigation of UFOs, was struck by the "strangeness" of UFO reports, the cognitive dissonance that characterizes experiences that don't fit our orthodox belief systems. He pointed out that all the old photographic plates in astronomical observatories had images of Pluto on them, but until Clyde Tombaugh discovered Pluto and said where it was, no one saw it because they didn't know where to look.

It is not too late—it is *never* too late—to explore new possibilities, in particular, the new ways of being in community, communicating, and accessing information that is symbolized by the Internet. Many of those who rushed into cyberspace to make money fast are closing up shop after losing lots of money. They remind me of the people who took off after gold in Alaska during the 1898 strike. A million men and women headed for Alaska. A hundred thousand crossed the border. Ten thousand made it through the mountains to the gold fields. A few of those actually struck it rich.

Who made money? The ones who sold picks and shovels to the greedy, driven prospectors as they came through the pass, the ones who bought up all the housing and rented it out.

The "robber barons" who built the railroads were mostly bankrupt a generation later, but the railroads stayed. The infrastructure that they built was used by the next generation as a framework for their lives.

What is failure and what is success? I don't know, but those who seem to be thriving are willing to take risks and fail into success again and again. The devil is always in the details. Real success comes through trial and error.

Edison invented a hundred filaments that didn't work before he found one that did. Every failure encouraged him. He knew that each one eliminated an incorrect possibility and brought him closer to his goal.

Listen to "Rogue Agent," a computer hacker who set someone straight who wanted to give simple rules to would-be computer hackers.

"You want to create hackers? Don't tell them how to do this or that. Show them how to discover it for themselves. Those who have the innate drive will dive in and learn by trial and error. Those who don't, comfortable to stay within the bounds of their safe little lives, fall by the wayside.

"There's no knowledge so sweet as that which you've discovered on your own."

The best engineers are like those hackers. Their endless curiosity and refusal to accept conventional wisdom is a declaration on behalf of the human spirit. Their failures are an affirmation of life itself, life that wants to know, and grow, and extend itself throughout the universe.

Computer programmers write software applications that are doomed to be as obsolete as wire recordings or programs for an IBM XT. The infrastructures built by engineers are equally doomed. Whether a virtual world of digital bits or a physical world of concrete and steel, we are building a Big Toy of a civilization. We are using up that Big Toy while we play and building another on top of it. The fun of the game is to remember that it is a game, and winning is just another name for the willingness to play the game, to give it everything you have got—all your energy, intelligence and gusto—and to be all used up when the game is done.

Generating Power   *April 1, 1997*

Too much change can make us feel powerless. Security comes from predictability and the world today is anything but predictable. Chaos for breakfast and doubt for lunch make for indigestion at dinnertime.

There's good news too, though. Creativity thrives on the murky edges. If we can stand not knowing for long periods of time, we feel ourselves filling up with power again. The powerful person, it turns out, is not the one who knows but the one who knows that they don't know. The powerful person is teachable, open, and has what Buddhists call "a beginner's mind."

Freedom and power are two things of which everybody wants more than they have. Yet freedom and power are two things of which every human being already has the most that they can have.

It depends on what we mean by freedom and power.

By freedom I do not mean the ability to do whatever we want whenever we want to do it: I mean by freedom our innate capacity to respond to whatever life brings with creativity and resilience.

By power I do not mean the ability to compel others to do our will: I mean by power our ability under any and all circumstances to use our resources to make a real difference. To have positive impact and know it.

Whenever we exercise our innate freedom and power, we find ourselves regaining the center. Powerlessness vanishes. We possess ourselves again.

Which brings us to the power industry.

There's nothing quite like watching a two billion dollar business falling through the air like an elephant pretending to fly, is there?

The power industry is moving into the looking-glass world of deregulation. When utilities look at the experience of other countries, it's like tumbling down the rabbit hole.

Consider Argentina: during the early stages of deregulation, competition among thirty-two Argentine electricity generators became so fierce that by the autumn of 1994, they were giving it away for free. That's right. For one month, the price of electricity was literally zero.

That sounds insane—until you remember what kind of Alice-in-Wonderland world we inhabit.

Scott McNeeley, CEO of Sun Microsystems, outlines a new business model:

First you achieve ubiquity, i.e. give away your product for free;

Then you capture mindshare;

Then you achieve brand equity;

And then you license the product and make ... profits.

In a world in which some genius looked at spring water bubbling out of the ground and said, "Hey! Let's bottle that water and sell it!" and Netscape built a web browser and gave it away for free; what used to be crazy sounds like common sense.

It's a marketplace, Bill Gates points out, that has never before existed on the face of the earth.

The days when utilities could make a profit by redecorating their offices are over. Profits will be made in the distribution of power, not its generation.

Beyond that, I hesitate to predict the future.

The number one object stolen from automobiles in Los Angeles, for example, used to be car stereo systems. So a booming business developed in anti-theft devices. Now the number one object stolen from cars is anti-theft devices.

Who would have predicted that?

I will predict, however, that applying intelligence and creativity to serving the end-user will build an infrastructure of loyalty and brand-equity that makes the system stable.

The infrastructure of customer service is like the physical infrastructure: it's never noticed when everything's working. That blinking VCR or digital clock is a sign that, while we were out, the power went off. At the least, we need products that don't proclaim our mistakes in such bald fashion.

But more than that, we need products that anticipate and meet the needs of consumers before they even notice them. Then they will be bound to us, as Shakespeare says, with hoops of steel.

The power industry will belong, I wager, to those who generate and distribute power reliably and link, bundle, and package power and power-related products in creative ways.

This means engineers must be engineers first, but must also look at products from the point of view of the consumer.

Think of computer applications you have used that were obviously designed by software engineers for themselves without a thought for the end user. People who don't care about communication will design products that don't communicate how to use them. They will write thick manuals that a Phi Beta Kappa can't understand.

Good computer interface designers build symbolic structures like Big Toys using digital information. They begin at the human being and build toward the computer, enabling end-users virtually to climb through a complicated arrangement of digital images and text into the machine. When they succeed, end-users are no more conscious of the interface or the computer than of their contact lenses.

I dream of a VCR I can program without a headache, a digital watch I can set, a smart house that turns on the light, warms the living room, and mixes a drink when I click my remote half a mile from home.

Look around the room at the light switches, the water fountains, the doors— is the function of every artifact clear to you? Were they designed with the user in mind? Can you use them intuitively without reference to a user manual, i.e. signs and instructions?

Freedom and power. Freedom means we have the ability to shift our point of view and see the system we engineer from the perspective of the user for whom it is designed. Power means making the decision to serve that user so thoroughly that they don't even notice.

One way to face challenges is to redefine problems so they no longer exist. British Rail couldn't get trains to run on time so they redefined "on time" to mean anything up to one hour late. Their record improved dramatically.

Another way is to start with customers and their real needs and build back to solutions.

Chaos for breakfast and doubt for lunch, indeed. Who wouldn't prefer simple answers? But these are crazy times, and in crazy times, power looks more like wisdom than winning.

The wise person steers their course by the torchlight of doubt and chaos.

Digital Civility   *July 1 1997*

Technology isn't about technology. Technology is about people.

The initial effect of every new communications technology is greater distance between people. But over time, the technology itself enables people to work and live in closer communion.

When the telephone was invented, no one thought of it as a personal communication device, not even its inventor. Bell is said to have answered when asked what use it might have, "Well, you can call ahead to the next town and tell them a telegram is coming."

Over time, the telephone taught us how to live the kind of distributed life it made possible.

The same is true of personal computers and other digital interfaces. We are still learning the rules of encounter that enable us to communicate through digital images and words in ways that work.

Learning how to use email is an art. Some companies have experienced disaster when people did not understand the rules that governed email and how they differed from telephone or face-to-face conversations.

We call them "flame wars" on the Internet, those explosions of incivility that make life online unpredictable. We're learning that our digital masks hide real human beings and the long term consequence of short term behavior is a break down of trust.

Free markets are often characterized as dog-eat-dog jungles, but it's just the opposite. Complex systems extended in time and space require a fundamental basis of trust in order to function.

The basis of capitalism is a handshake.

The trust implicit in contractual agreements ensures predictability. Without predictability, there is no security. Without security, we just don't do very well in the long term. Things don't work.

The first McDonald's restaurant in Russia after the collapse of the Soviet Union was built by a Wisconsin businessman. He reported astonishment at the conditions in which he had to work.

Lettuce and tomatoes were substandard so he had to buy a farm to grow vegetables. The same was true of beef. Materials for building were in such short supply that they had to be brought in by rail from Europe. He recalls freight cars filled with sand and gravel surrounded by armed guards to prevent hijacking.

He had to import personnel until he could train local workers in minimal standards of service and civility. The near-chaotic mob rule in Russia today reminds us what it takes to build strong, flexible institutions that ensure predictability.

Businesses are teaching civility too, not because they want to, but because they must. As the digital revolution undermines traditional forms of education, businesses are sponsoring their own schools, training programs, and apprenticeships. McDonald's "Hamburger University" teaches young recruits how to see customers as human beings worthy of respect and act accordingly.

As a young man, I remember watching a woman approach a counter in Woolworth's to make a purchase. She was greeted by a salesperson.

"How may I help you?"

The woman handed her a bouquet of plastic violets. The salesperson rang them up, accepted a bill and made change, and put the flowers in a bag. As she handed the bag to the customer, she said, "Thank you very much."

Period.

That's the essence of civility: How may I serve you? Then, thank you: thank you for the opportunity to be of value.

That's what works.

I worked my way through college with patronage jobs from the Daley machine in Chicago.

From time to time someone attacked the boss on what sounded like solid grounds. The newspapers would be full of accusations.

Usually the attacking politician was invited to the Mayor's office.

"What do you need?" the Mayor always asked. Then, after he had listened a while, he said: "OK. Now, what do you really need?"

The conversation always ended with a partnership characterized by mutual self-interest.

That political system worked because it factored in the real needs of real people and evolved a means for satisfying them.

A recent study at Harvard University revealed that most of the effectiveness of any worker at any job is attitude and people skills. Knowledge of the task had less relationship to long term success than working well with others.

A CEO of a large local utility told me he used to spend 15% of his time on leadership and other process issues and the rest on tasks. Now the proportions are reversed. Why? Because times of radical change require close attention to the people in a system. In fact, the people ARE the system.

Values are not add-ons. Values are intrinsic to effectiveness in the long term.

I once discussed values with the CEO of a Fortune 500 company.

"Why," I asked, "should we embrace the human dimensions of quality programs? Don't smart ruthless people really set the pace?"

Sometimes, he conceded, then said, "But I'm not that smart. I need other people. Besides, nothing else works today. Customers cross the street for a penny and just aren't loyal any more. Employees know that even if we promise them a steady job, we don't control our ability to make good on that promise."

Only the old virtues, he said—treating others the way you want to be treated—establish bonds of trust and build the long term loyalty we need to survive. It's not just a smart idea to include every stakeholder—customers, employees, suppliers—in our planning. It's the only thing that works these days.

A Zen monk once asked why monks bow in a temple. Some said, to acknowledge our divinity. Others said, to build respect. The monk listened patiently, shaking his head after every answer.

"We bow," he said, "because things work better when we bow."

"Getting" what someone meant because they made their email crystal clear ... hearing a warm sincere voice on the telephone ... knowing by their body language that a person's word is good ... that's what works.

Why?

Because things work better when we bow.

The Pattern of Community   *September 6, 1997*

Some of my older children have never been inside a physical bank. They know how to use ATM machines, write electronic checks, and carry smart cards, but think a trip to the bank is like a ride in a horse-drawn buggy.

Yesterday I walked to a branch bank, waited in line, and chatted with the teller as I deposited a check. I did that because it is still important to me to walk around the neighborhood now and then and talk to people. It isn't efficient, but it does provide the interface I need to feel part of the local community.

I learned to build community for myself by doing things like that as I grew up. That's what feels "normal" to me.

The patterns of community that feel comfortable to us, learned in early childhood, remain templates of "normal" for the rest of our lives. We do everything we can to replicate those patterns in our intimate and work relationships in the physical world and in cyberspace.

People in organizations that are morphing aren't simply resisting change when they try to retain the patterns of community that feel "normal" to them. They are acting out of lifelong behaviors that are almost as deep as life itself.

We are inundated this week with news of the deaths of important people – Princess Diana, Mother Teresa, and Victor Frankl, the author of "Man's Search for Meaning." We hear little of Victor Frankl, more of Mother Teresa, and endlessly of the Princess. These "death-events" are being transformed by the media—including the Internet—into archetypal "lives of the saints" that tell a deeper mythic truth about all of our lives: the roots of compassion are deep in our own suffering, and that compassion is the well-spring, pattern, and sustaining power of community as well.

Our patterns of community are learned first in our families of origin. Imprinting is deep, indelible. An Australian email friend recently wrote that we are imprinted in the first few years, spend the next twenty refining the pattern, the next twenty trying in vain to change it, and the next twenty coming to terms with it.

The Princess' brother noted that Diana's feelings of unworthiness, incubated in an environment of mutual loathing by her parents, were the source of her identification with and compassion for the destitute and outcast.

Winston Churchill too had a lonely childhood and fought off depression—he called it his "black dog" that followed him at every turn—by charging headlong into life whenever he suffered a major reverse. At every dark passage of his life, he responded with creativity and a burst of energy. The lifelong battle against depression for Churchill – as for Lincoln, who fought a similar war—generated a capacity for stirring words that led a civilization through its darkest hours. Churchill and Lincoln were both speaking first to themselves when they articulated their visions on behalf of their nations, then to the world.

We always speak first to ourselves, and if we are lucky, our words define a possibility for others as well. Teachers teach what they need to learn, clergy preach what they need to hear. The root of compassion is the pain in our lives that enables us to connect with others at the deepest levels of our shared humanity.

My father died when I was two years old, but his absence was more present in our family than many who were still alive. When I look back at my careers of teaching literature and writing, then serving as an Episcopal priest for sixteen years, now writing, speaking and consulting, I know that all my words were and are an effort to fill the resounding silence of his absence with symbols of possibility and promise. My passion to create meaning is an antidote to the threat of meaninglessness lurking always in the shadows, ready to spring.

I have seen as a consultant that a corporate culture usually issues directly from the personality of the CEO. The dynamics inside the organization often replicate the dynamics of the CEO's family of origin. The best leaders understand this and allow their weaknesses to become their strengths by compensating for the blind spots that are part of their heritage.

When CEOs describe the landscape seen from their desks, they are always describing themselves. The challenge of consulting, as in marriage or family counseling, is not to see what's happening but to say what you see at the right time, so the information is helpful. CEOs often sound like families or couples who want to change or fix something external to themselves, when in fact, nothing can or will change until they experience a contextual shift that immediately is felt throughout the organization. Anything else is a short-term fix that does not address the source of the problems that will keep happening.

To understand the world, we must first understand ourselves. Then, like the Hubble telescope when it first went into orbit, we can compensate for distortion and build a clear picture.

How we pattern our relationships with others—how we build community—is how we live and work in cyberspace. The words we have always spoken are the words we click and send.

Princess Diana needed to be held and comforted, and she held and comforted others. Churchill needed to speak words of light to his own darkness and spoke them to the darkest hour of western civilization. Frankl needed to survive Auschwitz and discovered in the depths of his soul a resilience, dignity, and capacity for heroism that became a map for the journeys of a million others.

Our weakness is our strength and the bond of our common humanity.

The task that confronts us in cyberspace is to allow ourselves to discover and create together symbols of real community that hang in the virtual world like stained glass windows through which light suddenly brightens, a moment of inexplicable splendor among wall-sized windows defining a luminous space. They hang suspended in the thin air, we hang suspended among them. The depth of our mutual need becomes ground zero for our mutual fulfillment. At the moment of ignition, the promise becomes the fulfillment of the promise. We engage in spite of ourselves—in spite of our childhood—in spite of everything—in joyful participation in the sorrows of the world.

Beanie Babies and the Source of All Things   *January 10, 1998*

Since this column is read in many countries, let me explain "beanie babies" to those who may not grasp their importance.

Beanie babies are toys, cute little animals with cute little names. They're manufactured here in the upper midwest, at least the real ones are. They're good examples of how to create artificial scarcity in a consumer economy. Some beanie babies are hard to find, so Peanut the Elephant or Chilly the Bear will sell for a thousand dollars.

Beanic babies illustrate the dangers of living in a digital world as well as a consumer society. When the value of a commodity or an idea is manufactured and therefore arbitrary, artificial demand inflates prices and invites fakes into the marketplace just as it does in the world of ideas.

Beanie babies are cute enough, but easy to fake if you don't mind inferior fabric or stitching. It's all in the name, and the name is on the tag, so beanie babies with fake tags are flooding into the United States. Collectors have paid a fortune for a "Grunt the boar" made in Shanghai, not Chicago. The fakes are sold over the Internet too, so people have paid a premium for an image of a copy of a stuffed toy.

That may sound insane, but ... we are good consumers, after all, and once our basic needs are met, what else are we going to buy but things on which we place an arbitrary value, making a market for goods or ideas, then acting as if they matter?

Living near the home of the Green Bay Packers (a professional football team), it's easy to see how sports and the digital simulation of fantasy games is one way to channel society's free-floating anxiety and hostility into an arbitrary activity. When entertainment (including professional sports) and information services generate the energy flow of a global economy, it is downright unpatriotic not to participate in the madness.

As one paid to make speeches, I see the speaking "industry" in the light of bogus beanie babies. Many speakers spend hours perfecting the presentation of someone else's ideas. They test the winds of popular interest and jump from horse to horse as they ride, following the wind. Of course, we all feed on each other's ideas, but unless we know the difference between snatching food and planting gardens, we live lives of debasing self deception, drinking from a dribble glass and wondering why we're always wet.

What *is* the real value of what we write, or say, or communicate through electronic media? Richard Dawkins popularized the notion of memes, contagious ideas that replicate rapidly. Some memes are life-giving and empowering, but how do we know which ones? In a world in which anyone can say anything, how do we know which beanie baby is real?

The answer, of course, is that no beanie baby is worth a thousand dollars, and only a willed belief in arbitrary value makes us think it is.

The creative ideas that transform our lives are always free.

One of my talks is called "The Stock Market, UFOs, and Religious Experience." In each of those domains, the menu if often sold as if it's the meal. In a world in which money managers take a cut of the total assets they invest regardless of performance, yet 87% failed to beat the averages last year, selling beliefs, images of God, and stories of communication from the mothership ought to be a snap.

The bottom line in all three is that there IS something real eliciting our projections, but the buyer had better learn to separate iron filings from a magnet.

In a knowledge economy, information is capital, but wisdom is gold. And gold is currently devalued.

Powerful ideas are rare, and those who see truths emerging over the horizon like the first light, long before the dawn is even a possibility in most minds, wade against the tide. In an information economy, the new business model is: ubiquity => mind share => brand equity => success. In the realm of ideas and values, we also begin by giving our best away for free. Give, give, give! and the coalescing of positive energy becomes a spiral like stars in a Van Gogh painting, enabling us to live on the energy that eddies back into our lives. How much will there be? Enough—there is always enough—enough to sustain us and remind us what matters most.

Springs of water that originate as trickles swell into life-giving rivers. Even in a world in which free spring-water is bottled and sold.

Which ideas matter most? Those that we can seize and make our own, creative insights or abstractions, the apprehension of which immediately changes our lives forever. Truths that set us free. Ideas that, like good mentors or good coaches, quietly put the reins of our lives back into our own hands.

We can't stop bottom-feeders from stealing ideas, nor software pirates from making CDs, nor thieves from faking beanie babies. But so what? If we understand the real value of ideas in the first place, anybody who disseminates them is doing ourselves—and the world—a favor. Powerful, life-giving ideas always diminish the need of our egos for a security, a permanence, a safe harbor that in this world simply does not exist. They transform the very context of our lives, that deep place from which we come to everything else, they create a platform inside our selves or souls on which we stand in the middle of the air and darkness through which we are always plunging. They give us the ability to live from the inside out, grounded in the source of ideas and capable therefore of always generating new ones.

Those real ideas enable us to grasp the patterns that point beyond mere data toward the energy that fills the universe and points in turn beyond itself to that which we do not know how to name much less invent or bottle and sell.

Why the Soft Stuff is Hard   *January 24, 1998*

I am currently consulting with a large diverse organization about technology and communication. Listening to the people on the front lines, I discovered once again that the collective wisdom of the work force is immense, but building structures to enable that wisdom to flow freely isn't easy.

Every introduction of new technology in the organization created problems. The "efficiency" of voice mail left people dangling. They didn't know if messages had been heard, action was being taken, or what. E-mail has solved some of those problems, but created others. You get a response, one said, but people often hide behind e-mail, staying out of reach. They use words to duck for cover, not communicate.

My mantra—"Mutuality-Feedback-Accountability"—holds true here too. Unless all three are maintained, an organization skews in predictable ways. Technology creates mutuality and feedback only if the leader holds people accountable to how it's used.

This particular business spent lots of money on hardware, less on software, and almost nothing on training people to use email effectively—not how to use email programs, but how to use words in a high-context medium.

When we need to communicate, we can walk down a hallway and speak face-to-face, or pick up a telephone, or send email. Each medium creates a different context. When building a virtual group, it works best to have plenty of face-time up front, then use email to sustain—not replace—those relationships.

Something that works when said face-to-face can feel like a boxing-glove coming out of a closet when an email pops up on the monitor and delivers the same words.

Computer networks are only half the solution. Computer networks are fused to people networks. We humans beings animate the network, making it alive. Otherwise it's a monster that over-controls us. How we manage, not the computer network, but the integrated human-computer system determines how knowledge is leveraged in an enterprise.

Because "soft skills" are harder to teach and supervise than tasks, we often spend more time buying chips and switches or choosing software programs than wrestling with the real struggles of the folks on the front lines.

We can use emoticons like smiley faces all we want—adding :-) or '-) or :-0. But emoticons don't convey subtleties or innuendoes. Besides, different cultures use them differently.

The best carrier of meaning in the digital world is text. Using speech—including virtual speech—and text effectively is seldom taught. Yet "soft skills" are more important than ever in a work place that relies more and more on computer technology.

The CEO of a large utility company told me he used to spend 85% of his time on the generation and distribution of power, only 15% on process issues. Now, he said, those percentages are reversed. He agreed that 85% of the effectiveness of anyone at any job is the "soft stuff"—attitude, working well with others, communication.

That CEO is not a touchy-feely kind of guy who can't wait to get to the office to get his hugs. He's a left-brain executive more comfortable with power grids than personnel. But managing people during times of change requires that we pay attention to how human beings link to one another, how energy and information moves through the human as well as the electronic system. That determines the real distribution of power.

The latest books addressing this issue call it management of intellectual capital. When so many books on a single subject show up on best-seller lists, it's best to treat the event as a symptom rather than a solution. The symptoms show up for good reasons, signaling a real need, but seldom provide the whole answer.

Re-engineering, for example. Re-engineering was invented (duh!) by engineers. They understood systems as if they were mechanical and taught a process that restructured businesses through brute force; a process better suited for rearranging marbles in boxes than human beings in cubicles. In a recent interview in the *Wall Street Journal*, Michael Hammer, one of the original re-engineering gurus, acknowledged that he added two days to his three-day seminar because he had not anticipated difficulty with people. When asked what to do with people who could not adapt easily to change. he had always replied, "Shoot them." He is learning that the people are the system, and the coupling of networked people and networked computers creates a single beast. Ignoring how that hybrid learns, grows, and produces value wreaked havoc in organizations that thought they were taking the easy way out.

The recent emphasis on the proper use of intellectual capital is one antidote to the excesses of re-engineering, a way to say that knowledge and wisdom have to be managed, not ignored.

Of course, good leaders always knew that the engine of any enterprise is the people who make it up, how they have learned to work together, how they train and sustain one another—in short, the culture of the organization. They know too that how a culture works is not always measurable. Their intuitive understanding of creativity is a butterfly that can't be caught with a calibrated net. So beware of books that reduce complex human processes to simple grids.

Any integration of human beings and their technologies requires that humans learn how to use those technologies effectively to minimize friction, generate and sustain energy, and keep tacking back and forth across a straight line to our goal or vision. That journey is a long-distance run, not a sprint, and a long-distance run requires a different kind of training and a different kind of discipline.

There are plenty of smart people in the work place, but sometimes we need perspective rather than a quick fix. Perspective is synonymous with wisdom. Wisdom may be scarcer than intelligence, but it's nuclear fuel that burns clean and burns a lot longer.

Professional Communicators   *July 4, 1998*

From one point of view, all we humans do is communicate. We broadcast information about ourselves all the time, just as our planet broadcasts information into space. Isn't there a better name than "space?" "Space" sounds like Greeks calling all the non-Greeks "barbarians." The Universe is teeming with life, and all we can call it is "space?"

But I digress.

All humans communicate, yes, but there are also men and women who call themselves "professional speakers." I am just back from a convention of two thousand of them. The National Speakers Association has been a tent for twenty-five years under which every conceivable kind of "professional speaker" comes to work and play.

Nick Carter, one of the great veterans of the speaking business, calls himself a professional communicator, not a professional speaker. By making that distinction, he captures the essence of life in the digital world.

The digital world is interactive, modular, and very much in flux, and because it is engineering the way we imagine everything, we see our selves as modular and transitory too. We imagine life as a kind of plug-and-play digital game. We build symbolic modules in our minds and live in those morphing modules even as our intuition tells us that there is a larger matrix of possibility from which they all emerge.

In a world of simulations, we achieve our goals by maintaining some consistency of artifact and design. We sustain a professional identity the way a business engages in branding. In a way that prior generations could not imagine, our intentions really do generate the landscapes of our lives. The primacy of intentionality extends far beyond tasks or projects to our selves and personas, the identities we present to the world. We become who we intend to become, and when we alter the matrix of our lives, when we move through any kind of dramatic passage or transition, we must build a symbolic bridge even as we cross the chasm to become the self we are imagining, adding modules to the modules of which we are already built.

Back to that great circus of "professional speakers." Enter the tent, the first thing you notice is that every single one of us is hopelessly neurotic. What a bunch we are, honestly. We traffic in symbols, nothing but symbols, and because we know that we're always dancing in the middle of the air, we pretend all the more that there's firm ground under our feet. We look around at all the beautiful people and compare our fluttering, anxious insides with the polished veneer of these practiced actors. We come together because we need one another deeply, but the minute we're together, we pretend we don't. We present images of accomplishment and success that would make even a Bill Gates doubt his vocation.

But then, that's all of us, isn't it? Isn't that life in a knowledge economy? What happens at that convention is what happens in the digital world. We can choose to believe the symbols or we can see through them to both the childlike fears and the real contribution of the people who invent them. We come back to both the digital world and that convention because every year we find more real connection, more modular structures to channel the flow of energy and information, and suddenly we discover that we have real friends in a world in which no one can know enough to make it alone.

Maintaining integrity in a world of simulations is, at best, pretty tricky. Integrity once meant "walking the talk," the congruence of action and speech. Now integrity means alignment of our selves and all of the digital images we create.

The worst mistake we can make is to confuse our presentations for the imperfect foundation on which they stand.

The story is told of a violinist whose notes were diced and spliced by an expert mixer until the concerto he had played a dozen times had been turned into one perfect performance. He was listening to the sound track with obvious delight and turned to a colleague. "Isn't that magnificent?"

"Yes," said his friend. "Don't you wish you could play that well?"

Our egos always airbrush our self-portraits. Our minds are like PhotoShop, making everything look better. The war between memory and pride, noted Nietzsche, is always won by pride. Session musicians are replaced by synthesizers, actors by their own more perfect digital scans. How can we believe those images represent who we really are? And yet … they do … because our images of ourselves are generated by interacting in and through the matrix of those digital symbols. Mental artifacts couple with digital ones. The simulation becomes the real landscape, perception becomes reality. The symbolic universe we inhabit defines our larger life in a way we can never escape.

"Professional speakers" had better become "professional communicators" and so had everybody else. The symbolic modules we construct are bridges between the thought of taking a step and the step itself, a Big Toy we can climb to the next level of self-representation and self-understanding. We need that bridge because we are headed for a cliff. The cliff is our extinction, the moment of our translation as a species into something else, something that we half-create and half-discover as we take control of our evolution, spread throughout the solar system and to the nearest stars, and become … utterly other.

Yes, we do need a better name than "space" for the gregarious universe. And a better name than "human" for what we are becoming. And a better name than "aliens" for the others we encounter. And a better name than "writer" or "speaker" for people who give names to emergent realities. Both the names and the realities have already been invented somewhere in the deeper matrix under us all. We ride a river of archetypal energy streaming from an underground canyon, rafting a white-water river that is a dream, not ours, under a sky of multiple moons.

Straight Talk   *October 22, 1999*

A reader wrote that recent columns emphasize sentiment, rather than technological issues, and he's right. So I found myself asking, what *are* the issues occasioned by technology as we experience them fired at us every morning at point blank range from the barrel of a gun?

The real issues, alas, *are* human issues. Due to rapid changes in technology, the possibilities of our lives fan out like the paths of sub-atomic particles. The ones that become real are those we choose to make real. But in the meantime, the number of options confronting every task from choosing a new television to resolving complex issues of work, parenting, or being in relationship cause much of the underlying stress so many feel.

We are realizing that reinventing ourselves is not a one-time event, but an ongoing affair. The task of asking who we are and how we will work and live is serious business that requires time and energy—the last thing we feel we have to give.

The digital world, like the print world before it, is assimilating us into its radical and powerful way of manipulating symbols, and since we are symbol-using creatures, every dimension of our lives is in transition. The digital world is interactive, modular, and fluid, which means that aspects of our lives that previously carried an illusion of fixity are becoming interactive, modular and fluid to a greater degree. So what we once experienced as optional—the need to step back and see the Big Picture, taking "time out" to journey into the deep places of our hearts by journaling, engaging in intentional conversations with trusted others, or just having the courage to pay attention to the disruptive events in our everyday lives—is no longer an option.

Some kind of personal or corporate retreat is as essential to intentional living as strategic planning is to business.

Nevertheless, because we often don't know how to build in the time or do the task, that "space" in our lives is something more often talked about than created and used effectively. We hire personal trainers to build up our bodies but hesitate to employ coaches to assist us in clarifying values or refining our personal vision and examining how our behaviors do or do not align with them. Yet those deeper realities affect our day-to-day lives more than the incidents and accidents to which we pay attention.

You know what? We can not have it all. We have to make hard choices and that often means real and painful sacrifice. So many popular modalities of spirituality and personal growth are popular precisely because they promise growth and fulfillment at little or no cost. But life is not like that. Life is not an endless cocktail party with gracious servants replenishing trays so we can eat whatever we want throughout the night.

Choices about technology begin with choices about people. Technology is about technology only in the abstract. It is in fact always about people—people who are changed by it, people to whom it discloses new ways of being human. Yet it is precisely the human dimension that is often ignored as we distribute workers into simulated nodal space in cubicle cities, where they sink into the quiet desperation of interfacing only with simulated digital humans over telephones and networks.

At a recent meeting of representatives from organizations working on Y2K issues at which I spoke, the moderator (a COBOL programmer) said:

"I have been working on Y2K for three years, but until I saw today's topic, 'The Human Dimension of Y2K,' it never occurred to me that there *was* a human dimension of Y2K."

The programmer surfed the Internet and was astonished to discover a cottage industry spreading FUD (fear, uncertainty, doubt) in order to increase their short term profits.

Think of it ... three years working on code without ever thinking of how those lines of code would combine into massive structures of behavior-changing modules that would constitute a distinct culture and demand of human users significant changes in thinking, feeling and behaving.

Implementing enterprise software like SAP restructures a human culture as radically as a merger between different businesses, yet the culture of the software – often implicit in the assumptions it brings to the humans who will use it – always wins. It is easier to dismiss employees who can't adapt to new software than adapt software to the humans who use it.

Take computer security, an area where it's easy to see how widespread our unacknowledged commitment to "invincible ignorance" has become. Computer security is a contradiction in terms. Those who work in the dark heart of the global network manifest an "appropriate paranoia" because they know; they really know. Yet again and again, real security is the last item on corporate priority lists. Quick fixes like firewalls or intrusion detection systems will cover the buns of anyone called to justify procedures after a theft or major act of espionage. But those in the know know that firewalls and intrusion detection systems in and of themselves do not do squat for real security because the weakest link in a network is the human user, how humans think about security, how humans love to outwit the electronic network.

Most users operate out of an obsolete trust model that is not congruent with how intelligence and counter-intelligence, disinformation, espionage and sabotage is done in the digital world. It is the difference between showing an ID to board a plane in the United States and showing up in Israel hours early to be interrogated. Israel knows what shadows lurk in the hearts of women and men and acts accordingly.

As the digital world assimilates us more and more into its looking-glass ways, we ignore the human dimension to our peril. We human beings, digitized and distributed, are not who we used to be, nor is human civilization. The real issues of computing are issues of identity and self, and that's where planning and strategy, personal and professional, should begin.

Time for Yoda – and Yodette   *April 18, 2000*

Yoda – that great guru puppet of the Star Wars stories – knew how to wait patiently as cycles unwound and possibilities emerged with some discernible shape from a sea of seeming chaos. That ability to wait involved the principle of wu wei or "not doing," a "wise passivity," as Wordsworth said, rather than mere inactivity – a kind of settling back into the rocking chairs of our souls as we lean forward at the same time with eager anticipation.

When it looked as if Luke Skywalker might not be up to the job, Yoda said, "There is another."

In a quantum universe, there are always other possibilities waiting in the wings. Seeing how to create them is the source of our real power. Our scripts, too, the ones we write for our lives, include alternative endings, and we contain inside ourselves an understudy for every role that we write. We are both star and understudy, teacher and learner, and wisdom means knowing when it's time for the star to step down and the understudy to step up:

When to catch the curl of a wave just as it breaks forth from the formlessness of the surging sea.

Here we are, after the rise and sudden plunge and rise again of the markets, surfing the currents of greed and fear that blew that bubble near to bursting, popped it, blew it up again.

Pop. Puff. Pop. Puff.

Greed and fear move markets. Long-term investors know that we don't manage money. We manage ourselves. We manage greed, fear, pride, and hope. We manage our sense of self-importance. Money is a blank screen onto which we project the contents of our souls. Then we treat those projections as if something other than ourselves is out there.

This is a good time to remember the wisdom of Yoda. Dot coms are falling all around us like the frog plague at the end of the movie "Magnolia."

Splat! Splat!

Reality is, after all, the final filter of our dreams. All excesses sift through the filter of real things. But reality is never what we think.

The net revolution will continue, of course, and the integration of a new kind of human being into the electric web will continue as well. But something else is being born, something we don't know how to talk about yet ... the collective experience of multiple generations that look at the world from multiple perspectives like facets of a fly's eyes. Longevity will soon stretch our lifetimes so that three, four, five, six, seven generations will occupy the same space—different perspectives that must somehow become cells in a singular matrix glowing with the wisdom and long view of a Yoda.

Or a Yodette. Like my online colleague, Kathleen Jacoby, author of the *Vision of the Grail* (serialized at Planetlightworker.com) who recently wrote:

"Living in Silicon Valley, where life and technology unfold at a dizzying pace, I watch my daughters being consumed by the industry and wonder where the idealic life is that we baby boomers envisioned. Being in the center of the new Athens of the world, I see cracks in the facade. People rush from activity to activity, overloaded, over-stressed, unable to process a growing amount of information.

"We need time for reflection. We need moments of pause and poise. We need observations that bring us back to soul purpose, reminders that we can take what is streaming forward and choose to ride gently with thoughtfulness, rather than jet ski upstream with nothing but dollar signs in our eyes.

"I feel as though our age group has somehow abdicated a position without giving a thought to the vacancy we're leaving. Well it should be that new energy refuels the life blood of a nation ... however, we abdicated too soon. The problem with our fading into the woodwork is that we have left a vacancy of maturity that we've gained through years of reckoning with life. We may not have the raw energy or money that the young here have, but we do have a viewpoint that is needed.

"In Silicon Valley, the lack of soul is evident. I think it's time to stand up and say, 'The Emperor has no clothes!'"

The voice of a minstrel, singing in the silicon wilderness.

Yoda had the viewpoint, Kathleen evokes. He watched entire planets explode as the evil Emperor surfed the currents of the dark side of the Force. Had he believed in fear (which is only faith turned inside out) he would have been impotent to mentor young Luke. He had to believe in a future and he had to believe in young Skywalker not blindly but because he saw his capacity for greatness of soul.

Wander through any hacker gathering worthy of the name, eyes closed and inner eyes open, and discern the essential excellence of the rising tide. Not merely intelligence obsession with knowledge passion or infinite curiosity but a gift of imagination and real soul power.

Yoda taught Luke levitation. Levitation is a way of saying that things rise according to the energies that lift them. Yoda taught Luke to use the Force. The Force is a way of saying that our hunger to engage with mysteries and manifest spiritual power is intrinsic.

Glimpsing deeper things puts everything into perspective.

There are more things in more heavens, on more earths, than we can imagine. Words like "miracle" fail to evoke what we see during moments of clear seeing: that consciousness is a sea in which we cannot help but swim, moving to the currents of our deeper intentions, deep below what we think makes the wheels turn and the cycles arise, the motive and soul power driving our real lives.

In a world of simulations, wise puppets make good mentors. Yoda knew that the bow the arrow and the target are just one thing. That the river curves to the contours of the earth. And that deep belief in the power that binds and transforms, binds and transforms.

For AJ: always more than meets the eye.

Whistleblowers and Team Players

January 17, 2003

It was only after whistleblowers came out of the closet during the Great Deflation that *Time Magazine* honored the practice of what team players call "ratting out your pals." Conservative magazines like *Time* may give lip service to whistleblowing in the abstract but never champion whistle blowers until after they have sung. Instead they support the conditions and practices which make whistleblowers a threat in the first place.

Whistleblowers are a reminder that ethics must be embodied in real flesh-and-blood human beings who put themselves on the line. Unless our deeper beliefs and values become flesh, they are words, words, words, designed to make us feel better, rationalize misdeeds, and send distracting pangs of conscience straight into space.

If you have never known a real flesh-and-blood whistleblower, see the film "The Insider" for a good portrait. The film confirms the conclusion of a Washington law firm specializing in whistleblower cases that lists motivations for whistleblowing—money, anger and resentment, revenge, justice—and eliminates all but one as sufficient to carry a whistleblower through the abuse they will face. Only acting from a pained conscience will sustain a whistleblower through the ordeal.

During a recent speech for accountants about ethics, our Q&A moved quickly into the gray areas where accountants spend much of their time. Outsiders think accountants live in a black and white grid with simple answers but in fact they wade through a swamp of maybe this or maybe that.

Accountants are paid whistleblowers. Accountants are intended to be in the corporate culture but not of it, to use company books like mirrors to reveal the truth and consequences of choices. That's why it is so difficult to do the job right.

The tension comes from the fact that only an individual can have a conscience. An institution or organization can develop a culture that supports doing the right thing only when a leader pursues that objective with single-minded intensity. Left to themselves, all cultures are based on survival, not telling the truth. Cultures reward team players, not whistleblowers. In all my years as a teacher, priest, speaker and consultant, I have never seen a culture with a conscience.

A cop friend reminds me that the first time a rookie cop sees his partners beat someone up in an alley or notices that money or cocaine doesn't always get back to the station, he is closely watched. The word goes out quickly that "he's OK" or "watch out for him." Those that are OK move up. The cop is a practicing Roman Catholic and noted that recent scandals in the church are symptoms of the same dynamics.

Institutions usually encourage disclosure only when it no longer matters. Operation Northwoods—the desire by the Joint Chiefs of Staff in 1962 to eliminate Fidel Castro by sinking refugee boats from Cuba, attacking our own base at Guantanamo, and planting terror bombs in American cities—was revealed by James Bamford in his book "Body of Secrets," but nary a peep of outrage greeted revelation of the treasonous scheme. When the Church apologized to Galileo for torturing him four hundred years after the fact, it raised the question of how an institution had so lost its moorings that someone might think an absurd gesture like that had meaning.

In Wisconsin a friend was nominated to head an arts board at the state level. His work on behalf of the party in power and his passion for art collecting made him a natural but he was passed over. I asked a confidante of then-governor Tommy Thompson why.

"He's not a team player," he said. "He isn't predictable."

The guy who told me this was a team player. He was faithful and steady and worked tirelessly to raise money for the party. When friends were "naughty," as he called it, he looked the other way. He called recently to tell me he was now a million dollars richer, having been compensated at that level for three years on the board of an energy firm. He had been recommended for the position by his friend, now-Secretary Tommy Thompson.

Thus has it always been. Thus will it ever be.

Why are so many of your heroes, I was asked, people who were assassinated? Why do names like Jesus, Lincoln, Gandhi, and Martin Luther King, Jr. keep showing up in your conversation?

I think it's because they embody what it takes to make a stand on behalf of the truth. They were all human but found the courage to blow the whistle on the cultures of death our institutions create. Their reward was getting whacked.

Make no mistake, those who articulate or embody an upward call always inspire ambivalence. A disciple of Gandhi said that even those who loved him most were secretly relieved when he was murdered because for the moment the pressure was off. Jesus as icon is malleable in the hands of his institutional custodians whereas Jesus the Jew in the street was a real pain.

In an era characterized by increasing secrecy by the government and the gradual but progressive surrender of our rights, it's only a matter of time until some malevolent design ripens and bursts into the sunlight because some whistleblower just can't stand it another minute. Some team player, their motives mixed but their conscience pricked, will tell the truth. That's the only way to have accountability when those with power and privilege remove transparency from the processes of government and business.

When a mainstream Midwest woman asks how she will tell her grandchildren what America was like before the Great Change, how she will explain openness and disclosure, the Freedom of Information Act, guarantees in the Bill of Rights … then I know that we don't need a weatherman to know the direction of the wind and see the firestorm on the horizon. Signs of the times grow on trees like low-hanging fruit, ripe for the picking.

We are all team players, all of us some of the time, some of us all of the time, but we each have our own particular crossroads where we must decide if our words will become flesh. It is never easy and there are always consequences. Only integrity will see us through to the bitter end and none of us really know if we have it until it is tested.

Chapter 4

Hacking and the Passion for Knowledge

Fear and Trembling in Las Vegas

October 1, 1996

It was my privilege in the summer of 1995 to deliver a keynote address at DefCon IV, an annual convention of computer hackers held every summer in Las Vegas. Daytime temperatures near 120 degrees ensured that casual curiosity seekers would be at a minimum. In heat that fries an egg on the pavement, you had better want to be there.

It was a surprise, then, when eight hundred people showed up, nearly double the expected attendance. It was an exciting convention, but above all else, it is fear that I remember: the collection of hackers inspired more fear and anxiety in the management of the hotel than anything I had ever seen. I felt as if it were 1968 and the security guards were Chicago police.

After the first night, for example, hotel personnel waited until three in the morning to install tiny security cameras in the ceilings of our meeting rooms. Numerous news crews from mainstream sources like Good Morning America were thrown out of the convention, their video tape confiscated. Concern over self-indulgence was extreme, resulting in my favorite convention photo: a 52-year-old man being "carded" in order to enter a hotel restaurant where alcohol was served.

What is it about hackers that provokes such fear?

It begins with the popular image of hackers as "evil geniuses," invading our board rooms and bedrooms at will. That image began with the movie *War Games*, and in fact the writer of that screen play, Larry Lasker, was at the convention, paying close attention to the latest trends.

But Lasker is the first to admit that alienated teenagers hunched over glowing screens as they attack the Pentagon are not the whole story. There were plenty of security experts at DefCon, plus intelligence agents, professional engineers, and thriving businessmen.

Real hackers are distinguished not by anti-social tendencies but by their hunger for knowledge. Hackers do not accept conventional explanations; they want to know, see, feel things for themselves. The only way to do that, they believe, is to enter our complex systems of information technology and look around.

Leonardo da Vinci was a hacker. He refused to limit his exploration of the universe to the constraints his more conventional neighbors called "the known world." He refused to limit his imagination. He did not ask permission before challenging conventional wisdom. This is why Bill Gates paid a fortune for the Codex Leicester created by that master hacker.

Are hackers criminals?

The short answer is no, not necessarily. Hackers distinguish between real hackers and crackers, or criminal hackers. Crackers use hacking skills to commit fraud, destroy or steal intellectual property, and vandalize the information systems of governments and businesses.

From here on, though, things get a little vague. On the highest levels of international diplomacy, it is difficult to distinguish not only hackers but crackers from government agents. Governments have bugged seats on transatlantic flights to glean important economic information. Governments—including our own—employ master hackers to spy and pry into the economic secrets of friend and foe alike. The busiest people at DefCon were FBI agents—"it's nice to be here for the first time," said FBI agent Andrew Black, "overtly"—who spent their days recruiting promising "brains."

Global information warfare has succeeded the Cold War. In the global marketplace, a marketplace characterized by increasingly semi-permeable national boundaries, information is ammunition.

This marketplace is appropriately likened to "the wild west" because there is often no legal authority to which to appeal when one has been wronged. In the virtual world, one is often forced to take the law into one's own hands. The Hacker's Code is a way to define for the online culture how bonds of trust, accountability to standards, and mutual self-interest can be sustained while the non-virtual legal world debates definitions of intellectual property that will never apply to digital constructs that are plastic and transitory, protean forms authored by online networks that have no names.

The printing press fixed information in forms that required "authors" as owners of those forms, and authors and authorship evolved. Electronic media are de-inventing those forms, those owners. We do not yet have a vocabulary of adjectives and verbs with which to depict a process that disappears when we try to nail it down with nouns.

Anxiety and fear are ubiquitous these days, but irrational fears of hackers are linked to more rational fears as well.

> In a global marketplace in which information is currency and knowledge capital, every organization is like an independent country. Intelligence and counter-intelligence is no longer a luxury. What you know must be protected; what others know about your business must be actively managed.
>
> Hackers are feared because their powers have been excessively magnified by the media. But their real knowledge of how the technological infrastructure works is also real power. Hacking is the creative exploration of the complex systems of information to which our lives are wedded. Hacking skills are essential to the well-being of organizations that intend to remain competitive.
>
> Competitive Business Intelligence 101 should be a required course at every business school.
>
> Hackers are not one-dimensional cartoon figures. They are complex human beings. They may play at night in the electronic Big Toy called the Internet, but most hold good jobs in security, intelligence, and high tech businesses. Hacking is where they got good at what they do.

"Tiger teams" of hackers often work collaboratively with government and business to identify holes in their networks and secure their systems. The teams for which I have served as an intermediary are composed of brilliant individuals using their skills in a beneficial way.

As life in the next century becomes unimaginably complex, the skills of hacking will be in demand. As the center continues to shift, we need those who know how to live on the edge. We need bushwhackers, pathfinders, scouts.

Hackers who know the territory make good guides on the electronic frontier.

The Enemy is ... WHO?   *August 2, 1997*

There are days I miss the Cold War a lot.

Things were so much simpler then. The world was divided into two great camps, ours and theirs, and everybody who didn't fit neatly into the schema could be made to fit with a shoehorn of twisted cold-war logic. Countries irrelevant to the ideological battle were either "with us" or "against us."

One day I looked at the map and realized that—even at the height of the Cold War—the geopolitical domination of the world by the United States was nearly absolute. The enemy controlled much less territory than the USA, but the more the United States controlled, the less secure Americans felt.

I wondered how much we needed in order to feel secure.

That reminded me of a seminar I attended. A man of obvious means was standing up and boasting of making his first million and working on his second. After listening for a long time, the seminar leader asked: How much will you have to have in order to have enough?

The guy was stopped in his tracks. He had obviously never considered the question. He sat back down and went away for a week to think it over.

The next week he stood up again but his manner was different. Finding the answer had changed the way he spoke.

"I realized how much I need in order to have enough," he said. "I have to have ... all of it."

The Cold War worked because it was written in big letters. The economic and political struggle was merely a foundation for the cosmic struggle. The Cold War was Armageddon, Good versus Evil.

Then everything fell apart. Our souls are working overtime to find templates onto which to project the evil that lurks in the hearts of all of us. We're not having much luck, but a couple of candidates are running hard—computer hackers and technology itself. Rational people—educated, thoughtful people—suddenly launch into tirades against "what computers are doing to the world" or how "hackers want to break into my computer."

I'll save "computers" for another time and focus on "hackers."

Hackers are often portrayed as whacked-out loners hunched over glowing monitors in the night, breaking into our bank accounts.

Those aren't the hackers I know. The men and women at DefCon V included some of the best and the brightest. Many wore the costumes of hacking culture but we know better than to stop there, don't we? Ask what they do for a living and you'll find ranking technocrats from Microsoft, IBM, banks and large consulting operations, makers of the best firewall and security systems. You'll find members of every intelligence agency around. Mingling with the hackers and exchanging information at DefCon and the Black Hat Briefings in Las Vegas were people from the military, CIA, FBI, NSA. In fact, those mingling with the hackers ... were the hackers.

Naturally.

Where else could agents of military and business intelligence learn their craft and subtle art but in the sleepless, passionate quest for knowledge in the networked world, tunneling through the gerbil tubes of the wired world? Hackers are need-to-know machines who go where they need to go to learn what they need to learn in order to understand how things really work.

In the knowledge economy, the people who know how to find knowledge and link it into meaningful patterns, not just amass collections of data but connect it in ways that illuminate and disclose the human reality behind the information—those are the people with their hands on the throttles of power, and those are hackers at their best. Even when they work for multinational corporations and intelligence agencies.

The revolution in information technology is one reason the boundaries of nation states are growing more and more permeable. Those boundaries evolved to define economic and political reality and protect populations. These days, when we can live anywhere and work everywhere, when multi-national corporations make decisions that transcend traditional political structures, when ideological and religious passions surge back and forth over borders like the ocean at high tide—how are we to identify the enemy?

According to the Chinese Army newspaper, Jiefangjun Bao, speeches at the new Military Strategies Research Center were summarized this way:

The goal is no longer to preserve oneself and destroy the enemy. The goal is to preserve oneself and control one's opponent. (*Wired*, May 1997).

Information warfare is the name of the game.

Remember Somalia? All it took was a thirty-second video clip showing one Marine being dragged through a crowd to undermine our will.

I miss those Cold War spy novels. Double agents unmasked at last, spymasters playing global chess. Today the game is more like ten-dimensional chess. Allegiance to who and to what? Our loyalties are nested like Russian dolls, and sometimes even we don't know on behalf of whom or what we are really acting.

Behaviors that are penalized in one context are sanctioned in others. The determining factor is not the action but the allegiance of the actor.

It is not the behavior of hackers that is threatening but their perceived allegiance. Ally themselves with a government, intelligence agency, or large corporation and they can hack their hearts out, with more computing power at their disposal than they can dream.

Ironic, isn't it? The "West" won the Cold War, the economy is the best in decades, and Americans have everything they thought they wanted. Yet people are more anxious and insecure than ever.

Security comes not from having what you want—even when you have all of it—but from stability and predictability. And that—in a world undergoing fundamental transformation—is in short supply.

So people will continue to project fear and anxiety onto templates provided by the media. Hackers—not criminal hackers, but real hackers—will continue to be demonized and misunderstood, because the nature of power, influence, and leverage in a global knowledge economy will continue to be misunderstood.

You can't write a 32-bit application for an IBM XT. It just can't handle the code.

I won't remind you that Pogo said "We have met the enemy and it is us" because everybody knows that. I'll just note that no amount of stuff, including knowledge, can give us what we need. Our desperate search for security in a changing world is really the pursuit of our own souls. That's all we can ever possess in its entirety anyway. We're like people wearing glasses running around frantically looking for our glasses. We have what we need, always, here and now. The enemy is anybody and anything that prevents us from seeing clearly what a crazy maze we have built to keep us from remembering that.

A Moment of Clarity   *February 28, 1998*

If we are fortunate, there occurs at least once in our lifetimes a "moment of clarity" in which we observe ourselves with our own eyes and see how narrowly we have lived in contrast with how we might live if we fulfilled the possibilities of our best selves. We see that we have come to everything - work, relationships, even the Internet - with an intention to use or exploit it to meet our needs. We see that it is possible to come tothe world with an intention to expand the options and possibilities of others instead of our own.

Most people familiar with hacking culture know the name of Richard Stallman, founder of the GNU project. GNU = "GNU's not UNIX" although it is a robust UNIX-compatible operating system that is - remarkably – freely available to the entire world.

Stallman was honored at the Computers, Freedom and Privacy conference for his consistency and the magnitude of his contribution. His speeches and informal conversation suggest that this particular Don Quixote is equal to the long-term demands of his improbable vision. The GNU project is no sprint for Mister Stallman.

What distinguishes Stallman from visionaries who have nothing but ideas is that Stallman is implementing his ideas. His words have become flesh, his vision is incarnate.

The GNU project is unfinished and needs programmers and donations, but even if another line of code is never written, GNU has achieved so much more than anyone—except Stallman—might have dreamed.

Some dismiss him as just another brilliant programmer stuck in the sixties culture at MIT where he learned what it meant to be part of a real hacking community in which everyone's work, ideas and computers were open and free to all. Like the source code that Stallman thinks ought to be available to everybody always.

Quixote's sidekick, Sancho Panza, would insist on a reality check, and maybe we ought to listen to him. I grew up in Chicago, after all, and people like Saul Alinsky, the late great community organizer, reminded us that we all act on our own self-interest. We may use the vocabulary of the righteous, he observed, but we always vote our advantage. He would have scoffed at Stallman's vision of free software owned by all who use it.

Alinsky's contemporary, Mayor Richard J. Daley, was often attacked by opponents from what seemed to be high moral ground. After they had screamed long enough, the mayor frequently invited them to his office. He asked one question: what do you need? And after he listened for a while, he asked one more: But what do you really need?

Alinksy knew what we needed, but Stallman knows what we really need. Once we have had that moment of clarity and our energy shifts, flowing out into the lives of others in a way that meets our own needs too, we experience a feedback loop that is mutually nourishing, that grows exponentially. Once we have experienced that shift, we can never again come to others only to exploit them without knowing it and knowing that we have a choice.

The GNU Project is wildly unrealistic. People just don't give themselves over to a project like that. Our economic system uses money to measure our contributions. Cash flow, like dye in the arteries of our efforts, tells us how we're doing.

At least that's how it looks from inside the old paradigm.

The digital world is changing how we use money. Not just replacing the exchange of paper for an exchange of electrons, but redefining how we do business. Electronic commerce, according to the vision of Robert Hettinga, a financial cryptographer, might bring into being a geodesic society. The intermediary between any two entities will be secure electronic commerce. Financial cryptography, secure electronic commerce, and a geodesic society, he suggests, might reinstate character as the true basis of financial transactions. If one person tries to defraud another in an electronic transaction, their identity would be exposed, but if their word is good, the transaction closes, their identity protected.

Stallman's vision of software owned by all is similar to Hettinga's vision of electronic commerce as a system that rewards trust. Yes, we are all self-interested, but when we act collectively, when our projects include and magnify the talents of everyone who participates and contributes, we discover a mutual self-interest that transcends our individual self-interest.

It's difficult to talk about all this from inside the old paradigm. We begin projects like programming thinking of our "selves" as individuals, authors of our "own" work, as the printing press and copyright law taught us to think. But when we lose ourselves in the digital collective, in the kind of fulfillment that Stallman upholds as the ultimate good of our lives, then the boundaries between reader and writer, software author and user community blur. The collective authorship of which Stallman speaks is similar to monastics working together on an illuminated manuscript. Who owns the perpetually unfinished product? We speak of software "authors" but a group creates the software and the whole world owns the code.

Sometimes what feels like going backward is really going forward. Sancho may be a realist, seeing through our fanciful dreams, but Don Quixote stirs our hearts and inspires our best selves. Quixote went crazy from reading too many books and believing them, only 150 years after the printing press was invented. Maybe Stallman has written too many programs. Maybe he's come to believe that what he feels when losing himself in something of inestimable value to the entire community is what we ought to use to measure all our efforts. It's difficult to distinguish a child's refusal to accept the adult world on its own terms from a crazy kind of sainthood, the kind that insists that we belong to one another, that dreaming and thinking take place today on a network, and that we are all cells in a single body.

If Truth Be Told   *August 1, 1998*

The press coverage of the Black Hat Briefings II and Def Con VI tells part of the story, but the fact that mainstream media covered those cons the way they did tells much of the rest.

Def Con is the biggest and most celebrated convention for computer hackers. The con has grown from sixty to two thousand in six years. The Black Hat Briefings, which grew out of Def Con, is a forum in which the best and brightest hackers engage in serious conversation with experts in computer security. The technical presentations are as good as it gets, and attendance at Black Hat tripled in a year.

Stories about Def Con in the *New York Times* and *L. A. Times* had similar slants: young hackers who a few years ago hesitated to reveal even their on-line handles now occupy critical positions in business and government. Which is certainly part of the story.

The crew from CNN, however, floating through Def Con like the bright shining bubble of the Good Witch of the North, was a symbol of a bigger truth.

Leon Panetta once said that CNN inserted itself like a filter between our minds and our own experience of reality.

Panetta recalled his arrival at the White House as Chief of Staff. One of the first things he wanted to see was the Situation Room. He wanted to know if it really looked like the one in "Doctor Strangelove."

So what did he find?

"Two guys in shirtsleeves sitting at a table watching CNN."

Now, think about it. A much younger Leon P sits in a darkened movie theater. Inside his head are "symbolic modules" generated by his youthful experience and education. "Doctor Strangelove" coupled an image of a hidden, forbidden reality— the situation room where life and death decisions are made—with that modular interface. With all his experience and political savvy, Panetta still wondered when he arrived at the White House years later if the image fit. He said it did not ... but in a deeper way, maybe it did.

Panetta saw two people interact with CNN, a medium that couples symbolic modules with our modular constructions of reality. Panetta had interacted with a movie that coupled a symbolic module with his construction of reality. In other words, decades later he laughed at two guys for doing what he had done ... and he had believed in his images all those years.

The CNN crew attracted everyone's attention. The camera and fuzzy mike on a long boom were huge, and every time they turned on the bright lights, attention in the room swirled around them like water going down a bathtub drain. Like physicists observing sub-atomic particles, they altered what they saw by the act of observing it.

The reporters who directed the process knew their business, but not hacker reality. "Three weeks ago, I had never heard of Def Con," said one. They looked forward to the Black-and-White Ball on Saturday night because they wanted good visuals. The visuals would be filtered to fit the expectations of the audience—expectations created by the media, where images of hackers have replaced Cold War spies as magnets of fear and fascination.

The media need modules that snap tightly together without being forced.

News and entertainment are virtually indistinguishable in the digital world. Their agendas are set by those who own the media and decide what is thinkable. Those who determine the questions that can be asked do not need to worry about the answers. The answers fly about in simulated opposition like birds flocking to a few recursive rules inside a digital cage. Because the birds have enough room, they do not even notice the cage.

At a deeper level, the structure of our information infrastructure determines how we think, the questions that we ask. That infrastructure is the context of our lives. Those who work at the nexus of context and content rule the digital world.

We don't notice those cages either, but that's what the real geniuses at Black Hat and Def Con are building. Those who code software and build chips (i.e. code in a harder state, like ice and water) create the contours or parameters of commerce, social interaction, and the kinds of wars we fight.

Although intrusion and data manipulation or destruction can be damaging, hackers are not threatening simply because they can break into systems. At the top level, it is their ability to piece together the Big Picture and see how the imaginary landscapes that we call "the real world" are constructed that constitutes a threat.

Hackers, spies and journalists resemble one another.

A reporter told me of her journey through ostensible coverage of the software industry to the unintended discovery of how things really work. Her off-the-record account detailed infiltration, collusion, and sabotage. "It wasn't what I was looking for," she said, "but I can't forget what I saw."

I mentioned something a hacker had uncovered, and she laughed. I repeated what I said and she laughed again.

"Ridicule is easy," I said. "The first line of defense of consensus reality."

"I have to laugh at that," she said, suddenly not laughing. "I would go insane otherwise."

If truth be told, that reporter is telling it. Wisdom and sanity depend on a context to give them meaning. When the context shifts, wisdom becomes nonsense, what is sensible sounds insane. And vice versa. The first line of defense of consensus reality is always to laugh, then ridicule, then attack.

Hackers don't live inside that consensus. Nor do spies. They live too close to the edge, the terminator on the moon where everything is thrown into relief, where intentionality creates consensus. In a world of pure information, intentionality is everything.

There's plenty of laughter at Def Con, but it's laughter at the paradox of the mind observing itself, watching itself build worlds in which—in spite of seeing marks of the tools on the raw material, the tools in our own hands—we lack the freedom not to believe.

Life in Space   *August 8, 1998*

There was so much hullabaloo at Def Con VI! (the recent convention for computer hackers, journalists, screen writers, producers, computer security and insecurity experts, programmers, federal agents, local police and sheriff's deputies, advertisers and marketers, hotel security guards, undercover agents, refugees from raves, groupies, and endlessly curious mind-hungry men and women of all sorts and conditions)—hullabaloo, that is, about how hackers have morphed from evil geniuses into respectable men and women operating at the highest levels of industry and commerce, the military, and the intelligence community.

The basis for comparison, of course, is an image of hackers as whacked-out loners hunched over glowing monitors late into the night, cackling like Beavis or Butthead as they break into our bank accounts—an image created and sustained by the media.

Well …let's be real. Some do, some are. That's part of the scene, the digital equivalent of growing up in Hell's Kitchen and living down these mean digital streets. That, however, is not the essence of hacking.

Hacking is curiosity, playfulness, problem-solving, motivated by the pleasure of browsing, following one's nose where others say it doesn't belong, looking for a constellation in the seemingly random stars. Following the luminous bread crumbs deep into the twilight forest. Building an elusive, always-hypothetical whole that forms and dissolves and forms again at every level of the fractal puzzle of life.

Hacking has its roots in Renaissance men like da Vinci and Machiavelli who saw clearly and said what they saw.

But something else is happening too. As I looked out at the audience of the Black Hat Briefings, I saw that the roles of journalists, specialists in competitive intelligence, spies, even professional speakers like myself, were converging, that roles in a digital world are as fluid as identities.

The skills of hackers and intelligence agents are the skills needed in the virtualized worlds we are learning to inhabit.

We hear endlessly of convergence of form and structure in the wired world. Every digital interface is an arbitrary distinction. Because we can reconstitute bits in whatever form we like, deciding to call an interface a PC, TV, or PDA is a job for marketing, not engineers.

But I'm talking about the convergence of roles. The digital world is engineering us in its image. Because that world is interactive, modular, and fluid, our lives are too. We don't even notice anymore that to choose to present ourselves to the world is a choice.

At one extreme, identity hacking—stealing identifiers like numbers and codes with which to gain access to the social and economic world or creating a new identity from whole digital cloth in order to disappear and surface in a new body—is a growing industry. But choices we take for granted—changing jobs, religions, marital status, changing our names, changing careers, changing who we essentially think we are – have become part of consensus reality. Not so long ago, people who did that were thought to be just plain nuts.

Once upon a time, the roles we were expected to fulfill were our destinies. Unless external crises intervened, people were expected to stay in one place, get a job and keep it, get married and stay married, be whatever religion they were told they were (as if something else were even thinkable), and live inside a single identity that was so much a fish in water that it wasn't questioned.

Identity is a social construction of reality that's noticed only when the external factors that shape it have changed.

The new consensus reality is reinforced by information sources from talk shows to the *Wall Street Journal*. We can choose careers, another marriage, another religion, another way of being ourselves, and we are everywhere surrounded by helpful advice about how to do it.

In the digital world, sanity means having the resources and capacity to know how to morph, changing presentations that are bridges between constantly shifting external factors and our own developmental stages. This is true for organizations as well as individuals.

The protean self, back-engineered from the structures of our information technologies, thinks of life as a creative act. The ability to distinguish who we are from our presentations, knowing how to use those presentations to exercise power, build feedback loops of energy and information to sustain us, that's a skill that used to belong to spies alone. Now it's asked of everyone who wants to remain viable.

Hackers call it social engineering, learning how to look and sound a particular way to elicit the information needed to build the big picture. In business, it is often called competitive intelligence. Some just call it "the way it is."

Every time I say, "the edge is the new center," I notice that the edge I had in mind is no longer the edge. A new edge is emerging. Turn-around time is about six months, not only for computers, but for viable constructions of reality.

We work and live in space stations, docking in modular fashion, then we're off again into space. That space is sheer possibility in which we create literally from nothing. The pull of the future creates the irresistible shapes of present possibilities with which we must comply. Every time we break through to a new way of seeing things it feels momentous, but breakthroughs are momentous for only a moment. Then they become commonplace, the background noise of the next stage of our lives.

Evil genius hackers? Give me a break. The hackers who have their hands on the throttles of power in the digital world were "kids" three years ago. That's about as long as a current generation lasts. And civilization too is ramping up toward a single point of convergence where identities are arbitrary. What we call "our species" will soon be a wistful memory in the molecular clusters of the progeny we design, an arbitrary distinction that served us for a while before we morphed. A noun turned into a transitory verb. Ice turned into a flowing river.

Don Quixote Goes Digital   *November 7, 1998*

Processing power is dirt cheap and Feds are crawling all over the Net. So why did Aaron Blosser use the network at US West to solve a 17th century math problem?

"Why?" repeats Aaron Blosser. "Why not?"

The question hangs in the air like the grin of the Cheshire cat, a koan posed by a 28-year-old programmer sitting in his apartment in Denver, Colorado. Aaron Blosser has a lot more room to stretch out in his place these days, now that the FBI took away his Pentium II (Blosser called it Big Boy), his 486 (Little Boy), and a pile of his CDs. It's all gone, perhaps forever. And so is his job as a computer consultant.

Blosser lost big because he went on a careless quest for a mathematical grail - the next Mersenne prime. Ever since Marin Mersenne identified a unique class of prime numbers in the 17th century, digit-searchers have been on the prowl for the next Big One. Their search reached the Internet a few years ago, with the release of Mersenne-hunting software that anyone can download. Blosser, a systems consultant working for US West, installed it on the company's customer service network in September. He should have known how to configure the software to run in the background, but instead he misconfigured the machines so that they checked for network activity every two seconds instead of every twenty minutes, flooding the system with packets in the process.

"We noticed a degradation of service at once," says a spokesman for US West. "We respect the pursuit of knowledge, but our workers tend to get irate if the network is not available for work." Thus, while the investigation of the case continues, US West is urging the FBI to prosecute Blosser as quickly as possible.

The Denver Post called him a hacker, but that handle is part of the problem. What Aaron did IS what hackers did do, once upon a time. But it's not what many older hackers do now. For them, the Golden Age of Hacking, which began in the sixties when mainframes at MIT became the Big Toy of a new generation, is over.

Like most hackers, Blosser wasn't trying to be bad. He was trying to advance knowledge, solve a puzzle, find out how things work. From Leonardo da Vinci to Dark Tangent, White Hat hackers are driven by a passion for knowledge, not a desire to foul things up. When Blosser loaded the Mersenne program onto the network at U S West, he wasn't trying to bring down the network. And he certainly wasn't trying to hide. (His name and e-mail address were all over the software.) But his so-called "hack" was unnecessary. Kids did this kind of thing when games were cracked using Apple IIs, then sent to friends via slow, acoustic-coupled modems at 300 bauds. Laws against unauthorized computer intrusion were all but nonexistent then. The challenges of playing the game and cracking the game were identical. Today, hackers play the game of life with real money on the table and the credible threat of prison sentences hanging over their heads.

Taking over a Baby Bell's network in the pursuit of pure Knowledge may sound romantic, but more experienced hackers say it no longer makes much practical sense.

"The media tends to portray all security breaches as 'hacks,' but hacking is not just about security," says security professional Yobie Benjamin. "It's about the whole domain of computer science—moving from node to node to see how things look. It's about harnessing the power of distributed computing." Benjamin laughs. "Blosser needs what Weld Pond calls a midnight basketball league to keep him off the streets."

That is indeed what Weld Pond and the rest of the gang at Boston's L0pht Heavy Industries call their enterprise—a midnight basketball game for hackers. Still animated by a passion for Solving the Puzzle and Seeing the Big Picture, the L0pht crew carries those hacker ideals forward by uncovering security holes in Windows NT or Novell products—without actually trespassing on anyone's system.

That's easier than ever to do these days, thanks to the open-door network of Windows, UNIX and Sun machines available at upt.org - the computer playpen descended from the BBS where some of hacking's best and the brightest honed their skills before graduating into corporate and intelligence ranks. "A lot of the old reasons to break in just aren't there any more," says security consultant Tom Jackiewicz, who helped administer the upt.org BBS. "Nobody can say they can't afford a UNIX box when all you have to do is throw some free LINUX onto a PC. You want to hack a Sun system? Break into ours—if you can."

Jackiewicz said it's more fun to secure a network against hackers than hack. Much more complex. You have to explore every single interaction among all the components, check out "all the weird shit that can happen.

"A guy called the other day to say he'd gotten root in our system," Tom laughed. "In fact, he was trapped in one of the five subsystems we created to look like the system." That's where hacking is at now, working at that level of detail, that level of complexity.

Likewise, if it was empty processor cycles that Blosser wanted, he didn't need to siphon off US West's resources. When the number-crunchers at Distributed.net decided to show that the US government's security claims about 56-bit DES cryptography were a sham, they simply created a software client that anyone could download. After 4000 teams contributed computing power to break the code, DES fell in 212 days. The next challenge, DES II-1, cracked in 40. As David McNett of distributed.net puts it, "I question Blosser's judgement, not his motives."

Hacking's "white hat" ideal lives on, but suitable targets for Robin Hood-style adventures have become increasingly hard to find. In 1997, a hacker and phreaker named Se7en went on a rampage against cyber-pedophiles, targeting their hangouts for network subversion. Nobody knows for sure how many web sites or IRC lairs Se7en and his cohorts took down, but nobody lifted a finger to curtail their vigilante attacks. And when Peter Shipley at dis.org uncovered gaping flaws in the Oakland, California fire department

dispatch system during a massive war-dialing project, authorities overlooked his campaign—in no small part because Shipley volunteered to fix the holes instead of bringing chaos to the streets of Oakland.

With all that in mind, Blosser's network-clogging "hack" was a throwback to the early 1990s, a ghost of hacking past, a Don Quixote apparition of a bygone age when the anarchist rhetoric of John Perry Barlow actually seemed to make sense. Cyberspace felt free then, even if it existed by permission of the military-industrial-educational complex that spawned it. Quixote became crazed after immersing himself in books. That was the paradigm-breaking technology then, 150 years after the invention of the printing press. Blosser's "hack" illuminates the splendid mythologies of a Golden Age of Hacking that have spread in the digital era on the Net.

Today, the laws have tightened, surveillance technologies are ubiquitous, big money is at stake, and the borderless economy is learning to regulate itself. Yet when asked why he loaded that software onto the network at US West, a kid who is nearly 30 laughs and says, "Why not?"

Why not? Because it no longer pays to sustain the illusion. The hackers who played in that club house are all going downtown, making good money while trying to keep their values intact.

Perspective, as Alan Kay said, is worth fifty points of IQ. Maybe we all looked just plain dumb as we lowered the lance and charged the turning blades of the wired world. Blosser's naive quest for the prime may be charming, but experienced hackers understand why it no longer pays to have that kind of innocence.

A note from Richard:
E-mail generated by the publication of this article turned on the real meaning of the word "hacker." In the Denver Post and the edited/published article, Blosser was called a hacker. Yet many hackers do not consider what he did as a hack. The edges are blurred further by the common use of the word "hacker" to mean what real hackers call "crackers," or criminals who use hacking skills in ways that are not congruent with the broader intentions of real hacking—

exploration, the pursuit of knowledge, building the Big Picture, solving the puzzle, serendipitous discovery, impish playfulness, and the sheer exhilaration of exercising power with intelligence, grace and some finesse.

The murkiness is murked up even more by the fractal-like replication of hacking generations every decade or so. Each hacking generation is true to the values of real hacking, but the forms of their exploration are determined by the structures of our technologies. The near-thirty generation quoted in the article is not the first generation of hackers to move into positions of power and authority but they are the first to have "grown up digital." So the essential question is, as technology changes and redefines the "space" in which we hack, what forms will real hacking take?

But that question is for another time

Knowledge, Obsession, Daring

December 26, 1998

The best of times, the worst of times.

Governments prepare for the worst, ramping up toward New Year's Eve 2000 and the dislocations expected at the ticking of the millennial clock.

And yet ... so many of my colleagues, out of nowhere, have recently said: "I can't believe I'm paid to do this for a living!"—"this" meaning the many ways the wired world enables us to work and play.

While others feel excluded or intimidated by new technology, many in the knowledge business are giddy from successive explosions, burst upon burst, of possibility and opportunity. It feels like summer in the long daylight close to the poles.

Writers, for example, have discovered that we work in the world instead of one country. A few decades ago, our readers were defined by our coasts or cultures. Engaging with electronic networks revealed the entire world as our playground.

Yet even to speak of "the entire world" is constraining.

I visited a Protestant Church for a post-Christmas service. The liturgy spoke of God's love for "the world," meaning our planet. But that's not where we live now. Exploring routes to Mars, to the moon and the asteroid belt, to the tempting moons of Jupiter, coupled with years of living in the funhouse-mirror-world of UFO investigation, has shifted my perspective. It happened as Hemingway said bankruptcy happens, gradually then suddenly. Now I live in a universe teeming with life, knowing that a real Encounter, once we allow ourselves to become fully conscious of what is happening, will shatter our status as the "apple of God's eye" and all the parochial notions that derive from it forever.

Columbus, McLuhan reminded us, was a mapmaker before he went exploring. Mapmaking transformed his sense of the possibilities of life. When we interact with new technologies, with complex networks or systems, we discover radically new ways of being in the world.

No wonder so many people are having so much fun.

Artists are creating new virtual worlds, reconstructing the gateways of perception. Corporations that scale up to trans-global dimensions are absorbing enterprises still trying to live in niches that no longer exist. Pan-national religious cultures like Islam or Christianity are trying to dig in, but they too live on borrowed time.

Nostalgia for what is vanishing is a symptom of the evolution of all organizational structures. What is lost—not only forms and structures, but clusters of values, sensibilities, ways of framing realityÂis turned into touristic space. Theme parks replace living villages. When we enter Disneyland, filters created by landscape design eliminate telephone poles, dynamos, strung wiresÂeverything connected to the infrastructure of our lives. Disneyland religion, too, screens out experience that doesn't fit its archaic ways of constructing belief.

To be engaged in a real spiritual quest asks more of us than acquiescence or simple consent.

Edward O. Wilson in Consilience: The Unity of Knowledge reflected on the motive power of scientists at their creative best. They shared, he said, a passion for knowledge; obsession; and daring.

Knowledge. Obsession. Daring.

At a recent hacker con, I was struck—again—by the fact that hacker culture is the space in which everyone will live in the next century. Hacking is not about breaking into locked rooms. Hacking is about mapping, then exploring; or perhaps exploring, then mapping. Hacking is a mandate from evolving technologies to enter a play space characterized by limitless vistas. Properly understood, hacking in its essence is a kind of spiritual quest.

Hacking is not just hard work. It is playfulness at its very best.

An article in the *Boston Globe* described the scene at a toy store before Christmas. "Board games line an entire wall, but they draw so few customers that visitors could hold a race down the aisle without risk of hitting anybody." Across the aisle, however, "shoppers are jamming their carts with GameBoys and Nintendos."

No doubt there will be days when families play board games around physical tables. But the brave new world we foresaw only a few years ago is already morphing toward something else. Children's games prefigure the kind of world adults will inhabit.

We grieve for the loss of one kind of community, back-engineered from particular technologies, until we awaken to a new kind—just as real, immediate, and meaningful—created by new technologies ... and created, as always, out of our alienation and need. New media distance us from one another, then enable us to connect at a deeper level than ever.

Hackers worthy of the name have a passion for knowledge; are obsessed with following luminous breadcrumbs through the darkening forest, solving the puzzle, and understanding the Big Picture before it morphs into a piece in a bigger picture still; and hackers are nothing if not daring.

But hackers do not only explore the electronic innards of a system. Top-level hackers work with images and symbols as they emerge in the hive mind of a self-conscious digital civilization.. They hack the network that we call culture, cobbling together meaning from broken tablets and dead language.

The boundaries between networks—electronic and human—are illusory, ways of differentiating everything from nothing. We are all linked inextricably to everything that is alive, we are the mind of a conscious Being creating and discovering the structures through which we will manifest our will and intention.

How we define or imagine our connection to the Ground of that Being is, quite simply, up for grabs.

Techno/spirituality is the search for our "human nature" as it is transformed and expressed in new structures of possibility. We are primates recognizing their faces in the river for the first time. Our gaze however is mirrored by a digital river, flowing through our collective mind.

Knowledge. Obsession. Daring. This is our genetic heritage, a gift from the earth. The courage to let go of what we were, endure the passage through a zone of annihilation to what we are becoming, and emerge onto the next level of the rising spiral of life.

In Defense of Hacking   *February 16, 2000*

Let's get our definitions straight. Last week's attacks on dozens of Web sites were not the work of hackers. They were the work of script kiddies, and the difference is everything. Script kiddies download ready-made tools and use them to damage the network. Script kiddies criminally distort the essential ethos of hacking, which is to pass through the network without a trace. Hackers read the unknown, sense the contours of the codes that make tomorrow's booms and busts.

It's no wonder that last week hackers everywhere cringed when the media confused them with script kiddies. Not less than ten years ago, the word hacker conjured a dedicated geek, hunched over a glowing terminal, working late into the night to solve an intractable dilemma. Now hacker means something akin to cybercriminal.

The semantic shift is regrettable, not only because the distortion inhibits clarity, but because it buries a piece of history we'd be wise to keep fresh: It was hackers who cobbled together the Internet.

Hacking is a quest for knowledge. You can see the essence of the activity in meetings at security firms like Secure Computing, where hackers are a key part of the professional services team. With clients in the Fortune 500 and three-letter government agencies, like DOD and NSA, the stakes are high, and when the firm faces a perplexing problem, brainstorming sessions go late into the night. Ideas fly from one person to another like pinballs off flippers, as the group mind turns over and examines the puzzle from all sides.

The concept of a "group mind" flows from the structure of the Internet itself, parallel processor harnessed to parallel processor to achieve a single goal. It's no coincidence that information technology professionals often think in a style similar to the way computers calculate. The network taught them how to reason digitally; it imprinted itself on their minds just as they imprinted their minds on it.

Is it any wonder, then, that hackers are the leaders of the new millennium? By leader I mean someone who forges ahead and names the emergent realities of the dim future. Consider Tim Berners-Lee, who designed the first Web protocols and wrote the first browser code. Berners-Lee was a hacker. Or consider Richard Stallman, the evangelist of Open Source software. Stallman is an extraordinary hacker.

I recently consulted with a major mutual fund, and after the meeting I traded war stories with its head of IT. He fondly recalled the old days of hacking Unix systems. That this former "delinquent" now runs a system executing billion-dollar transactions is not shocking. Most of the bright people in the IT business learned how to hack by—what else?—hacking.

Let's go back to Open Source for a moment. It's now the conventional wisdom that the Linux operating system and GNU Project are miracles of modern computing, which may one day triumph over the clunky software produced by the Microsoft-Apple cartel. Stallman launched the GNU Project by asking hackers to volunteer their services. Of course, they did. Likewise, Linux was founded on the belief that complex systems must be open, evolving, and free in order to reach their full potential. In other words, they must be hackable and they must be hacked.

Continuously.

Now comes the FBI and President Clinton with criminal sanctions for these script kiddies. It's right and just to keep the peace, but let's remember that in the Internet's embryonic stage, hacking, far from being criminal, was encouraged. When computers were first networked through telephone lines and slow modems, bulletin boards emerged as crossroads where cybertravelers could leave messages and valuable information about how the phone lines intersected with microprocessors. By these postings, the network formed a symbiotic relationship with its users, and through the give and take of countless exchanges between hackers, the network bootstrapped itself to a higher level of complexity. As Tom Jackiewicz, who helps administer upt.org, an outgrowth of the hackers' favorite, the UPT Bulletin Board, recalls, "In the old days of a decade ago, no kid could afford a Solaris workstation. The only machines available were online. You could learn only by roaming the network."

Today the stakes are higher, security tighter, but the basic modalities of hacking and its relationship to innovation remain. The challenge du jour is the gauntlet thrown down by Microsoft, which claims that Windows NT, the operating system of many businesses, is secure. What a claim! For a baseball fan it would be like hearing the Yankees brag that they could play an entire season without losing a single game. Hackers love to find flaws in Windows NT. For them, the payoff is the power rush of the thunk! when the stone hits Goliath in the forehead.

One of the sharpest stones to leave a hacker's sling is a program called Back Orifice 2000. Developed by a group called Cult of the Dead Cow, the program can be loaded stealthily on a Windows network, giving a remote user control over the network. Why develop such a weapon? In the current environment of ubiquitous distributed computing—that is, networks and nodes everywhere—the hackers argue that no operating system protects against stealthy executables like Back Orifice. So the program is a form of shock therapy. It jerks Microsoft into action, stirring an indolent industry into making the Internet more secure. The upgrades that come as a result benefit every Windows user.

As a culture we are just beginning to recognize this dynamic. One of the first hacker groups to benefit from our grudging acceptance of the craft is LOpht, which crossed over from the computing underground to the mainstream after finding flaws in Windows NT. Their transition has been so successful that when Congress conducted an investigation into Internet security it asked two LOpht members, Mudge and Weld Pond, to come to Washington for a briefing. Now LOpht has teamed up with former Compaq Computer executives to form @Stake, a security firm that has the media and Wall Street swooning.

So when is a hacker not a felon? When he receives $10 million in venture capital? When Congress invites him to a hearing?

When we lump all hackers into a criminal class we are liable to forget their essential role as architects of the information age. Edward O. Wilson said that scientists are characterized by a passion for knowledge, obsession, and daring. Hackers share that passion, the hunter-gatherer gene for restless wandering, wondering what's beyond the next hill. They hack because it's fun, because it's a challenge, and because the activity shapes their identity. Their strengths—love of risk, toleration of ambiguity, and ability to sift meaning from disparate sources—power the very network we all rush to join.

Hactivism and Soul Power   *November 21, 2000*

The danger with taking the moral high ground is that, once you take it, you no longer have it.

Saul Alinksy, a great community organizer, was committed to delivering power into the hands of the powerless. He worked to create structures that would shift the flow toward the dispossessed. He was an engineer of the Tao, or "Way," which is often likened to a waterflow seeking its own level. The Tao is impossible to resist because it's how energy in the universe flows, it's the flow, and it's the energy, all at the same time. So when we align our energies with the Tao, our actions are boosted beyond anything we might achieve on our own.

Alinsky focused on the flow, not the organizational structures. The structures were necessary but temporary, like irrigation ditches designed to channel the waters of a river. He helped organize the Back of the Yards Council in Chicago, for example, to give power to neighborhood people but when, a decade or so later, the Council has become reactionary, he organized others against it.

Once we seize the moral high ground, we lose it if we try to hold it. We become what we are fighting. Organizational structures become constraints instead of means of liberation. When we identify the right with organizational structures and then act on behalf of those structures, we can justify anything. Once we think we're right because we belong to the organization instead of determining right action by the context, we turn the Tao into a river of blood.

Enter hactivism.

We hear a lot these days about hacktivism. One form of hacktivism is the use of hacking skills to crack web sites and deface them or replace them with political messages.

During recent Israeli–Palestinian battles, criminal hackers or "crackers" affiliated with both sides attacked one another's Web sites. In one incident, a Pakistani stole the credit card numbers of members of a pro-Israel lobbying group and posted them on the Web.

A single computer in the hands of a child has more leverage in the digital era than a rock in the hands of a rioter. Destroy one node in the network and another node becomes the center.

Hactivism is celebrated by some as a sign that young technophiles are growing up and using their skills to a purpose. Instead of leaving graffiti, they are "hacking with a higher purpose."

If we mean that technophiles are creating software like "Hactivismo," a program that enables oppressed people to access human rights information or news reports blocked by their governments, that might be true.

But the use of cracking skills to defame and deface, regardless of one's side, always defeats the higher purpose. Whatever sense of righteousness motivated the act in the first place is lost in the act itself.

Such hactivism is "hacking-and-hiding," throwing stones, then ducking for cover, which merely escalates the level of virtual violence. It's a power play on behalf of a power rush.

Action on behalf of the Tao, that is, action on behalf of the powerless, the dispossessed, the genuinely victimized, always transforms the battlefield by revealing injustice in the bright light of undeniable revelation. Such action manifests what Gandhi and Martin Luther King, Jr. called "soul power," which is the power of a human being with integrity, focus, and high intentionality to expose an unjust law by confronting it ... and accepting the consequences.

King's letter from a Birmingham jail sounds like it was written on the Internet.

"We are caught in an inescapable network of mutuality," he wrote, "tied in a single garment of destiny."

This "systems approach" to human consciousness ought to resonate with people who live on the Web. But for that to happen, we have to not just live in a web—we all do, online and off—we have to see the web in which we live, we have to see the luminous threads connecting us indissolubly into a single field of consciousness. We have to see that "injustice anywhere is a threat to justice everywhere" because life in our quantum world is non-local.

"Whatever affects one directly," said King, "affects all indirectly."

A hacker once suggested to me that the chat rooms in which he once hung out resembled an island of lost boys, bootstrapping themselves into adulthood without benefit of counsel. They needed an image or icon of higher possibility, he said, which could disclose, illuminate and called forth their hidden possibilities into the light of day.

He too was talking about "soul power."

First, said King, collect the facts to determine whether injustices are alive. Then negotiate. Then comes self-purification, and only then, direct action.

Self-purification has a quaint ring to it, doesn't it, after decades in which we extolled greed and self-indulgence?

But listen to the words of a man who spent his life as a spy.

"We need something like a 'holy knight,'" he said. "We need people trained in the deepest spiritual truths. In some of the situations in which we put our agents, the only thing preventing a horrible death is their capacity to tune into multiple levels of awareness.

"We looked to the east, to martial arts and generic spiritual disciplines backengineered from other cultures, to train them in those spiritual arts. But I think we have models in our own traditions, we just don't know how to use them."

He was talking about the will and discipline to act on behalf of what we see in the depths of our souls. The structures we build on behalf of liberation may constrain us or set us free, but ultimately, it is right action that creates freedom: Right action on behalf of real victims of injustice, after which we have the courage not to mistake the means for the end, the tools for the task, or the people now set free for the freedom they sought.

Hacking Chinatown   *May 15, 1997*

"Forget it, Jake. It's Chinatown."

Those are the last words of the movie "Chinatown," just before the police lieutenant shouts orders to the crowd to clear the streets so the body of an innocent woman, murdered by the Los Angeles police, can be removed.

Chinatown, with Jack Nicholson as Jake Gittes, is a fine film: it defines an era (the thirties in the United States) and a genre—film noir—that is a unique way to frame reality.

"Film noir" is a vision of a world corrupt to the core in which nevertheless it is still possible, as author Raymond Chandler said of the heroes of the best detective novels, to be "a man of honor. Down these mean streets a man must go who is not himself mean, who is neither tarnished nor afraid."

"Chinatown" also defines life in the virtual world—that consensual hallucination we have come to call "cyberspace." The virtual world is a simulation of the "real world." The "real world" too is a symbolic construction, a set of nested structures that—as we peel them away in the course of our lives—reveals more and more complexity and ambiguity.

The real world IS Chinatown, and computer hackers—properly understood—know this better than anyone.

There are two themes in "Chinatown."

1. People in power are in seamless collusion. They take care of one another. They don't always play fair. And sooner or later, we discover that "we" are "they."

A veteran police detective told me this about people in power.

"There's one thing they all fear—politicians, industrialists, corporate executives—and that's exposure. They simply do not want anyone to look too closely or shine too bright a light on their activities."

I grew up in Chicago, Illinois, known for its political machine and cash-on-the-counter way of doing business. I earned money for my education working with the powerful Daley political machine. In exchange for patronage jobs—supervising play-grounds, hauling garbage—I worked with a precinct captain and alderman. My job was to do what I was told.

I paid attention to how people behaved in the real world. I learned that nothing is simple, that people act instinctively out of self-interest, and that nobody competes in the arena of real life with clean hands.

I remember sitting in a restaurant in a seedy neighborhood in Chicago, listening to a conversation in the next booth. Two dubious characters were upset that a mutual friend faced a long prison term. They looked and sounded different than the "respectable" people with whom I had grown up in an affluent part of town.

As I grew up, however, I learned how my friends' fathers really made money. Many of their activities were disclosed in the newspaper. They distributed pornography before it was legal, manufactured and sold illegal gambling equipment, distributed vending machines and juke boxes to bars that had to take them or face the consequences. I learned that a real estate tycoon had been a bootlegger during prohibition, and the brother of the man in the penthouse upstairs had died in Miami Beach in a hail of bullets.

For me, it was an awakening: I saw that the members of the power structures in the city—business, government, the religious hierarchy, and the syndicate or mafia—were indistinguishable, a partnership that of necessity included everyone who wanted to do business. Conscious or unconscious, collusion was the price of the ticket that got you into the stadium; whether players on the field or spectators in the stands, we were all players, one way or another.

Chicago is Chinatown, and Chinatown is the world. There is no moral high ground. We all wear masks, but under that mask is ... Chinatown.

2.   You never really know what's going on in Chinatown.

The police in Chinatown, according to Jake Gittes, were told to do "as little as possible" because things that happened on the street were the visible consequences of strings pulled behind the scenes. If you looked too often behind the curtain—as Gittes did—you were taught a painful lesson.

We often don't understand what we're looking at on the Internet. As one hacker recently e-mailed in response to someone's fears of a virus that did not and could not exist, "No information on the World Wide Web is any good unless you can either verify it yourself or it's backed up by an authority you trust."

The same is true in life.

Disinformation in the virtual world is an art. After an article I wrote for an English magazine about detective work on the Internet appeared, I received a call from a global PR firm in London. They asked if I wanted to conduct "brand defense" for them on the World Wide Web.

What is brand defense?

If one of our clients is attacked, they explained, their Internet squad goes into action. "Sleepers" (spies inserted into a community and told to wait until they receive orders) in usenet groups and listservs create distractions, invent controversies; web sites (on both sides of the question) go into high gear, using splashy graphics and clever text to distort the conversation. Persons working for the client pretend to be disinterested so they can spread propaganda.

It reminded me of the time my Democratic Party precinct captain asked if I wanted to be a precinct captain.

"Are you retiring?" I asked.

"Of course not!" he laughed. "You'd be the Republican precinct captain. Then we'd have all our bases covered."

The illusions of cyberspace are seductive. Every keystroke leaves a luminous track in the melting snow that can be seen with the equivalent of night vision goggles.

Hacking means tracking—and counter-tracking—and covering your tracks—in the virtual world. Hacking means knowing how to follow the flow of electrons to its source and understand on every level of abstraction—from source code to switches and routers to high level words and images—what is really happening.

Hackers are unwilling to do as little as possible. Hackers are need-to-know machines driven by a passion to connect disparate data into meaningful patterns. Hackers are the online detectives of the virtual world.

You don't get to be a hacker overnight.

The devil is in the details. Real hackers get good by endless trial and error, failing into success again and again. Thomas Alva Edison, inventor of the electric light, invented a hundred filaments that didn't work before he found one that did. He knew that every failure eliminated a possibility and brought him closer to his goal.

Listen to "Rogue Agent" set someone straight on an Internet mailing list:

"You want to create hackers? Don't tell them how to do this or that. Show them how to discover it for themselves. Those who have the innate drive will dive in and learn by trial and error. Those who don't, comfortable to stay within the bounds of their safe little lives, fall by the wayside.

"There's no knowledge so sweet as that which you've discovered on your own."

In Chinatown, an unsavory character tries to stop Jake Gittes from prying by cutting his nose. He reminds Gittes that "curiosity killed the cat."

Isn't it ironic that curiosity, the defining characteristic of an intelligent organism exploring its environment, has been prohibited by folk wisdom everywhere?

The endless curiosity of hackers is regulated by a higher code that may not even have a name but which defines the human spirit at its best. The Hacker's Code is an affirmation of life itself, life that wants to know, and grow, and extend itself throughout the "space" of the universe. The hackers' refusal to accept conventional wisdom and boundaries is a way to align his energies with the life-giving passion of heretics everywhere. And these days, that's what needed to survive.

Robert Galvin, the patriarch of Motorola, maker of cell-phones and semi-conductors, says that "every significant decision that changes the direction of a company is a minority decision. Whatever is the intuitive presumption—where everyone agrees, "Yeah, that's right"—will almost surely be wrong."

Motorola succeeded by fostering an environment in which creativity thrives. The company has institutionalized an openness to heresy because they know that wisdom is always arriving at the edge of things, on the horizons of our lives, and when it first shows up—like a comet on the distant edges of the solar system—it is faint and seen by only a few. But those few know where to look.

Allen Hynek, an astronomer connected with the U. S. Air Force investigation of UFOs, was struck by the "strangeness" of UFO reports, the cognitive dissonance that characterizes experiences that don't fit our orthodox belief systems. He pointed out that all the old photographic plates in astronomical observatories had images of Pluto on them, but until Clyde Tombaugh discovered Pluto and said where it was, no one saw it because they didn't know where to look.

The best computer consultants live on the creative edge of things. They are pathfinders, guides for those whom have always lived at the orthodox center but who find today that the center is constantly shifting, mandating that they learn new behaviors, new skills in order to be effective. In order to live on the edge.

The edge is the new center. The center of a web is wherever we are.

When I looked out over the audience at DefCon IV, the hackers' convention, I saw an assembly of the most brilliant and most unusual people I had ever seen in one room. It was exhilarating. We all felt as if we had come home. There in that room for a few hours or a few days, we did not have to explain anything. We knew who we were and what drove us in our different ways to want to connect the dots of data into meaningful patterns.

We know we build on quicksand, but building is too much fun to give up. We know we leave tracks, but going is so much more energizing than staying home. We know that curiosity can get your nose slit, but then we'll invent new ways to smell.

Computer programmers write software applications that are doomed to be as obsolete as wire recordings. The infrastructures built by our engineers are equally doomed. Whether a virtual world of digital bits or a physical world of concrete and steel, our civilization is a Big Toy that we build and use up at the same time. The fun of the game is to know that it is a game, and winning is identical with our willingness to play.

To say that when we engage with one another in cyberspace we are "Hacking Chinatown" is a way to say that asking questions is more important than finding answers. We do not expect to find final answers. But the questions must be asked. We refuse to do as little as possible because we want to know.

Asking questions is how human beings create opportunities for dignity and self-transcendence; asking questions is how we are preparing ourselves to leave this island earth and enter into a trans-galactic web of life more diverse and alien than anything we have encountered.

Asking questions that uncover the truth is our way of refusing to consent to illusions and delusions, our way of insisting that we can do it better if we stay up later, collaborate with each other in networks with no names, and lose ourselves in the quest for knowledge and self-mastery.

This is how proud, lonely men and women, illuminated in the darkness by their glowing monitors, become heroes in their own dramas as they wander the twisting streets of cyberspace and their own lives.

Even in Chinatown, Jake. Even in Chinatown.

Hacker Generations   *August 1, 2003*

First, the meaning of hacker.

The word originally meant an inventive type, someone creative and unconventional, usually involved in a technical feat of legerdemain, a person who saw doors where others saw walls or built bridges that others thought were planks on which to walk into shark-filled seas. Hackers were alive with the spirit of Loki or Coyote or the Trickster, moving with stealth across boundaries, often spurning conventional ways of thinking and behaving. Hackers see deeply into the arbitrariness of structures, how form and content are assembled in subjective and often random ways and therefore how they can be defeated or subverted. They see atoms where others see a seeming solid, and they know that atoms are approximations of energies, abstractions, mathematical constructions. At the top level, they see the skull behind the grin, the unspoken or unacknowledged but shared assumptions of a fallible humanity. That's why, as in Zen monasteries, where mountains are mountains and then they are not mountains and then they are mountains again, hacker lofts are filled with bursts of loud spontaneous laughter.

Then the playful creative things they did in the protected space of their mainframe heaven, a playfulness fueled by the passion to know, to solve puzzles, outwit adversaries, never be bested or excluded by arbitrary fences, never be rendered powerless, those actions began to be designated acts of criminal intent.. That happened when the space inside the mainframes was extended through distributed networks and ported to the rest of the world where things are assumed to be what they seem. A psychic space designed to be open, more or less, for trusted communities to inhabit, became a general platform of communication and commerce and security became a concern and an add-on. Legal distinctions which seemed to have been obliterated by new technologies and a romantic fanciful view of cyberspace a la Perry Barlow were reformulated for the new not-so-much cyberspace as cyborgspace where everyone was coming to live. Technologies are first astonishing, then grafted onto prior technologies, then integrated so deeply they are constitutive of new ways of seeing and acting, which is when they become invisible.

A small group, a subset of real hackers, mobile crews who merely entered and looked around or pilfered unsecured information, became the definition the media and then everybody else used for the word "hacker." A hacker became a criminal, usually defined as a burglar or vandal, and the marks of hacking were the same as breaking and entering, spray painting graffiti on web site walls rather than brick, stealing passwords or credit card numbers.

At first real hackers tried to take back the word but once a word is lost, the war is lost. "Hacker" now means for most people a garden variety of online miscreant and words suggested as substitutes like technophile just don't have the same juice.

So let's use the word hacker here to mean what we know we mean because no one has invented a better word. We don't mean script kiddies, vandals, or petty thieves. We mean men and women who do original creative work and play at the tip of the bell curve, not in the hump, we mean the best and brightest who cobble together new images of possibility and announce them to the world. Original thinkers. Meme makers. Artists of pixels and empty spaces.

Second, the meaning of "hacker generations."

In a speech at the end of his two terms as president, Dwight Eisenhower coined the phrase "military-industrial complex" to warn of the consequences of a growing seamless collusion between the state and the private sector. He warned of a changing approach to scientific research which in effect meant that military and government contracts were let to universities and corporations, redefining not only the direction of research but what was thinkable or respectable in the scientific world. At the same time, a "closed world" as Paul N. Edwards phrased it in his book of the same name, was evolving, an enclosed psychic landscape formed by our increasingly symbiotic interaction with the symbol-manipulating and identity-altering space of distributed computing, a space that emerged after World War II and came to dominate military and then societal thinking.

Eisenhower and Edwards were in a way describing the same event, the emergence of a massive state-centric collaboration that redefined our psychic landscape.

After half a century Eisenhower is more obviously speaking of the military–industrial–educational–entertainment–and–media establishment that is the water in which we swim, a tangled inescapable mesh of collusion and self-interest that defines our global economic and political landscape.

The movie calls it The Matrix. The Matrix issues, from the fusion of cyborg space and the economic and political engines that drive it, a simulated world in which the management of perception is the cornerstone of war-and-peace (in the Matrix, war is peace and peace is war, as Orwell foretold). The battlespace is as perhaps it always has been the mind of society but the digital world has raised the game to a higher level. The game is multidimensional, multi-valent, played in string space. The manipulation of symbols through electronic means, a process which began with speech and writing and was then engineered through tools of literacy and printing is the currency of the closed world of our CyborgSpace and the military–industrial engines that power it.

This Matrix then was created through the forties, fifties, sixties, and seventies, often invisible to the hackers who lived in and breathed it. The "hackers" noticed by the panoptic eye of the media and elevated to niche celebrity status were and always have been creatures of the Matrix. The generations before them were military, government, corporate and think-tank people who built the machinery and its webbed spaces.

So I mean by the First Generation of Hackers, this much later generation of hackers that emerged in the eighties and nineties when the internet became an event and they were designated the First Hacker Generation, the ones who invented Def Con and all its spin-offs, who identified with garage-level hacking instead of the work of prior generations that made it possible.

Marshall McLuhan saw clearly the nature and consequences of electronic media. It was not television, his favorite example, so much as the Internet that provided illustrations for his text. Only when the Internet had evolved in the military–industrial complex and moved through incarnations like Arpanet and Milnet into the public spaces of our society did people began to understand what he was saying.

Young people who became conscious as the Internet became public discovered a Big Toy of extraordinary proportions. The growing availability of cheap ubiquitous home computers became their platform and when they were plugged into one another, the machines and their cyborg riders fused. They co-created the dot com boom and the public net, and made necessary the "security space" perceived as essential today to a functional society. All day and all night like Bedouin they roamed the network where they would, hidden by sand dunes that changed shape and size overnight in the desert winds. That generation of hackers inhabited Def Con in the "good old days," the early nineties, and the other cons. They shaped the perception as well as the reality of the public Internet as their many antecedents at MIT, NSA, DOD and all the other three-letter agencies co-created the Matrix.

So I mean by the First Generation of Hackers that extended or distributed network of passionate obsessive and daring young coders who gave as much as they got, invented new ways of sending text, images, sounds, and looked for wormholes that let them cross through the non-space of the network and bypass conventional routes. They constituted an online meritocracy in which they bootstrapped themselves into surrogate families and learned together by trial and error, becoming a model of self-directed corporate networked learning. They created a large-scale interactive system, self-regulating and self-organizing, flexible, adaptive, and unpredictable, the very essence of a cybernetic system.

Then the Second Generation came along. They had not co-created the network so much as found it around them as they became conscious. Just a few years younger, they inherited the network created by their "elders." The network was assumed and socialized them to how they should think and act. Video games were there when they learned how to play. Web sites instead of bulletin boards with everything they needed to know were everywhere. The way a prior generation was surrounded by books or television and became readers and somnambulistic watchers, the Second Generation was immersed in the network and became surfers. But unlike the First Generation which knew their own edges more keenly, the net made them cyborgs without anyone noticing. They were assimilated. They were the first children of the Matrix.

In a reversal of the way children learned from parents, the Second Generation taught their parents to come online which they did but with a different agenda. Their elders came to the net as a platform for business, a means of making profits, creating economies of scale, and expanding into a global market. Both inhabited a simulated world characterized by porous or disappearing boundaries and if they still spoke of a "digital frontier," evoking the romantic myths of the EFF and the like, that frontier was much more myth than fact, as much a creation of the dream weavers at CFP as "the old west" was a creation of paintings, dime novels and movies.

They were not only fish in the water of the Matrix, however. They were goldfish in a bowl. That environment to which I have alluded, the military-industrial complex in which the internet evolved in the first place, had long since built concentric circles of observation or surveillance that enclosed them around. Anonymizers promising anonymity were created by the ones who wanted to know their names. Hacker handles and multiple nyms hid not only hackers but those who tracked them. The extent of this panoptic world was hidden by denial and design. Most on it and in it didn't know it. Most believed the symbols they manipulated as if they were the things they represented, as if their tracks really vanished when they erased traces in logs or blurred the means of documentation. They thought they were watchers but in fact were also watched. The Eye that figures so prominently in Blade Runner was always open, a panoptic eye. The system could not be self-regulating if it were not aware of itself, after all. The net is not a dumb machine. It is sentient and aware because it is fused bone-on-steel with its cyborg riders and their sensory and cognitive extensions.

Cognitive dissonance grew as the Second Generation spawned the Third. The ambiguities of living in simulated worlds, the morphing of multiple personas or identities, meant that no one was ever sure who was who. Dissolving boundaries around individuals and organizational structures alike ("The Internet? C'est moi!") meant that identity based on loyalty, glue born of belonging to a larger community and the basis of mutual trust, could not be presumed.

It's all about knowing where the nexus is; what transpires there at the connections. The inner circles may be impossible to penetrate but in order to recruit people into them, there must be a conversation and that conversation is the nexus, the distorted space into which one is unknowingly invited and often subsequently disappears. Colleges, universities, businesses, associations are discovered to be Potemkin villages behind which the real whispered dialogue takes place. The closed and so-called open worlds interpenetrate one another to such a degree that the nexus is difficult to discern. History ends and numerous histories take their place, each formed of an arbitrary association and integration of data classified or secret at multiple levels and turned into truths, half-truths, and outright lies.

Diffie-Hellman's public key cryptography, for example, was a triumph of ingenious thinking, putting together bits of data, figuring it out, all outside the system. But Whit Diffie was abashed when he learned that years earlier (1969) James Ellis inside the "closed world" of British intelligence had already been there and done that. The public world of hackers often reinvents what has been discovered years earlier inside the closed world of compartmentalized research behind walls they can not so easily penetrate. People really can keep secrets, and do. Do you really think that PGP was news to the closed world?

In other words, the Second Generation of Hackers, socialized to a networked world, also began to discover another world or many other worlds that included and transcended what was publicly known. There have always been secrets but there have not always been huge whole secret worlds whose citizens live with a different history entirely but that's what we have built since the Second World War. That's the metaphor at the heart of the Matrix and that's why it resonates with the Third Generation. A surprising discovery for the Second Generation as it matured is the basis for high-level hacking for the Third.

The Third Generation of Hackers knows it was socialized to a world co-created by its legendary brethren as well as numerous nameless men and women. They know that we inhabit multiple thought-worlds with different histories, histories dependent on which particular bits of data can be bought on the black market for truth and integrated into Bigger Pictures. The Third Generation knows there is no one Big Picture, there are only bigger or smaller pictures depending on the pieces one assembles. Assembling those pieces, finding them, connecting them, then standing back to see what they say—that is the essence of Third Generation hacking. That is the task demanded by the Matrix which is otherwise our prison, where inmates and guards are indistinguishable from each other because we are so proud of what we have built that we refuse to let one another escape.

That challenge demands that real Third Generation hackers be expert at every level of the fractal that connects all the levels of the network. It includes the most granular examination of how electrons are turned into bits and bytes, how percepts as well as concepts are framed and transported in network-centric warfare/peacefare, how all the layers link to one another, which distinctions between them matter and which don't. How the seemingly topmost application layer is not the end, but the beginning of the real challenge, where the significance and symbolic meaning of the manufactured images and ideas that constitute the cyborg network create a trans-planetary hive mind. That's where the game is played today by the masters of the unseen, where those ideas and images become the means of moving the herd, percept turned into concept, people thinking they actually think when what has in fact already been thought for them has moved on all those layers into their unconscious constructions of reality.

Hacking means knowing how to find data in the Black Market for truth. Knowing what to do with it once it is found. Knowing how to cobble things together to build a big picture. The puzzle to be solved is reality itself, the nature of the Matrix, how it all relates. So unless you're hacking the Mind of God, unless you're hacking the mind of society itself, you aren't really hacking at all. Rather than designing arteries through which the oil or blood of a cyborg society flows, you are the dye in those arteries, all unknowing that you function like a marker or a bug or a beeper or a gleam of revealing light. You become a means of control, a symptom rather than a cure.

The Third Generation of Hackers grew up in a simulated world, a designer society of electronic communication, but sees through the fictions and the myths. Real hackers discover in their fear and trembling the courage and the means to move through zones of annihilation in which everything we believe to be true is called into question in order to reconstitute both what is known and our knowing Self on the higher side of self-transformation. Real hackers know that the higher calling is to hack the Truth in a society built on designer lies and then—the most subtle, most difficult part—manage their egos and that bigger picture with stealth and finesse in the endless ambiguity and complexity of their lives.

The brave new world of the past is now everyday life. Everybody knows that identities can be stolen which means if they think that they know they can be invented. What was given to spies by the state as a sanction for breaking laws is now given to real hackers by technologies that make spies of us all.

Psychological operations and information warfare are controls in the management of perception taking place at all levels of society, from the obvious distortions in the world of politics to the obvious distortions of balance sheets and earnings reports in the world of economics. Entertainment, too, the best vehicle for propaganda according to Joseph Goebbels, includes not only obvious propaganda but movies like the Matrix that serve as sophisticated controls, creating a subset of people who think they know and thereby become more docile. Thanks for that one, SN.

The only free speech tolerated is that which does not genuinely threaten the self-interest of the oligarchic powers that be. The only insight acceptable to those powers is insight framed as entertainment or an opposition that can be managed and manipulated.

Hackers know they don't know what's real and know they can only build provisional models as they move in stealthy trusted groups of a few. They must assume that if they matter, they are known which takes the game immediately to another level.

So the Matrix, like any good cybernetic system, is self-regulating, builds controls, has multiple levels of complexity masking partial truth as Truth. Of what else could life consist in a cyborg world? All over the world, in low-earth orbit, soon on the moon and the asteroid belt, this game is played with real money. It is no joke. The surrender of so many former rights—habeas corpus, the right to a trial, the freedom from torture during interrogation, freedom of movement without "papers" in one's own country—has changed the playing field forever, changed the game.

Third Generation Hacking means accepting nothing at face value, learning to counter counter-threats with counter-counter-counter-moves. It means all means and ends are provisional and likely to transform themselves like alliances on the fly.

Third Generation Hacking is the ability to free the mind, to live vibrantly in a world without walls.

Do not be deceived by uniforms, theirs or ours, or language that serves as uniforms, or behaviors. There is no theirs or ours, no us or them. There are only moments of awareness at the nexus where fiction myth and fact touch, there are only moments of convergence. But if it is all on behalf of the Truth it is Hacking.

Then it can not fail because the effort defines what it means to be human in a cyborg world. Hackers are aware of the paradox, the irony and the impossibility of the mission as well as the necessity nevertheless of pursuing it, despite everything. That is, after all, why they're hackers.

Thanks to Simple Nomad, David Aitel, Sol Tzvi, Fred Cohen, Jaya Baloo, and many others for the conversations that helped me frame this article.

Chapter 5

Digital Spirituality

A Silent Retreat

June 27, 1997

The mind is like a chattering monkey, some Buddhists say, and one goal of disciplined spirituality—i.e. doing "what works"—is to quiet that mind.

Spiritual tools are practices validated by generations of trial-and-error that more or less work, that allow the "ambient noise" of our lives to diminish, and finally—in a grace-filled moment of enlightenment—disappear. Then we see our selves as we really are, instead of believing the images of ourselves we present to our own egos, as well as others as if they are us.

Although one hesitates to speak of that about which one cannot speak, the quieted mind is like a still pond that reflects the full moon, with not so much as a ripple to disturb its tranquility.

Moon mirrors moon on a windless night.

If the mind is a chattering money, the Internet—our hive mind—is like a million monkeys pounding away at keyboards all over the world. The Internet is proof that a million monkeys unleashed at the same time will not produce the works of Shakespeare. They produce home pages by the thousands, images of our egos run amok, advertisements for our hopes and dreams. The dream life of humanity—and not a few nightmares—pours into the Internet, the uncensored, unabridged contents of our psyches.

And noise. A lot of noise.

One of my sons taught me how to listen to noise. He's a sound artist. He records the cacophony of industrial life and uses those tones to create layered or textured sculptures in sound. Electronic noise is one media he uses to focus our attention on what is always there but never heard because we filter it out. Noise is like the power lines of urban civilization; looking at a tree in front of a power station, we erase the power lines until they disappear into the background and we almost convince ourselves that we're in a park.

When we listen to the noise and allow ourselves to become conscious of it, we can free ourselves of it. When we listen to it, we have a choice. When we can't hear it, we don't even notice the noise. We think its reality.

People sometimes go on a silent retreat to "shut out the noise" and quiet the mind. Like beginners at meditation, what we first notice is just how much noise there is.

We just finished a week of thunderstorms in southern Wisconsin. First we had seven inches of rain overnight. The storm just stalled and poured, the loudest thunder in the history of the world, all night long.

Then a second thunderstorm came through with 70 mph winds. A huge whole side of a tree above our patio twisted and came down, amazingly missing the house and garage. The power went out from early evening until the following afternoon.

My car was locked in the garage, the electric door down. The lights and air conditioning were off. Above all, the computer—THE COMPUTER—was off. There was nothing to do but go outside.

The darkness was charged not only with the energy of the storm, but with the quiet conversation of neighbors. Usually glued to their television sets or held suspended in the lighted life I glimpsed through windows, they were all out in the darkness, talking.

Like our lives, the Internet is filled with noise, but we don't hear it until the power is off. Suddenly there is ... only ourselves. A rhythm of life issues naturally from the bodies that we are. The world that we saw in the familiar glare of overhead lights looks different in candlelight. My wife was aware that my steps did not turn toward the office to check e-mail one last time before crossing the hall. Instead we lay in the summer night, in the warm darkness, shadows flickering on the walls, the storm passing.

We listened deeply to the absence of noise.

The next morning I walked several miles to a breakfast appointment rather than driving. Returning to my office, I realized that all of the interior urgency—meeting deadlines, preparing a speech, working the telephone—was gone. There was nothing to do but whatever there was to do. The compelling pressure of necessity was lifted.

Instead of leaning forward anxiously into my life, I relaxed back into the rocking chair of my own soul.

The lights came on again, of course. It was a real let-down. Everything was normal again. At once I was sucked at once back into the world of e-mail, researching an article using the Net, then writing it on a word processor, pausing now and again to connect with electronic colleagues.

A periodic retreat from the Net is a necessity. To unplug and listen to the noise, and then, as the noise diminishes, to the silence. Coming back to the Net, you roar with laughter at the antics of a million monkeys jabbering away day and night ... and all too soon, there you are again, hands dancing on the keyboard, jacked into the noise.

But something is different.

At first the Net was ... the Net. Then, during that moment of tranquility and insight, it was not the Net. It was what it had always been.

Now it's the Net again. But not in the same way. Now I can see that we construct it from nothingness, from thin air ... we create the Net together so we can play in it. Creation from nothing.

What a game! What a life! What an extraordinary silence!

A Nightmare in Daylight   *September 12, 1997*

In a recent column, I wrote:

"We can't think the unthinkable; from inside the old paradigm, we can't imagine what the world will look like from inside a new one.

I wish I knew a better term than "paradigm change" to describe our movement through a zone of annihilation—as individuals and as cultures—in order to experience genuine transformation. But I don't. We have to let go of the old way of framing reality in order for a new one to emerge. ...

Asked how people go bankrupt, Hemingway said, "Two ways: gradually, then suddenly."

That's exactly how transformation happens.

A subscriber to the list e-mailed:

"What do you mean by the 'zone of annihilation?' Do you mean that all our old beliefs and ideas are destroyed by change, and then reformed 'gradually, then suddenly?' Please elaborate on this."

The short answer to the question is "yes."

This week's and next week's columns are the longer answer.

It is difficult to exaggerate the real impact of personal and cultural transformation, our collective response to "the shocks and changes that keep us sane," as Robert Frost put it; those jolts to the soul that compel us to rethink everything.

Today those jolts are more and more frequent. Exponential change is a wild tiger we try in vain to tame. We speak of "paradigm change" casually, over coffee or in seminar rooms, so the facts will fit into our framework instead of our framework fitting into the facts. We want to have "it" instead of letting "it" have us.

The truth is, though ... it has us. All we can do is come along for the ride.

The fancy name for our various styles of riding through life is "spirituality." Our challenge is not to find the form of spirituality that's right. Our challenge is to find one that works.

Change can make us uncomfortable, but real transformation can be terrifying. It threatens our deepest beliefs, our notions of what's real, even our sanity.

Sanity is contextual, a consensus determined by circumstances. Beliefs and behaviors that make sense under one set of circumstances look crazy under others. That consensus reality must break down before we can cross the militarized zone, studded with land mines, that I call a zone of annihilation, and arrive at another (temporary) consensus.

It is like swimming from island to island to island. If our perspective is narrow enough, we think each island is an entire continent. As Hawaiians living in relative isolation and stability for hundreds of years discovered, however, there always comes a Captain Cook into Kealakakua Bay, and everything changes forever.

Since long before the computer revolution, too much data has streamed into our lives. We perceive much more than we "see." Henri Bergson thought the brain was a filter that screened out nearly all reality so we could pay attention to the mundane tasks of daily life.

One definition of religious or mystical experience is that suddenly flung-open doors of perception allow all that data and daylight to come in.

When our filters are overwhelmed by anomalous data that doesn't fit, we deny it, reject it, ridicule it, kill it. But sooner or later the facts will have their day. Our discomfort grows acute, and we have to pay attention.

The twenty-five year-long marriage of a couple I know was coming apart. For several years, they did everything they could to keep it together. They tried this kind of counselling, that kind of church. One night, the husband, having tried everything else, rearranged all of the furniture in their house.

It didn't work. The next morning he packed his bags and left.

We do everything we can to sustain the structures of our lives—our beliefs, our framework of reality—until we finally let go and move into a new possibility. That moment has been in the process of arriving for a long time, but it often seems to happen suddenly, like a ripening pear coming off its stem at a touch.

It is happening today in our individual lives, our organizations, and our societies, at every level of life. Naturally. Any way you cut an apple, you get apple.

A religious conversion is one form of paradigm change. Individuals going through an experience of religious conversion often feel as if they are "going crazy." In a way, they are. They are letting go of one center or organizing principle and reaching for another. It is not that the content of their thinking or their lives is changing, but the context, the means by which they hold all that content. It feels as if the ground under their feet is opening wide.

The metaphors used by different religious traditions to talk about this experience do not pussyfoot around. Jews speak of slavery and freedom, exile and return. Zen Buddhists say enlightenment is a "nightmare in daylight." Christians use crucifixion as the metaphor for transformation.

The system, whether an individual or a culture, must come to the end of itself. Things fall apart. There is a moment of freefall during which one literally does not know if things will come together again. Everything we believed true is called into question. Then everything coalesces at a higher level of organization around a new center.

Some think a psychotic break is a conversion experience that is incomplete, the fragments of the psyche in some kind of chaotic elliptical orbit.

The risks of transformation are real.

Describing the new rules in an information economy in *Wired* (September 1997), Kevin Kelly speaks of how difficult it is for executives who think in traditional ways to let go of what's working and move into chaos in order to reinvent new products and processes. Yet the network economy demands that kind of courage. We must let go in order to be reinvented in ways that disclose new possibilities once we are open to them.

An article on business and the information economy, sounding like a primer on spirituality? Surrender, letting go, living on the edge of new possibility?

Sounds like we're talking about faith, doesn't it?

Of course. Life on a changeable planet has always invited a spiritual response. Coping with exponential change means using traditional spiritual tools: Tools for staying flexible, effective, open to possibility in the face of chaos. Tools we had better carry to work ... except these days, life itself is our work, and faith is getting out of bed in the morning and just showing up.

Mutuality, Feedback, and Accountability

September 20, 1997

"Coping with exponential change means using traditional spiritual tools ..."

If we're lucky ... after we have exhausted every other avenue ... we turn to the traditional tools of spirituality to cope with stress and rapid change. That is, with life on earth.

You won't hear a word like "spirituality" in many Fortune 500 board rooms, but businesses, too, are figuring it out.

It makes sense. These practices are the result of centuries of reflection on our collective experience, sifting and sorting everything we've tried in order to find out what really works.

Some things seem to work across the board.

Effective organizations have: (1) a high degree of mutuality; (2) mechanisms for frequent, widely distributed feedback; and (3) accountability to mutually-agreed-upon goals and to a vision of leadership. I have said that before but let me spell it out.

MUTUALITY.

The individualism that many of us were taught was axiomatic to being human was, in fact, generated by a print culture. Before the Gutenberg era, nobody thought that way.

Digital culture undermines individualism and our ability to act as if we exist apart from our communities.

A representative of a school district told me they received good grades from corporations that hired their graduates, except in one area: cooperative learning. I asked for a definition of "cooperative learning" and realized that in my day it was called "cheating."

This indicates how completely the assumptions of post-World War II America have been turned upsidedown by the digital revolution.

Independent learning, apart from the learning of the group or organization, is not viable because the individual—one of many modular units in the network— must correlate with the activity and trajectory of the group.

This means learning new behaviors.

A CEO of a utility told me they used to spend 85% of their time on task and 15% on process issues: leadership, team work, and the like. Today the percentages are reversed, not because utility executives want hugs on Monday morning but because that's what mandated by conditions.

As a young hacker said, looking back nostalgically on the days when he could know everything about hacking a system: "These days, there's too much for any one person to know. That's why the most important thing I need to know is what I don't need to know. The second most important thing is, who knows it? So I can get it when I need it."

He needs to know: people-skills, networking, cooperative learning. The electronic network has back-engineered a culture that must work as the network does in order to be effective and in order to function in a symbiotic relationship with the network.

FEEDBACK.

An organism in a rapidly changing environment must know what is happening inside itself (the smaller system) and outside. As we climb a spiral toward more and more complex organization, the feedback loops must grow larger, and those inside the boundaries of the smaller system must make us aware of internal changes in equilibrium. That's why quality programs insisted the system must include suppliers, customers, and ultimately all "stake-holders"—to remain current with conditions and to capture the knowledge of everyone relevant to the success of the organization.

All the way up the spiral, every living organism is part of the system, and ultimately the universe must factor in the input from every living creature. That's another way of saying what mystics have always said, that all life is interdependent and the energy and information that constitutes the visible interaction among all parts of a system are an image of a universe that is unified, self-conscious and evolving.

On a more mundane level, we can not adapt to changing conditions or "morph" unless our sensors are out there in the multiplicity of environments that impact our well-being.

And ... we must hold ourselves accountable for what we learn.

ACCOUNTABILITY.

When things are going well, accountability diminishes. Then when things don't go well, there's chaos.

Many financial managers are riding the crest of a remarkable bull market. They receive handsome fees to manage billions of dollars. Yet only 7% of professional fund managers beat the S&P index over the past year.

So long as benchmarks are not used to align performance with stated goals, those managers can continue to benefit from the rising tide that is lifting all boats. But when the turnaround comes, mutual funds by the hundreds will merge or collapse in a shake-out that imposes stricter accountability.

Without accountability, there is no way to look back and see how we have done and no way to look forward to see where we want to go.

The absence of any of these essential qualities skews an organization in predictable ways.

Mutuality and feedback without accountability result in team-work and data-exchange to no end. The system has no compass and no means of realigning itself when it gets off course.

Feedback and accountability without mutuality characterize a top-down system driven by goals. But the feedback becomes fragmented, undermining the security we need to function. An anxious and fearful system becomes rigid and isolated; feedback does not result in purposeful action.

Accountability and mutuality without feedback characterize a closed system that is blind. Cults work well for those inside them until they don't. When something new gets in—an idea, a fact, an event—it's a debilitating blow. The cult either commits suicide or is transformed into something else (a business can be a cult, too).

To surrender one's illusion of individual well-being in order to participate in a larger structure for the good of all (including oneself) is, paradoxically, an individual decision. It is a moment of insight into one's real nature and destiny that so threatens our illusions and habitual state of denial that it has been called "a nightmare in daylight." Once it happens, however, we can never again think of ourselves as we did before. When the paradigm changes, there is no going back.

This template is not a recipe. It simply identifies some of the marks of that perilous journey, undertaken with fear and trembling appropriate to the real risks and real rewards.

The Illusion of Control   *October 3, 1997*

Microsoft did it again.

Some users of the beta version of Explorer 4.0 were surprised to learn that, after they went to sleep, their computers were dialing Microsoft and telling it secrets, downloading information from Microsoft's web pages and uploading information from the sanctity of their homes.

The San Jose Mercury News reports that Microsoft says such calls only happen when the feature is activated, but admits that users can activate it without understanding the consequences. Said one beta tester who had wandered in search of a midnight snack, "I was completely freaking out. I pulled the phone plug right out of the wall."

Microsoft insists that the system is under the user's control, but many users didn't know that. The users can be forgiven a little skepticism. Microsoft is widely believed to have a history of gathering data about users secretly, but at the least, the company was indifferent to the concerns of the human user at the end of the connection. They did not allow the user to maintain an illusion of control.

The truth is, our computers are sending and receiving all sorts of information back and forth automatically all the time. As Edward Felten, head of the Secure Internet Programming Laboratory at Princeton University, said, "I think part of the concern here is the feeling that you've lost control of the computer when it's doing stuff in the middle of the night. The feeling is that you've got control of the computer if you're sitting in front of it. The reality is that you only have the illusion of control."

Psychologists tell us that dominance and submissiveness are two traits that we immediately recognize in others. Of course, submissiveness is often a way of dominating others too, so its safe to say that all human beings expend energy on dominating others and avoiding being dominated by them.

The computer isn't a person, but we treat the computer like a person and react to it as if it's a person. The network invites powerful projections, some of them straight out of the Frankenstein legend. We fear the monster we created and can not control. The more we resist domination, the more we hate symbols of the dominator—Microsoft, in this case, often called "the Borg" and the "Evil Empire," as well as all computers and networks.

When I lived in Hawaii, I "crossed over" sufficiently to the way that blend of Polynesian and Asian cultures sees things. I sometimes could see "haoles" like myself—the Hawaiian word for ghosts or pale North Americans—as the Hawaiians saw us.

I recall a recent arrival to the islands holding forth one day at the tennis courts. The local people listened quietly as he explained what needed to be done to improve the islands. He believed their silence was agreement and kept talking until he grew tired. Then the small crowd scattered and he went off to look at the surfers, thinking he had accomplished something.

"Haoles" think talking is doing, that by telling others what we think or intend to do, we have engaged in action. In fact, the crowd was politely waiting for him to finish. They had heard it all before and learned how to absorb the words of well-meaning tourists as the sea absorbs our energy when we swim.

The principles of aikido, both a martial art and a spiritual discipline, underscore that approach. There are no aggressive moves in aikido. Instead one aligns one's energy with the energy of an attacker, enabling them to complete a move with as little damage to oneself as possible.

All spiritual traditions talk about real power as an alignment of our energy with the energy that is already flowing, the "tao" or the movement of the universe. The advice of Jesus to turn the other cheek has been distorted to mean that people being beaten should keep taking abuse, but that isn't what it meant. It's more on the order of "turn to align yourself with the energy coming at you" in order to increase, rather than decrease, your real control of the situation.

In a workshop demonstrating the principles of gestalt psychology, a group of us were asked to join a loose circle and let our arms fall naturally around one another's waists. Then we were told to "make the circle go where you want it to go." Everyone pushed in different directions and we all fell down. It felt fragmented and chaotic. Then we reconstituted the circle and were told to allow the circle to move as it chose to move. We found ourselves engaged in a natural back-and-forth rhythm, and we experienced deep feelings of well-being as we allowed ourselves to be part of something without having to impose our will on it.

In hierarchical structures, we learn to exercise power by dominating and controlling. In webs or networks, we can't do that. Our energy is diffused along the strands of the web.

The way to exercise power in a network is by contributing and participating. That's why leadership in flattened organizations requires people who know how to implement a vision by coaching, rather than giving orders. Like the CEO who called the troops together and told them, "You are all empowered," then returned to his office, thinking as haoles do, that he had accomplished something.

Much of what we call power is the illusion of control. Whether connected to a network, sitting in front of a computer that has an antonymous operating system, engaging in a relationship with a person, or trying to make the world move as we want—it is all an illusion of control. The only thing we can control is the quality of our response to life. We have an innate capacity to respond to whatever life brings with dignity, elasticity, and—when the chips are down—genuine heroism.

The way to rule the world, as Lao Tzu said, is by letting things simply take their course.

The Day the Computer Prayed *October 24, 1997*

When a computer prays, is it really prayer?

And I mean real prayer, I don't mean some mood-altering self-manipulation. I mean, is there an intentional focus of energy and intelligence, the intelligence of the heart, so that something happens beyond the merely subjective, something that percolates powerfully through all the levels of our consciousness?

Nor do I mean merely ritualistic prayer. As T. S. Eliot said, "... prayer is more than an order of words, the conscious occupation of the praying mind, or the sound of the voice praying."

Not that anything's wrong with that. We human beings need repetitive symbolic acts to comfort or sustain us. No matter how spontaneous we think we are, our habits dig ruts in our psyches, and the wagons of our lives—including prayer—roll in those ruts.

That's at the top level. That's what happens when a conscious mind thinks or says words. Which means that one assumption of prayer is that telepathy is real.

A clairvoyant moment returning from the moon became a new axis for Edgar Mitchell's life. The astronaut experienced a silent communication that disclosed to him the unity of all things. It was a moment of transcendent communion that told him he was right where he belonged, at home in a gregarious universe.

When enough people have that kind of experience, they come together and struggle to articulate what they believe. Our individuality is expressed fully in community. That makes for corporate rituals. Our religious institutions and organizations are grievously flawed, but they do bridge the generations and pass on a legacy of the symbols of possibility and promise that can then explode once again into our real experience.

Or devolve once again into ritualized prayer.

Monasteries sometimes send notices saying they are praying for me on a particular day. The names for whom they pray are in a book or rolodex, and as the wheel of time turns, so does the rota. Names are plugged automatically into the blank spaces.

It's natural for computerization. That monastery, executing its structured top-down program for ritualized prayer, is a symbol manipulating machine. All human beings are symbol manipulating machines, and so are computers. We're interlocked in a symbiotic embrace that is taking both networked computers and networked human beings up a spiral of mutual transformation. As we are changed by this process, the symbols we use to express our understanding of the process also change.

Whenever there is a transition from one "technology of the Word" to another, there is always resistance. In an oral community, prayer and ritual were alive as the words were uttered. When the words were written down, they seemed a pale reflection of words that had potency when spoken. Same thing when the printing press with movable type was invented. Some people just couldn't read what was printed.

One of my favorites is the Duke of Urbin. A passionate manuscript collector, he refused to read printed books, but when he heard of one that he wanted, he had it delivered to the monastery where the monks copied it over by hand.

So there will be resistance to prayers on a computer, as if they are somehow "not real." Anyone who has reached out on-line during a crisis, however, as I did recently when my brother was deeply depressed and threatening suicide, knows that the words that show up on the monitor in the middle of the night are words of light and life. The response I received to my late-night invitation to a few colleagues and friends resulted in action that saved my brother's life.

Some of those people prayed and communicated their prayer via e-mail. Some lighted simulated candles in the digital darkness, no less candescent for being words or images. Some typed advice or encouragement. And some, like those monks that turn that rolodex, plugged in our names to programs they had written and let the computer just keep on praying for us, day after day.

OK, you tell me: Did the computer pray?

But remember, the "computer" is not some stand-alone machine, a brain in a bottle on somebody's desk, the computer is the global network, alive not only with energy but also with intentionality.

Intentionality transforms what would otherwise be rote into prayer. Whether people are reading in a chapel or communicating on the Network, the symbols—printed words or luminous pixels—are turned to flame.

Prayer becomes real, according to Hasidic Jews, when the words on the page become flame. The words on the monitor too.

The Network is a symbiosis, a global community of human beings interlocked with a global network of millions of computers. The symbiosis—digital humanity expressing itself through an electronic network inseparable from itself—prayed and keeps on praying.

How can we separate a mediating structure from that which becomes incarnate in and through it? The medium is the message, the context is content, and words becomes both silicon and flesh. Physical objects are permeated with memory and meaning, and then they become sacred. Sacred places are spaces bracketed in the physical world—which is nothing but energy also—transformed by the energy and intelligence of the heart.

There are moments—aren't there?—when we feel the presence of someone interacting with us through the monitor, through the modem, through email or IRC, so palpably that we feel them there in the room, we feel their energy, their intention focused on us, and we feel it as well when their focus shifts and the energy wanes. Being is manifest through the wires and electromagnetic energy of the digital world.

So yes, prayer happens, but the initial question—does a computer pray?—dissolves into finer distinctions as our sensory extensions are fused with our will and intelligence. Prayer happens, luminous sacred spaces glow in the night, the sudden candescence of a million monitors transformed into altars and sacred groves, a roar of flame in the darkest hour.

Climbing Down the Iceberg   *October 31, 1997*

I am told that the Japanese word "rikutsuppoi" means "an idea or position smacking of such a high degree of logic that it ignores reality."

Granted, too little logic is a dangerous thing. During times of change like ours, when the connections between the stabilizing matrix of our world views and our daily experience are torn like weak ligaments, we can drop into a black hole of confusion and project patterns onto the universe that aren't really there.

A professor once found a diary in a secondhand book shop in London that was written in code. He pored over the arcane marks until he cracked the code and translated the text. A fascinating world emerged, full of details of court intrigue and daily life. When he published his findings, colleagues asked for a look and discovered that it wasn't code at all. The diary had been written in English but the ink had dried and cracked over the years, and the desperate professor had projected all that rich content onto the meaningless squiggles.

An intriguing phenomenon plagued code breakers during World War II as well. When they came up against a code they couldn't crack, some of the codebreakers cracked instead. They doodled instead of dithering and drew pictures of the implacable enemy they believed had created the unbreakable code. The pictures were usually warrior women, armored goddesses like Wonder Woman, unknowable, aloof.

The kink of code-breaking aside, something similar happens in the midst of religious experience, when the rational mind is overwhelmed and from the depths of our souls there emerges an image of a being beyond comprehension who we believe created the uncrackable code of life on earth.

When logic breaks, strange things happen. It is an unfortunate fact that those who torture others to extract information or to conduct state terrorism, know there is a point they must avoid, when pain overwhelms the capacity of the conscious mind to cope or make sense of what is happening. After that break-point, the victim looks out at their torturer through eyes blazing with gratitude, having dropped into a place in their souls that is deeper than pain, deeper than life itself.

Next time you find yourself in an art museum with portraits of saints by El Greco, look at the expression in the eyes of the blissful martyrs.

So ... during times of radical transition, when the way we construct reality just doesn't fit our experience, there is a tendency to fall into all sorts of irrational belief of conspiracies, sidebar spiritualities that promise easy salvation, and extraterrestrial plots to kidnap our neighbors.

We surrender the light of logic to our peril. Yet ... we humans are more than logic machines. Supra-rational or trans-rational experience is not identical to irrational. The former includes and transcends our rational faculties, illuminating a larger life that we have filtered out.

Synchronicity is Carl Jung's word for events that connect in a way that befuddles simple notions of causality. All spiritual traditions have words or practices designed to remind us that the bulk of the iceberg of life is well below the surface.

Yesterday the telephone rang at the end of a long work day. I had worked mostly alone and was feeling … strangely becalmed, at the end of a trajectory I had been following, unsure of the next move.

The caller was Ralph Blum, a man I had never met. He had received one of my "Islands in the Clickstream" columns by email from a colleague and called to talk about it. We discovered many things in common, moving from life history to spirituality to competitive business intelligence and computer security. I mentioned that I was speaking at Pump Con, a computer hackers convention, this weekend, and added that I believed that Odin was one god of the hackers (Odin had hung, cold and alone in a windswept tree for nine days and nights, sacrificing himself in order to seize the knowledge of the runes). Ralph said he had written *The Book of Runes*, and as we spoke he "cast my runes." He said, "Interesting. The same one has come up twice. That's unusual.

"Your life is at a poise point, the moment when a system has fulfilled the momentum of a particular direction. You're waiting now for a new direction to emerge.

"Don't miss the richness of this time," he added. "Waiting can be a splendid experience."

There is a time before the beginning, when new possibilities are ripening, what Hebrew scriptures mean by "brooding over the darkness of the deep" like a mother hen, what Christian scriptures mean by "the fullness of time."

That call, coming from nowhere, was the right thing at the right time. We can trace the steps, how his friend had received the column from a friend and sent it on, but all of those pieces won't add up to one.

Was it only a coincidence that he received a column and acted on impulse and called? An unconscious response to the subtext of my words? An intuitive apprehension of feelings in my voice? Or was it what it seemed, a glimpse of the connections among all things, usually hidden by the veil of the mundane?

Ninety-eight percent of the Internet is invisible, operating sight-unseen "out there" in the world. That means it is also sight-unseen "in here" as well, in the collective mind and unconscious that we have become by virtue of interaction in the digital world. Our hive mind is the unified consciousness of humankind learning to observe itself in digital symbols like Indra's jewels, nodes of a net that each reflect the entire web.

Beware of too little and too much logic. The Net is a moving map of the human mind like a mobile over a baby's crib. Through its worm holes we slip now and then like quicksilver to experience the necessity of connection, the illusion of solitude, the gregariousness of the wired world.

A Digital Fable

November 14, 1997

A sacred canopy of shared belief used to soar above our heads like a large umbrella, keeping us warm and dry as the contradictory data of real life beat down.

A canopy doesn't have to be sacred—any canopy will do—but because our understanding of the cosmos and our place in it is such an important part of our stance toward life, a canopy always has a sacred component. What we believe determines how we act.

No model of reality contains everything. Life is larger than our models of life. All we need is an umbrella that is good enough to manage the odd drops by keeping them irrelevant. As long as our model of reality makes enough sense of the world to let us act, we hold to our beliefs.

But there is an awful lot of rain these days, forty days of rain—more than forty days—and it keeps on raining...

Our trans-planetary network of computers is a rain-making machine that—finally!—works. There is no snake oil this time, no flim-flam man. It's really coming down out there. More and more data just doesn't fit. Our umbrella has more than a few holes in it, and the water is trickling through.

At first we act as if we don't notice. The real experience of our lives contradicts what we say about life. When we hear ourselves speak, we sometimes sound like ... someone else, someone we used to be or someone we're overhearing. If we refuse to believe our experience and believe our beliefs instead, we get a headache. A very very bad headache. We crawl into bed or pop a Prozac, but we keep getting wetter and wetter.

Alas! we're all too human—stubborn, blind as umbrellas, frightened out of our shivering skins—so we still insist that we're not wet. We hold the handle of the umbrella more and more tightly, telling ourselves and everyone else how dry we are, what an excellent umbrella we have found. Others politely suppress giggles and move on.

It's so easy to see holes in someone else's umbrella.

Finally the umbrella is so battered that we can no longer deny what everyone else has seen for a long time; that we're holding nothing but shreds of wet black cloth on a skeletal metal frame and we're soaked to the skin.

We all want to stay dry, but one legacy of living in the twentieth century is that no canopy spans us all. We join organizations to experience the momentary consolation of agreement, but we can't live there. Life today is like living in a village of grass huts in which everyone has a radio tuned to a different station. However high we turn the volume, we can't shut out the other songs.

I recently spoke about "The Stock Market, UFOs, and Religious Experience" to an investment conference. The speech distinguishes between things we think we see out there and things we really see. It's about the psychology of projection and the psychology of investment.

I noted that in the United States and increasingly in the world, an attitude of respect for other religious traditions creates a good deal of tension. We have to both believe in our own belief system and acknowledge that others are entitled to contrary views. Holding mutually exclusive truths simultaneously in our minds is difficult. We're not even always sure which is the umbrella and which is the rain.

We will try to surrender our freedom to those selling cheap umbrellas, but we cannot avoid our destiny: we are each responsible for inventing ourselves, for creating our own lives. There is no high ground on which to hide.

Our calling is made more difficult by the digital world. The digital world consists of simulations, models so compelling we mistake them for reality. Sometimes the digital symbols refer only to other symbols, what Baudrillard called simulacra, simulations of simulations, copies with no originals. All those simulations are umbrellas, and all those simulations are rain.

Nietzsche saw it coming at the end of the last century. It's what he meant when he said, "God is dead." He wasn't talking about the creator of the universe, but about the gods in our heads, the cultural artifacts that we invent. He saw that our sacred canopy had shredded and the rains were pouring down.

Prophets are people who get wet before everybody else and start sneezing. We try to quarantine them, but reality is a cold it is impossible not to catch.

As did speech, writing and printed text, electronic media are transforming what it means to be human, what kinds of gods we are likely to worship. Gods. Not God. God is always God, and God is with us, out here in the rain, getting wet.

In the digital world, Nietzsche's questions are more urgent than ever. Never mind that he asked them long ago. As Kafka wrote slyly in "The Great Wall of China," it can be many years before an edict of the emperor is heard out here in the hinterlands. Civilizations take lots of bullets and walk dead for a long time before they fall.

Some treat the digital world as if it is an umbrella, as if simulations can be more than an umbrella, as if they can be stitched together into an ark. And who can blame them? Who does not want to be warm and dry? But the words "warm and dry" will not keep us warm and dry, nor will digital simulations of 3-D umbrellas dancing and singing on the screen. The digital world is water, a rising tide, a tsunami impacting our consciousness with revolutionary force, levelling our villages, sweeping away our shrines and altars, sweeping everything, everything out to sea.

What games, asked Nietzsche, what festivals shall we now invent? Indeed, my friends. And what games shall we simulate? What games shall we play? What games shall we dare to believe?

Digital Religion   *December 1, 1997*

If we take a step back from our own religious beliefs and observe them for a moment, we can see that they show up in our minds and imaginations as images and symbols. It follows that the technologies that manipulate and generate those symbols have a profound impact on the content of our religious lives.

This is true of religious organizations and institutions as well as the psychic contents of our religious experience.

It has become trite in business circles to speak of the transformation of organizational structures and the need to "work smarter." That phrase is seldom defined. It seems to mean anything from making yourself open somehow to flashes of intuitive genius to learning how to do things you don't know how to do. It's a scary phrase because most of us think we are being as smart as we can and if we could have fuel-injected our intelligence we would have done so in fifth grade, just to get that teacher off our backs.

Telling people to become "coaches" rather than managers, when that command is not accompanied by the patient training and mentoring that enables them to do that, is like telling us to work smarter. Educational circles are rife with anxiety as schools confront the need for training as a budget item at least as important as buying hardware and software and setting it up.

Still, educators and businesspersons alike can feel in their bones the extraordinary impact of the computer revolution, even if they can't yet articulate its real depth. We know that the virtualization of organizational life means more people are working everywhere in the world from anywhere in the world and the task of using digital symbols to manage them—via wired and wireless networks—makes oversight of those amorphous, shape-shifting structures a real challenge.

If we know that is happening in the world of work and education, we have merely to widen the circle of our understanding to realize that the same thing is happening in religious organizations and communities.

This is relevant even to those who care nothing for religion or spirituality because the cosmic mythology of a culture or civilization determines its values, behaviors, and perceptual lenses. How we think about the universe and our place in it determines our possibilities for action, and that in turn is determined by the structure of our information technologies.

If we accept Hindu hierarchies, for example, and our place in them, we accept what it is possible for us to think and do with our lives. That structured thinking is not far from the way western European Christians thought about society before technological change turned the medieval worldview and its great chain of being on its ear.

Or we can note that it was probably not an accident that all of the great religious founders or patriarchs of contemporary religions—Moses, Jesus, Buddha, Mohammed, Confucius, Lao Tzu—emerged during a narrow bandwidth of historical time that corresponded with the emergence of writing. They were translated, in effect, from flesh-and-blood individuals into "textual beings," and it was in and through the text that their followers or disciples encountered the "person" of their guru or their god. Those gods were structured by the parameters of text, disclosing possibilities for human life that the receding horizon of the text made available. Those possibilities literally did not exist in the world before writing.

Oral cultures have smaller vocabularies, seldom more than 40,000 words, and those words exist only when spoken. That limited vocabulary defines the boundaries of the world and the self that perceives the world.

Walter Ong, a Jesuit theologian, notes that the Roman Catholic practice of "self-examination prior to confession" did not exist before the printing press. The explosion of English, for example, to more than a million words, meant that the self coming to confession could observe itself in more subtle detail. That self literally did not exist before it could see and say what it saw through the lens of expanded language. Ong concludes that the printing press generated a new kind of self-conscious self that in the process of self-examination and confession overcame the alienation that the technology itself had also generated.

Information technologies distance us from ourselves, one another, and our gods and at the same time make available the means for greater communion among those more nuanced selves. But the new self is genuinely transformed, unimaginable from within the parameters of the prior technology. The new self includes and transcends all that came before.

Electronic media are generating in an analogous way new selves and the means by which those selves will come into new kinds of community. Interaction with digital technologies is changing who we are and how we experience ourselves as possibilities for action.

This means that the images of our deities are being transformed as well. We are learning to encounter the persons of our gods as well as other people in and through the transformative experience of digital interaction. As technology makes available immersive 3D virtual environments, the structures of our religious experience and organizations will continue to morph.

Digital images of our gods will be evolutionary, modular, and interactive, with theologies that follow suit. As the strands of many oral traditions fed into the religions we can name, the strands of our current religious traditions are flowing into the fractal landscape of emergent religious experience in the digital world. What we call "spirituality"—the tools that more or less work to keep us more or less sane—

will also be shaped by the contours of the digital world. And so will the images of ultimate meaning, power, and possibility around which our new distributed communities coalesce.

What the Platypus Dreamed   *January 3, 1998*

The paradigm or model of reality according to which we operate determines the questions we can ask and therefore the answers we can hear.

My extended family includes people from four or five major religious traditions (depending on how we count) and a dozen denominational flavors, so I don't have the luxury of forgetting how religious beliefs filter our experience, leaving patterns of tea leaves in our various cups that all look like "reality."

Different scientific domains build the same kinds of filters. Scientists in different disciplines inhabit radically different landscapes, but their discoveries stream into the public domain where, somehow, we must integrate them into our larger understanding of life on our home planet.

Dozens of the year's significant discoveries were reviewed by Science News. They include: the heart of the milky way pumps a fountain of antimatter and hot gas into the halo of material lying several thousand light years above it; apes walked upright about eight million years ago, upsetting notions that only the human branch of the family had this posture; researchers deduced the presence of planets orbiting other sunlike stars; a computer program designed to reason in a general way solved a problem that stumped mathematicians for 60 years; scientists took movies of the world's smallest rotary motor, an enzyme that makes fuel for biochemical processes.

Et cetera. Many disciplines, many maps.

But what is the key to the unified kingdom? To continue to speak to one another with civility, we need shared paradigms, modules of integrated understanding that knit the diverse perspectives of the human species into a single latticework, a network of reciprocal symbols. Then we can imagine a shared heritage and a common destiny.

And then our species can find the courage to continue to learn together, managing the anxiety caused by ambiguity, complexity, and exponential change.

I think one of the discoveries cited by Science News is the key to that kingdom:

"The platypus experiences REM sleep."

Now, the platypus is a primitive mammal, and scientists had thought that REM (rapid eye movement) sleep evolved fairly late in mammalian development. They thought REM sleep aided dreaming or memory. Now they think it may assist very basic brain stem functions.

In short, we share with the lowly platypus a function previously believed to be a mark of human uniqueness.

That's why the REM sleep of the platypus is both a symbol and an example of our revised understanding of our place in the universe.

Like Alice eating her magic cookies, we grow smaller and larger as we nibble on the fruit of the tree of knowledge. The more we learn, the more we see how much we didn't know, how tentative our hypotheses, how incomplete our classification of everything from subatomic particles to cosmic events.

Paradoxically, the more diminished our uniqueness, the more genuinely powerful we become. Real progress in directing our own evolution—genetic engineering, nanotechnology, our first steps off our home planet—gives us the confidence to admit that the special niche we thought we occupied was the vision of an infantile ego compensating for feelings of inadequacy. Now that we know we are specialized ants dancing on a commonplace planet in a classifiable galaxy, we may have the humility we need to begin to mature.

The boundaries between plants and animals, humans and other animals, animals and machines, grow fuzzier and fuzzier. Yet many religions still claim that human beings are the apex of creation, our planet the center of the universe.

That narcissistic cosmology may have made sense in the Bronze Age but in the twenty-first century it is a symptom of pathology.

Human beings are one path by which matter is becoming conscious and intentional, and we travel that pathway with increasing speed. Our self-conceptions are always abstractions, blurred snapshots of hurried travelers; by the time we realize it is our face in the photograph, our real face has aged and changed.

There is a struggle between our desire to hunker down in the darkness and a convergence of evidence from every direction that cries out for the integration of commonsense knowledge and scientific data with a viable religious myth that includes our real shared heritage and our real, more comprehensive destiny.

Now that we know that the uterus produces a marijuana-like compound called anadamide, we can understand why human beings hate to forsake the darkness for the bright light of life. Not only are fetuses nourished and protected, they're sustained in a mellow high that makes the chaos and cacophony of birth a sobering experience.

Religious quests sometimes sounds like a yearning to return to the blissful oneness of the womb. Mood-altering practices conserved in religious rituals accomplish some of that. But religious rituals are also threaded with symbols and narratives that must bear more than a passing resemblance to experience. Otherwise we divide our lives into "reality" and "religion," undermining our own integrity.

To say that humankind cries out for a religious myth that integrates common-sense knowledge and scientific data with life-giving symbols of promise and possibility is to ask for clarity and awareness, pure and simple.

Clear thinking saves trouble.

Yet ... we cannot just think our way into new religious structures. Every major earth religion has come to us through flesh-and-blood human beings who were transformed into "textual beings," i.e. translated into written images or personas. That transformation initiated a sea-change for civilization.

Now we are carried along in a different kind of sea-change. Deeper waves are bringing forth digital images of gods, the transforming power of electronic media is giving birth to divine agents, disclosing life-giving possibilities more congruent with new ways of framing reality. And ... those divine agents will be incarnate, those digital images linked to flesh-and-blood human beings who can expect to receive the same warm welcome from the gatekeepers and thought-police that prophets have always received.

Keep your belt buckled and your virtual lamp lit.

What Is, Is   *March 28, 1998*

Many of the more profound insights into both digital and non-digital realities sound like bumper sticker slogans, and whether they are truisms uttered by a well-intentioned friend or the sudden illumination that recontextualizes ... everything ... is due more to our readiness to hear them than anything else.

For example, I was expressing anxiety the other day about something, and my friend said, "let go and let God." That happened to be what I needed to hear, and my concerns dissolved.

Here's another one, equally simple: What is, is. What isn't, isn't.

So long as we operate in the domain of conceptualization, this is obvious. Things that are true are true. Things that are not true are not true. But this isn't about things that are true. This is about things that *are*. It is the relationship between the representations of things that are in our heads—mental artifacts, Marvin Minsky calls them—and things that are or are not—that creates confusion. The amount of energy needed to turn something that is into something that isn't is infinite because it can't happen. And vice versa. What is, is, and what isn't, isn't. I was thinking about that here in Honolulu where I came at the invitation of St. Andrew's Episcopal Cathedral to speak and keynote a workshop on the larger issues of technological impact and specifically the transforming effect of computer technology on spirituality and religion.

Keep in mind that I am a former Episcopal priest who feels deep gratitude and reverence for the Anglican tradition, for the way it "constructs reality," for its symbols and rituals. But keep in mind too that a primary reason for leaving the ordained ministry was my need to explore the impact of computer technology in a free and unfettered way. Had I remained a custodian of the institution and its traditions, I would have been constrained to incline my insights in the direction of its construction of reality. And central to that construction is the exclusive claim that Jesus alone is the path to God.

Most other religions do not ask that others either convert or get out of the way. The Judeo-Christian God is indeed a jealous God. Buddhists revere Buddha as an image of enlightened possibility and allow others to walk their own paths. Jews do not ask others to become Jews. Hindus believe that God has many names and forms and invite them all to the party. But Christians claim that there is no other way to come to God, which makes the journey into cyberspace so perilous for Christianity.

The journey into digital reality explodes our boundaries, threatens our imaginary walls, from the borders of nation-states to the creeds that contain a religious community. I don't know the answer to the question, but I do know that this is one of the questions: Is Christianity bigger than everything else, or is there something bigger than Christianity?

Entering cyberspace changes everything. Local communities become global. Power is exercised in a network, not by dominating and controlling, but by participating and contributing. When a community creates structures that invite and sustain real growth, it is subversive of the structure that exists when the invitation is issued. Control of the process must be surrendered.

The simple fact of other viable spiritual traditions is a conundrum for Christianity. Seventy percent of the world's inhabitants are not Christian and seem to develop spiritually using other traditions. That they exist is an ineluctable fact, a way of saying something about God's generosity and graciousness as a host of the party called the universe, that threatens all of our efforts to define "Truth" from the top down, rather than the inside out.

It is not God who is as stake, but our images of God, our constructions of reality, the names and forms and symbols that we use to move toward God. The Judeo-Christian tradition calls those images idols, mental artifacts as culturally relative and transitory as fetishes. Buddhists say that the finger pointing toward the moon is not the moon. That's a way of saying that all religious traditions formed and sustained by writing and printed text are engaged in a transformative process of which digital reality is the catalyst, and may in that process be transformed into something entirely else, something that includes and transcends all that came before. Digital reality is interactive, a moving process rather than a fixed tradition, shape changing or "morphing" in its essence, and those intrinsic qualities determine a different kind of experience and a different kind of human being (at least in how we conceive of ourselves and construct ourselves as possibilities for action in the world) than entered the process in the first place.

There always comes a moment in those workshops in which that paradox is encountered. I see in the eyes of spiritual pilgrims the same light that I see when teachers realize that incorporating computers into education means that teaching and education is changed forever. The same light that I see when leaders and managers realize that bringing technology into the workplace changes their role and function forever.

That's why it matters to distinguish the representations in our minds from the real thing. Those representations are the only things that *can* be threatened. Our inviolable selves are never threatened. The God who created and sustains us is never threatened. Only our way of constructing reality, that walls both in and out specific possibilities, is threatened. And the Good News that speaks to that fear and anxiety is that good old bumpersticker slogan: What is, is, and what isn't, isn't.

Power consists of seeing and saying what is simply and deeply true. When we speak that truth, as much as the Truth can be spoken, we move with the Tao, the power of the universe, the Truth that will and does set us free.

Showing Up

June 20, 1998

Most of us have not lived very long in the digital world, yet the debris of the past is all around us.

One of the kids took an old Apple 2 and shoeboxes full of floppies when he left. An XT sits on a stand in our living room, an object of art. A neighbor bought it for $3400, then we bought it from him for a hundred bucks and sent it with one of the kids to college to use as a word processor. ("You expect me to take an IBM XT to college?!?") There's an AT that we use as a doorstop, a 386 with Linux on it. Why go on? The detritus of our digital play space is everywhere.

Why do we keep that hardware around? I guess we think it isn't used up, that maybe we can connect again using ASCII Express at 300 bauds and download warez before it was called warez.

The name of the game, we learned early, is to get inside. See how it works. See what we can learn when messages are exchanged silently in the night, more like signing than sound.

Well past midnight, when all the distractions of the day have faded and our minds are focused with clarity and high intentionality on the project at hand … listening to the whisper of our own minds and the clicking of the keyboard as we navigate the maze of data, not quite knowing what we're searching for … until we find it. For one bright shining moment, the dissonance that drives our need to understand is relieved and everything seems to connect, a missing piece completes the puzzle, the game dissolves and reconstructs itself at a higher level.

We know that the developmental stages in our lives have ended when the illusions that sustained them disappear. It happens again and again. Increasingly we detach from our constructions of reality, seeing them as temporary, not worth dying for. We seek common ground in the bonds that transcend content or form. Eras end too, according to Arthur Miller, when their illusions are exhausted. And planetary cultures. And trans-galactic civilizations. Galaxies explode. Light to light. Atoms to atoms. Dust to dust.

What knowledge is worth knowing? What puzzles are worth solving? What connections are worth the effort to drive our tired minds through the night toward what we believe is the light of another dawn? What matters most?

Premature death always feels, well, premature, as if something barely used is wasted. But even a timely death can be a reminder that ultimately life wants nothing more than more life.

Those of us who thrive in the digital world love to manipulate symbols. We hope that the world they disclose has some relationship to what we call "reality." The laughter that echoes in the enlightened mind and the laughter that rattles through cyberspace is the laughter of Zen monks contemplating the paradox that the mind that knows can not know what the knowing mind would know.

When I notified my column's mailing list that my wife's mother had died, many of you responded with words of condolence, encouragement or wisdom. My wife was astonished by the degree to which your words, forwarded to her email box, became transparent to the reality of so many human beings behind the visible symbols. Windows were thrown up and the fresh air of genuine connection filled the house.

Out of nowhere, many of you simply chose to show up. The joke is that nine-tenths of life is showing up, but showing up means more than moving our bodies from here to there. Faith is the willingness to get out of bed in the morning and just show up, because implicit in the decision is the belief that somehow, something new can emerge in our lives that is redemptive or transforming.

All knowledge is configured to the hard-wiring of our genetic heritage, the contours of our minds and cultures. We think and see only what our ways of thinking and seeing allow us to think and see. So what do we really know?

There are moments in the silence of the night when an unexpected communication or chance discovery connects the dots into a bigger picture. We see more deeply how our civilization works. Or we realize that we are not alone in the universe, that our delusions of grandeur are mere hubris, the fantasies of a toddler at the top of the steps of his front porch, getting ready to go downstairs for the first time.

The impulse at the moment of knowing is often to share what we know. The destiny of a cell is to be part of a body it can never comprehend. Yet we see in that moment of knowing that our language is inadequate to the task of real communication.

"My life belongs to the world," George Bernard Shaw said, "and I want to be thoroughly used up when I die. I rejoice in life for its own sake. It is not a brief candle for me but a sort of splendid torch which I have for only a moment and I want to make it burn as brightly as possible before handing it on to future generations."

To understand what we think is happening within the parameters of our inherited modes of knowing is one way to be conscious. Another is to see that we are momentary configurations of energy and information and we always have the option to become transparent to our destiny, the desire of the heart to belong to one another. When we exercise that option, then cyberspace glows, an explosion of inexplicable splendor magnifies our light before it is transformed. (Light to light.) We are present to ourselves. (Atoms to atoms.) We are more than what we think we know, more than digital symbols, more than the prison of our dead language, the binding constraints of archaic code. (Dust to digital dust.)

In memory of Bernice (1904 – 1998), who never knowingly used a computer.
But knew, nevertheless, how to show up.

Millenium's End   *December 10, 1999*

My machinery is wired to move pretty fast, and all my life people have told me—bless their hearts—to slow down. It always comes from people who move more slowly, never from those who are faster, so once in a while I reply, no, *you* speed up. But then they think I'm rude.

It's fashionable to equate being slow with being spiritual. There's something to that, but popular culture turned it into the Forrest Gump School of Wisdom, where life is never complex and wisdom is rules for the first day of kindergarten.

Fast and slow are relative. For some projects, cycles of a thousand years work best, for others, nanoseconds. Yes, we twitchers often find serenity when we take things down a notch, when we focus on something outside ourselves that induces a state of flow and short-circuits our habitual thinking. But it's also true that we relish those moments when our brains or bodies twitch like the fingers of a teen genius at a game of Quake, lost in light-speed heaven.

Chariots of Fire told the story of two runners, one a Scottish missionary (Eric Liddell) and one a Jew (Harold Abrahams), preparing for the 1924 Summer Olympics. The Jew was a sprinter ("neurotics make the best sprinters," said his coach) who itched to explode out of the blocks at the gun and burn it up.

Liddell ran a longer race but he too loved speed. His religious commitment was absolute, but when urged to go into the missionary field instead of competing in the Olympics, he said:

"I know God made me for a purpose, but He also made me fast, and when I run, I can feel His pleasure."

Now, *that's* spirituality.

I sometimes become impatient with people who divorce technologies like network computing from "spirituality" as if "reality" can be separated into pieces. They moan like Eeyore about the downsides of technology as if they are not obviously the downsides of civilization itself. When they work themselves up about genetic engineering, for example, they attack biotechology instead of the decision to domesticate wheat a few thousand years ago. Technology is a problem only if it was invented after their birth.

Spirituality means "what works" and it comes as we explore and reflect on the depths of our lives. Yes, we twitchers are sometimes astonished at the sudden thunder of an inner epiphany when we quiet our minds. But we are equally astonished when we seize or are seized by an insight on the fly, our fingers twitching on the joysticks of our lives. Yes, we know, God made us for a purpose, but God also made us fast, and when we run—or whatever it is we do that equates to running—we feel the exquisite pleasure of the universe pulsing through our hot blood.

So whatever "running" is for you—do it, do it with all your heart and mind and soul. Come out of the blocks at the gun and burn it up.

The universe honors our commitment to use our gifts in ways that enlarge the lives of others and enhance their possibilities. To participate in that transaction with its endless loops of self-sustaining energy is what I think it means to be fully human.

In a simulation of artificial life, it was observed that life is a function of the velocity of information inside a system. When information moves too slowly, the system freezes. When information moves too fast, the system becomes chaotic. When the accelerating speed of information pushes the data almost to overflow its banks ... there at the edge where order almost dissolves into chaos ... life is optimized.

Leaning over the edge of the cliff but not toppling.

We neurotics love that story. Whether or not it's true, the story supports risk-taking ... as does our current life situation.

The long bull market and expanding global economy have created an environment that rewards taking risks. Millions have lived so long in this context they can't easily imagine anything else. At a recent planning retreat for multi-billion-dollar money managers, I asked how many of the thirty managers in the room had lived through a bear market. Only the founder of the firm, a man in his fifties, raised his hand.

My family tried to teach me the lessons of the Depression, but I came of age during post-war prosperity and discovered that much of their wisdom didn't apply. The context in which I lived rewarded different behaviors.

My children, too, make decisions based on their life experience. There have always been plenty of jobs around, so they make choices based on the length of a commute, time off for travel, or other quality-of-life issues that didn't exist during the Depression or the fifties.

So what was there to teach them? Not a program, but how to design their own program. How to trust the process of life to deliver what they need. How to learn how to learn.

The millenium is wobbling to its anti-climactic end. I have no idea what lies ahead. So I look to the past for its lessons. In the long dim hallways of my memories I see, like lighted busts, my private panoply of saints, those people whose presence, acceptance, and availability made the difference at critical turns of my life.

What else is there to say at millenium's end except that there is not enough gentleness and kindness in the world? Or that we ought to be endlessly grateful for the gift of people willing to overlook our flaws and remain loving and present in our lives?

Your speed is probably the right speed for your life. If you go slowly, go slowly with a high intentionality, aware of every step. If you twitch, twitch for all you are worth. Sail as close to the wind as you dare. Fly as close to the fire of self-knowledge, risk flying high. Risk the furnace of the devouring sun.

And be all used up when you're done.

An Owl in Winter: Millenium's End II

December 17, 1999

Late last night, I was walking alone on a path leading toward a footbridge that crosses a ravine near my home. As I approached the bridge, I expected to hear the familiar echo of boots on wooden planks but instead I heard, in a moment of silence just before I walked onto the bridge, the first owl of the winter.

I looked at the shadowy branches but couldn't see him. Last winter I saw an owl only once. I looked up from the icy snow and saw him perched on a low branch against a full moon. Then he opened wings that expanded unimaginably as he lifted off into the darkness.

That owl is a bird of prey, not some cartoon bird wearing glasses.

My wife recently attended a speaking engagement with me in Des Moines, Iowa. She had not returned to her home town since we buried her mother fifteen months before. We went to the cemetery and looked for her parents' graves. The markers were already overgrown with grass and covered with leaves. I pulled out the grass and brushed away the leaves so she could see their names, feeling like King Canute ordering the tide to recede. The grass will grow back, but next time no one will be there to pull it away.

We walked afterward in a park where my wife had ice-skated as a child. It was one of those lingering twilights when we feel deeply the transitoriness of all things, that all sanctuary is a momentary turning from the wind toward a temporary refuge. We followed a path in the woods along the Raccoon River until it grew dark, and when we turned back, we saw against the sky the silhouette of an owl in the low branches.

Dylan Thomas wrote in Fern Hill that all through the summers of his child-hood, "as I rode to sleep the owls were bearing the farm away in the moon that is always rising ..."

Owls. Rising moons. Images of death. But not of death only, images too of life, life lived on a razor's edge, life thrown at us, fired at us point blank from the barrel of a gun.

The millenium's end *is* an ending, of sorts: We will never exactly come this way again, if we do, we'll all be different. An owl in winter signifies the cold darkness surrounding the solace of our conversation, built of illusory pixels and made lumi-nous by the sheer force of will and desire. Eros in its digital essence, binding us together. A fusion of fact and imagination.

I wrote a few weeks ago about Digital Autumn, and a reader commented that it is one thing to embrace the ambivalent longings of autumn when love and loss are inextricably intertwined, when the wet earth is redolent of spring and autumn alike. But it's something else to embrace winter when it finally arrives.

How, he asked, do we welcome the real winters of our lives?

I thought of my first winter in England. At that northerly latitude, as the winter solstice neared, the sun rose lower and lower in the sky, looking like a distant pale candle seen through a frosted windowpane. I understood why Celtic legends tell of the twilight of the gods and eternal winter. There was an icicle of fear in our hearts that the sun would not bounce, but would sink lower and lower and finally disappear.

But the sun did bounce. Winter-blossoming cherry trees flowered. Love unex-pectedly melted our hearts once again.

There is no yin without a dot of yang, no yang without a dot of yin. Winter and summer, fire and ice. A figure-eight held in paradoxical tension, traced by a skater on thin ice.

Leafing through a friend's fortieth high school reunion book, I noticed that almost everyone said the same thing when asked what made for a wonderful evening. It was always dinner with family or friends, a quiet evening at home, an afternoon off with someone we love. Now it sounds like many of us are planning the same kind of quiet celebration for the last night of the millenium, just as we would if the universe were ending.

There will be parties too, of course, and a few crazies will do what they can to ruin everything, but most of us just want to be with people we love as we begin not so much the next thousand years as the next few minutes of our lives.

We don't live for millennia. We live for now.

Digital winter is the hollowness we sense outside the warm glow of our ingathered circle. These digital symbols comfort us with intimations of promise and possibility. Sometimes late at night when we can't sleep, we sit in front of our monitors as before a dying fire, hoping for a sign of communion. We build a digital bridge but before we cross it, we hear in the late-night silence the sound of a solitary owl. We realize that loss and grief have built the hearth on which we light this blazing fire, made up of air, nothing but thin air.

The loss of those we have loved has an icy core but contains a trace of consolation, the suggestion of a tide that will rise once more. Winter-blossoming cherry trees flower. A river of fire flows through these wires. We are alive. Here and now, we are alive. The sun and the moon are rising. And the fact of our being transfigures the threat of annihilation into a bonfire celebrating the end of everything and nothing, destroying and creating worlds.

For Karin/Krystalia – a bright young hacker girl who died too young - In Loving Memory

Night Light   *January 3, 2000*

All my life I have explored imaginary landscapes. From short stories to hypertext and interactive fiction, I have been fascinated by the way narratives are knitted together, ensnaring our minds in complex webs of luminous symbols and deceiving us into mistaking those illusory landscapes for reality itself.

Brains filter out as well as filter in. We wear our brains like blinders, protected from the splendor of the universe so we can keep our noses to the daily grindstone. Most of what matters most is beyond our grasp.

The deeper meanings of our lives manifest themselves as intimations that show up not in words but in the silence between words. Maybe that's why Buddhists say, those who know do not speak, those who speak do not know. Our images and symbols can take us to the gates of that nether-domain of darkness but then we must lower ourselves alone down into the caverns … hang like a spider on a thread … and let go of the rope.

And plunge into the cave of unknowing. Into darkness brimming suddenly with radiant light.

The midnight of the millenium has passed. It is still a ticklish world out there, but for the moment we are all breathing a little easier.

I asked myself, if this were my last opportunity to say what I have learned, to leave these words as a legacy for my children, what would I say?

Of that of which we cannot speak, said Wittgenstein, we must be silent. And humility, said Eliot, humility is endless.

But still, I would like to try.

Computer programmers often learn to think in terms of top-level languages like C, but nested in those friendlier languages are languages like assembly that describe the operations of computing at a different level of precision. These days, assembly language is often difficult to distinguish from machine language. That makes it hard to say what computers are "really" doing.

Machine language organizes how logical processes operate. But the process of manufacturing logic is too complex for humans alone, so the chips themselves contain many of those processes. Our network is manufactured by a symbiosis of human beings softwired into designs in turn hardwired into millions of invisible switches.

When we try to look under the level of machine language to the flow of electrons or photons, we spin dizzily down into the depths. When we try to look under our lucid explanations of biological processes to the genetic code that generates them—a code to which it seems we must only add water to grow symbol-manipulating machines like ourselves—we grow equally dizzy. Our identities cascade into a recursive process that spirals down into the darkness.

What is the ultimate source of our identities?

Our identities both as individuals and as civilizations seem to emerge from a recursive process acting on an unknowable initial condition. That's a way of saying that our origins are mysterious. "We" have bootstrapped ourselves from that unknowable condition into the light, hauling ourselves up by our own symbols, just as the universe has bootstrapped itself through successive levels of complexity via sentient beings distributed throughout all of unknowable space.

So when we look into that luminous darkness ... who are "we?" If we try to respond to that question, language breaks. All we can say is that "we" are not who "we" thought we were.

We are more than a community or a collective. Sentient life is woven in a singular web shot through with the light of luminous symbols. We are part of one another and of everything. We belong to one another and we belong to the universe.

We are not merely "fulfilled in community"—we are fulfilled when we so yield ourselves that we lose ourselves and our power is transformed into the power of others like ripples amplified endlessly in the still pool of the universe.

Here at top-level, high up at the level of language, all we receive are hints. At an immense distance—even at opposite ends of the universe—when those we love are hurting, somehow they let us know. At the moment of death, they often manifest themselves. Our connections are protected. We feel their presence as certainly as we know when someone has entered a room. And they have, in a way, entered a room, they have etched themselves indelibly in our souls. When we are socketed deeply into the love of others, we experience their energies whenever they extend in our direction and we know it.

Prayer is a name for clairvoyance radiant with omni-directional power. Telepathy means that we "get it" when it happens. Mystics have described this domain with precision, but a mystic is just an ordinary person who said what was so.

It can be startling to find our words, posted long ago to a newsgroup, archived at Deja News. Or old email stored on a server. Or the pattern of our lives linked and mined and sold to a list. So it ought to be even more surprising when we learn for the first time that all of our words and actions have a life of their own, that our lives are feedback loops of actions and reactions in which we live like ghosts in machines, going along for a ride. Yet paradoxically, our deepest intentions have always generated the patterns of our lives. Freedom and necessity fuse in a way that only the language of paradox can say.

So our ultimate task seems to be to try and try again to align our actions with our best intentions. Our lives will reflect our intentions anyway no matter what. Our lives tell us what we really meant if we have the courage to look at what we did.

And once we know, we can never forget.

An inner compass points always toward True North. The universe is a gesture intimating generosity and gregariousness, the primacy of what we call "love." Life is an invitation to discover somehow despite the seeming evidence to the contrary the means of unceasing affirmation.

Of course we love stories! Stories tell stories, after all, that cannot be told. Every technology of the Word—spoken, written, printed, transmitted—makes this real matrix in which we live a little more visible. These digital images that string us like beads or drops of dew on a spider's web are like dye in the arteries of our Soul(s).

The ghost in the machine is no pale shade. It is more than a luminous mist, more than a demented spirit hungering for its home. It is an intelligence transcending nested levels of insight into the darkness in which wings of the spirit infold into a single point of light and almost disappear.

For Julie, Barnaby, Rachel, Aaron, Scot, Susan, and Jeff

Breaking the Code   *October 3, 1999*

"Original ideas" have always incubated in a matrix that outputs similar insights through minds thinking in similar ways. It's more than a dialogue or conversation, it's a kind of mindfulness that includes and transcends our sense of being individuals. This matrix is more visible in the digital world, projected onto screens where we can see it. The digital world is constitutive of "selves" that are cells in the honeycomb of the "hive mind." We are still aware of ourselves but aware of ourselves as part of something much larger than our "selves."

The longer we live in this world, the more difficult it becomes to think of ourselves only as individual selves because the energy and information that constitutes the matrix flows with such fluidity between and among us. In moments of deeper seeing, we realize that we too are organizations of energy and information, recognizing a dependence on others and on the matrix itself that is daunting. We see ourselves seeing ourselves, and we are abashed.

That a column like this is a "work" created and owned by an individual author is a fairly modern concept generated only after the printing press was invented. Writers are encouraged to search for their own "voice" but we discover in our most creative moments that the voice that speaks is not our own. We may be need-to-know machines, but the real result of our needing to know is that we are more known than knower. We think we are speaking the words but the words in fact are speaking us.

The mass of humanity moves today through fields of information organized into honeycombs of cells toward new emergent realities. We like to call people who name those emergent realities "original thinkers," but the whole mass of humanity really arrives at the same time. Early adopters and late adopters simply have different seats on the same bus.

Everything, anyway, always happens at the same time.

Outside my office window, the world is bathed in autumn light, making the leaves translucent, suggesting that the world is a kind of computer animation projected through the multiple lenses of our brains, a holographic image of everything seen one slice at a time.

Something new is growing in the distributed Network, quickening in our collective enterprise. Because we can predict only the predictable, we can't say what it is. The readiness is all. In the fullness of time, both our individual lives and entire civilizations swell and burst with new possibilities that always seem to dawn with stunning suddenness. In retrospect, we impose on the events that seem to lead up to them a kind of compelling necessity, but life is always more complex than our explanations.

When our brains or eyes have evolved to a sufficient level of complexity, we apprehend what has always been there, but hidden. The neural net grows until it can grasp the pattern of more complex structures of data. Then we say, "Now I under-stand. Now I see." But we never really understand. We never really see.

"Out of the box thinking" is just a name for climbing out of one box into a little bit bigger box.

We are like miners tunneling through an immense mountain, seeing only the earth in front of our faces. What we don't know is so much bigger than ourselves.

The digital world, with all its circus animals and mythical beasts, is simply a new way for the human brain to deceive itself into thinking it Knows.

Why do so many Silicon Valley millionaires keep working when they can go to the beach? I think it's because we realize that once we have won by the terms of the game we thought we were playing, the game shifts to a new level. Toys just don't matter very much. Nobody is counting and nobody cares.

An IPO of Red Hat Linux created some new millionaires. Linux is Open Source software, which means the source code is available so anonymous program-mers can keep growing and tweaking the code. Open Source software presumes that people are motivated not primarily by money but by participation in projects that give their lives meaning. The success of Linux seems to support that assumption.

But the truth is never simple. Red Hat stock options loomed large. Our motives are always mixed. At one level of description, we look like individuals acting on self-interest, and at another, we look like cells in a body deriving identity and purpose by participating in efforts that transcend self-interest. We can describe what we see at the level of the individual programmer or at the level of the code.

The ego is a modality of self-control, while the Self is a modality of self-tran-scendence, built to surrender control. When we lose ourselves in life in all its won-derfulness and flowing, we find ourselves, but when we try to hold on to what we find, we lose it again. Victory comes only in moments of surrender.

We flicker back and forth between these two ways of being like holographic images. Wanting to quietly eat our cake and wanting to quietly have it, too.

It takes energy to maintain balance, doesn't it, to hang poised between life as it flows and noticing suddenly that it flows. We become suddenly fearful and reach out into the empty air to regain control. But there's no there there.

Look at the rocks in the rapids, says a friend who loves to kayak, and you'll hit the rocks. Look at the water flowing around the rocks and you'll go where the water goes.

What does it matter what name is pasted on the voice or the words if the words are worth speaking? Jews refuse to spell out the word "God" because the mystery at the core of our being is unspeakable. So is the pattern of the pattern of the program and our lives. The closer we come to the mystery, the intensity depth unknowability and richness of life, the more we melt into the code itself. Our existence is a recur-sive call of the pattern of the pattern of the code. When we relinquish the search for a pattern that our brains can grasp in symbolic notation, we experience more than contentment, we experience peace beyond all understanding, letting ourselves only be spoken, only be Known.

Invitation to a Seance   *May 31, 1997*

The e-mail message came literally out of nowhere.

"Hi this is new to me is th5s how yuo do it/?"

The return address contained the first name of a friend I had not heard from in years. I'd heard he was married now and living in San Diego. Beyond that—nothing.

Yet here he was again ... I think.

Wasn't he?

I admit I can be a little cynical. I sometimes feel like Jane Wagner, who said, "I'm getting more and more cynical all the time and I still can't keep up." Sometimes that seems like a reasonable response to the things our species does.

A cynic, however, is really a disappointed idealist. A realist, someone who takes life exactly as it is, on its own terms, fired at us at point blank range from the barrel of a gun, and is never disappointed. What happens is just "what's so."

A cynic, on the other hand, is always hopeful but frequently disappointed. My head is a cynic but my heart is naive. My heart is always ready to believe in the highest possibilities. An attitude of forbearance, generosity of spirit, and hope for reconciliation may not always be supported by the evidence, but it does help us get some sleep.

What does that have to do with that e-mail?

Hanging out with hackers who really know their stuff has given me a profound appreciation for the illusions of cyberspace. An e-mail can be easily forged: e-mail address, routing information, IP address, everything in the header. Web sites can be altered or simply appropriated, complete with a URL that brings unsuspecting email to your dummy site.

Cyberspace is full of Potemkin villages.

So ... without a context for that e-mail, how did I know who had written it? How could I know?

I wrote back, "Mike??? Is that really you?"

He wrote: "yes i am jst lrnig how to do this i cnt type"

Flashback to when I lived in England, a young man in a village in Surrey near London. I had made the acquaintance of an elderly woman named "Mrs. Frazier." I don't remember her first name.

Mrs. Frazier lived in a nursing home and from time to time, we invited her to our home for "high tea." She loved "getting out of prison," and from my point of view, the visits were always interesting.

Right in the middle of a sentence, as she lifted her teacup to her lips, Mrs. Frazier would suddenly pause and freeze, her eyes fixed, then set down the teacup and begin sputtering, shaking like a large wet dog coming out of a pond. Then she said, "That's all right, friend," to the air just behind her left ear, and to us: "He's here. He's with us."

That meant her "Indian guide" had manifested himself, and for the next while, she passed along tidbits of information about "life on the other side" and insights into our progress at our current "level of vibration."

Sometimes the guide brought messages from the dead. I never believed them, and I always wanted to believe them. They were always encouraging, but seldom specific. Once in a while I asked a test question that required knowledge of past events. The answer was always too vague to be evidential.

So we were left with Mrs. Frazier, a dear lonely woman who loved her outings and "specialness" so much she would let her imagination take over, and, for a few moments, become the center of our attention.

I sent test questions to my e-mail friend. One requested "the name of the mascot of the high school social athletic club that you belonged to, and where did it live."

Mike did better than Mrs. Frazier.

"It ws a chickn," he replied. He added the unprintable nickname we had given the hapless fowl. "It lved on the roof of the apartment bildng you lvd in untl they found out and made us give it away because of livestock laws."

He passed the test. My old friend really was new to cyberspace and learning how to represent himself as a digital construct interfacing with other digital constructs, like a ghost after it leaves its body.

He types better now. In one e-mail, he mentioned a woman we both knew and asked where she was. To my astonishment, an e-mail from her arrived—out of nowhere—that week.

"It is amazing," Mike wrote, "that you received an e-mail from her at the very time we were talking about her. Is it possible that e-mail is just a way of communicating with one's self? i.e. it doesn't get sent anywhere except into the brain of the sender?"

I think he's right, but the Self with which we communicate is the larger Self, the overSelf in which we all participate, the single organism constituted by all of our humanity. Of that Self, the Internet is a collective representation, the echoes or reflections of our digital dreaming and thinking.

The Net is an imaginary garden with real toads in it. We create it together literally out of nothing, then forget that we made it up so we can play in it.

The eyes with which you read this message are one pair of the multi-faceted eyes of a single honeybee looking at a digital simulation of our hive mind.

This digital transmission can be faked or hijacked, text changed in transit, images scribbled over with graffiti, but I don't think that's the last word.

Connection is the last word, genuine connection, and the community that blooms when we socket.

Maybe that's what dear Mrs. Frazier was trying to say when she started shaking like a great wet dog. Who knows why we play in cyberspace? Maybe we too need some feedback or attention, maybe we need to hang out, get out of ourselves, and connect. Yet what we create together out of our mutual need is a magical realm where anything can happen. Lost friends magically appear. The long-dead walk and talk.

So who knows?

When the final delete key is tapped, maybe we still reside in long-term memory, and a good hacker can recapture that data and undelete us with a single keystroke. Fix whatever was broken or lost.

And still remember our first name.

Getting Real   *September 19, 1998*

The themes of the digital world often involve fantasy and reality, illusions and truths, game-playing and "getting real." In cyberspace, we traffic in abstractions, digital images and symbols that represent printed text—these words, for example—which represent writing which represents speech which represents thoughts and affective states. These images become as fixed in our memory as photographs once were "fixed" in a chemical solution. We mistake our representations for the "real thing," the truth of our own experience, which devolves into an elusive, mythical being like a unicorn or the firebird.

Recent studies suggest that many complex organisms—not just human beings—represent the world to themselves. This is easier to visualize when we think of monkeys, for example, always using one sound to mean "danger in the sky" and another to mean "danger on the ground." Our nervous systems seem to have evolved so we can present to ourselves those representations of streaming photonic data that we call "experience." But when we live in a world that is more manufactured than remembered, a world that simulates simulations like computers making recursive calls, it becomes increasingly difficult to know whether we have really experienced something. Or not.

And yet … at the highest level of our experience, we do know when we are being real.

I am often a guest on a local radio program hosted by Jean Feraca, an interviewer so accomplished after a dozen years of doing it ten hours a week for Wisconsin Public Radio that her crafty artfulness has dissolved into her technique. She creates a context effortlessly that invites her guests to be forthcoming, anticipating the directions of their thinking intuitively so she can lead them to the next paragraph.

Today we spoke about the "outing" of humanity by the digital world, the difficulty of engaging in civil discourse when we all know whatever there is to know about everybody else.

The presupposition of the conversation was, of course, the President's recent humbling. Now, separate from the details of the situation, some people hate our American President the way others hated Roosevelt or Nixon, with a lacerating visceral rage. One caller railed at his improprieties and demanded punishment. "Don't you think," he said, "there should be consequences for this kind of behavior?"

It seems to be the nature of cause-and-effect in the moral domain that there *are* consequences whether I think there ought to be or not, of which the President's prolonged ordeal is one obvious example. Bill Clinton is reaping a whirlwind and his life is soaked with the anxious perspiration of public humiliation. But the caller wanted more. He wanted blood.

Now, I was immersed for years in people's lives at a deep, intimate level as a parish priest, and I learned that we judge and vilify most the things we have done or think of doing. We "whip the whore," as Shakespeare said, while lusting for her body. And when we do, our self-righteous anger has a tone of voice that is unmistakable.

When we stop attacking, however, and tell the truth about ourselves instead, the tone of voice changes. It becomes softer … more self-effacing, more … real.

All I could ask was, what in the world had the caller done? What real or imagined guilt fueled his pitiless fury?

I didn't expect a confession on the air. But there might have been a pause. There might have been that blessed hesitation that discloses that we have become conscious of our own history in a way that tempers our vindictiveness. When that happens, our voices downshift, and we speak from a deeper awareness that the truth includes the rest of us as well as the one we assailed. And when we do, it does. Others are welcomed back into humanity instead of demolished.

Civil discourse can't happen without that level of self-knowledge. It's as true of public debate as a disagreement in a marriage. Political discourse does not need to emulate a twelve step meeting in order for the conversation to get real. The details do not need to be part of the dialogue, just the deeper self-knowledge that includes others in the conversation as well as ourselves.

Digital symbols, like all abstractions of our experience, are neutral. They simply reflect and refract the truth of our lives. We human beings radiate information all the time. We can't help it. A good observer can spend ten minutes with someone and discern the essential truth of their lives. A few words and gestures does it all. The truth of our lives begins at the core of our experience and being, and however we obscure or disguise that core, it wants to be known. It wants to declare itself to the world, and when it does, the barriers created by our prideful posturing vanish. Whether speech or writing or digital typing, all the levels of abstraction collapse into a single point as if we had jerked the drawstring of a purse.

By "getting real," we mean that we speak with humility because we speak first from the truth of ourselves. When we know who we are, we can see clearly who others are. Then we can speak of accountability and compassion in the same tone of voice.

The digital world is transparent. Every key I hit declares who I am. The digital world is a Big Toy made up of video and audio and morphing animations which all collapse into light and color when we speak from the heart. The media with which we try to hide ourselves become a magnifying glass for all that we are.

"Truth" is a dangerous word. It all depends who says it, and how. The real truth is what it always was. And the truth can be said or sung by any voice, any time, any where. In that moment, we break into an invisible communion, and our digital words becomes law in the world because they're congruent with the deeper truth and our larger life.

A Dry Run   *November 14, 1998*

It depends what e-mail lists you read, what kinds of information you get.

Doomsayers still fill the Net with cries of alarm over Y2K, but more missives are arriving that show evidence of nuanced reflection. There may well be some disruption, they say, but maybe it's not the end of the world.

When the electricity went down last week, I thought of all the dire predictions of the imminence of the twilight of the gods.

One minute the lights in my office were bright, the computer screen luminous with simulated cards. I was winning at solitaire, too, a necessity before I log off for the night, when—a crackling of static—the screen flared, the lights died, and the background noise of the furnace and television downstairs disappeared.

When warm fronts and cold fronts war in November in the upper Midwest, it can be exhilarating, just before it gets serious. I had left a meeting of usability professionals earlier that evening, the sky low and moving, luminous clouds flowing over the city. My meeting-mates leaned into the wind as they pushed toward their parked cars. Garbage cans and traffic cones bounced around the pavement, signs hung crazily and clanged on their metal poles like bells. The wind was nearing seventy five miles an hour, gusting to more, so we had (technically) a hurricane. When I stopped for red lights going home, the car rocked like a cradle in the hands of a deranged parent.

But I made it home. That warm well-lighted place, that lantern-glow in the blowing dark, was an archetypal cave. Coming inside from the garage, I slammed the door and shut out the threat of chaos that lives just under the skin of every facsimile of ordered life.

"That wind is so unsettling," my wife said. We remembered the wind in Wyoming that never seemed to die. We had no tranquilizer darts to blow into the heart of the storm. The wind was an emblem of everything we could not control, joining the images of breakdown, terrorist attack, and hoards roaming the frozen landscape in search of food that fuel millennial fever.

I sat in the dark for a moment when the lights went out. My first thoughts were of data I hadn't saved. The cursor on the screen vanished into thin air like everything around me. There was nothing, after all, at which to point. My hand slid from the dead mouse.

Last summer I wrote a column, "A Silent Retreat," after the lights went out in a storm. But that was summer. Neighbors gathered outside in the warm night, and the next day, we ran errands on foot. Life was time-rich without our usual obligations. This time it was November, and the only sign of neighbors in the blackness that stretched as far as we could see were flickering flashlight beams on drawn curtains.

This time it went on for several days. A hundred thousand people in our corner of the state were without heat or light. The winds continued the next day, and as fast as crews could upright a pole or raise a downed power line, another fell.

In the morning we realized that our cars were locked in the garage. My wife took a taxi to work. A pile of printed material was waiting for just such a break in my seamless wrap-around world. Stephen Hawking notes that a human being would have to travel at ninety miles an hour twenty-four hours a day to keep pace with what's being published, just to stay at the interface. But it wasn't easy to concentrate.

Instead, I became aware as the day progressed of how unplugged I felt. The computer was dead, with all my contacts and e-mail. The television was dead. The car was inaccessible. The temperature was dropping steadily, and I moved like a cat toward the sunlight that slid across the sofa through the day. When an early dusk brought no sign of the restoration of power, we ate bread and cheese and fruit, then huddled under blankets, a dozen candles lighting the room. We located a radio with batteries and listened to love songs, gentled by candlelight flickering in the chilly dark.

Of course, this was not really a dry run for disaster. It turned into a lark. We knew they were working sixteen hour shifts. We figured out how to jimmy the window in the garage and crawl in and liberate our cars so we could have gone to a friend's house in a part of town that worked. But still, our sense of disorder was real. The degree to which we lived in a simulated world, plugged into interfaces feeding us with images, sounds, and illusions was revealed by contrast with the silence of the night.

The simple truth is, we drifted into an altered state. We were more than quiet. The night was more than dark, the candles more than adequate, because they enabled us to see just enough. The music on the old portable was beautiful and clear. The warmth of our bodies under an afghan was more than enough.

That deep quiet joy is accessible always, we have to believe ... but once the lights were back on and the house too warm, despite the fact that we lighted candles the next night, the mere possibility of turning on lights was a barrier between ourselves and the stillness we had touched.

Community is more than dependence, more than noticing that different skills keep society alive. Community is the simple truth we discover when we huddle in the darkness keeping ourselves warm by the fact of our closeness rather than emblems of connection. It is beyond electronic symbols, beyond printed images and text, beyond written words, beyond the capacity of speech to reach. Those are symbols, and symbols are a menu, while what we had tasted was a real meal. An affinity for the truth of another, the fact of pattern in a plausible chaos.

Words, Words, Words   *January 23, 1999*

Last week's column, "When Computers are Free to be Computers," was a jazz-like riff using images in words in the search for an image of a world of images beyond words—life as we might live it inside a grid of virtual communication, our thoughts like electrons traveling on interlacing wires.

A reader named Michael Goldhamer (www.well.com/user/mgoldh/) challenged that vision: He wrote:

```
Dear Richard Thieme,
        I too have dreamt of something similar to what you dis-
cuss, how computers could widen our communicative powers, but
reading your letter forces me to doubt it. Look at how quickly
and easily words bring up images and permit our attention to
move freely down all sorts of different channels in rapid suc-
cession with little ambiguity.
        While it is true that words might be augmented by pic-
tures, language has been perfected over thousands of years.
Language itself is multi-modal and I doubt we shall ever be
```

```
able to convey images faster than we can in language. You can
take me on your little image-filled joy-ride in words far more
easily than any other way. In fact, the Internet may prove to
be the renaissance of text....
```

.....as the Renaissance was, in fact, the renaissance of writing, as writing was the renaissance of speech, speech the renaissance of gesture and guttural utterance ...

Now, far be it from me to deride this textual medium in which I live and move. I am probably the last of the print-text people. Most colleagues in the speaking profession use slides in their presentations, but I prefer to make pictures out of spoken words. That creates a completely different kind of transaction between audience and speaker. It's like building a virtual fire, then lighting it. When it works, we engage with one another with intransitive attention, enmeshed in a dynamic flow. To follow intuitively the energies that flow back and forth between a speaker and an audience, surfing the currents of the group mind that emerges in the moment, is more like reading Tarot cards than lecturing. When an audience looks at slides or reads words in sound-bite bullets, it engages another part of the brain, and unless images have been so well integrated into the presentation that a new unity is created, that flow is broken.

When I am in the presence of an artist—or a web site—that successfully integrates words, images, sounds in a coherent whole, something new, something rare is taking place. But speaking about that new unity using only words is like "dancing about architecture."

In his latest book, "Visual Language: Global Communication for the 21st Century," Bob Horn claims that a new auxiliary language is emerging that integrates words and visual elements. Horn's book contains nearly 3000 visual elements in 270 pages, so it's a book about our new visual language composed in visual language. He tries to describe in images and words the syntax and grammar of this new sea in which we are just learning to swim.

Still, Horn's book is only a baby step along the way. I was imagining life well into the next century, as different from ours as robots on Mars are from steam engines. I was trying to illuminate something that includes and transcends whatever infrastructure might evolve. I was searching for a way to describe that deeper conscious intentionality that underlies all real communication.

Remote viewing, by way of example, is a kind of clairvoyance that intelligence agencies explored for several decades. Remote viewing is migrating now into the domain of competitive intelligence. It seems that RV is a primitive function located in the brain stem. Impressions of distant places or events are received as images. "Higher" brain functions immediately begin to interpret those images in words. Our beliefs skew our experience so that our experience will seem to support our beliefs. Part of the art of remote viewing consists of learning how to compensate for those filters so the first impression can be held lightly in a kind of freeze frame and clearly seen. It's like listening around the corners of your mind for quanta that come from all directions.

Communication is a function of the intention both to send and to receive. Everyone, everything, is radiating information always, and all we have to do to receive it is learn how to pay attention. Listening closely is a learned skill.

We have all had the experience of someone trying hard not to hear us. We know what we have to do to get their attention. We raise the level of our intentionality and penetrate their defenses. We discover that communication is a function, not of the media we use to communicate, but of our intention to connect. When I intend that you "get" it, you get it, even when "it" is a wordless communication of love, compassion, or deep respect.

Talking about communication on this deeper level is inseparable from talking about spirituality. Once we know that life is a web in which we are all enmeshed, we discover an obligation to become as conscious as we dare of what we are sending, then accept responsibility for modulating the signal if it sounds like static or noise. The evolving electronic infrastructure—the immersive 3-D virtual collaboratory landscape in which we will live—will replicate primitive brain stem functions like Remote Viewing at a higher level of the fractal of life. The infrastructure will disappear through habitual use and become background noise, just as our hardwired language-making brains have become the presupposition of human conversation.

The universe is an open-ended system, always evolving, always free to find new ways of arranging molecules in self-conscious clusters. We use words like "sacred" to mean those moments when we experience a nexus, self to Self. The connection itself is experienced in silence, but we seem compelled to express it, telling stories, storing memories in clusters designed to remind us of the deeper possibilities of life when we have slipped back into the routine slumber that we call our lives.

What Works?   *February 6, 1999*

I was reminded this week of the time a Zen monk greeted an audience with a bow. After we returned his bow, he asked, "Do you know why we bow here at the monastery?"

All sorts of answers came back at him, most true enough, but none of them on the mark. Some thought we bowed to acknowledge divinity in one another, others thought we bowed to indicate mutual respect. The monk did not refute any of the answers, but turned them aside as an aikido master turns aside an attacker. When no more answers were forthcoming, the monk said, "We bow because things seem to work better when we bow."

Our postures, in other words, express a deeper truth than we can tell, even when we connect those postures to explanations that purport to make sense of them. Good tools work regardless of why we say they work. Technical tools and spiritual tools alike.

Two very different meetings this week brought that monk to mind.

The first was a conference sponsored by the American Bible Society and the University of Chicago Divinity School on the future of scriptures and religion in the next century. The sixteen-member panel included public figures like Bill Moyers and noted academics like Gregor Goethals, Dean Emeritus of the Graduate School of the Rhode Island School of Design. I went along for the ride as an explorer of techno/spirituality, the struggle to articulate names for emerging spirits in the digital world.

One dilemma against which we kept bumping our heads was, how do we reconcile a multiplicity of voices in a pluralistic world with any attempt to define "truth" by doctrine or creed? How can we be true to the depths of our experience yet not fuse that experience with stories that make sense of them in such a way that we become incapable of listening to someone else's story ... which also makes sense?

The process of telling our stories and listening to one another's points toward the emergence of a larger story that includes and transcends them all, a story that is still being written and does not yet have a name. The next level of the fractal spiral of our story-telling life.

Panel members represented a diversity of points of view, but we shared at least one presupposition in common. We all believed that truth is discovered in dialogue. That's why we were there, having that conversation. People who know they know the truth, once and for all, would never be on that panel. Why would they bother?

We did not reach a conclusion, because we do not have the vocabulary yet to describe the emergent realities blossoming in our digital gardens. But we can see dimly the images and hear faintly the music that is weaving beings of spiritual depth and power in the loom of those sacred groves.

The second event was a meeting of our Wisconsin Year 2000 Group, a monthly gathering of IT leaders focussed on Y2K solutions for businesses and government agencies. Representatives of large corporations discussed their contingency and disaster recovery plans, and as they moved from node to node, they repeated the mantra, "Of course, we don't expect this to happen and hope it won't, but in case it does, this is what we plan to do."

By the time they had traversed every 'if this-then that' branch of possibility, they had fleshed out quite a scenario. I was reminded of a high ranking military officer describing plans for world wide martial law if "social unrest" became pervasive. The shadow of breakdown like the total eclipse of society moved around the globe from the first Australian city to tick millennial midnight. If all those readiness plans become real, our downtown will consist of large office buildings secured by small armies of private police. Illegal diesel generators will fill the parking lots and sidewalks, maintaining buildings at forty degrees so the buildings will function in the Midwest winter. Shivering inside, hundreds of emergency workers will try to restore order. Their families, of course, will have to be cared for so needed workers won't stay home to protect them . That means day care, food, water, and medical staff on site, all guarded by well-armed mercenaries.

"Of course," they kept saying, "we don't expect this to happen and hope it won't, but in case it does ..."

Both explorations—the future of religion in the next century (as organizational structures and the internal structures we use to frame our subjective experience are transformed in the digital world) and planning for the worst-case scenarios at the turn of the century—remind us that major transitions are always loaded with unknowns, and the ways we frame reality, identity, and self are all up for grabs.

Each of those meetings was a snapshot of the insides of our heads as we try to reconcile opposites and impossibles in a single narrative skein. The panel consisted of people struggling to hold in tension systems of belief that are mutually exclusive. The IT people are planning for contingencies that force us to think the unthinkable, that a Soviet Union that imploded into more than a dozen countries may be a better template for the next century than a prosperous Island America. Both meetings invite the same question: during times of transition (and all times are times of transition), what works?

Zen Buddhists sometimes respond to questions that invite a logical answer by saying, "not this, not that," pointing toward a supra-rational response that issues from a deeper place than logical thinking. What works? is that kind of question.

Do we think that being right is what really works? Fill-in-the-blank answers blur in the sustained downpour of complex realities, messing up our certainty. What works is to remember that we are bound to one another by a common struggle and a common destiny, and so long as we are, things do work better when we remember to bow.

Two Ways of Looking at a Network   *February 27, 1999*

There are more than two, of course, but let's start with two.

A computer network can look like a collection of stand-alone machines, just as humans in a community can look like a collection of individuals benefiting from economies of scale. It all depends on the POV from which you describe the system, and whether you notice the individual or the network. Without the individual, nothing happens. But without the network, nothing persists. The network organizes and stores information so it lasts a little longer than the span of our short lives.

In all high-level systems, from religious systems to business systems, symbols are stored and transmitted. Some are preserved through rituals, some through records or narratives, some through one-on-one teaching. We preserve them so they can be there like fruit ripening on trees so we can eat them when we're hungry. Symbol systems are like complex intertwining stairways in an Escher etching. Even symbols that have become stale or flat through habitual use are time bombs that can suddenly explode and shock us with visions of possibility beyond anything we had imagined.

Religious systems do not collect people who are virtuous or good. Religious systems collect individual people who need a training program to become more fully human beings.

Seen as individuals, we always start with self-interest. I learned growing up in Chicago that we're all in it for ourselves. No other presupposition seemed to work. The most exalted moral position dissolved when someone's ox was gored. I learned that no one has the high moral ground, that we all enter the arena of life, as Saul Alinksy said, with blood on our hands.

But who, as the caterpillar said to Alice, are we? Who is "us?"

I was talking with Steve Straus, a personal performance coach at a workshop sponsored by the National Speakers Association. It was one of those hallway conversations that are the real reason we go to those meetings. We were talking about "giving it away," as this newsletter is sent to anyone who wants it. But we were talking about more than turning a commodity into a loss leader. We were talking about how things work.

"It reminds me of the saying," I said, "give and it will be given to you. The more you participate or contribute, the more you experience a feedback loop of incredible value."

Now, here are some of the presuppositions of my statement: that there is something to give, that I have it, that I have, that I am an "I" and "I" can own whatever it is that is given away. As if what we give when we contribute to others is a "thing" we can possess.

That's the way the world looks when we think "we" are collections of individuals, bounded by parameters, when what we see when we look into a mirror is an edge, a boundary, a separateness.

"It's deeper than that," Steve said.

I don't remember his exact words, because as soon as I grasped what he meant, my construction of reality dissolved into something else. But although he used only a few words, I think he said something like this:

When we participate in something larger than ourselves, we experience a more complex truth about ourselves ... that the network really is the computer, that humans are cells in a single body. That as Marvin Minsky said, a person alone, like a desktop computer unplugged from the network, is nearly useless, a brain in a bottle. A person who isn't connected to how information and power flows in the network is like an abandoned infant raised by wolves in a cave, unable to speak the dialect of the tribe.

Power in a network is not exercised by dominating or controlling. Power in a network is exercised by contributing and participating.

So this is about more than managers morphing into coaches or organizational structures flattening into branches on tall fractal trees. It's as if we are staring at our image in that mirror, when suddenly the doorways of perception are cleansed, and instead of seeing a hard-edge shape created by eyes and minds designed to delimit a mass against a background, we see that we are energy and information exchanged in a self-similar system. Our edges blur, we see that the center is everywhere, the merely local focus of everything that exists. We see that the monitor through which you read these words is the stem of the leaf that you are on a single tree.

When we know this and live out of that knowledge, we become so integrated with the flow of all things that we experience ourselves as part of it. We are transformed then into what we always were. The desire to align ourselves with what we know in those moments is not virtue, it is merely self-interest, the only way we can be our real selves.

When we lose ourselves, we do find ourselves, we discover a deeper identity as a dimension of something inexplicable, an "it" we can never master, although we can master our willingness to be part of "it." Then feedback loops load energy into the system until it ramps up into something entirely else and transforms.

Networks manage packets of meaning. But the boundaries of those packets are hackable, made up of arbitrary meanings themselves, meanings that flow.

So this is not about religion. Even religion is not about religion. True, religions will evolve in cyberspace that are interactive, modular, and fluid, but the essence of those digital religious systems will be what it always was: to find appropriate forms for symbol-manipulating systems with which we symbol-manipulating sentient beings can interact, so that when we least expect it, the meaning of those symbols can ignite in our lives.

I think that's what Steve Straus meant when he said, "It's more than that." But I'll never know. To grasp the meaning of those moments is to squeeze a handful of water that drips away in the effort to keep it. As we, ourselves, like bright drops of water, slip into an ocean beyond our capacity to fathom.

Christmas 2001 – The Base   *December 25, 2001*

It's a shame when words like "The Base" or "Homeland Defense" are associated in the first instance with Al Queda and in the second with the Third Reich, because then they're difficult to recapture.

Oh well. We can still say what we mean and hope it connects.

Al Queda and the Third Reich share at least one common ground; the high-jacking of religion in order to twist it into something powerful but destructive. In Christian mythology, an angel of light, his stature enhanced by his formidable intellect, turns to the "dark side of the force" because he can't stand being second banana, which in a way is the same story.

I think I have some insight into how official religions work. My father was a Christian and my mother was a Jew. I served as an Episcopal priest for sixteen years, and not because I got drunk one night and thought it might be fun. Because it was the fullest way I could express, in action, a transformation that had turned me literally inside out and changed the way I thought about everything.

Today I am a Jew who speaks Christianity fluently, but I hope I am more than that. My wife and I have seven children who range from Christian to Jew to Neo-Pagan to Buddhist to agnostic, and there is no more holy ground than that created by our energetic discussions about our paths. The core of spirituality does seem to be, as that splendid imposter Carlos Castaneda wrote, does your path have heart? If it does, you always find common ground with others whose paths do too.

But having been in the religion "business," which all organized religion is, one way or another, I know deeply the truths that lurk in the shadows and how easily an impulse that begins with the best intentions is turned into something destructive. How easily any religion can inflate the egos of its adherents until they believe that they, and they alone, are right. The dehumanization of the Other is a precondition to killing the Other, regardless of which group is hated and which does the killing. So knowing we're right and justifying our evil deeds go together.

The greatest evil in the world, it seems to me, is done in the name of righteousness and religion. Every banner that drips with blood has the word "God" at its center.

The spirituality that makes sense to me, on the other hand, begins with knowing that I haven't got a clue. Those aren't just words. Deeply, deeply, as I have grown older, the realization that I know absolutely nothing about those "Big Truths" is the only thing I do know. I am also left knowing that in moments of genuine communion, I am heard and understood and am listening at the same time, in the depths of my being, to the truth of the humanity of the Other.

Why don't you write a "spirituality book?" I am sometimes asked. The simple answer is that I just said everything I know about that. The closer I grow to myself, others, and to what we call "God," the more of a mystery everything becomes. It's bright, but it's darkness too.

In the presence of that mystery, there is nothing to do but fall down and shut up.

So when I responded to recent events by suggesting a "homeland defense network" in which we practice the meaning of "be alert!" I meant above all the practice and creation of a spiritual base on which everything else rests. I meant the development of awareness by first learning to use the tools that all religions and spiritual traditions give us. I meant the day-in and day-out discipline of putting those tools to use under each others' watchful eyes so feedback helps us correct excesses. I meant sharing our wisdom and experience in a robust open-source model of life.

A conversation with a former FBI computer security friend this weekend turned to the practical matters of "being alert." We agreed that his work as head of a "Tiger Team" and spiritual work are both practical efforts to build on a strong base and make things as secure as we can. Spirituality is the most practical thing in the world when it isn't distorted. It's a way to face the insecurity and uncertainty of life and build meaningful community through practical action as a way of affirming unity in the face of chaos and meaning in the face of meaninglessness, building a web or network that glows with its own inner light in the otherwise cold and lonely darkness of the Void.

In the process of building that network, the distinctions that we thought defined us disappear, the boundaries that we thought were limits dissolve, and energy and information flows at the speed of light. Critical mass is achieved, then ignition, and light explodes outward in the darkness toward the receding edges of everything.

The dark forces that justify creating chaos and destruction know no national boundaries. This is bigger than national boundaries. This is about a species at a critical moment of its evolution knowing the difference between the darkness and the light, not in a naive or trivial way, but deeply, from knowing ourselves intimately, then making the right choices.

It begins with daring to be aware. That in essence is a spiritual task. The Homeland Defense Network in essence as well is about choosing to do what we know how to do but need reinforcement to do right and persist in doing over the long term. Awareness is transformed into action that makes flesh what is otherwise sentiment or whimsy. It means the fusion of being, knowing and doing.

That's one meaning of Christmas, whether or not it's the story you tell. I like to believe it's the meaning of Ramadan and Hanukkah, too. It is, at any rate, the meaning I wish for you and yours at this dark but enlightening time of year.

Looking for Paradise   *March 25, 2003*

This morning on a private list, the moderator expressed concern that the word "peace" was being used without regard to its real meaning.

"We throw the word peace around too casually," he said. "We claim we are aiming for peace in Iraq, peace in the Middle East, peace in Afghanistan."

Another participant asked, "Has there ever truly been a peaceful time on this planet? I don't think so. Has any major country ever had an extended period when one could say they experienced peace? By peace I mean a state of tranquility, freedom from concern, anxiety, the dedication of significant resources, energy, and attention to a threat from others."

That definition of peace triggered a memory of living on Maui, an island marketed to visitors as a piece of paradise, a haven of peace. While living there, I read a fascinating study of how the psychological archetype "paradise" works. An archetype is an image deeply embedded in our collective psyches; paradise is an image of that state described by my friend in which striving, desire, anxiety is absent, leaving only "the peace that passes understanding."

We project an archetypal paradise onto mythical states of being, like the Garden of Eden or Heaven, that exist before and after life here now. Paradise is a projection of bliss-in-the-womb when all needs are met in that warm dark surrounding fluid.

One particularly stressful and difficult day (yes, even in Hawaii, there are difficult stressful days) I felt like I really needed a break. Now despite being Episcopal clergy at the time, I lived reasonably well (like the earlier missionaries, I came to do good and did well) and the parish owned a house that was a five bedroom beauty on the beach, three steps down to the water, with views of Lanai and sunsets and the harbor. It was on that beach, in front of that house, surrounded by palm trees and plumeria, that I stood with a guidebook for Kauai, a neighbor island. I showed my wife a picture of Hanalei Bay and felt a great tidal yearning for the peace it suggested.

"That beach," I said with feeling, "looks wonderful. Do you want to go?"

My wife laughed. "Will you please lift your eyes off the picture?"

Above the picture of the beach, as I raised my gaze, there was the real beach on which I stood, the waves breaking over the reef where I snorkeled or went diving nearly every day. It was like a Magritte painting where the edge of a small canvas painted on a larger one holds a picture of a beach, the easel itself standing on a beach that extends to the edge of another canvas.

What became crystal clear in that instant was that I did not long for a "beach" at all but for the full rich blissful content of "paradise" and the peace it promises.

That yearning for wholeness and peace resides deep within, but when we project it onto an external reality—anything, a place, a person, a political situation—we always find that the possession of that thing does not lead to peace at all, because it can't. Peace is an internal condition often sought as if it is out there somewhere. Peace can never be captured or conquered. Peace can only be experienced as a letting go of the futility of trying to turn what is into what isn't and what isn't into what is.

The kingdom, in short, is inside, and in my experience it is that for only a short while at the level of intensity and heartfelt yearning we seek.

A carrot nevertheless worth trotting after, so long as we know that the eating of it somehow magically restores the carrot out in front of us even as we eat it.

The genuine spiritual battles I observed in visitors to Maui were often caused by coming to that isolated place as if it would provide that peace, when in fact a beach with thousands of miles of ocean on the other side of it only delivers us more deeply into our selves. Whatever chaos we use to lose ourselves in our daily lives is stripped away and there's more of ourselves to feel, not less. Visitors who stay long enough either use that discovery to face themselves, integrate what they learn, and achieve some real peace. Or they run faster than ever from the reality of themselves; they do more coke, smoke more pot, drink or eat more, or roll into more beds because those drugs of choice are default positions for momentary release.

So the short answer to my friend's question is, no, there has never been a permanent state of peace like that on this planet, nor in this comet-pocked solar system (ask the dinosaurs who probably had an illusion of peace-through-dominance after a hundred and fifty million years, just before impact), nor in this turbulent galaxy, nor in this explosive and catastrophic universe.

I have no answers to the truths and lies of this crazy world. If you want answers, do a google. The internet is full of answers. I don't even have answers for the truths and lies of my own life. The older I get, the only thing becoming clear is that I haven't got a clue.

Ask a Zen adept, where will I find peace? and he might say:

Not here, not there.

Where, then?

Oh ... (he might say) ... here and there ...

Chapter 6

Mostly True Predictions

A note from Richard:
I was invited by the Wisconsin Society of Professional Engineers to write a column on cyberspace for their monthly magazine. I began offering my columns to subscribers through e-mail, prompting USA Today to designate my web site a Hot Site of the Day (in those days it was easy to get noticed). The first featured column in this section was the inspiration for Islands in the Clickstream. The articles to follow include insights into current or future realities that turned out to be pretty much true.

Learning to Live in Cyberspace *August 1, 1996*

A clickstream is the record of every transaction we make on the World Wide Web, that visible and notorious dimension of the Internet we access through a friendly graphical interface called a web browser. Every click of our mouse leaves a trace in the melting snows of cyberspace. Those tracks make up a clickstream, a trail through the virtual worlds we are all learning to inhabit.

"Islands in the Clickstream" will examine ways that life in the virtual world is changing life in general.

The Internet is both a symbol of and a vehicle for the transformation of work and life. A few years from now, the Internet may well evolve into something else—the forms of electronic connection are not inviolable—but the fact of connection is.

The human species is growing a new nervous system.

The Internet does not demand merely a new set of skills; the Net is a new culture, with mores, customs, and its own rules of netiquette. Learning to do business in cyberspace requires patience, attentiveness to how things work in the virtual world, and a willingness to call into question some of our fundamental assumptions about how we do business.

"Islands in the Clickstream" is a travel guide to that new culture. Privacy and surveillance, personal and corporate security, marketing and sales, PR and disinformation, how to avoid netscams—we'll look at all this in future columns. This month we'll look at how we experience change due to the revolution in information technology and what we can do in response.

It is said that someone once asked Ernest Hemingway, "How does a person go bankrupt?"

"Two ways," he replied. "Gradually and suddenly."

That is also how individuals and organizations experience transformation. Inside the old paradigm, it feels as if we're learning little by little, adding each new fact onto the last ... until the paradigm snaps. Then we struggle together through a threat of impending chaos to learn new behaviors or new ways to frame reality.

Paradigm change is easy to manage in the seminar room. In real life—where it translates into downsizing, bankruptcy, and new rules for utilities, government, manufacturing—it isn't as easy.

Individuals and organizations everywhere are going through this passage. Radical change is traumatic. It always causes fear, rigidity, and isolation. We've lived with fear, isolation, and rigidity so long,. we think it's the normal condition of life. The high level of stress turns our offices and cubicles into zones of "fight or flight." We turn colleagues and customers—the very people who should be our allies—into enemies. We collude to create an artificial scarcity of affirmation and power in the work place. Internal competition undermines our best intentions and drains our energy.

There is an antidote, however: the creation of structures of mutuality, feedback, and accountability.

Every quality program—from quality circles to re-engineering—builds structures of mutuality, feedback, and accountability. This is not an accident. All three are necessary for organizations to remain viable through times of accelerated change. The absence of any one of them skews organizational life in predictable ways, with predictable consequences.

Structures of mutuality, feedback, and accountability keep us flexible and effective under rapidly changing conditions. On the human level, they provide the security we need to keep building the bridges—even in the middle of the air—that we're using to cross the abyss. As a worker in a bank told me, they enable us to build the airplane while it is flying.

New paradigms call us forward through successive zones of transition. The center is constantly shifting. People who had have grown comfortable living at the center find themselves on the edge. They need to learn new skills, or, at the least, make alliances with people whose skills are relational and whose gifts include creativity and knowing how to make connections. Traditional "outsiders" can help center-dwellers learn how to live on the edge that is always arriving. They can help "traditionals" move out of the rigidity of hierarchical thinking into the more transitory and flexible structures mandated by change.

Paralleling the change in how we work, the revolution in information technology is changing our basic experience of ourselves. Just as the printing press was a catalyst for the Renaissance and the Reformation, life in cyberspace is changing what it means to be a human being.

Networks are subversive of hierarchical structures.

When we connect to a network, we experience ourselves as a point of presence at the center of the web. Our ongoing experience in a web changes how we think about possibilities, how we frame options for action, how we behave.

Persons in hierarchical structures, for example, talk about those structures as if they are external to themselves. They complain about the organization as if it is doing something to them. When they grasp that they are the organization, they move from the edge to the center again.

In a network, there is always more than enough power and affirmation to go around. Nobody is ever displaced from the center.

Think of how characters in modern movies change shape, like Jim Carey in *The Mask* or the bad robot in *Terminator 2*. That special effect is called "morphing." It is said that the only competitive advantage a business has today is the capacity to morph like that into new forms.

The same is true of individuals. Only the self-conscious creation and nurturing of structures of mutuality, feedback, and accountability will give us the security we need to risk changing so we can move together in the right direction.

Reaching the Honey   *November 1, 1995*

Hanging under his balloons beside the honey tree, we are told that Winnie the Pooh "could see the honey, he could smell the honey, but he couldn't quite reach the honey." After another night hanging in cyberspace, I know how he feels.

There has been such an explosion of possibility and promise on the Net that it's easy to become cynical about the content it often delivers. New technology always excites bigger dreams than can be realized—at first.

Remember the claims made for AI a decade ago? The spirit of Pappert's Mindstorms and the MIT lab made us dream of robots, ubiquitous by the end of the century, doing slave labor. Those dreams disappeared as the vaporware of AI vanished into thin air.

But wait a minute. Before we sneer at the predictors, look at what AI is in fact doing. Every time another chip takes over a dozen functions in my new car, it's invisible. Expert systems and neural nets don't do everything, but in the right domains, they do more than we imagined. Every time there's another breakthrough in AI, it devolves into an "incremental change" in the tasks we hand over to computers. Another miracle made tame by integration into what we already know.

The contextual shift promised by prophets of AI has in fact happened—smart machines are everywhere—and is now the ground on which we stand. How quickly we forget.

Every revolutionary technology takes a long time to teach us how to use it. The visionary "futurists" always miss the big picture. A bright man said when the telephone was invented, "I can foresee the day when there will be a telephone in every city."

Socrates feared that writing would destroy civilization. How can one evaluate the validity of an argument, he asked, unless one is face to face with a known person? No one would remember anything if everything is written down.

Similar objections were raised against the printing press in the fifteenth century. Identical arguments are raised against computers. In a way, they're right. Civilization as we know it is coming to an end and something new is breaking out of a cracked egg.

Futurists can't help it, and neither can we. We don't know what we don't know and we can't see what we can't see. Bound by the constraints of how we've been taught to frame reality, the advent of revolutionary technologies can feel like the end of the world.

You wouldn't know it, though, from much of the content of CD ROMS and websites. The rush to stake out territory in cyberspace has meant a lot of pretty pictures, some video clips that take too long to download, and little of the innovative content that the Net must now teach us patiently how to create. I'm sure that smart catalogs and talking billboards will not remain the normative forms of the content of cyberspace.

No wonder I'm disappointed. I find hundreds of pop-up books on the WWW. Now, books are fine. I love books. But when I'm on the Web, I don't want books. I want creative interaction. I don't want to dig through mountains of ore looking for a little gold. I want to discover not only new content mediated by new forms but also new dimensions of my self as I interact with the Net in a symbiotic relationship that takes us both up the rising spiral of a self-conscious dialectic.

Maybe I'm jaded. My eyes have been trained by fractals, after all, cycling through millions of colors, kaleidoscopes of unimaginable complexity. I want the same rush, the same insight into the nature of things, when I click from site to site searching for wisdom.

It's a shame, really.: It's a natural fit, cyberspace and our hunger for growing our minds and training our brains. Our minds expand naturally into the shimmering non-space of the Net. The glowing screen seduces us into a night that never ends. I stay up way too late, following luminous breadcrumbs through the forest. But those breadcrumbs seldom make a full meal.

I need to be patient. Like written documents and printed books before it, the Net, as it evolves, will feed back to us reflexive knowledge about the journey itself. The Net will continue to become self-conscious and replicate fractal images of infinite possibilities at higher and higher levels of abstraction. Then we will encounter our hive brain in a way that lets us recognize ourselves, included in something bigger that is at the same time reduced to symbols that enable us to see our new selves.

The content of the Net will ultimately be the content of our transformed selves rendered in symbolic form. The Net is a new kind of community. Every transformation of the Word increases our distance from one another and paradoxically makes available at the same time the means for connecting with one another at deeper and more intimate levels.

So what is our task? To appreciate the enormity of this contextual shift through which we are living. To have the courage to think and imagine the genuinely new content that will enable the Net to discover its potential. To be co-creators ex nihilo, from the nothingness that is sheer possibility, of the synthesis of sound, images, text, and motion that will define the virtual spaces we are building like modules of a space station.

There will continue to be plenty of garbage. Hucksters will continue to sell the menu as if it's the meal. Our job as creatives and technicians is to fill that space nevertheless with the heights and depths of ourselves as we discover and create the interior landscapes of the virtual world.

No More Pencils, No More Books

December 1, 1995

We are children of our times. We frame our worlds as they are given to us by our language and the structures of our education. The frame is invisible until there is a change so pervasive that we see by contrast what we took for granted. The education I received in the 50s and 60s was not experienced as a *choice*. It's what education *was*.

I thought adolescence was a universal developmental stage. But adolescence is a modern invention. When the printing press invented school—collections of benches on which to sit and read—it invented adolescence. Learning had been accomplished through apprenticeship. Young people worked beside adults, learning by doing. Then textbooks necessitated a prolonged period of time to learn the art of symbol manipulation. The real American aristocracy—the upwardly mobile masses—postponed adulthood.

It was called "education."

Today the structures of education are out of joint with the structures of adulthood. That's why so many businesses are educating workers. More education takes place today in conference rooms, meeting rooms in hotels, and via remote telepresence and onsite computer-assisted learning than in classrooms. The need for continuous lifelong education is now an unquestioned assumption.

Apple flooded schools with computers, but didn't provide teachers who knew what to do with them.

I know a fourth grade teacher who was supposed to teach computers but didn't know how to turn them on. She asked her class, "Who knows how?" Hands waved in the air. She turned the task over to a student and hid behind her desk.

But she couldn't hide forever. So she asked her three brightest students secretly to teach show her after school how to use (and teach) the new computers.

Older managers and as well as older teachers, must learn from younger adults, as well as teach them. The wisdom of experience is relevant, but relevant in a different way. Command-and-control behaviors do not make for good coaching.

At least that teacher knew how to get out of the way, but that didn't make her a coach. She needed to learn how to be present but not controlling, available but not directive. Like the best computer- assisted learning, good coaches provide information not at the convenience of the curriculum, but when learners are most teachable.

Teachers threatened by this challenge take away computers and lock them up. They call it a "computer lab" and let the kids in there an hour a day.

Imagine being a teacher when pencils were invented. You pass out pencils and watch as the children discover that pencils can do anything because a pencil is a symbol manipulating machine.

Afraid you're no longer needed, you collect the pencils and lock them in a Pencil Lab, letting the children use them an hour a day. The rest of the time they write with rocks on slabs of broken concrete.

The structures of education, like the structures of work, are moving through a sea-change. Symptoms include:

> **Rising drop-out rates**. Racial minorities, the canaries in the coal mine of society, die first. The irrelevance of school to life in the world was experienced first in ghettos. Now blue-collar workers and middle-aged managers are feeling the pain so it's a "crisis."
>
> **A growing "black market" in education**. We give lip-service to traditional structures but barter for "educational goods" on the job and over the Internet, in the global marketplace.

Businesses become centers of education, not because they want to, but because they must. McDonald's teaches politeness and civility because the traditional structures of home, family, religion, no longer do the job.

Conscientious teachers who can't see the forest for the trees redouble their efforts. They become exhausted , working harder and harder, but it's like drinking from a dribble glass. The gears of the system don't mesh with the real world. Veterans count the days until retirement. Burn-out abounds.

Work-to-school programs grow as apprenticeship is re-engineered for the 21st century.

Is there hope? Of course. The solutions begin with understanding the depths of the transformation we are experiencing and asking questions relevant to our real lives. The process of finding answers together will generate the security we need to remain effective during revolutionary times.

Nowhere to Run,
Nowhere to Hide   *June 15, 1997*

Data—mere information—is neutral. The power of information that is linked and accessible is magnified by many orders of magnitude. The pattern is what matters.

Technology advances. Software that matches patterns and flags anomalies is getting pretty good. But ultimately, computers aren't about technology. They're about people.

The real power of the Net derives from the intention and intelligence of the people who use it. When we choose our response to what we learn online, that's when we bite the apple. That's when we engage our capacity for good and evil.

Consider the cookie, how it works.

Netscape's little "cookie file" is a snapshot of a clickstream, the tracks we leave in the virtual snow whenever we go online..

The "cookie" is left on the hard drive. Any site can access the cookie and therefore our history. This is a marketer's dream.

Alex Zoughlin, President of Neoglyphics Media Corp., described the value of the cookie file for a catalog company.

"As soon as we know where you're calling from, a response is customized. Say you call from Chicago in January. The first pages you'll see are winter coats, tropical getaway vacations.

"If you visited the site before and spent three minutes looking at a snow-blower but didn't buy it, we'll show you that snowblower on sale.

"Then we can use the data on the cookie-file to cross-reference the clickstream with everything in databases built from the electronic transactions in which you've engaged."

Our social security numbers, admission tickets to the world of virtual purchases, is an index number, a universal identifier linking our interactions with governments, schools, and businesses, building a composite portrait of our habits and our lives.

That pattern is in turn enhanced by surveillance.

Consider ITS, the Intelligent Transportation System.

The Gary-Chicago-Milwaukee corridor is being wired with transponders, sensors, video cameras. The plan calls for quiet incremental implementation, then a propaganda campaign to explain why what's in place is good. ITS will be sold in the name of safety and efficiency,

Zoom past a toll booth at highway speeds, letting the sensor debit your account. Sounds good. But now there's a record of who, where, when.

Speeding? Trigger a sensor that snaps a camera that prints a picture of the license plate over the radar readout and sends you the fine. The ticket gets home before you do.

Trucking companies are ahead of the curve. Console computers and satellite dishes tell the home office the location, speed, and fuel consumption of every truck. The trucker is transformed from a road warrior into spam in a can.

"They say it's to empower the trucker," a caller told me during a recent radio interview, "but that's crap. It's more centralized, more hierarchical than ever. All that data feeds back to command central. As long as you stay within the guidelines, there's no red flag. But deviate an inch and you're juice in a blender."

That's the new paradigm. Life in Singapore is a model for life in the barb wired world.

It's called the Panopticon.

The Panopticon is a prison dreamed up by Jeremy Benthem in the 19th century. Cells with glass doors are arranged in a ring, a watchtower in the center. Prisoners can see neither one another nor the guard, but the guard can see them—all of the time.

The panoptic sort is the name for how every computer transaction is cross-referenced, then used by persons we don't know for undisclosed purposes.

Color your life inside the lines and stay safe. Deviate and set off the sirens.

Once our medical records are on smart cards, a swipe through the authorization reader can liberate the data. Or say you visit a tailor and your charge card entry includes the fact that your waist grew four inches. That data is tagged for the insurance company that owns the bank that issues your card. Your rates go up or your policy is cancelled and you never know why.

If something has value and can be sold, it will be sold. Banks do it now. So does the government.

"Remember, it isn't the technology," says Dean Schober, a Milwaukee cyber-sleuth. "It's the mind using the technology that makes the difference.

Schober is connected to more than 15,000 data bases in 123 countries. His value doesn't lie in accumulating data but in putting it together for clients. Competitive business intelligence is the growing edge of his business. Clients pay big bucks for the Big Picture.

You don't even need to be inside the computer to get the data. Suppose it was possible to aim a device at your apartment or home from across the street or down the block. Suppose you were working on a confidential business project on your PC. Suppose that device could read what you were typing and viewing on the CRT.

Such a device does exist. You can buy one. It monitors everything you do on your computer by collecting electromagnetic radiation emitted from your computer's CRT, CPU or peripheral equipment, then reconstructs those emissions into coherent signals and stores them.

One agent reports that he was able to view the CRTs of computer users from 300 yards away. He observed CRT screens at ATM machines, banks, a doctor's office, the police department doing a DMV license plate check, and a branch office of a securities trader making a trade. Then he borrowed an office near the World Trade Center and read passwords, files, proprietary data and records right through the glass walls.

Who's surprised? The French government bugged every first class Air France seat to eavesdrop on foreign businessmen. The battlefield is the global economy. "Privacy brokers" who know how to encrypt, decipher, capture, or secure communications and proprietary information are growing in numbers and sophistication. Building the mediating structures that protect our data is big, big business.

What should we do? It's a waste of time to cry for the past. Privacy as we once knew it is over. Better to learn to defend ourselves, engage in disinformation if need be, protect our boundaries. Teach our children how to hide. Build virtual scarecrows in the wired world to confuse the enemy.

Turn around street signs.... don't call attention to yourself.... and above all, be still... be very very still ...

Where Do You
Want To Go Today?   *December 6, 1997*

"The first two weeks in a new culture are so profoundly impactful," Margaret Mead told her friend Ralph Blum, the author of *Runes*, that you have to stay in that culture another full year to learn anything more."

Our first two weeks in the digital world are almost up.

Have you noticed how the excitement has faded, how normal it feels to exchange e-mail, to live anywhere and work everywhere, to know that the virtual rooms we inhabit comfortably might grow larger or have better furniture or nicer pictures on the walls, but will have nevertheless essentially the same feel?

Back in our apple days, when we were green and being blown away by every new application, I remember waiting anxiously for a new game from Infocom because it disclosed a whole new world. A few weeks ago, chatting with one of the producers from Jellyvision, the company that brought us 'You Don't Know Jack,' I realized that the sound effects and clever interactive text of the game show were direct descendants of those old games, rather than something altogether new.

This week I listened to Abby Cohen, prognosticator of prognosticators, speak of the United States as a "supertanker economy," dependable and immense. She gave examples of American companies that no other country can match: Disney in entertainment, Intel in chips, Microsoft in software.

Those three companies are building a virtual world, a framework for designed experience that we inhabit—near the end of our first two weeks—without even noticing.

The theme parks of Las Vegas, animated landscapes inside our heads, the transformation of "real life" into touristic space—it's all of a piece. All skin on the scaffolding of a virtual world.

Tourism, for example. Tourists used to visit a foreign country and live in it while they were there. Then the natives put up signs and markers that defined "touristic space" as art galleries, museums, certain restaurants and parks. Books and brochures to guide us through those spaces were a virtual map, telling us what was interesting and safe for us to see.

That grew boring. Tourists wanted an experience of "real life" lived by the natives. So tours of factories and farms were added to the mix—but they weren't "real" factories. The factory was a simulation of a factory, and tourists moved through it on conveyor belts. Behind the appearance of a factory, a real factory still happened, but the workers in it took a step back from the touristic space they propped up from behind like a Potempkin village. As when we stay with a local family and they put on company manners until we're gone.

When I lived on Maui, I noticed that tourists loved to attend luaus at which real Hawaiians danced. The people on Maui, however, are mostly Korean, Filipino, and Japanese, followed by "haoles" (ghostly pale people) and various kinds of other Asians, Pacific islanders, even a few Hawaiians. The hula is often danced by recent arrivals from Manilla.

To know the real Hawaii, you have to stay … and stay. There are successive barriers defined by time, and on the other side of each, locals waiting to welcome you into a deeper experience of what it really means to live on a multi-racial island devoted to simulating itself.

We are tourists in our own territories, accessing our lives through simulations designed like drugs or high fashion to be wrapbe wrap-around immersive virtual worlds that feel so real we forget they're invented.

The symbols with which we manipulate our constructions of reality point increasingly to other symbols. It is no longer a case of remembering that the finger pointing toward the moon is not the moon, but that the finger is pointing toward another finger that is pointing toward another finger ... and we call that recursive experience ... the moon.

Disneyland is a prototype of a designed environment from which realities like telephone poles are intentionally filtered. So too with Disneyland religion. The truths of our lives are filtered out as we enact pageants or tell stories that provide a vicarious experience of transformation. It's like drinking from a dribble glass, but we wonder why we're wet ... and still thirsty.

The points of reference of much of our experience are movies, television, multi-media, the virtual world of computer networks ... designed contexts and therefore contents in which we increasingly live and move and have our being.

I stood one day with my wife on the beautiful beach in front of our Hawaiian home. The palm fronds blew in the sea breeze, but I was unhappy about something, and I opened a Kauai guidebook to a picture of Hanalei Bay. "Look!" I said, "at that beautiful beach. *That* would be a great place to visit."

My wife laughed and said, "Look at the blue and blue of sky and sea, whitecaps breaking over the reef, the clouds over Lanai across the water." I had to laugh too. The beach in the picture was an image of peace and contentment, an archetypal image of paradise and a magnet for my yearning—the same yearning that lured tourists to the beach on which I stood in their own elusive search for peace.

The virtual world is an image of a beach onto which we project ourselves. We are like people searching frantically for their glasses while wearing them. We're really in search of ourselves, and to find ourselves we must simply look up from that image of a beach to the bright sky and feel the salt spray, the hot sand, the velvet caress of the tropical air.

The digital world is a landscape painted from a palette of a million pastel colors, a big toy made not of plastic, but of simulated plastic. Under its red and blue balloon-like skin is a sky the color of television, tuned to a dead channel.

I guess I'm suggesting that, now and again, we take more than a vacation and turn that television off.

The Digital Forest

December 21, 1997

When the Viking lander sent the first pictures from the surface of Mars, I watched with my neighbor, a video ham, as the Martian desert painted itself slowly down his monitor in narrow bands.

That desert was compelling. I burned to go to Mars, and even imagined that I might. So I was deeply disappointed when space exploration went onto the back burner.

Yet, only twenty years later, the exploration of near-earth space by tele-robotic sensory extensions of ourselves is happening at every level of the electromagnetic spectrum. Human beings will certainly follow.

The exploration of what Europeans called the "New World" excited plenty of interest too. Then things died down. Europe went about its business as usual, but beneath the surface, the structure of the world had indeed shifted. After a lull, Europeans poured onto the continent.

I write this column in Wisconsin. It's only been a few hundred years, but the landscape I see from my window is a design that reflects the rectangles and planes of the male European mind.

After any breakthrough, we fall back into our comfort zone. Growth for individuals, as for civilizations, moves in waves.

I remember this as I read an article by Gary Chapman in the Los Angeles Times, "The Internet May Be the Latest Media Darling, but It's No Baywatch." Chapman is disappointed by the gap between the hype about the Internet and the reality. He debunks "myths" about the Internet's impact on society.

I don't think he can see the forest for the digital trees.

Myth 1: Everyone will be online.

> **Chapman:** Use of the Internet is limited. "An astonishing 1.6 billion people, worldwide, tune into Baywatch every week. The entire global Internet-using population is 4% of the Baywatch audience."
>
> **Bigger picture:**

1. The Internet, only a few years old in its current incarnation, is being adopted faster than any previous technology. People weren't watching Baywatch when television was four years old; they weren't watching anything.

2. "Internet" is the current name for the network of networked computers. The realities behind the name are evolving into new forms, many hidden in the infrastructure itself. Just as automobiles are becoming electronic devices riding on mechanical platforms, we live increasingly inside an electronic

infrastructure. The Internet is not just e-mail or the World Wide Web. It is the entire matrix of electronic connectivity.

Myth 2: There will be a huge increase in the varieties of opinion expressed in society because of the ease of online publishing.

Chapman: "There is an almost limitless variety of opinion to be found on the World Wide Web and in online forums," but , "the dynamic range of opinion in mainstream America appears to be narrowing, not expanding."

Bigger picture:Chapman is still looking to the "space" defined by the mainstream media to see what's "real." Multiple sources of influence ARE evolving on-line but they're butterflies that can't be caught in that net. Their very transitoriness and fluidity makes them difficult to define.

Myth 3: There will be lots of cool jobs for creative people who will work in cyberspace.

Chapman: The hope that the World Wide Web would foster a renaissance in writing and art appears to have died. Writers who flocked to the "new media" are disillusioned.

Chapman again: Nobody makes money from the new media. Most information-rich sites lose money like crazy, or, at best, break even. If you want to get wealthy, he says, write a screenplay, a mystery novel or a computer game.

Bigger picture:

1. Every transformation of the technology of the Word—writing, the printing press, electronic media—magnifies rather than eliminates the media that came before. There are more books and magazines than ever, but that shouldn't be a surprise. Writing did not eliminate speech; the printing press did not end writing. The inability to quickly predict which creative jobs will be viable in cyberspace does not mean that they aren't emerging. We always try to port forms of the old technologies into the new media. That never works. The new media teach us over time how to use them. The dynamic marketplace incubates the forms that are viable.

2. Some sites are making lots of money, like sex sites. It's no coincidence Chapman cites Baywatch as an example. The cutting-edge work to make streaming video and audio easy and seamless is being done at sex sites because people are willing to pay for it. This was true too of VCRs, first

used for x-rated films. Mass markets for Hollywood movies and educational videos followed.

3. The Internet will not replace anything. It redefines the relationship of symbolic content (text, images, sounds) to itself and to the human symbol-user. The Internet, as McLuhan said of the electric light, is pure information, an example of context as content. The Internet is redefining how we use other media.

Myth 4: Government will fade in significance, perhaps into irrelevance.

> **Chapman:** Government, at all levels, is actually becoming bigger and more powerful.
>
> **Bigger picture:** Shortly before the French Revolution, had you suggested that the monarchy, the aristocracy, the church, everything, would come down all at once, you would have been thought crazy. The sudden reorganization of everything at a higher level of complexity is called hierarchical restructuring. Because the changes leading to it are exponential, happening everywhere at once, it is invisible until it happens. The Berlin Wall. The Soviet Union.

Governments will evolve into forms appropriate to the economic and social structures generated by the technological transformation of our planet, just as nation states emerged in the past few centuries.

Chapman was probably once as excited as he is now disappointed. Gary, just you wait.

In the short term, predictions are always exaggerated; in the long term, they're always short-sighted. As Alan Kay said, perspective is worth fifty points of IQ.

It *is* all happening, but we don't know yet what *it* is. Emergent realities must wait for the language with which we can discuss them and the seers and prophets who give them names.

The Challenge to Our Humanity *May 9, 1998*

I ran into my neighbor this morning at the supermarket. She works in "logistics" for a large retail chain. I asked how they were doing with the Year 2000 (Y2K) challenge.

"We're afraid," she said.

"It isn't us, it's our suppliers, manufacturers, the whole big chain. We receive 20% of our merchandise from outside America, mostly by ship. If we put every single ship in dry dock today to make them Y2K compliant, there wouldn't be room in the world to hold them all.

"Some manufacturers tell us they're just starting to do assessments. Which means, of course, it's already too late."

We looked at the frozen food, the lights, the cash registers, the shoppers going about their business. "People just blow it off when you tell them what could happen. Everybody's in denial."

Well … not everybody.

The future's market, making big bets on either side of the millenium, is not in denial. The wolves of Wall Street are betting on catastrophe.

The scene outside the supermarket is tranquil. Ornamental trees are blossoming, lilacs blooming, and the sun on this crisp spring day is radiant. The local multiplex movie theater is showing another disaster movie, this one about a comet hitting the earth. I remember *On the Beach*, the last days of remnant nuclear-boomed humanity, the end signified by newspapers blowing through empty streets. In *Y2K – The Movie*, the final image is a dead computer, not newspapers no one is left to read, and the streets will be full, not empty.

In *Y2K – The Reality*, humanity is again being called to measure and declare itself. The real issue is, are we up to the challenge? Are we up to fighting this war?

Every one of us is a philosopher. We all make decisions about what matters most. Usually it's not words but our lives that testify to our deepest beliefs and the commitments that elicit our passion.

For atheistic existentialists like Jean Paul Sartre, who believed that extreme conditions illuminate the truth of our souls, the battle cry is "No excuses!" For explicitly religious people, the mandate is to take responsibility for living rightly. The results in both cases are the same: men and women who refuse to be seduced by trivial distractions or lesser goods, living and who live from the depths of their quest for meaning.

The week that Princess Diana and Mother Theresa died, we also lost Victor Frankl. Frankl's belief that the search for meaning is our ultimate motivation was discovered in a concentration camp. The Nazis took Frankl's livelihood and made him a prisoner. They took his clothing and replaced it with oversized striped pajamas. They took his name and replaced it with a number. They took his family and replaced them with nothing. They took the predictability of daily life and replaced it with a constant threat of starvation and torture. They took every single thing that we use to make life "human" yet he clung to the belief that life, even in hell, had meaning. He embodied the truth that, especially when the chips are down and our backs to the wall, we are capable of responding to whatever life brings with resilience, dignity, and in our best moments, genuine heroism.

Life in the United States has been for many a long sunny ride on a tame horse. The "haves" seem lost in euphoric fog, oblivious to our radical contingency. After a run of good luck, people think they deserve it. That can make real threats to our well being seem like special effects, digital manipulation that we watch on a distant screen, warm and dry as Manhattan floats away when a tidal wave hits.

In Hilo, Hawaii there is a large green park on the oceanfront. There used to be buildings there. When the warning came of a tidal wave, people gathered to watch it slam into the town. Then the water receded, thousands of fish flopping in the mud flats as the ocean disappeared. Hundreds of people rushed onto the reef to gather fish. Then the second wall of water came, moving at hundreds of miles an hour, fifty feet high. A third wave cleaned up whatever was left.

The current warnings of Y2K are the first wave. We go to the movies, shop, live our lives, happily gathering fish flopping in the shallows.

This is a war. Wars require organization, rationing of scarce resources, hard choices made in light of the big picture. This crisis will reveal who we really are. Some will engage in quiet heroics and no one will ever know. Some will discover how shallow and venal they really are. The American Civil War brought us both Abraham Lincoln and those he called "the wolves of Wall Street," who bet against their own country to leverage their advantage.

How do we access those depths from which human beings respond with their best efforts? Religious people use symbols and beliefs to access in a primary way the capacity for self-transcendence. Having faith, using those symbols sincerely, is like solving a puzzle in a computer game, taking ourselves to the next level. Belief moves people to move mountains. If not, the mountains themselves. Yet those who have no explicit religious beliefs also have, innately within themselves, intrinsic to their humanity, that same capacity to respond in ways that dignify our species. That capacity is accessed when we choose to access that capacity.

No excuses.

To know what *can* happen means we can make choices now about critical systems and plan for the long haul. In the long haul, humanity does quite well. We'll learn from this experience, although slowly, and maybe we'll pay attention a little more closely in the future. The future is not fixed. The future is a spectrum of possibilities fanned out before us. It may be too late to reprogram everything, but we can still choose the wiser options, but only if we have the will to do so before the next wave hits.

A Vision of Possibilities   *October 24, 1998*

It is one thing (some would say the only thing) to apprehend that clear focus inside our own field of subjectivity that enables us to aim our lives with greater precision, and another thing to begin building a different construction of reality based on the modular building blocks provided by our society. But that construction—ultimately defining a very different universe—will still be animated by our intentionalityintentions. The ghost in the machine will still be a ghost.

Three domains that currently converge in a way that radically redefines our possibilities are:

(1) The transformation of our perceptual field by virtue of our interaction with technologies of information and communication;

(2) The redefinition of what it means to inhabit a "human space" as we begin to genetically engineer our field of subjectivity, affective states, and modalities of being; and

(3) The evolution of a trans-planetary civilization including our designed descendents and other intelligent species in our galactic neighborhood.

Those of us old enough to straddle the icebergs of rapidly diverging paradigms know that sooner or later we have to jump and live inside a relatively consistent model of reality. The digital model, the model enabled by digital interaction, is becoming dominant. We internalize a view of the landscape by internalizing first the forms of the media that convey images of that landscape to our brains. The medium is the message, as McLuhan said. Both the eye and our extensions of the eye define our field of view. We can see this because we still live near the terminator on the moon, where the contrast between light and darkness throws mountains and rills into sharp relief. When the moon is full, its features dissolve, and when it's all darkness, there's nothing to see. Liminal vision is razor-sharp.

The digital landscape is interactive, modular, and fluid. So how we construct reality is, too.

This is noticeable when people complain about the loss of security that they once felt. A friend said last night with some resentment, "Organizations used to be loyal to employees, and employees to organizations. Not any more." What he meant, I believe, was that the construction of reality he used to share with others in an unexamined consensus sustained the illusion that cultural artifacts, including organizational structures, were more permanent. Our organizational structures—including nations, world religions, and "the earth" as a point of reference for our thinking—are top-level consensual constructions fused with the media that filter the data of our lives. The media create the infrastructure of our collective thinking in their image.

But so do our genes. We are discovering that thinking and feeling are expressions of our genetic code.

A consumer society in which we swap simulations like children trading baseball cards has long conditioned us to accept the "manufacture of consent" in every domain of our lives. A generation before Chomsky wrote "Manufacturing Consent," Edward Bernays, the "father of spin," wrote "Engineering Consent." Bernays understood that creating a particular context always generates a particular content. He assisted book publishers whose sales were declining, for example, by soliciting testimonials on the importance of reading, then took the affidavits to architects who agreed to build houses with built-in bookshelves. New homeowners, not even noticing, stocked those shelves with books.

The use of images to collect individuals in groups, then move those groups, is an ancient practice. But now we will engineer the kinds of human beings available for binding and bonding in the first place.

The practice of genetic engineering will dovetail with refined practices of social engineering. Most of it will go unnoticed. Subcultures that pride themselves on independent thinking, for example, are a good gill net in which such people can be collected, observed, or manipulated. That's much more effective for social control than repression of such tendencies and their social expressions. We may find it desirable to build larger percentages of people amenable to such manipulation.

That practice would simply extend what we call "education" onto the practical level of biomechanics. Fractal levels of self-control by the body politic will manifest in whatever media are available. Ethicists will object, but the cries of ethicists always follow the emergence of the practice they decry.

Last but not least, our identity as "citizens of the earth"—which intensified as a point of reference when the first photograph of the earth seen from the moon became part of our collective awareness—will be, in the not too distant future, a historical memory, much like biblical tribes in the memories of Jews, Christians, and Moslems. Whether we persist as a distinct identity, like Jews, or vanish in the gene pool, like Jebusites and Perizzites, is impossible to predict.

Our constructions of reality will change when we couple our current modular thinking with the modules of beings who have different genetic structures and reference a different cosmology. The challenging process of negotiating realities as we engage with the perspective of other species will reveal what it means to be human-on-earth. If a "human" point of reference persists, it will be profoundly altered by that encounter.

My experience in Hawaii taught me that the Hawaiian construction of reality shattered when Captain Cook sailed into Kealakekua Bay. Nearly two hundred years later, in the nineteen sixties, when consciousness-raising activities became pervasive in the dominant culture, their descendents reconstructed Hawaiian culture, but as it was seen through the prism of the dominant culture. Hawaiian culture today is a reflection in the eye of the assimilating culture, a simulation built to the blueprints of archeologists and imagineers.

The moment we see ourselves as we are perceived by another, we become someone else; neither who we were nor who they think we are.

How we design the reality factories of our genetic structures and link them in digital simulations in a trans-planetary context so much more vast than the thinking life of our little planet has imagined—well, at the least, life in the next century will not be devoid of interest.

A Flashlight in a Haunted House
October 31, 1998

In a shorter daily column, "Imaginary Gardens," I referred to the dire forecasts of *The End of Civilization as We Know It*, which is linked these days to the Y2K computer glitch. The growing contagion of fear and unreason reminds me of the Fallout Shelter episode on *Twilight Zone*, when fragile bonds of community shredded in the face of a nuclear disaster that never happened.

Survivalists are buying up caves and generators, stockpiling food, checking ammunition. The Y2K bug is the intellectual's version of millennial fever. Amplified by the Internet, their primordial fears raise hair on the backs of our necks like a scream in the night.

What actions are in our real self interest? We all do what is in our self-interest, however we disguise our actions, but altruism itself seems to be in our self-interest. Those who go it alone have less of a chance to survive in the long run, although in the moment they may make it into the hills.

That's what I meant when I concluded that column with these words from a study of birds:

"... When flocking birds are looking for food, it's best not to be near a glutton. The bully birds grab all the good grub. But, the study suggests, smart birds know which piggy-birds to avoid."

Dominant siskins, for example, have larger markings on their chests, so savvy siskins look for birds with smaller spots. When they eat next to a less aggressive neighbor, there's plenty to go around.

That's something to remember as the Y2K bug begins to make inroads. Hang with friends who are willing to share, who live in modest houses, drive smaller cars. Humans who know that enough is a feast. Maybe come the millennium, the meek who stick together really will inherit the earth."

A practical reader responded: "Richard, you know as well as I that the strong, brutal and well-armed will dominate after this crisis as after every other throughout history."

That made me think. I long ago learned that any spirituality worth its words must be realistic. It doesn't help to live in a dreamscape floating above the world like a Sky City. But the "facts" have to be held in tension with the extraordinary capacity of humanity to transform its landscape—physically, emotionally, spiritually—by acts of belief, faith, will, or intention. The words differ, but it comes down to the same thing. We are co-creators of our lived experience, and we are resilient, even heroic when the chips are down beyond our capacity to grasp.

My reader must have copied his response to another friend, because I next received a response to his response:

"Hal [wrote Rick],

Upon first reading, the truth of your comment was obvious. Then I recalled the story of Tom Brown, the tracker who wrote in The Way of the Scout that he was asked by police to track and capture a murderer, regarded as an expert survivalist. This survivalist had a ton of tools--rifle, pistol, knife, dehydrated food, water purification tablets, sleeping bag, etc. He was loaded up like a lunar astronaut as he fled through the woods.

Tom Brown had nothing but his clothes and maybe a pocket knife. His power was his knowledge of how to live with the wilderness--how to build brush huts for a warm sleep, where to find clear water, which plants were edible, how to track. He stalked and harassed this violent murderer until the man was completely broken.

Brown set a trap that the killer fell for, causing a painful sprained ankle. Then he poured swamp water into the murderer's canteen, giving him violent cramps. Then the gun disappeared. Then the backpack. Then the pistol. Then the warm jacket. Then the knife.

Finally, all of the murderer's clothes disappeared while he was bathing. He had nothing left, and he had never once laid eyes on Tom, nor heard a sound, nor saw a single footprint. Up to this point, Tom Brown was an invisible, terrifying ghost.

Then Tom allowed the naked murderer to see him. Keeping his distance, Tom led the broken, sick, injured, whimpering survivalist into the arms of the police. Without his arsenal, he wasn't so tough, after all.

Survivalists may be able to go several months on stored foods. But they too are highly reliant on the manufactured products of civilization. The people with the best odds of long-term survival are those who know how to live with the wilderness. When things finally quiet down, the humble will have inherited the Earth, with their profound reverence and respect for the living Earth."

The original word for "meek" didn't mean what we mean by "meek." It's meaning was closer to the root of aikido, the martial art that suggests that we align our energy with whatever's coming at us, rather than confronting it directly. It's a way of saying that the universe moves with its own momentum, and if we can align ourselves with that flow, it'll take us where it wants us to go.

Meek means the strength at the heart of humanity—and the universe. Some traditions call it God, some don't. Some call it the Tao, the flowing of the universe. Others call it ki, as in aikido. Those are merely words, meant to be levers under the rocks of our denial and resistance. Words are either walls that imprison us and keep others out or tools that move boulders that block the flow of our lives. The words are less important than that to which they point, the ability of life itself to recall its strengths recursively, strength within nested strength. Not knowing, but knowing that we know, and knowing what we know, moves mountains.

Our fears dance on the walls like shadows. Alone in the cold in the dark is the moment of knowing, candescent and expansive. Digital simulations, nothing but illusions, waking dreams, all disappear, leaving only light illuminating pixels, showing us patterns we created then believed.

When Computers Are Free To Be Computers   *January 16, 1999*

Which, for the moment, they're not.

Computer technology is still brand-new, relatively speaking. We're so aware of how much has changed that we can't see how much hasn't.

Take this column, for example.

I am whacking away at a keyboard designed for a typewriter, playing on keys that are built to slow me down. My fingers dance as fast as they can, but my mind is way ahead of my fingers. When images emerge, instead of simply intending that they blossom on your monitor or in your mind, making them flow as fast as I think, all I can do is describe them in words. Our minds are constrained by this ancient tool, bent to its cramped dimensions.

They say that if all you've got is a hammer, every problem looks like a nail. Communication looks to me like words, like text to parse, and always will. So when I try to define the qualities of an interactive game or even a great film, I don't have the vocabulary. I lean heavily on words given to me by the study of philosophy and literature, when I was immersed in a canon that's been completely redefined.

I can see in my mind's eye something like luminous neurons emerging in this space we are creating by our digital interaction, linked by lines of light. But our tribe does not yet speak a common tongue so we can't say what it is. The most visionary among us look like miners crawling through a tunnel in a dark mountain, their little lamps illuminating a square foot of dirt.

On a long ride through a cold snowy landscape last weekend, I listened to tapes from the Teaching Company, a wonderful set of lectures by Stanford's Seth Lerer on the history of the English Language. Lerer recalled that when William Caxton brought the printing press to England in the 1470's, society changed over centuries, not overnight.

People wrote manuscripts by hand for at least 150 years and both written manuscripts and printed text co-existed. The first printed books were expensive, hardly meant for the masses. Their type fonts were designed to look like writing.

A new technology always tries to look like an old technology. The first "horseless carriages" had whip sockets in their dashboards, Lerer observed.

When the infantry was first mechanized, men continued to be posted near large artillery pieces, one hand raised in a fist. Long after cavalry officers gave up horses, those men had to stand there when the canon boomed, their empty hands holding the ghosts of a horse's reins so it wouldn't bolt.

Real computer literacy will extend far beyond our screens of scrolling text, dictation to a little mic, the evolution of book-like containers to hold our words ... beyond a mouse in our cramped fingers, clicking icons like hieroglyphics ... beyond images pasted on a flat panel display ... beyond dancing applets, clever animations, snippets of film.

When we live inside the space created by real computer literacy, the pixels on our screens will turn to flame.

Computers will be free, free at last to be real computers and won't have to pretend to be televisions or books. The generations immersed in that modular interactive world will experience multi-modal constructions of meaning and possibility, adaptable and plastic—right here, right now—with communication like balloons in comics that pop up in your mind as well as mine, the result of a nod or a wink, not a click. Seemingly instantaneous meanings happening in the matrix of spacetime, our conscious intentions like gravity wells, bending vectors of electromagnetic energy toward our nodal selves. And we will be inside.

Inside the rooms of a digital castle, its walls made of mist as we are, dreaming ourselves deep in the interior of a single mind.

We are not the first generation to be alienated from their own childhood memories, Lerer reminds us, estranged from what we once thought was "human nature," which we see now is simply the way we constructed identity and self in the context of prior technologies. The abrasion of the present against our evolving souls is the price of a digital future.

In 1490, William Caxton wrote that language had changed beyond recognition since he was a child, two generations earlier. Dialects evolving in the countryside forced people to choose the way they wanted to be human. They lived, Caxton said, in a variable world of transitory forms, including the structures of power.

Five hundred years later, compressed by digital technology, our world presses us against choices like that too. The Computer, like the printing press, inaugurated a contextual shift in how people wield power. To know that we can choose identities, choose how to be human ... that throws us for a loop. We too live in a variable world of transitory forms, our boundaries dissolving. We are old men, old women, clinging to tribal identities and gods carved in words as we wash out to sea in a tide of digital transformation.

A seachange, then and now. What does it mean to be "English?" asked Caxton like a newlywed trying on the strange word "husband." What does it mean to be ... "human?" And who will *we* be, living inside those fluid powerful selves that extend themselves in immersive 3-D virtual collaboratory landscapes (our monitors, keyboards, and modems in museums) ... when poetry, art and dance are difficult to distinguish, and the evidence of the senses blurs ... when the electromagnetic spectrum visible to our modified eyes extends to unimaginable lengths. We realize that we don't write code; our code writes us, defining the extensible horizons of our conscious life.

But that will be then. This is now. And for now, there's nothing to do but bang away at these keys, waiting for more spacious bandwidth ... and click and send these little e-mail bombs to explode with a flash and a bang and drift like acrid smoke in the night sky and disappear.

Distortions   *March 18, 1999*

"We all know the same truth. Our lives consist of how we choose to distort it."
— Woody Allen

A couple of weeks ago, it was reported by Reuters News Agency that hackers had taken control of a British military satellite and demonstrated control of the "bird" by changing its orbit. The report said the hackers were blackmailing the British government, and unless they received a ransom, they would take action. The demonstration was frightening for those who were just waiting for a blatant act of cyber-terror.

A few days later, the Hacker News Network, an underground alternative to CNN, reported that the hijacking was bogus.

The Hacker News Network got it right while Reuters got it wrong.

Just as business managers increasingly supervise IT workers who know more about networks than they do, traditional news sources often cover subjects they don't understand, and they often get it wrong.

A few weeks ago, I wrote an article for *Forbes Digital* on the unique culture of the professional Services Division of Secure Computing, where a number of former hackers help government agencies and large financial institutions secure their networks. Many articles have appeared recently about former hackers who have swapped underground lives for stock options, but that wasn't what my article was about. It was about the mindset that hackers bring to their work, a map or model of reality that is becoming the norm in a borderless world, where intelligence operatives are migrating into competitive intelligence in growing numbers. It's a mindset characterized, said one, by "paranoia appropriate to the real risks of open networks and a global economy."

Businesses used to decide on a course of action, then inform IT people so they could implement the plan. Now our thinking must move through the network that shapes it, not around it. The network itself—how it enables us to think, how it defines the questions that can be asked—determines the forms of possible strategies. So those who implement strategy must participate in setting strategy, not be added on after the fact, just as information security must be intrinsic to the architecture of an organizational structure, not added on as an afterthought.

The mind that designs the network designs the possibilities for human thinking and therefore for action.

Every single node in a network is a center from which both attack and defense can originate. The gray world in which hackers live has spilled over the edges which used to look more black and white. The skies of the digital world grow grayer day by day.

In that world, we are real birds fluttering about in digital cages. Images—icons, text, sound—define the "space" in which we move. If the cages are large enough, we have the illusion we are free and flying, when in fact we are moved in groups by the cages.

Example: to prevent insurrection during times of extreme civil unrest, government agencies created groups whose members were potentially dangerous, building a database of people they intended to collect if things fell apart. These days, many digital communities serve this purpose.

Example: Last week an FDIC spokesperson provided data on the readiness of American banks for Y2K. Tom Brokaw of NBC had recently announced, he said, that 33% of the banks weren't ready, but in fact, 96% of the banks are on schedule, 3% are lagging a little, and only 1% are seriously behind. The biggest threat to the monetary system is a stampeding herd, spooked by the digital image of a talking head giving bogus information.

The digital world is a hall of mirrors, and the social construction of reality is big business, fueled by the explosion of the Internet, a marketplace where the buyer of ideas—as well as items at auction—had better beware.

This is not just about the distortion of facts by mainstream (or alternative) news media, nor the exploitation of fear, because we know that fear sells. More and more, we are seeking and finding alternative sources of information from sources we believe we can trust. Believable truth must be linked to believable sources, or else we will make it up, pasting fears and hopes onto a blank screen or onto images built like bookshelves to receive our projections. Because we like to live on islands of agreement, receiving information that supports our current thinking, we live in thought worlds threaded on digital information that isolates and divides us. But the network is also the means of a larger communion and the discovery of a more unified, more comprehensive truth.

We live on the edge of a digital blade, and the blade cuts both ways.

"We all know the same truth," said Woody Allen. "Our lives consist of how we choose to distort it."

Except Woody Allen didn't say it. Rather, he said it through the mouth of Harry Block, a character in "Deconstructing Harry" named Harry Block. Except Except Harry Block didn't say it either. He said it through the mouth of a character he created in the movie.

Hacking is a kind of deconstruction of the combinations and permutations available in a network. Deconstruction is essential in a digital world. The skills of critical thinking, the ability to integrate fragments and know how to build a Big Picture are more important than ever. Those skills are critical to hacking and securing networks and critical to understanding who is really who in a world in which people are not always what they seem.

Plato feared the emerging world of writing because anybody could say anything without accountability, but he did not foresee the emergence of tools to document and evaluate what was written. Our world may seem, for the moment, to be a historical, fragmentary, multi-modal in relationship to the world of printed text. But something new is evolving—a matrix of understanding, a set of skills, a mindset that lets us sift through disinformation and use the same technology that lulls us to sleep to wake ourselves up.

Generations   *April 10, 1999*

Back in the old days, it was exciting when new software came out. Every day, we hurried to Computerland, hoping it was there. I remember a new version of WordStar with a million control-everything commands. I remember new interactive fiction games like Hitchhiker's Guide to the Galaxy from Infocom.

I don't remember the first time I skipped an upgrade on a software application, but now I skip them all the time. I seldom need the less-than-essential new features that require close perusal of an eight hundred page manual to master.

Same with life. Living life at different speeds, we inhabit different temporal niches. Generations no longer last a generation.

I wrote an article, "In Search of the Grail," in 1993, describing the impact which playing that Infocom game with my oldest son on an Apple II had on my understanding of what would happen to the world as the world played games with distributed networks.

I believed that interacting with the different world of symbol-manipulation in a context of distributed computing would change how we thought in fundamental ways. In retrospect, my intuition was correct. But six years later, it is also dated, at least three (digital) generations removed from the present.

A generation now in its teens or twenties has been so thoroughly socialized by interaction with the digital world that it doesn't see the lenses through which it sees. What was revolutionary a few years ago is ho-hum, the stuff of wild-eyed speculation now the platform on which that generation stands.

Last week I delivered a keynote speech for a web-based training conference. I said that the symbiotic relationship between networked computers and networked humans had spawned a large number of people who think they're working for the human side but in fact are working for the electronic network. "You're working for HAL," I said, "teaching people how to speak HAL's language."

A woman approached me after the speech.

"Many people in the audience," she said, "don't know what you mean by HAL."
Or what I mean by an Apple II. Or interactive fiction. Or Infocom.

No narrative chronicles the social history of popular computing. The way it came to us like an unexpected birthday present. And nobody seems to want one.

My wife came upon an "ice box" yesterday as we toured a Victorian house. She told a guard that she remembered a real "ice man," how she waited as a child until he had hacked ice into blocks for delivery, then picked up the shattered splinters to eat as a treat.

The guard listened politely and looked away, checking his watch for closing time.

They said it would happen, but they didn't say it would happen again and again, faster and faster. But it does. The points of reference that define the shared experience of a generation are changing more rapidly than ever.

"The Big Picture changes," a mentor once said, "about every ten years." I discovered that, indeed, every decade or so, I transitioned into a new developmental stage which re-contextualized everything that had come before.

Now, I am finding that I must reinvent myself; that is, revise the points of reference of how I think, every eighteen months to two years. The leisurely pace of an evolutionary life cycle that changes by the decade is a vanished luxury.

The fact of history itself as a shared point of reference has morphed into an indifference to the historical perspective entirely. History as a discipline, threaded through textual narratives and how text defines time and causality, has morphed into a world of hyper-textual images, in which our personal interests determine the path we travel through images of meaningful events. The patterns of our explorations either connect at intersections or they don't. A shared vision is less important than the machinery which enables us to search in the first place.

I can hear a dissenting voice, pointing out that people *always* did that. We *always* chose which books to read and created a unique pattern from our study. But—and this is a huge "but"—readers in a universe of printed text did not know that's what they did because they shared a vocabulary with which to discuss their experience. That vocabulary imposed what felt like a shared perspective. Only in retrospect— only after images and words had been reorganized in digital space—did we see our former experience as computers have taught us to see it.

The singular prism that bent all light in a print text world has been shattered by a hyper-text world that perceives that prism as a prison.

The excitement of my vision in 1993 is gone. Merchants, circumspect and wary, prowl the digital world. They have taken the gold from the pioneer miners who had to use it to buy food, shovels, and hovels. Merchants are always the pragmatic parents of the next generation, defining the real possibilities of their offspring. They even sell their children uniforms sewn with symbols of rebelliousness, the symbols each generation needs to pretend to break new ground.

So what is the value of experience? A broader perspective? Patience, as Yoda suggested ... what? Who, you ask, is Yoda?

Yoda is a puppet invented many years ago by a film-maker to represent purveyors of ancient wisdom. Yoda articulates wisdom in sound bites that we can snatch on the fly.

I remember diving on the reef, chasing the quick fish and never catching any. One day I swam out over the reef and sank in thirty feet of water. Then I just sat there, waiting, and all sorts of fish, wondrous and strange, came to me.

The digital world can be exploited or pursued, dreams of stock options feeding our greed. But it can also simply be observed. We can just sit there, under the ascending bubbles of our deep breathing, listening to the subterranean clicking. Not even learning the wisdom of not doing. No. Not even that.

Child's Play   *April 3, 2001*

"Games Engineers Play" was one of the first *Islands in the Clickstream* columns I wrote. In it I observed that a society socializes its young through games, teaching them through play the attitudes and skills we want them to have.

Those of us who have grown to middle age through the current technological revolution have learned to partner with the young. We know that they know intuitively things we have never learned. We listen to how they frame the world for clues to where new technologies will take us. Executives at Sony bring in children to test prototypes of the Playstation, watching them do things with the platform that its inventors never imagined. In exchange for their insight and perspective, we offer them our insight and perspective, knowing that all partnerships are quid's-pro-quo in which something of value must be exchanged.

We need to go to the edges, I often tell audiences, to see what's emerging outside of our conventional thinking. The edge is the new center. We must be dislodged from our comfortable niches, our snug little cubbies, in order to see what's real.

The edges I encourage people to explore are the latest military technology, commercial sex sites, and children's games. All three offer clues to what's coming next.

This is not rocket science, really. The military needs the most current technologies. Five years ago, an Air Force report on war in space in 2025 referenced the use of holographic image projection, cloaking devices, multispectral camouflage, and the creation of synthetic environments which the attacker believes to be real as necessary for the defense of the battlespace. If we consider those technologies metaphors for what will be needed in all competitive environments, we can anticipate some of the directions from which new winds will blow, just as ten years ago the migration of intelligence agents from government to industry signaled the growing power of trans-national corporations and dissolving geopolitical boundaries. The manipulation of perception itself, not just the concepts which frame those perceptions, will increasingly inform the arts of government and commerce. The masters of illusion will be masters of the space.

Nor is it rocket science to know that human beings love sex and will pay for it, real or imagined. We buy what looks or feels like love. New technologies of communication—books, photographs, VCRs, the Net—are always used to sell sex. So consumers fund the R&D that will bring the next advances, knowing that what the sex trade develops will migrate into the daylight commercial space.

And I try to pay attention to the games children play and anticipate how they will evolve into the playspace of the next generation of adults.

Last weekend I waited in line for an IMAX movie next door to a museum shop. I noticed posters on the window inviting children inside. This is what they advertised:

offworld gear,

weapons for the mind,

cyber-pets,

idea generators,

cosmic debris,

alien life forms,

space armor,

space junk,

thought reactors...

I flashed back to the Viking Lander settling down on Mars. When it began transmitting the first pictures from the red planet, I waited with a neighbor, a video ham, and watched as the first image of the Martian desert painted itself pixel by slow pixel across his monitor. I looked at that desert and yearned to be there,. I burned to climb Olympus Mons, to hike across the plains of Mars with the red wind at my back.

When I heard that the third successor to the Survivor television series planned to take contestants to the cosmonaut training center at Star City where the Russians would eliminate one each week until the finalist went to Baikonur in Kazakhstan to be launched to Mir, I wrote my application in twenty minutes and e-mailed it to the network. They said I was one of the first to apply. I knew that if I were a contestant, I would do anything, anything to go into space.

When we tack back and forth on our clear intention like a shark on its prey, nothing can stop us.

Or almost nothing. Mir no longer exists, having flamed to an ignominious end after its glorious moment in the sun. Since I don't have twenty million to pay the

Russians for a ride, I had better find another route out of the gravity well of the earth.

Offworld gear ... alien life forms ... space armor ...

I felt like I was looking through a shimmering window onto the future that is here now, but just out of reach. I felt like Winnie the Pooh hanging under his balloon next to the honey tree. He could see the honey, he could smell the honey, but he couldn't quite reach the honey.

So the military tells us that the practice of deception will be more and more important. A friend who taught cover and deception to intelligence experts says: "Deception consists of illusion, misdirection, and ridicule, these three." Then he smiles. "But the greatest of these is ridicule."

Ridicule is how we defend ourselves from the first images of the future as they crawl out of the darkness. Ridicule can be defeated, however, with the right tools, the tools that track down the truth, the real weapons of the mind. There is plenty of cosmic debris out there, plenty of illusion too. Talk about alien life forms and off-world colonies and the herd might think you're odd. The herd loves illusions, after all, loves being a herd. But for us little cyber-pets frolicking in a greater cosmic glory, what we see on that monitor is Mars, what we see in that museum window is right here, right now ... don't you see? It's within our reach.

It's only a matter of going.

Chapter 7

The Psychology of Digital Life: Identity and Destiny

In Search of the Dancing Bee   *July 27, 1997*

The accelerating pace of our lives contributes to the feeling that there is no firm ground under our feet.

Since the average American worker in the 90s works one month per year more than the average worker in the 60s, it's no wonder we feel pressed.

And once upon a time our forebears lived under a single "sacred canopy," a shared construction of social reality. Their core beliefs were never called into question; supported by consensus wherever they turned, our ancestors swam in their shared assumptions like fish in water. Their everyday sense of "reality" was never challenged.

In the Middle Ages, European towns devoted generations of effort to building a cathedral. The cathedral was a physical image of the sacred canopy under which they lived. They built over hundreds of years because they had all the time in the world. One generation died and another grew, but the symbolic structure that mediated day-to-day as well as cosmic meaning stayed in place.

Imagine a movie of that cathedral-building process running at the accelerated speed of time-lapse photography. Villagers rush about frantically, build a cathedral, and disperse in minutes instead of centuries.

That's what online communities look like and, increasingly, off-line communities too.

On-line communities coalesce, persist for a while, and dissipate. We give them names—usenet groups, listservs, web sites—and connect with each other like shuttles docking at a space station.

Off-line, too, in the "physical" world, we dock at modules more like space stations than cathedrals. Our communities come together, disperse and regroup continuously like time-lapse flowers.

Virtual organizations live and die at accelerated rates. We co-create them as opportunities for meaningful human interaction, building a context that quickly fades into the background. If we believe those structures are "real," we forget that we invented them. We notice them by contrast only as they replace one another in rapid succession.

I am writing this column on a jet. I am on the last leg of two large circles. The first took me from Milwaukee to Las Vegas, where I keynoted two conventions—the Black Hat Briefings, a forum for dialogue between the computer hacker underground and members of the computer security, intelligence, and IS communities, and DefCon V, an annual hackers' convention. Then I went to Boston to speak at MIT before a conference of academics and religious on technology and spirituality.

Then I plugged into the home module for two days.

Then I attended the convention of the National Speakers Association in Anaheim. Then I spoke at a conference in Chattanooga on education and technology.

During these weeks, I also exchanged e-mail with people from Sweden, Belgium, Holland, Germany, South Africa, Australia, Great Britain, Canada, Ireland, Singapore, and the USA.

I am a little dizzy.

I am more than ready to dock at the home module once again.

Each of those modules is a distinctive community with its own mores, language, assumptions about reality, and behavioral expectations. Jet lag was incidental compared to the necessity of understanding and participating meaningfully in the different "constructions of reality" that characterized each community.

Moving in and out of modular communities requires an ability to live between and among paradigms. That challenge calls forth moments of striking illumination, when we see how our "selves" flicker back and forth like holograms between different constructions of reality. We see or sense the persistence of a protean Self that unifies our experience.

The challenge is to remember who we are and to whom we are speaking.

The interaction between distinctive paradigms is giving birth to a new paradigm, a new construction of reality, that cannot be described from inside any prior paradigm.

Hebrews encountered Greeks and a new reality emerged in western civilization. Neither could have predicted the new reality before it happened. It included and transcended what had come before.

Trying to speak to the old paradigm from the new paradigm is like writing a 32-bit application for an IBM XT. The old OS just can't handle the code.

We can react to the clamor of clashing paradigms like children pulling the covers over their heads to blot out the noise of someone banging at the door, but our denial simply testifies to the loudness of the knock. Inevitably we must take our stand in the new paradigm, the emergent reality we are co-creating, and align ourselves with the pull of the future rather than the drag of the past.

Some observations:

- Context is content. What is not said is as important as what *is* said and gives meaning to what is said.

The cues with which individuals and cultures signal their beliefs must be read quickly and fluently. That's easier to do when you enter a roomful of hackers, educators, or professional speakers than when opening an e-mail.

Creating the context in which e-mail communicates clearly is one of the great challenges of online life.

- Churchill noted that we shape our buildings, then they shape us. The structures of life in the physical world resemble the simulated structures of life online. It's a chicken-and egg kind of thing. Our symbiotic relationship with networked computers is a dynamic process in which we rise together up a spiral of mutual transformation.

- Although I only docked at the "home module" for two days, that module defined the context in which I experienced everything else. In the new paradigm emerging from our encounter with "otherness" everywhere, we are driven inside ourselves to seek the center that serves as an anchor, a "psychic home," wherever we go. As we talk to each other about that experience, we will discover new symbols, new images, new concepts for identity and community.

That new community, too, will be simulated online and from our online interaction we will continue to engineer new ways of living in the physical world.

- New ways of living require new ways of talking about our evolving selves and the real spiritual needs of those selves. The Internet is a mediating structure of symbolic interaction. It is more than one of the space stations at which we dock. It is an emergent reality in which that conversation and that community are evolving.

The Internet is an opportunity to create and discover a new multimedia language of sound, images and text, "a language of the heart," as Andre Gregory said, "a new kind of poetry, the poetry of the dancing bee, that tells us where the honey is."

Beyond the Edge

August 29, 1997

There comes a point in our deepest thinking at which the framework of our thinking itself begins to wrinkle and slide into the dark. We see the edge of our thinking mind, an edge beyond which we can see ... something else ... a self-luminous "space" that constitutes the context of our thinking and our thinking selves.

As a child I tried to imagine infinity. The best I could do was nearly empty space, a cold void defined by a few dim stars, my mind rushing toward them, then past them into the darkness.

The same thing happens today when I think about energy and information and the fact that all organisms and organizations are systems of energy and information interacting in a single matrix.

I try to imagine the form or structure of the system, but the structure itself is a system of energy and information. I try to imagine the structure of the structure ... and pretty soon the words or images are rushing into the darkness at warp speed and my mind is jumping into hyperspace.

When we see our thinking from a point outside our thinking, we see that our ideas and beliefs are mental artifacts, as solid and as empty as all the things in the physical world—things, we are told, that are really patterns of energy and information, that our fingertips or eyes or brains are structured to perceive as if they are objects—out there—external to ourselves.

That is an illusion, of course. There is no "there" there.

Makes a guy a little dizzy.

At the recent Hacking in Progress Conference near Amsterdam (HIP97), there was a demonstration of van Eck monitoring. That means monitoring the radiation that leaks from your PC. Hackers do not have to break into your system if the system is leaking energy and information. They just have to capture and reconstitute it in useful forms.

A participant at HIP said, "It was nice to see a real demonstration of analog van Eck monitoring of a standard PC, which meets all the normal shielding and emission control standards, via an aerial, via the power supply and via the surface waves induced in earthing cables, water pipes, etc. Even this simple equipment can distinguish individual machines of the same make and model in a typical office building from 50 to 150 meters or more with extra signal amplification."

He is saying that the radiation leaked from your PC monitor, even when it meets all the standards proscribed by law, can be reconstituted on a screen at a distance greater than the length of a football field, and everything you are seeing at this moment can be seen by that fellow in the van down the block as well.

And he can get the radiation from the water pipes under your house.

We are radiating everywhere and always the information and energy that constitutes the pattern of what we look at, what we know ... who and what we are.

All of the great spiritual traditions teach practices of meditation. They teach that those who enter deep states of meditation soon discover that paranormal experience is the norm at a particular depth of consciousness.

At first this discovery is fascinating. It is like scuba diving for the first time. The beauty of the underwater world is so compelling, you can stop at twenty or thirty feet and just gaze in awe at the beauty of the fish. But if you do, you won't go deeper. You'll get stuck.

So we are told simply to note that what is happening is real, then keep on moving.

In those deeper states, we observe more and more clearly the thinking that we often mistake for our real selves. We see that we are usually "inside" our thinking, living as if our thoughts are reality itself. We see the edge of our thinking and then ... something else beyond the edge.

We see that the structures of our thinking—our culture—are mental artifacts.

When we think that, and catch ourselves thinking about the illusion of thinking, we laugh.

That's why laughter peals so often from the walls of Buddhist monasteries. Enlightenment is a comic moment. Enlightenment includes the experience of observing our minds in action and seeing that we are not our minds. Our minds may be as automatic as machines but we are not machinery. We are the ghosts in the machine.

We see that in our essence we are more like stars in a spiraling galaxy. We are not just radiating energy and information always, we are radiant energy and information, a single matrix of light that is darkness visible.

Back in my days of doing workshops and long weekends, we used to do an exercise of looking into each other's eyes until we were lost in a wordless communion. By playing games ("feel a feeling and communicate it without words, the other receive it and say what it is") we discovered that what we were feeling was always transmitted to anyone and everyone around us. All a person had to do was stop for a moment and pay attention and they would know who we were. Even when we thought we were providing high-level descriptions of ourselves that fooled everyone, we were leaking energy and information.

It is dawning on us that privacy as we used to think of it is over, that the global village is a community in which the data of our lives is available to anyone who wants to gather or pay for it. It ought to be dawning on us as well that the ways we think we mask ourselves are as transparent as the shielding on a PC monitor.

The initial distancing we experience when we first connect via computers is soon replaced with the realization that our willingness to be present—to communicate via symbols like these—means that we are transparent in our interaction, that the global network is a mediating structure through which information and energy is transmitted literally as well as in symbolic forms. We show up in cyberspace, not just representations of ourselves. We are here, alone together.

The structures of energy and information in the universe are the universe.

How can we speak of what we see beyond the edge of our collective selves? It seems to be a ground or matrix, a glowing self-luminous system of … nothing … there is no "there" there … and we rush through the darkness toward the few stars defining the limits of our thought then past them.

The Perils of Parallax   *September 26, 1997*

In last week's column I wrote: "The individualism that many of us were taught was axiomatic to being human was in fact generated by a print culture. Before the Gutenberg era, nobody thought that way. Digital culture undermines individualism and our ability to act as if we exist apart from our communities."

A reader wrote: "What about assessment in the age of mutuality? We may need to work as a group, but we are measured as individuals. As a collaborative writer I know plenty of horror stories about people misappropriating another's work and taking full credit."

That reader describes an inevitable tension as we try to catch an avalanche coming downhill. No matter how wide-eyed we think we are, things show up at the edges and catch us by surprise. Sound waves become visible on the wings of an airplane just before it breaks the sound barrier, McLuhan reminds us. To the blind, all things are sudden, and in some ways, we are all blind to the deeper implications of the digital revolution.

- In the middle of the clickstream, we see things now from this point of view, now from that. Our perception flickers back and forth like a holographic image.

Parallax is the apparent displacement of a single object seen from two different points of view. The "object" is human beings living in community in a digital world. From one point of view we are a collection of individuals with rights. From another, we are cells in a single body.

- Only as we engage with new technologies over time do they disclose to us the possibilities they make available. It is difficult to imagine today that when the telephone was invented it was not seen as a personal communication device. The telephone became a distributed medium that taught us how to use it and we became extensions of the system. When the movie camera was invented, it was set on a tripod in front of a proscenium arch. We used it to frame reality the way stage plays taught us to frame it. Over time the camera taught us how to move around, change focus, see through its lenses, and perceive reality differently.

We live in the meantime between different models of reality, straddling icebergs that are slowly drifting apart.

- When we read the translated words of sacred texts from only a couple thousand years ago, we assume they meant then what we mean by them now. They don't.

When Hebrews spoke of divine justice, for example, it was justice for an entire tribe. It was literally impossible to think of individuals separately from the community that provided the context for their identity.

Only after print was invented were the Reformation and Renaissance possible. Only then were individuals able to conceive of salvation or destiny as a private enterprise. Only then could they read scriptures to themselves and interpret its meaning privately, inaugurating a proliferation of religions and denominations.

- Ownership of literary property did not exist when the work was not fixed in text. An "author" did not have "rights" to a "work."

These columns are distributed on the Internet and published in print. In print form, fees are paid and the copyright is enforced. In digital form, it is hoped they will be replicated and distributed, but not published for gain by someone else.

Such is the new marketplace.

Ubiquity = > mind share = > brand equity = > sales.

We give away products for free, as the Grateful Dead invited fans to record concerts, creating a bootleg market that broadened the context for their tours.

The "rights" of "authors" to their "work" are in flux.

- When we work collaboratively online, ownership is blurred, and so are the boundaries around the selves that create the work. It's like an exploration of paranormal phenomena. Once we discover telepathy or clairvoyance to be possible, the "self" having the experience begins to lose its boundaries or definition in something bigger. If reincarnation is real, the self that persists cannot be the "little self" that pops at the moment of death like a soap bubble.

- A recent Wall Street Journal article on self-governing work teams spoke of how hard it is for some workers to accept responsibility ("accountability") or hear the feedback that is necessary for teams to function. Ralph Stayer of

Johnsonville Foods in Kohler, Wisconsin, reports that among the painful casualties of the perilous journey toward self-governing work teams were executives who could not morph from command-and-control generals into real coaches.

A professor at Carnegie Mellon estimates that such teams have been adopted by 40% of US manufacturers. Rumors of the demise of hierarchical structures, however, are greatly exaggerated. Hierarchy conserves energy and eliminates role confusion. The initial impact of the digital revolution is a flattening and broadening of horizontal structures but those branches grow on taller trees. Hierarchical structures are replicated fractal-like on a larger scale.

- During epiphanies—moments of revelation—we see that all of our cultural assumptions about identity and community are "consensual hallucinations" like cyberspace itself.

A friend recently recounted a vision he had years ago. He saw the whole earth as a large sphere, millions of lines radiating from its center until, when they arrived at the surface, they became millions of tiny patches of land. On every patch was a minuscule person proclaiming, "I own this land. It's mine."

My friend, of course still flickers back and forth between paradigms. We all do. His safety deposit box holds deeds to "land" that he "owns." He will never forget that, underlying that arbitrary abstraction, we belong to the earth, rather than vice versa.

Our descriptions of reality are true at different degrees of precision. The streams of our truths are continuous, like the flow of the strands of a fractal, and replicate at all levels.

We work in groups but measure ourselves as individuals. We need one another without qualification to create the community in which our individuality is fulfilled, but we act as if we are independent isolates. The truth is not just one thing, ever. Our minds make up the maze of distinctions through which we make our various ways until, suddenly, the walls explode and we find ourselves in a midnight garden, "the heaventree of stars hung with humid nightblue fruit."

Nodes of a network, individuals interlaced with their glowing monitors, luminous leaves of a single tree.

The Power of Projection, The Power of Digital Presence *June 20, 1997*

Welcome to the blank screen.

A computer monitor glowing in the dark. Pixels constellated as an image of printed text. The belief that behind those images is a human intelligence, whose energy and presence you sometimes swear you can "feel." Once that belief becomes our shared or consensus reality, you believe that "I" am talking to "you."

Believing is seeing. Believing is the precondition of a possibility.

So ... here I am again.

Twenty years ago, I moved to Mutton Hollow, a rural area of northern Utah. Since I had lived only in Chicago, London, and Madrid previously, this took some getting used to. The pleasures of a big city were far, far away.

We were high against the Wasatch Front, and the winter skies were magnificent. I bought a telescope with a long barrel. Since the seeing was best at the top of the sky where the air was clearest, I often lay a tarp on the frozen snow so I could lie on my back and look straight up.

I moved slowly through the star fields, pausing at a cluster or the Great Nebula in Orion before losing myself in the three-dimensional darkness among the blue, white, yellow, and blood-red stars.

The stars and the vast spaces between them became my companions. I still can't identify most constellations, however. A constellation is an arbitrary pattern imposed on a random scattering of stars. I guess I can see it's a bull, but it might as well be a bear or a crawling baby.

The images our forebears used to connect the dots were projected from within their own psyches. Once there was a consensus reality about what they were, the projections became "real." It really was a herdsman or a bear "out there."

The computer monitor at which we are both looking right now is a powerful invitation to project a pattern onto what we are seeing.

Haven't you read an e-mail or an IRC communication when your emotion was running high, and you could swear you felt the presence of the sender in the room? As if they were right there in the words you were reading? Hasn't it sometimes seemed beyond coincidence when you went online with someone on your mind and ... bingo! There they were.

Or there their words were. But were they in the words you read? And did the words mean what you thought they meant?

It is a perpetual dilemma of the human condition that we can not easily distinguish our projections from genuine perceptions. Carl Jung said the soul or psyche projects its contents onto archetypal symbols that invite them. You can tell there's projection, he said, when there's secrecy, fascination, and high energy.

A speech I have given for portfolio managers and others interested in the psychology of investment is called "The Stock Market, UFOs, and Religious Experience." What do those three things have in common? All three domains invite powerful projections, and we think we see "out there" in the economy or the markets, in the night sky, or in the universe itself that which we have projected onto it.

Something is out there. Something elicited the projection, but we can't see what it is until we withdraw our projections and integrate them once again into our selves. Then we can see where we end and someone else begins.

Confusion of boundaries bedevils online relationships as well as those in the flesh.

All religious and spiritual traditions have tools designed to help us integrate our projections into our selves. We call the process "getting it together," the end result "integrity." We say we "feel centered," when we take back the power we have projected onto another or given away.

The pixels on your monitor invite projection.

Secrecy, fascination, and high energy.

How about it? Have they characterized any of your online exchanges or adventures?

If there is a context for a personal or business relationship before e-mail is exchanged, the online exchange is anchored. Face-time and telephone-time too ground the exchange. When people connect online and do not mitigate their encounter with a context that grounds it, the projections, and the sparks, can fly.

The greater your intention to crate a context that grounds your e-mail, the greater the likelihood you will not be misunderstood. That requires imagination, an ability to see different interpretations for your words. You may think the words you sent were crystal clear, but the person on the other end, returning to their cubicle in a dour mood, may receive them like a boxing-glove coming out of a closet.

The fewer words you provide, the greater the invitation to project. The stars can be a bull or a bear or a crawling baby. In business as well as personal online communication, we are responsible for creating a context that enables our words to vibrate with obvious meaning.

The digital image at which you are looking is a simulation of printed text, which simulated written words, which simulated spoken words. Reading silently to ourselves is a relatively late practice. T. S. Eliot may have thought that his "words echo thus in your mind," but only a few generations ago, schoolchildren read aloud, all together, so the schoolmaster would know they weren't shirking. The only real words were spoken words.

Some think spoken words are a specialized kind of gesture. Gestures are feelings felt so strongly they make the whole body vibrate like a violin.

When I intend to communicate to you in this medium, all I have is my intention to focus energy and information so you "get it." We human beings are nothing but organized systems of energy and information. That's what computers are, too. The words on your screen are merely the echo of a gesture, feelings felt so strongly they show up and glow through the words. It isn't words alone, though, it's the energy or the shape of the energy seen and felt through the words that you "get." A spirit making the electrons coalesce by sheer force of will so you see, and sometimes feel, my presence in the room, in your life, in your head and heart.

Believing is seeing.

So ... as I said ... here I am again.

The Voice of the Computer *October 10, 1997*

I was disappointed when hour-long cartoons of Peanuts were made for television. I had been reading the comic strip for years, and when I read the words in balloons above the characters' heads, I heard their voices inside my head as a kind of echo—the way you probably hear "my" voice inside your head as you read these words.

That voice—private, well-modulated, always just right—was replaced by a real child's voice that didn't sound right at all. It sounded like a child—a real child. Not the Charlie Brown in my head. By providing too much information, the movie makers yanked Peanuts from the world of imagination and turned it into one more concrete thing in the world of sensation, a fetish stripped of its magical properties.

Computer engineers pay close attention to the world of sensation as they struggle to develop computers that act like human beings. The more they try, however, the more it seems they miss the mark. Artificial intelligence and robotics experts design crabs that scuttle around their labs like low-grade idiots. Few laypeople are excited when a robot distinguishes a cube from a ball and lifts it off the ground.

The best robots are designed for tasks, not to look like living creatures. Let them do their jobs, and we'll provide the personality.

A decade ago, Joseph Weizenbaum of MIT became upset when an employee interacted with ELIZA, the simple interactive "therapist" he designed, as if ELIZA were a real person. The employee even asked him to leave the room so she could have a private conversation.

Weizenbaum was alarmed at the ease with which people projected personality and presence onto the computer. He thought it was bad, instead of just what's so. Now, two men from Stanford, Byron Reeves and Clifford Nass, have carried out some wonderful studies that reveal how and why we respond to computers as if they are real people ("The Media Equation: How People Treat Computers, Television and New Media like Real People and Places"—Stanford and Cambridge: 1996).

Their studies state the obvious, but, as usual, it was so obvious, we missed it. Our brains evolved to help us survive, and we react, unconsciously and automatically, as if something that looks or acts like a person is a person. Our "top-level" program may say something else— "it's only a movie," for example, when we're frightened during a horror flick—but that wouldn't be necessary if we didn't think it was real.

Artificial intelligence and virtual reality are not necessary to make us think a computer is smart. Less is more. Too much detail, too much information, overwhelms our imaginations.

Computers are inherently social actors, Nass said at a Usability Professionals Association conference. He used flattery as an example. "We're suckers for flattery, even when we know it isn't true." So computer programs that flatter the user are consistently judged to be smarter and better at playing games, and users enjoy using them more. And ... people always deny that's what they're doing.

We act the way we act, not the way we think we act.

We need friends, we need allies, Nass explained, and when they tied blue armbands around both users and computers and said they were a team, the users believed their computers were friendlier, smarter, better, just as we do about our human team-mates. Again, no one knew they were doing it.

The voices of our computers—the ones we hear in our heads—are always just right. If designers simply provide the opportunity for projection and facilitate the transaction in a seamless way, we'll do most of the work and add emotional richness and content. Get in the way too much, it's like that little paperclip guy on Windows programs, always in your face. I don't know anyone who wants that animation dancing on their screen all the time, like a fly you can't swat.

The Infocom interactive text games from the 1980s were powerfully evocative. Games like "Trinity", "A Mind Forever Voyaging", and "Hitchhiker's Guide to the Galaxy" used clever text and poetic imagery to invite us to co-create landscapes as magical as those I remember from children's books. With larger platforms and memory devices, games evolved into interactive movies that shut down that process. When graphics dominate the interface, there's less room for the activity of the imagination.

Children imagine so much, Eleanor Roosevelt observed, because they have so little experience. As our experience grows, the magical landscapes of our childhood vanish, replaced with interstate highways, convenience stores and power lines. A little more imagination and a little less information wouldn't hurt. It gives our souls some room to maneuver. If computers provide just enough cues to elicit our projections, we'll do the rest. We'll endow distributed networks, human and non-human alike, with personality, presence, and intentionality as the ancient Greeks saw gods in every rock and grove and thunderstorm.

Cyberspace is "space" indeed, brimful of gods and goddesses, angels and demons waiting to become flesh. That's neither good nor bad, it's just what's so. Digital deities are emerging now in the brackish tidewaters of cyberspace, where all life begins. If we accept responsibility for understanding how we co-create them, how we interact with the Net and the entire universe unconsciously and automatically, then we can cooperate with how our brains work anyway. They make up the game whether we want them to or not. "Out there" and "in here" are metaphors, defining preconditions of perception as "space." The grid is imaginary, and the grid is real. That's the playing field of our lives so we might as well learn the rules, then work and play the game with gusto.

Memory Storage   *October 17, 1997*

The story making the rounds this week about the decline of President Reagan is poignant. The worst terrors of Alzheimer patients—rage, paranoia, uncontrollable outbursts—are not in evidence, but we do have an image of a man looking into a mirror, not knowing that the man looking back had been President of the United States.

When Alice was underground, the caterpillar asked, "Who are you?" and we might imagine the face in the mirror asking the President the same question.

And what is any self, after all, but a momentary arrangement of information and energy? A "dissipative structure," like a whirlpool that holds its shape while exchanging its atoms. Where is that self, when our memories have been "lost in time like tears in rain?" as Roy says at the end of the movie *Blade Runner*, just before he dies in the rain under an acid sky.

Blade Runner is a dystopian view of the next century, an inquiry into the blurred boundaries between humans and machines. Roy is a replicant, a machine so human it develops an instinct for survival. Driven by a fear of mortality, some rebellious replicants need to be "retired." Deckard is the "blade runner" given the task of killing them.

Deckard is asked by Eldon Tyrell, who dreamed up the code for the replicants, to run an "empathy test" on Rachael, an employee, to determine whether or not she's human. Deckard concludes that Rachael is a replicant, but it takes him a long time.

"She doesn't know, does she?" he says. Then, "How can it not know what it is?"

Tyrell explains that implants of false memories supported by faked photographs convince Rachael that she has lived a normal human life. The illusion of memory and the seamless interface of an artificial and a real self enable her to live a lie.

Later Deckard sits in his apartment, surrounded by photographs, and wonders if he too is a replicant that doesn't know what it is.

Memories are internal representations of experience that no longer exists. So how can we know if they're real? Biography morphs into history, and history morphs into myth. History, in fact, is our corporate myth, as biography is our individual myth.

So how can we know what we are? How can we not know what we are?

My brother called not long ago to ask about a childhood incident. Our parents are long dead, and we're the only two people on earth who remember that event. That shared memory makes us family.

As he talked of what he remembered, I said, "I don't remember it that way." Our memories were contextualized differently, skewed to fit the interpretation of life congruent with our individual stories.

That memory file had become corrupted, but had it ever existed in a pure form? Our beliefs determine our perceptions and our memories, and we gather evidence for our beliefs throughout our lives, turning our life stories into self-validating circles.

Those chemical traces in the brain caused by photons and other vectors of energy that we call "events in our lives" might be convertible to digital storage. Then we can save our memories—ourselves—and download ourselves into new bodies, ensuring the same kind of immortality we'll derive from teleportation, the creation of a copy from source code while the original is destroyed.

Who exactly will it be, then, that remembers "my" life? And when we pool our memories to form a tribe or community or nation, who will it be that remembers our history?

My first office computer was a Zenith running on CP/M. I used WordStar and its thousand-and-one commands to keep records for the church I served as an Episcopal priest.

Parish records had been kept in a book , and when someone died, a line was drawn through their name. Their name and maybe the person was still there, somehow, "in the book of life" (to use an archaic print metaphor), but different—the way I think many people vaguely imagine the self to persist after death.

When the records were computerized and someone died, however, I hit the delete key. The person vanished without a trace. There were no undelete keys then, no way to restore a lost file.

The first time it happened, it felt like a chill wind blowing through my soul.

A biblical scholar, Joachim Jeremias, thinks the words of Jesus at the last supper were misunderstood. He did not say, "Do this in remembrance of me," in Aramaic, but "Do this so that God may remember me." At his last meal before execution, he suggests, the condemned man implores his God not to delete him from long-term memory.

We still distinguish between people and machines because it's convenient. We may have artificial hearts, wear contacts, have hair transplants, plastic skin and artificial joints, but we think "we" are somehow separate from all that. We still locate ourselves in our mental activity. The genome project promises to map that mental activity—the source code of our memories, temperament, modalities of perception—and then we can make up digital pictures to support our memories. Maybe we'll make the pictures first, then invent the memories to match, the way news media do.

Deckard's question—how can it not know what it is?—is a simple inquiry into the nature of the landscape in which we live. There is always a lag as human cultures take their sweet time catching up to human experience. The Vatican only recently apologized to Galileo, after all. But soon enough our civilization, like President Reagan, will look into the mirror and not know who or what it is. The familiar names of our nations will join those of lost tribes—Philistines and Jebusites, Czechoslovakia and the Soviet Union—and we will evolve a bold new way of understanding what has happened on our planet.

When the caterpillar poses its koan, "Who are you?" to our replicants and clones, perhaps the simulated face gazing back from the digitized mirror will have an answer.

Detours   *November 24, 1997*

When Carl Jung was an old man, the fifteen-year-old daughter of a friend asked, "Dr. Jung, could you please tell me the shortest path to my life's goals?"

Without a moment's hesitation, Jung replied: "The detours!"

My wife was taught by her parents that trips began at the front door and headed straight to their destination. The first time I said, "Let's try a different road and see where it goes," it was quite a stretch. Now we both think the most interesting parts of a trip are often the detours.

Here in the upper midwest, people used to map a straight-line trajectory from cradle to grave. When you left school, you were supposed to get a job and keep that job until you retired. People who deviated from that plan were ... well, suspect.

I remember a childhood friend who decided to be an accountant. He outlined his life straight through to retirement. He never moved, seldom travelled, and built up a nest egg. End of story.

Some people log onto the Internet and know exactly what they want, get it, and log off. I don't browse as much as I did because of intermediate structures like directories and search engines, but the pleasure of browsing is still driven by the feeling that I might find something wonderful and unexpected. Often enough, I do, and like a slot machine with a high pay-off, that keeps me pulling the handle.

Sometimes something I find feels like it was planted, that I was always intended to stumble upon it.

I wonder if detours really exist or if that's just a name for essential legs of the journey that can not be predicted from what comes before. The whole journey, including detours and dead-ends, might all be right there when we start.

"In my beginning is my end," said T. S. Eliot.

I was once scheduled by my family to be an accountant, too. On the eve of my junior year of college, I looked at that semester's books and recoiled. I ran around changing courses, majors, schools. I never regretted that decision nor any subsequent decision that emerged with such clarity from the inside out. I learned to consult my internal compass and go where it told me to go.

In my twenties, I wrote a novel about a young writer (naturally) who wrote a short story with a limited vision. Over the course of a single night he rewrote that story and rewrote it until his vision—embodied in a final story that included everything that came before—was comprehensive and mature.

Some of the paths he tried along the way turned out to be dead-ends, but at the end of the novel, even the dead-ends were integral to the structure.

When I look at that novel now, thirty years later, I see that it outlines the trajectory of my life. Everything I needed to learn in the flesh I already knew, but I had to live my life so I could learn it, not just know it.

Jungian psychology is full of archetypal images, universal symbols that transcend our cultures. Archetypes show up in stories, paintings, sacred rites, and movies, and computer games, and now the Net.

One archetype is the "wise old man" or "wise old woman," an image of the part of ourselves that always knows. In guided meditations we can imagine a forest (of life) and a cave in that forest and a wise old man or woman in the cave. We can approach them as Greeks approached the oracle of Delphi with the puzzles of our lives. Their answers are always mysterious, always right.

The seed contains the tree. The seed knows from the moment of germination where it is headed. It may twist in response to drought or flood, but knows how to become the mature tree. And we know how to become who we already are.

Fate is character, the Greeks concluded, and our destiny, already determined, has only to be chosen to turn necessity into freedom.

It is no accident that "management by objective" has been eclipsed during the computer era by "scenario planning." Management by objective presumed a straight line to the future and a series of steps by which to get there. Scenario planning involves cross-disciplinary teams that define three or four possible futures and the conditions that must hold if they're to exist. That branching fan of possibilities is then compared to what emerges so adjustments can be made.

There is, of course, no such thing as a "future." The future, like all descriptions of spacetime, is a human construction, in part, engineered from our interaction with our structures of information technology. As management-by-objective echoed the straight line of printed text and mechanization, scenario planning is shaped like a computer program and the logic that governs it. The context becomes the content and then dissolves, forgetting itself.

Any parent who thinks they will determine who their children will become is taught by life to forget it. Children emerge with personalities, temperaments, set vectors of energy. The most we can do as parents is help them grow.

Individual psyches are wise and know where they want to go. Societies are wise too and grow organically, knowing more than their individual members, and so are cultures, and species know what they're destined to become, and life knows where it is headed, knitting itself on the loom of the universe into the billion possibilities that have all been present from the beginning.

The Internet, imaged with reflexive symbols, is a mirror of our individual minds and collective Self, one way by which consciousness is becoming conscious of itself. Consciousness can always call recursively its own ancient wisdom and self-correct. Seeming detours, wise old men and wise old women wait in caves in the forests of cyberspace, real simulations of the wisdom of the heart.

Christmas Presence   *December 26, 1997*

It's the day after Christmas, and we're all a bit tired. I am sitting at the computer, listening to a voice on the telephone.

"She didn't know how to turn it on. She turned on the monitor but not ... hello? Are you there?"

The voice on the telephone had noticed, although I hadn't said a word, that my attention was back on the e-mail I had been reading when the telephone rang. It wasn't my noises—they were the right ones in all the right places—but how I was "there" somehow communicated that I had slipped away from the conversation.

I was trying to do too many things at the same time, like an old Windows PC. When we do two things simultaneously, we take about thirty percent of our attention off the primary task. Like the car last week that was wobbling in the roadway and almost hit me when I passed, making me turn to see a driver staring at a point in front of his gaze, speaking with animation on his cellphone.

All we're asked to do is stay present when talking to someone or even doing anything at all. But we do drift, don't we?

Civilization is a mediating structure designed to facilitate the exchange of energy and information. The new hardware—the electronic infrastructure of our civilization—is, for the moment, just a little bit in the way.

Electronic networks mediate communication. Yet no one thought of computers or telephones as personal communication devices when they were invented.

It is reported that Alexander Graham Bell, when asked how the telephone might be used, said, "Maybe you could call ahead to the next town to tell them a telegram is coming."

It is also reported that Western Union was not interested in the patent on the telephone because they believed the device had no practical value.

When the telephone was invented, the simulated voice sounded unnatural. Now we think we're talking to a "real person."

But there's no one there. The "space" in which we converse is cyberspace, the consensual hallucination defined by William Gibson, a space that doesn't exist until we make it up and act as if it's real. We're like mimes building walls in the air, then living in the rooms.

We know we're working in virtual space during a conference call or an online meeting. But we don't realize how much that has changed us even when we're face to face. Virtual meetings have changed how we relate to one another when we're all in the same room. We have been "virtualized" by our experience and have internalized the structures of relationship that has taught us.

Professional sports, for example.

When I was a child, I attended Chicago Cubs baseball games. I sat in the stands. I felt the weather. The game took place on a grass playing field with real ivy on the walls. We watched a scoreboard where a human being physically moved numbers each inning to keep score. During the game, we talked to each other.

I attended a professional basketball game the other day. The stadium was indoors. Huge video screens facing four directions demanded my attention. I tried to look under the screens at the players but there was no way to avoid those immense images hanging in front of my face. When the game started, it was easier to watch the players on the screen than on the court.

I knew the introductions of players would be loud, but I didn't expect the decibel level to remain high throughout the game. Even during halftime, the noise level was so loud I couldn't talk to my friends.

Between watching the game on television and watching the game at the stadium, there was little difference. Compared to my childhood experience, it felt like I wasn't at the game at all. I was at a digital simulation of the game. The simulation was inserted between myself and my own experience, even at the stadium.

Someone who attended their first large convention in decades might report a similar experience. They might feel as if they weren't at a convention at all but at a digital representation of a convention. The tiny image of a speaker far away at a tiny podium is dwarfed by video images all around the hall. The audio and video equipment often makes it impossible to see the speaker even when you try.

We bring our digital experience into a physical room as the psychological space in which to interact. It is a modular interface that we port into all our relationships, a consequence of "virtualization."

We had to learn how to stay present on the telephone and we have to learn how to stay present in and through computer networks. When I drifted away from the person on the telephone, I really drifted away from myself.

When I speak to an audience I try not to watch the next paragraph turning itself over in my mind like an index card because then I cease to be present. When I'm on the radio or communicating through this column, I often imagine a person listening or reading and stay present to that persona, focusing my energy and attention toward them.

Any meeting—from a tête-à-tête to a convention—is a structure for the exchange of information and energy, and we have to learn how to use mediating structures, including telephone systems and computer networks. Not to hide, but to show up.

Presence is a gift, perhaps the only gift we have to offer. Energy and information is who we are and what we have to contribute. Hoarding our energy shrinks the soul and makes it look like a puckered prune—black hole from which no light can escape.

I'm with Shaw. Life is a splendid torch, I want it to burn as brightly as it can before handing it on, and when I die, I want the fuel to be all used up.

Winter Dreams
January 17, 1998

How we experience winter depends, firstly, on where we live. Here in the upper midwest it is a low gray sky over a white landscape. When the snow began to fall on Christmas Eve, and the shapes of everything recognizable went under like a tired swimmer who stopped struggling, the snow fell inside too, transforming an interior vista that had been sharp and hard-edged into a whitened sky.

I missed that feeling of "having to go inside" when I lived in the tropics. Winter there means ten degrees cooler and a less intense sun. It doesn't encourage withdrawal into our depths like a midwest winter, letting our lives lie fallow for a season while engaging in "wu wei"—not-doing—instead of frenetic activity.

Cold snowy weather is a kind of relief that lets us retreat and think things over.

When the landscape remains gray and white for weeks, however, it is also like a sensory deprivation tank. I tried that, too, and watched with fascination after several hours as my mind generated its own brightly colored animated graphics. Against the blackness, it was easier to see what was coming from inside out. We live in a kind of equilibrium with the input from our senses, providing from within what doesn't arrive from outside. We live suspended, as Wordsworth said, between what we "half create and what perceive."

So how we experience winter depends too on what we bring to the experience.

When things get too quiet, some people twitch. A reader in Brazil, responding to my column on "presence," suggests that we are "constructing an ADD (attention deficit disorder) society" with too much stimulation and an inability to pay attention. Channel surfing on cable television, telephoning from cars, or networking through multiple windows—we do too many things at once. But some people—the twitterpated, as my step-son called his sometimes addled younger brother—feel right at home in that. And who's to say they're bad or wrong?

The world can be understood as a polarity of twitchers and contemplative thinkers. That dichotomy is an oversimplification, of course, as are all divisions of the world into matched pairs.

It's easier to make distinctions at the edges of the bell curve than in the murky middle where most of us live.

What we now label ADD, a psychological disorder, is an inability to attend to one thing very long. The psyche switches channels constantly. From a broader perspective, however, perhaps we ought to be grateful for twitchers and ask what value they bring to the species.

In unpredictable or unstable environments, a twitcher at the point of patrol will outshoot a dreamy contemplative any day. That advantage probably helped us survive. In the digital world as in our cave days, a twitcher at the trigger scores more points.

A doctor who was manic-depressive wrote a book asserting that a condition present in 4% of the population has obvious survival value. She contended that many past geniuses were manic-depressive, and not coincidentally. It's impossible to psychoanalyze the pages of a biography, so we'll never know, but it's worth considering. Psychologists are diagnosing more and more people as ADD. Maybe transitional families and virtual organizations reward those who don't know how to sit still. Maybe it's the "stables," who find change difficult, that are having the toughest time.

Our cultures seem to invent the antidotes we need to external conditions. In anxious times, spirituality is defined as calming or quieting our noisy minds. In the seventies, on the other hand, when people were dispersed far and wide and needed to invent "instant community," the human potential movement generated the intensive encounters we needed. The encounter may have been a hothouse flower, but hey, in a world of genetic engineering, all human beings will be hot house flowers and the question becomes: What kinds of flowers do we want to grow?

Our spiritual traditions provide, not so much answers, as templates for processes that generate answers. The digital world is a good place to look for that to happen. But the symbols of our diverse traditions must be translated into interactive experiences that speak to our real lives.

A weekend intensive I developed in the "old days" translated the six seasons of the traditional church year into experiential processes that enable people to internalize and understand the recursive stages of spiritual growth. The church calendar is a mnemonic device, letting us remember the paradigm that carries us like a rising spiral through our lives. The first season, Advent, for example, is a time of ripening prior to the arrival of unexpected, often unthinkable truths. But we have to know how those ritualized seasons correspond to our inner seasons.

Good preaching is like a Tarot card reading. Liturgical churches have calendars that turn the wheel of lessons to be read on a regular basis. Those lessons are archetypal images of healing, deliverance and transformation that it is the task of the speaker to interpret in terms of the experience of the community. It's like shuffling a Tarot deck, which also consists of such symbols, then "reading the psychic space" of the community as reflected in the depths of those images.

Communicating in cyberspace feels as much like speaking as writing. We can feel the tidal energies of real people flow in and out of our virtual lives. As advertisements ironically describe telephone calls, we "reach out and touch someone," using a simulation to encounter a real Other. Our digital symbols mediate real intimacy and real community.

All human experience is mediated through a matrix of symbols and myth. That shared network glows like images on our monitors, a web of sustaining grace, veined with light. We are held in tension, suspended momentarily between the light of the snow and the light of the low clouds, and only when the moment has passed and we exhale again do we notice that we had been holding our breath.

Summer Nights *July 11, 1998*

The evocative power of summer nights in northern latitudes is intense.

Different climates, like different constructions of reality, fuse so completely with how we experience our lives that we are like fish in water.

When I lived in Hawaii, I missed the first chill in the air that came in mid-summer, an intimation that long daylight might not last forever. An intimation that the luminous humid darkness of this particular summer night is an unappreciated gift.

Why are so many feelings interlaced with memories of summer nights? And why am I sitting at two in the morning in front of a computer when the sky is clear, Scorpius is rising, and the warm night is an invitation to go outside and do nothing, absolutely nothing, while the symbols of the universe written in the sky say more than I want to know of what's passed and passing and to come?

Memories in their molecular matrix trigger chemicals that make me wistful. I remember the smell of the summer hair of the first girl I loved. I remember a night in a back yard behind the home of an uncle and aunt, surrogate parents that I visited in southern Indiana, their neighbors visiting and the hollyhocks growing wild and how it felt to dream to sleep with their warm house around me. And I remember summer in the city, a promise of excitement that was always kept.

Memories … I remember Deckard in *Blade Runner*, murmuring "Memories. You're talking about memories." Trying to grasp that memories implanted in repli-cants cushioned the shock of their brief lives.

These memories of which I am writing are not memories at all. They are digital images coupling with your own. Those stars in the summer sky are pixels darkening on your monitor. Or ink squeezed onto a white page by a printer. The moment these words are written and sent into cyberspace, they become part of something else. Part of a different molecular matrix, part of a larger mind.

Memories … cushioning the shock of our brief lives.

The digital world that so many of us loved just a few years ago is already gone. It has become the ubiquitous sub-text of our lives.

These days, we are all in the business of the construction of reality. Literature—the creation and discovery of meaning and value—used to be a special case. Then the Romantic poets said that everyone was a poet, that all reality was "half perceived and half created," and poets simply did it a little better.

When Vance Packard told a popular audience in the fifties of "hidden per-suaders" in advertisements, it was a revelation. Now we don't have to board a plane to go to Disneyland, we merely have to get out of bed. We live inside simulations, in a sanitized landscape, under which imagineers are pushing buttons, flipping switches, smothering alternative voices. They can even make things vanish.

"The Disappeared," those thousands of men and women that vanished into unmarked graves, ceased to exist, their presence no longer magnified by the minds of those who knew them. In the digital world too, we cease to exist when our images are no longer magnified or replicated.

The CIA-drugs-Contra connection, disappeared by a swarm of false assertions. The reality of UFO phenomena, disappeared into the manufacture of crazy worlds inhabited by "useful idiots." The horror of war, disappeared into "cool" images of smart bombs smoking down chimneys, digital images insulating us from our own experience.

Leon Panetta, former Chief of Staff at the White House, said he was once awakened in the middle of the night by the Secret Service.

"A plane has crashed into the White House!"

Panetta roused himself. "What kind of plane?"

"Well, according to CNN …"

Panetta exploded. "Will you stick your head out of the window and look at the plane and tell me what you see?"

Somalia was the first invasion covered by cameras and lights already on the beach to welcome soldiers wading through the surf. But the digital world is a two-edged sword. The will of the Last Great Superpower was broken by a thirty-second videotape of a Marine dragged behind a jeep.

Outside on a summer night, the stars look still and timeless, as if nothing is exploding. Nothing disappearing.

The other night, several of our many kids came and went. The house was alive once more with their noisy life. Then they scattered again. We must have looked to them as they left as I remember that uncle and aunt in southern Indiana, an image of reassurance that stays there after they're gone.

Now I am outside, looking up at Cassiopeia. On a good night, the Andromeda galaxy is a smear of light, but beyond the reach of my telescope, galaxies explode and civilizations vanish. That house in Indiana has had several other owners now. The neighbors who came and went have moved away or died, as all of my family died. The trees they planted have grown tall, but someone else sits in their shade.

What do we know of our place in the scheme of things, of secrets kept not only by those who think they have good reasons but by the universe itself? What has the digital world done but accelerate the construction of realities, the dark bars of our locked cage?

Memories … the mystery of a molecular nexus, a biomechanical process turning into a meaningful image. The digital world is a repository for memories fading fast, oh fast, in media that flake and peel, software that can't even turn the corner of a century without a shrill hysterical shriek.

Digital dreams, under the silence of indifferent stars. The sound of footsteps far away disappearing into an imaginary house. Clocks melt, trains race out of chimneys. E-mail is deleted, systems go down. Yet the will to build and persist persists, life loving life, mystery and passion of which even digital images dare not dream.

The Power of Love   *October 10, 1998*

Cyberspace hangs by a thread, a tenuous connection not always visible when we focus on chips and switches, the speed of connectivity, the sizes of our drives. The hardware is a visible image of something less tangible that quickens our network life, making us skip and hop like spring lambs.

The ubiquity of electronic connectivity is the context of our lives. As the interface becomes more seamless and invisible, we notice it less and less, like the fact of speech. It becomes "space" in which we live and move and have our being.

Context is content. McLuhan said it clearly in the guise of a digital prophet, but others have said it before. That is a truth the apprehension of which immediately causes a contextual shift in our lives. We see the landscape from a new point of reference.

When Yobie Benjamin, Chief Knowledge Officer of Cambridge Technology Partners, says that real power consists of moving from node to node within the network, seeing the system now from this point of view, now from that, he is speaking of the freedom of multi-nodal scanning, the capacity to "hyperjump" inside a system by an exercise of will and intention. In cyberspace, however, the mind exercising that prerogative is the hive mind of collective humanity. That may have always been true but today the images and symbols of the Net function as dye in the arteries of that hive mind, visible and outward signs of a real and inward animating spirit.

Columbus, McLuhan reminded us, was a mapmaker before he explored. Interacting with technologies that made maps possible, he internalized a new set of possibilities that percolated into his heart and mind until they ignited. Then he set sail. But he was merely an aperture, one opening through which a new horizon of possibility was disclosing itself. It was humankind in its restless quest for mapping space and time that set sail for a new world.

Columbus did not really think he would fall off the edge, but plenty of people live their lives as if they do. During times of radical change, the edge is the new center, speeding toward the dissolving center at a faster and faster pace. Maybe that's what Robert Galvin meant when he said that every idea that made a critical difference at Motorola began its life as a minority opinion. Or Shaw when he said that all great truth begins life as blasphemy.

Two hundred years ago, the English conceived of themselves as the center of everything, their colonies as the edge. In fact, for those who had eyes to see and ears to hear, colonies like the United States were already the new center. Today, we think of our island earth as the center and "outer space" as a whirligig of concentric planes or rings turning wildly about ourselves, when in fact the orbital slots of the earth, the colonization of near earth space, our evolution toward participation in transgalactic civilization, already constitute the center. Just as "the Soviet Union" was recently the name of a country that vied for dominance in "outer space," the names of all of our bases are passing into the inconstant storage device of historical memory.

When all things are morphing into goal states that we individuals have difficulty imagining but which our hive mind seems to anticipate, it is more important than ever to trust the process. Trust mitigates our fear of the edges. Once we break through fear, there is nothing but space, sheer possibility. Then we can fly.

Because of my different history—the early loss of parents, a self-conscious search for identity on the margins of other cultures—I have lived much of my life on the edge. That can be said of any minority group as dominant cultures define them. But marginalization is a gift. Those inside a dominant culture do not need to know when their self-perception blurs into a comforting myth, but minorities must know the difference between statement and behavior. Their well being, if not their lives, are at stake, and they do not have the luxury of not knowing what people in the dominant culture really mean. I am useful as a consultant to people who have always lived at the center because center-dwellers need edge-dwellers as pathfinders these days to name the behaviors that work in a world that is always on edge.

Because the center of a network or web is wherever we are, and no one else is displaced by our presence at the center, power is exercised in a web by participating and contributing, not by dominating and controlling. We know that our own heads are not the universe, we know that the symbols and images of our belief systems are maps and not the territory. We know that we are nodes or modules in a web or network vast beyond our comprehension. We are moments of self-luminous knowing in a transitory pattern made up of the conscious conversation of sentient life everywhere.

Still, we must take care of ourselves, we must manage practicalities, because if we don't, who will? But if that's all we do, we diminish ourselves. We are more than selfish little clods of earth, as Shaw said, whining and complaining that the world will not devote itself to making us happy. We do not own the world, we are owned by it, and our real fulfillment lies in making this firefly moment burn as brightly as we can.

The field of subjectivity, a skein of self-consciousness, animates our lives even as it knits us into a single diaphanous fabric. Human nets and electric nets connect at a nexus where the sparks fly, but power in that Net derives from our will and intention. How we set the arrow of our lives in the bow of intentionality creates the shape of the target. When intentionality is fused with the deep knowledge of contingency and belonging, we have ignition, we have blast-off.

That's when mountains move.

The Field of Subjectivity   *October 18, 1998*

Back in the days when the Human Potential Movement emerged on the West Coast, we heard a lot about the "technology of consciousness." That was a way of saying that the structures of human possibility are definable, and those who leverage their understanding of how humans work are "power up" on those who stay asleep.

Those intensive weekends were big on "intentionality." The concept was taken, perhaps, beyond the limits within which it made sense, but that's how we discovered what those limits were. We would never have reached so far had we not tried to reach further. And, that's how we learn. We seldom get it perfectly right. Aristotle described the Golden Mean as a plumb line across which we tack back and forth, headed for the source of the wind. The goal is to sail closer and closer to the wind, and the wind is the Tao, the energy of the universe. Aligning ourselves with the Tao is like catching a wave. Maybe that's what Jews, Christians and Moslems mean when they talk about being aligned with "the will of God," i.e. God's ultimate intentions.

The Human Potential Movement was also a way to invent communities. In the absence of extended families and stable communities, we needed to make them up. When castles crumble, we learn to live in space stations, docking in modular fashion. Those weekends were opportunities to define norms and symbols, create some kind of structure, a sense of coherence, in a new world in which we were all immigrants. Traditions had to be created from nothing and sustained by agreement—sustained, that is, like all social constructions of reality, by our deeper intentionality.

I learned the meaning of intentionality when planning an all-day intensive experience for a parish I served in Salt Lake City as a young Episcopal priest. I designed a day that I hoped would deliver an experience of real transformation. A week before the event, only twenty people had registered. I was disappointed and resentful. Those feelings made it easy to blame the people of the community for not doing what I wanted. But there was a small gap, a critical synapse, between those feelings and that "space of possibility" from whence cometh our deeper intentions. I saw that I had a choice: I could use their non-response to justify doing nothing more or I could choose to manifest my real intentions.

I spent every day of the next week from early morning until late night telephoning every one of the 250 families of the parish to enroll them in the event. When I hung up from the last call, I knew that even if the event were cancelled, the transformation had already happened. My willingness to take responsibility for manifesting my real intention made it happen.

Eighty-five people showed up instead of twenty. The event worked. But more important, every time I subsequently heard myself try to justify not doing what I said I intended to do, I knew I was lying. I discovered that my real limits were far beyond what I previously thought.

Interaction with our technologies helps to frame how we hold ourselves, individually and collectively, as possibilities for action in the world. The "technology of consciousness" is a way of defining the field of subjectivity that enables us to leverage the truth about ourselves, that we have as much freedom and power, as Charles Rike said, as we can have, which is more freedom and power than we like to believe. When we finished those long weekends, we not only knew that but knew that we knew.

These themes—intentionality, intentional communities, life in cyberspace—will be explored in coming weeks. Today I just want to say that we live within a field of subjectivity that defines our essential qualities as intelligent living beings. Within that field is the power of intentionality, that is, the capacity to seize once again the reins of our lives when we have dropped them.

A friend e-mailed a story this morning about an implant in the brain of a paralyzed man that enables him to move a cursor on a screen. This is the first direct communication between the human brain and a computer.

"It's like we're making the mouse the patient's brain," said Roy Bakay, one of the doctors who developed the technology. Because the device is implanted in an area of the brain that produces signals that cause movement, researchers told the stroke victim to think about grabbing a glass. His brain signals are amplified and transmitted from a coil on his head, which points the cursor at icons.

We are walking on shaky ground here, because the Cartesian belief that the mind and body are separate has died hard. We are learning to understand that we live inside a field of subjectivity defined by our genes, a designed capacity for structuring the world. Like the ape that learned to draw and sketched the bars of his own cage, we are learning that every thing we say about the "world" in fact reveals how we construct that world in the first place. And how we are constructed to construct that world.

The network that is the computer is linked to the human network or perhaps to all intelligent life or all life or, for that matter, all matter. A complex pattern of energy and information, life blurs at the edges into its raw materials. But the engine is intentionality, that quality within our field of subjectivity that lets us aim the arrow of our lives. When the arrow hits, we discover that we have also created the target.

The energies of the universe are mutable and plastic. We think, therefore the cursor moves, whether moved by a mouse or an image in our minds. The universe is a point-and-click wraparound multi-dimensional interface in which we are immersed, multi-dimensional point-and-click beings whose capacity for creativity and meaningful action is so much greater than we think or dare to dream.

But To What Purpose?   *March 20, 1999*

A scientist writes that the way we humans evolved as hunter-gatherers is how we are still built. Another writes about the "intelligence of vision," noting that seeing takes up nearly half our brain and generates the structure of the world we take for granted. Another struggles to imagine how alien species might interpret our civilization, discovering as he does some of the presuppositions of our perceptual field.

We bring our built-in apparatus for seeing and perceiving to the world on a computer monitor, where we build a simulation in its image. Because that simulated space is fresh, we can still see the roadwork, but the infrastructure of the digital world is becoming as invisible as the infrastructure of literacy and speech. Chips are disappearing into every aspect of our lives—communication, transportation, physical environments, clothing, and ultimately, ourselves.

The imaginary gardens on my monitor often seem more real than the trees in my back yard. Most of the time I don't even notice the real trees. We don't yet live in the world constructed by computers that way, but we will. The world created and disclosed by computing is becoming an essential dimension of who we believe ourselves to be. And who, therefore, we are.

Most of us who love online life remember the first time we tumbled into the rabbit hole, falling headlong into a domain as magical as Alice's underground. I remember downloading the first browser around ten o'clock at night. When I next looked up it was four in the morning. That knowledge engine rearranged data into forms that coupled effortlessly with my perceptual apparatus. It was a world of digital symbols filled with projections of myself as it moved among them, thinking it was leaving the room and extending itself "out there." The exploration was really, of course, inside the consensual space we agree to hallucinate together.

What is it about this domain that compels such a response? What seduces us to stay up all night, fooling around for hours as we build communal worlds or play with these symbols, using them as levers to turn gears in the "real" world?

The nexus between nested levels of symbolic reality and the field of human subjectivity, the extensible domain of human consciousness, haunts me. It is the point at which consciousness connects with any or all of those levels, which unfold like a pop-up book or—perhaps—spiral up like a fractal, open-ended, evolving, and free. From sub-atomic particles to machine language to top-level symbolic constructions called "culture," they fold into one another like steps in an Escher stairway, creating a world we half-create, as Wordsworth said, and half-perceive. And then believe.

This week I spoke with Joe McMoneagle, a "remote viewer" for many years in military intelligence programs. Remote viewing is the ability to be present in our consciousness to events or places at which we are not physically present. Called a "natural" by observers because of the detail of his best "hits," McMoneagle engaged in a disciplined kind of clairvoyance using structured protocols.

McMoneagle discovered that the world is not what he thought it was. He had to reinvent continuously the images he used as maps of reality as his psychic adventures exploded the consensual reality he had been taught to believe.

The images of the world we internalize from life online also become obsolete each time we turn off the computer.

McMoneagle's exploration of the deeper levels of consciousness was like learning to dive. We are unaware of the ocean until we hear about it or see pictures of a reef. Then we go to the coast and look down into the water. Arriving at the land/water interface is crucial: we learn firsthand that oceans are real, find guides to teach us the rules, and practice.

When we dive for the first time, we're astonished. We learn to go deeper, stay longer, deal with real dangers. After a while, we're as comfortable under water as on land, and when we speak of the "world," we mean life under water as well as on land.

Symbols are like face plates on our masks, invisible themselves but enabling us to see. Symbol-making and symbol-using constitutes the technology of consciousness as tool-using constitutes the technology of a culture. Human physiology is a kind of technology too, as invisible as language, defining the way we evolved to gather and hunt.

Online life changes what we mean by "reality." McMoneagle has difficulty talking about "reality" with people who have not experienced what he has. He has to build a modular interface that somehow connects both his experience and the experience of someone who has never gone diving. In the same way, building a computer interface that lets ordinary users couple with the many levels of the digital world is more than "usability." It is participation in a revolutionary act of mutual transformation.

Computer codes are languages, mental artifacts, and modular units of shared perceptual worlds, all at the same time. McMoneagle's description of exploring the deeper waters of consciousness is a template for learning how to move with clear intentionality among the nested levels of symbols that fold into one another in the digital world. Remote viewing is a function of the intentionality of the viewer, not the so-called "physical" world. Nor is a computer network fully defined by chips, switches or code; the network is defined above all by the intentionality of the users.

It is easy to lose ourselves in the act of building simulations that our brains think are real and forget that intentionality animates the network like a ghost in the machine. Inside the domain of human consciousness—and we are always inside—we are bow, arrow and target. We define ourselves as a spectrum of possibilities, choose one, and do it. The symbols we think we use as tools disappear, the nested levels built of those symbols collapse, and we see in that moment our responsibility for what we are building instead of pretending we're merely technicians or just along for the ride.

A Model for
Managing Multiple Selves   *September 19, 2000*

Just about everybody knows by now that our interaction with networked computers has created a different sense of ourselves. Our lives are affected powerfully by what we experience online and we think and act as if we are online even when we are off. The wiring gets changed around inside. We become nodes in a network.

One way offline life calibrates with online life is modularity. The various dimensions of our lives are modular now. We can mix and match them as we choose.

In the conservative upper midwest where I currently live, people used to live lives that were all of a piece. If you were raised in a religion, that's what you were. You chose a career and stuck with it. You married someone and (mostly) stayed married. And of course, identity was fixed. To think of reinventing one's core identity was literally impossible.

Now, however, we reinvent ourselves again and again. We change careers or vocations, we marry several times or not at all, we convert to other religions, and above all, we sometimes experience a strange kind of dissonance that accompanies the realization that—within limits—we are who we choose to be.

Our identities and selves are modular and fluid.

Even if we do not drop out of sight and surface in some witness protection program of our own making with new digital identities and simulated histories, life is experienced more and more as a sequence of developmental stages that are growing in number. When Daniel Levinson wrote "Seasons of a Man's Life" in 1978, the landscape beyond middle age was shrouded in mist. "Old age" was an undifferentiated haze rather than a sequence of distinct segments, each with its challenges and tasks.

Not any more.

Our life span has increased 100% in the past 300 years. In this century, a life span of 150-200 years is likely.

With so many modular segments to couple together into a coherent life, how will we maintain the useful illusion, the necessary fiction of a coherent Self that includes and transcends all of those modules? Will the process by which experience devolves into an integrated self, transformed alchemically into wisdom, continue for two centuries? Will it stretch to fit the elastic lives our selves must learn to lead?

As we augment memory, cognition and sensation through computer networks, biotechnology and genetic engineering, and nanotechnology, we bring new cyborg selves into existence. The distinction between natural and artificial is nearly gone. As we press toward the limits of inherited long-term memory storage, like hunter-gatherer brains, we might well confound the ability to link seamlessly the diverse experiences of multiple selves over the span of many careers, families, and identities. It isn't the "atoms" of experience that we risk losing but the way they collaborate to build a mature self.

As we switch off the symptoms of aging and replace parts that we don't even know yet are parts, we will need a new model for identity and self. Our ancestors did not have to reinvent themselves. This challenge is less about technology and more about the spiritual dimensions of our lives.

I suggest using the reincarnation model to imagine and design a transcendent Self that persists, an integrated Self that survives the changes and chances of an attenuated life.

During past life regressions, a person enters a meditative state and uses memory, imagination, or both to move through images of a lifetime until one passes right through the moment of birth and begins remembering or imagining images of other lives.

If those images are only imagined, that's the end of the quest. But in those cases in which images can be corroborated with historical details from other sources, the useful and familiar distinctions of parapsychology immediately vanish.

If one "remembers," calls into consciousness, an image of an event that is "real," then one might be (1) remembering one's own experience or (2) telepathically accessing another's memories or (3) clairvoyantly reading a record—a tombstone, a ship's register, a diary—accessed on the unconscious level.

In other words, if an image is "real," it can be correlated with objective historical records, then the boundaries between categories vanish just as the distinctions between illusory selves disappear. The images exist, not in a the mind of a little self, but in the mind of a transcendent Self that includes all the little selves and all their little lives.

Reincarnation can never be proven but some do recover memories or images during deep meditative states that point to the transmigration of those images in the medium of a larger consciousness.

Arthur Koestler said that all organisms are holons, which are characterized by differentiation, cooperation, and boundaries. A cell is a holon. A cell may look like a community of interdependent parts or like a unit in a more highly organized body. A principality may look like an independent duchy or like part of a unified Europe. In the same way, a self may contain differentiated modular dimensions of consciousness or a self may be one of many selves contained by a Self.

Merely to imagine this model is to bring it into being. To describe it is to create it. That's how consciousness works. Creation and discovery are one thing seen from different points of view.

Naming our Selves is a creative act, but it's not for the faint-hearted. The faint-hearted ask others who they are, exchanging their identities for an illusory security, selling themselves cheap.

Identity is destiny. Our task is to name ourselves, and we will, once we know who we are.

To plunge into the darkness of inchoate possibility and say, let there be light, then let that light play across a landscape of multiple possibilities ... this is the joy of intentional acts of creation. Deriving an identity from history, which in turn is merely a suitable myth, and a vision of a future that bounces us into the life we design like a springboard or trampoline. We are who we think we were, but we can always—with a mere word—transform who we think we were into who we choose to be.

The Next Bend of the River   *December 5, 2000*

A younger friend called recently to discuss his perplexity as he moves through what we sometimes call "the age thirty transition." This is a time of coming to terms with the growing awareness that our twenties, which we thought meant adulthood, was really a kind of post-adolescence.

Around thirty, the upward call of taking our place in the world as an adult is felt more keenly. It is often accompanied, as it was in my friend's case, by the dissolution of the model or map of the world he had created in his twenties and thought would be permanent.

In his case, the playing field is the world of "computer security." A brilliant young technophile, he had previously defined his horizons of possibility in the depths of computer networks. Now that "computer security" is morphing into one aspect of security-in-general, its power to seize his imagination is waning.

In short, he is growing, listening to the whispers of other voices in other rooms of his soul, discovering dimensions of himself which arrive with the fresh surprise of a real tequila sunrise.

In retrospect, I think he will find greater continuity between the larger Self he discovers himself to be and all those "little selves" we invent in the process of adapting to internal as well as external changes. Yet that Self too changes appearance as we grow.

This process is happening in the wider world too. Humankind is not what it thought it was. Our species is having an "identity crisis."

We have options for choosing identities thanks to various technologies that we never had before. In the film *Blade Runner*, an android who thought he was human wondered about an android who thought she was human—"how can it not know what it is?"

That question is being asked of us by our cyborg face in the funhouse mirror.

We are transforming ourselves through enhancements to cognition, memory, and our senses, then looking at ourselves through those enhancements. There's a momentary disconnect between what we see and what we used to see, a parallax view of our Selves.

So which is real? The world seen without glasses that we have been taught to call "blurred" or the sharply focused world seen through the "corrective lenses" of our technologies?

If we told someone from the twelfth century about "developmental stages" like adolescence or middle-age, they would find them unthinkable. As we extend longevity toward 150-200 years, our designer progeny will find our developmental stages equally unreal.

During transitions that call our identities into question, we often look to organizational structures to define who we are. We surrender autonomy in exchange for the comforting illusion that an identity derived from a corporation, a nation, a religion, will provide security. But those structures too are in transition, their boundaries dissolving. Religions are dividing, merging and emerging, forming alliances. The conflicting norms, intentions, and agendas of countries, multi-nationals, and NGOs (non-government organizations) make our loyalties uncertain, our social roles ambiguous, our identities confused.

Looking backward toward organizational structures that made sense in the past for self-definition does not solve the real questions of our lives. Yet the new organizational structures that are emerging at a higher level of complexity do not yet have names.

The intentional construction of identity is one of the biggest challenges facing individuals, nations, and our trans-planetary society.

Some will shrink in fear from ambiguity and complexity, falling back on tribal identities defined by dissolving religious, ethnic, or national boundaries. To become aware of the transitory nature of those structures would make them feel lost. They are lost anyway, but refusing to become conscious provides the consolation prize of not knowing they are lost.

Someone in a seminar recently objected that my description of a cyborg future made him feel helpless. "Good!" I said. "When we started, you were just as helpless - you were at minus two—but didn't know it. Now you're at minus one: You're helpless and you know it. The next step is Ground Zero: What will you do about it?"

The only thing any of us can really do is move through a zone of annihilation that challenges everything we believed to be true about ourselves and experience the vertigo of freefall as our new identities emerge.

An astronaut on his first spacewalk outside MIR described a feeling of vertigo that never left. He felt the whole time he was clinging to the exterior of the space station that he was falling off a cliff. He had to use considerable mental energy to locate himself in the void in a way that anchored him.

That anchor is the Self we discover and create in freefall.

A field of gravity merely disguises the truth that we are always in freefall. Developmental stages, those nested identities that emerge fractal-like as we grow, create that kind of field, letting us ground ourselves in the void.

New organizational structures will be defined by boundaries big enough to be functional (for now) at the level of complexity appropriate to current social, economic, and political circumstances, just as nation states emerged in the past few centuries to organize commerce and political life at a different level of complexity.

Then Humankind will look into the mirror of its collective consciousness and see a new Self, a Self that is multi-nodal, multi-dimensional, and non-local. Today that Self is still vague and inchoate, a mist on the mirror. But one day that spirit will quicken and become flesh.

Courage is the willingness to look into that mirror and not to forget what we see, then say what we see, thus defining new possibilities for Humankind. The second level of courage is the willingness not to confuse ourSelves for that image ... to persist in freefall, fixed in the void, aware that our flicker of self-consciousness is a wrinkle in spacetime, a firefly like MIR, a fold or flow in a larger fabric.

What's His Name   *August 12, 2001*

I have never had a single original idea.

I recently came to this humbling truth from two directions.

The first was triggered by a recent article on the evolution of modular programming. Alan Kay is a name frequently connected to that event. Kay has had a brilliant career. One biography states that he is "one of the fathers of the idea of Object Oriented Programming."

But Kay learned about modular programming from an anonymous Air Force programmer before he went to Xerox PARC.

We know Kay's name ... but we don't know the name of the man who made that breakthrough. He is the Unknown Programmer, one of the million minds that created the hive in which we are buzzing today.

Identity is a function of boundaries. Identity is destiny.

Who we believe ourselves to be determines what we think we are capable of being and doing. That's why seminars, intensives, or retreats designed to blow away our presuppositions about ourselves and replace them with farther horizons can have so much power in our lives. When we draw the boundaries out farther, we can imagine ourselves doing what our larger identities allow us to do. We are exhilarated at the feelings of renewal and rebirth that attend such events.

That's also why the only way to deny another person their intrinsic freedom and power is to convince them that their boundaries are constrained. When we believe that our power is limited, we don't use it.

In times like ours, when boundaries are dissolving and redrawing themselves in ways more appropriate to the social, political, and economic complexities of our trans-global and increasingly trans-planetary culture, most of us are not bored. We may be exhilarated, we may be terrified—we imagine ourselves hiking the red deserts of Mars or we think that the Taliban are pretty good role models—but we are not bored.

Many breakthrough discoveries are indexed in cells in the matrix we call "history" with the names of "geniuses" attached. Genius is a relatively new concept, one of the consequences of the Renaissance, along with notions of individuality, ideas of rights and intellectual property, and boundaries around "nation states." One can imagine monks toiling in medieval monasteries to create illuminated manuscripts having a hard time trying to conceive of a "genius" creating a "work" the rights to which he "owns."

The output of their collective effort was the result of an open source model of reality. The truth is that, like Alan Kay inheriting principles from a nameless programmer who hacked modular programming, the transmission of ideas is the result of aggregated intelligence that creates conditions in which ideas grow and prosper, a culture that fosters tinkering and the search for ingenious solutions, one that encourages the sharing of information. That culture is hacking culture in its essence.

Ideas want to be free because it is their essence to be free. Every breakthrough idea is always the result of thousand of minds adding their little bit to the process until one day the critical mass of converging possibilities is focussed through a "genius" who stumbles into a solution. We don't know how to give a Nobel Prize to everybody in the world.

Our model of reality matters. Our model of reality determines the questions we can think, how we define problems, look for solutions. Our model determines who we think we are.

Our model of reality determines our identity. And identity is destiny.

I mentioned coming to this from a second direction as well.

Life is humbling. The longer we live, the shorter the time we have to live. That foreshortening of perspective does interesting things to the clarity of our vision.

Every time I have an insight, it's only a matter of time before I read or hear of someone else having that insight too. My original thinking is always a symptom of the spirit of the time looking for minds through which to articulate itself.

When I was in college, I saved what I wrote, wanting to preserve my original insights for posterity. Now I can't get ideas into the world fast enough, hoping that someone may find them useful for the moment, the way a chimpanzee will pick up this or that stick to get honey from a beehive.

Nobody owns that stick. Nobody owns ideas. Humanity is a hive mind processing data and experience, creating transitory models of reality in which energy and information momentarily flow.

Individuality is an illusion, a convenient illusion, true, but an illusion nevertheless. We are all part of a single evolution in which the elements of the earth seek to become conscious. Now that we inhabit our planet like a brain outgrowing its head, now that we know that evolution includes the elements of all planets seeking to become conscious, we are realizing that boundaries around our species or any species are a convenience appropriate to our current stage of growth or understanding.

Every time we encounter the Other with a full awareness of what is happening, we flip into another way entirely of understanding our identity, our destiny.

Meanwhile, I still act as if I know, because I must. It helps to move the day along. It's still how "I" think about things.

Within that model, what can I articulate in the local dialect of my tribe? That we are not who we think we are? That our origin and destination are not what we think?

Not this. Not that.

Everything I know is a gift from others, here there and everywhere.

The herd is a peasant culture, hunkering down, eyes on the ground, suspicious of the new. Despite my exhilaration, I too share the destiny of the herd. The herd's beating heart is my heart, its hot flanks my flanks, trembling with anticipation.

Eyes on the ground as it brightens suddenly in the night, unwilling to raise my gaze, risk blindness in the inexplicable splendor of a midnight sunrise.

No No No   *September 10, 2001*

That may not sound like an affirmation, but it is.

Sometimes No is the shortest route to Yes.

A colleague, for example, recently included this quote from a "success expert" in his newsletter:

"Whatever you vividly imagine, ardently desire, sincerely believe, and enthusiastically act upon ... must inevitably come to pass!"

That sounds like a lot of heavy lifting for a mere mortal. We hear this kind of advice a lot from seminar leaders, inspirational speakers, and fire-walking gurus as we channel-surf infomercials, shopping networks, and religious TV.

I think life works the other way around, inversely in proportion to the effort of the ego. So I reversed it, giving that fortune-cookie message a Taoist twist, flavored with wu wei or "not doing."

"Whatever you can not imagine, do not desire, in which you do not believe, and do not act upon ... inevitably comes to pass."

The first saying focuses on the figure in the ground; it speaks to the little ego-tipped pyramid-of-self that we think we are. The second focuses more on the ground, the four fifths of the iceberg under the surface.

That's the problem with oracular truth: the opposite is nearly always just as true. Oracular truth is more like a mobius strip than a yes/no binary system. When we look inside its bent reflections for the "inner truth," we confront our own fun-house image sliding along the twisting strips. It's all all true and it's all all false.

Untruth lies in things not mentioned, said John Steinbeck, but maybe truth does too. Context creates content, but once the context is visible, it too becomes content in an unseen context. Russian dolls, Chinese boxes, fractal landscapes. Distinctions are a matter of convenience. The "ultimate truth" is just another approximation.

I listen in my car to audio tapes of college lectures on all sorts of topics. Keeps the brain engaged inside that sensory deprivation tank.

Focusing on the words of a complex presentation is like staying with the flow of your own mind during a period of meditation. When you catch yourself watching a leaf on the surface of the river as it moves downstream, you detach yourself and come back to the still flow in the center of your mind. In the car, you think you're listening but suddenly notice that you slipped into "rain man space," driving automatically for minutes or miles while your mind went somewhere else. While it was elsewhere, the part of you that always pays attention paid attention to the road.

Maybe that's what always drives, even when we think the steering wheel is in our hands.

Anyway, the lecture series was about relativity and quantum physics. The professor had arrived at the necessity for connecting the very small and the very large, particle physics and cosmology. His vivid word-pictures of the universe at various stages of development were like a movie-in-reverse as it rewound toward the Big Bang. The cooler universe became hotter, complexity and distinctions between things became simpler and simpler ... and suddenly everything erupts from the non-point of the Big Bang, boundaries identities and distinctions exploding from behind the false face of the first trillionth of a second when everything was just one unified still-mysterious Thing.

Our intellectual journey in search of "ultimate reality" parallels that moving picture. Electricity and magnetism became electromagnetism. Then electromagnetism and the weak nuclear force became the electroweak force. Soon the electroweak force will include the color force, and one day when that grand unified force includes gravity too we will describe in a few equations the unity of all things.

But try to do that now and the universe retorts: no no no.

Not this. Not that.

No. No. No.

When I experience such moments, it's better to pull over and think about things. Safer, too.

The older I get, the more I find that reflection and contemplation become the locus of my spirituality rather than the joyful participation in the sorrows of the world that characterized my earlier years. Love consists more of understanding or waiting patiently or saying nothing at all. These days, the late summer flowers, the first fall of a few leaves, the earlier sunsets, remind me that autumn is delicious, a crisp memory of summer gone that tastes like a tart apple straight from the tree.

The great lake along the trees and ravines near my home has been tranquil. It almost looks like the ocean if one doesn't think too much about it. Tall cumulus clouds obscure the vanishing point just behind the sky and the horizon as I kill the engine and turn off the words.

The complexity and distinctiveness of everything is of course a function of my brain and its favorite interface, my eyes, as they have been taught to discern and design the sensory input of my life. Language teaches us how to see, our hive teaches us how to dance, how to tell one another where to find the honey.

What enters a black hole in our current conceptual model becomes infinitely dense, which we know is crazy. We know it goes somewhere, but we don't know where. Our minds stop at the vanishing point. Our distinctions collapse into a few forces defined by mathematics and then, one trillionth of a second before the beginning at the end of our trek, the vanishing point skips a beat and disappears over the horizon.

Behind its mask, Medusa waits. If we tear off her mask, before we can say what we see, we turn to stone.

It's not because we don't know how to say it. Oh, we do. We know. We know that it must be like knowing how to drive when our mind is elsewhere, then suddenly noticing. We went away and returned, but that to which we returned was not the little ego-topped self that thought it left.

It's something else. It's …

No. Not that.

No. No. No.

Absolutely not.

Political Implications

Freedom and the Net   *July 4, 1997*

The recent decision by the Clinton Administration to advocate a free and open Internet and the U. S. Supreme Court decision in favor of free speech on the Net are acknowledgements that you can't catch an avalanche coming downhill.

It's always wisest—and takes less energy—to ride a horse in the direction it's going. The nature of the Net undermines control of the free flow of information. When computer hackers say that "information wants to be free," they don't mean we ought to loot cyberspace, but that ideas and information in their very essence will propagate, that powerful ideas are contagious and multiply in the petri dish that is human culture.

A single idea, ripening at the right time, cannot be stopped by all the NOs in the world.

For freedom to be meaningful, of course, we need a guarantee of privacy. Only strong encryption can guarantee the secure boundaries we need to be free. But that's another conversation.

The partisans of social control who want to impose mandatory rule-based behavior on the world are marshalling their forces for a counter attack. When your own safety requires that everyone live under the same rigid structure, you can never rest. Until the Ayatollahs have the guns and can write the rules, their anxiety keeps them awake at night, no matter how well the rest of us are sleeping. When one side is willing to compromise and the other can't, real dialogue is impossible.

Rules aren't bad, but rules are the beginning, not the end. Beyond all rules, there are meta-rules. Rules spell out exactly what to do in every situation. Meta-rules say, "Evaluate the situation and do the right thing."

How we position ourselves between rules and meta-rules determines our ability to tolerate ambiguity and complexity, trust the process of life, and trust others to regulate themselves without the benefit of our advice—letting parents accept responsibility for using net censors, for example, rather than censoring the Net for them. Trusting others to learn how to be experts at living their own lives.

Which brings us to expert systems.

Expert systems are programs that attempt to capture the "rules" according to which human experts make decisions. Before neural nets and fuzzy logic, expert systems were strictly rule based.

"Knowledge engineers" attempted to codify the behavior of human experts as a series of if-then rules regulated by logic gates. When they elicited the heuristics or rules of thumb by which experts came to conclusions, however, they discovered that experts broke the rules all the time ... and knew WHEN to break them.

Beginners need context-free rules because they lack the wisdom of experience. Experts engage with the flow of life in all its complexity and richness. Experts respond intuitively to the bullets of real life fired at us every day at point blank range.

Example: Tim Hoeksema, President of Midwest Express Airlines, one of the great examples of a quality program in action, spoke of how hard it is for beginners to catch the "meta-rule" behind the written rules.

A ticket agent responded by the book when a woman at the counter requested a senior citizen discount. The rules required a picture ID to verify that she was over 65. Since she did not have one, the agent told her to pay full fare and send a copy of her ID later to get a refund.

Hoeksema received an angry letter from the woman's daughter, who had been with her at the counter. The daughter was in her 70s and noted that anyone could see that her mother was well into her 90s. But the ticket agent went by the rules because he did not know how to transcend the rules and access the reason for which the rules were written in the first place—to ensure fair, incomparable customer service.

Example: Huckleberry Finn, at the end of the novel of the same name, was told to return the slave Jim to his rightful owner or face (1) legal sanctions for harboring stolen property and (2) eternal damnation for breaking God's laws.

Huck agonized all night before choosing to break the rules. "I'll go to hell then," he concluded.

The meta-rule—"do the right thing" or "do the loving thing"—required that he break the rules sanctioned by society and conventional religion.

Trusting people to "do the right thing"—or learn from their mistakes how to do it next time—can drive rule-based people crazy.

So the one supreme rule is ... if you don't know when to break the rules ... don't break the rules.

We only feel a need to impose a rigid structure on the flow of life when we are afraid that in our cores we are chaotic, that we are in danger of losing control at any moment, and without training wheels, we will never keep the bicycles of our lives upright. Those who live life out of a more secure center concede to others the freedom to learn from their experience. They trust the process of life to be self-correcting. Ultimately that trust is the ground of real faith, a faith that intuits an intelligence and energy animating and sustaining the universe and trusts it to do what it does best.

The Net, a simulation and celebration of life, invites the same kind of trust. That doesn't mean that anything goes. "There are roughly zones," wrote Robert Frost, boundaries that we recognize when we cross them. Aristotle defined the Golden Mean as a plumb line we need to "true ourselves up" but which we see over our shoulders as we tack back and forth across it. The trick is to tack closer and closer to the wind, measuring progress by our speed and the exhilarating experience of real freedom. We can't do that if we don't have room to maneuver.

The Internet—like the world—is best ruled by letting things take their course.

Life in the Nudist Colony *January 31, 1998*

A funny thing happened on the way to the panopticon—a transformational SNAP! changed all the rules. Life in the nudist colony may never be the same.

Let me explain.

A panopticon is a kind of prison dreamed up by Jeremy Benthem, a nineteenth-century English prison reformer. The cells are wedges, like slices of a pie. In the center rises a tower from which guards can see the prisoners, but the prisoners can't see the guards, or one another. Surveillance is either taking place or may be taking place. Prisoners never know which, so they internalize the possibility of surveillance and behave always as if they were being watched. They become their own guards, what we call "model prisoners."

That used to be a prototype for a totalitarian state. In the electronic era, it's a prototype for the world.

Technology that turned the world into a panopticon invaded our lives quietly, one sensible function at a time.

Take the loss of privacy. Employers always owned work produced by employees but once it was done on networked computers, they could see everything at a glance. Clandestine "sniffers" intercept mail, filch memos. As the NSA listens to the electronic communications of the world, flagging key words or patterns of activity, any person—employer or not—with the means, the motive, and the opportunity can observe the virtual life of a network.

Global Positioning System satellites mean that a vehicle need never get lost again. And also that no one can go so far as to get out of sight.

The intelligent transportation system is being sold as a reasonable way to manage overcrowded corridors. Video surveillance of highways to monitor traffic jams turns into video surveillance, period. Electronic scanning of ID numbers as cars speed through toll booths becomes a universal record of who went where when. It's called "function creep," how things created for one purpose migrate into other domains.

Interlace the data gathered by surveillance with databases that cross-reference every electronic transaction, then mine that data for patterns of behavior ... and we inhabit a panopticon. We are all prisoners and guards, as Andre Gregory said in "My Dinner With Andre," preventing one another from escaping.

Next add the speed (i.e. light) with which behaviors that used to be called "back-stage" (the original definition of "obscene" is an action performed off stage) are brought into our living rooms twenty-four hours a day. The Internet and satellite and cable television are really one thing: a single medium that fuses news and entertainment.

Now let's reflect on the current state of affairs (so to speak) in the White House.

America is a pretty puritanical place. We drool over violence and sex and condemn them at the same time. Anchors on the "nightly news," speaking with the pinched tones of those who hold the high moral ground, told all the details of Diana's death in the guise of an exposé of sleazy tabloids. Last week they rushed every snippet of hearsay onto the screen the minute someone whispered a new accusation. MSNBC sneering at the Drudge Report, Tweedledum reproving Tweedledee.

So far, so good. Business as usual. Public outrage mounted as lurid images were manufactured then magnified by the media. We all have our favorites. Mine was the news-anchor telling parents to "turn down the sound"—psst! psst!—because what followed was going to be soooooo titillating.

But then there came not just a bounce, but a huge elastic bunjee bounce of popular sentiment against the press ... not all of it manipulated, I don't think, by the president's men turning the herd like a pack of dogs. Some of it was caused by the fact that we have simply lived long enough now inside a nudist colony.

The rules are different in a nudist colony. Before we lived in the panopticon, there really was such a thing as privacy. People could have what was called a "private conversation," reasonably certain that no one overheard. There were boundaries between private and public life.

Not any more.

Now everybody knows everything about everybody or can if they want to or pay enough. For a while, we still lived by the old rules and rushed to judgment whenever we saw that someone was naked. But in the brave new digital world, we're all naked, and besides, it's happened so many times, we're a little weary of it all.

In a nudist colony, people act as if everybody is wearing clothes. We have to. What someone else looks like doesn't matter any more, or if it does, it can't matter in the same way.

That's the SNAP! that happened last week. Just as the English and Japanese, crowded onto small islands, learned to be polite so they didn't kill one another, people who live in a panopticon will find ways to respect boundaries ... precisely because we can see everything. Civility and politeness, as William James said of wisdom, consist in knowing what to overlook.

The rigidly righteous can march from left or right; it isn't a question of politics but of the means by which a civil society organizes itself when everyone's life is transparent. The data isn't all in, of course, and this particular story isn't over. But at least for the moment, the media can't say with a straight face that the "news" consists of gossip and hearsay because the people demand it.

The wisdom of democracy is the belief that common people in possession of the evidence and allowed to consult their own minds and hearts will reach a reasonable consensus. The presumption is that those hearts are filled with common sense. Common sense that agrees with Gandhi, "an eye for an eye" means a world in which everyone is blind. That issues an invitation to those who are without sin to cast the first stone.

What Is To Be Done?   *February 7, 1998*

I think it was Disraeli who said: show me a person who is not a liberal at twenty, I'll show you a person with no heart. Show me a person who is not a conservative at fifty, I'll show you a person with no mind.

That's a funny way of saying that when we are young, we believe we can change much more than we can—and a good thing too, or we would never reach so far—but we come to believe, with experience and maturity, that the larger life of our community knows more than reason alone can know. So we acknowledge traditions and institutions as repositories of wisdom, necessary structures that factor in the negatives as well as positives of human behavior.

Something else happens too. As we grow, we shed self-righteousness, recognizing our stake in the order of things and our collusion with societal structures—unjust though they may be—because they give us an advantage.

The spirituality that supports this point of view is passive.

Now, there is certainly a time for "letting go and letting God," a time for "wise passivity," as Wordsworth calls it, a time for aligning our energies with the Tao or the flow of the universe, what Christians call seeking the will of God.

But isn't there a time too to question how a spirituality of acquiescence rationalizes our silence or inaction in the face of sustained terror?

The Internet can be the Mother of Lies, enhancing campaigns of disinformation or creating simulations of reality that we visit like Disneyland, suspending our disbelief in talking mice and ducks and dogs, pretending that the world floats like a sky-city in pastel clouds. The Internet can be a soporific that keeps us sleep-walking, dreamily happy.

But the Internet as a global forum can also be a threat to those who would keep things quiet, whitening out of the landscape the bloodstains we would rather not see. That's why every repressive government threatened by free speech is trying to control access to the Net.

Now, this is the dream-world: as you read that black-and-white description, to the degree that you identified your own society with freedom and the "other side" with repression.. to that degree, we live in cloud-cuckoo-land, where wishes are fishes and all have a fry.

A draft report was released this week by the European Parliament's Office for Scientific and Technological Option Assessment, "An Appraisal of Technologies of Political Control."

The report details the economics and politics of using advanced technologies for population control, surveillance, and torture. The details are chilling, not because we are ... surprised, exactly, but because we prefer not to know so we can act as if we are (1) safe, and (2) innocent.

The United States, joined by other first world countries, regularly exports the most sophisticated instruments of torture and terror to the outlaws of the world. The United States intercepts the world's electronic communications. The United States trains governments who align themselves with our economic and political interests in the efficient use of technologies of torture, electronic surveillance, and population control.

A friend suggested that it might be better not to know. He may be right. I would prefer to sing always a song of daisy-love in the sunlight. But what are we to do when—while we are singing that happy song—we suddenly hear screams coming from the closed room at the end of the hallway? Yes, we wish we had not heard them, but once we have ... what are we to do?

If we refuse to hear, we lose the power to choose. To choose, we must know, and to know, we must stay awake so we can at least ask one another ... shall we ignore what we heard? Or is there still a way to redeem the bloodstained night?

Technology is indifferent to how it is used. The answer to those questions lies in the domain of human freedom and choice. Information and knowledge are preconditions of freedom. In a global society, there must be a global forum in which we can dare to become conscious and deliberate and choose. For all the nonsense on the Internet, it is still the world's one relatively free public forum.

Does anyone really expect the conglomerate mass media to create a forum in which we will learn what is real, engage in reasonable discourse, and make sane and informed choices? Does anyone really believe that their daily newspaper or local news will provide the details—name names, connect the terror to the companies that sell it—instead of filling our minds with sex, street crime, sports and other forms of entertainment, and trivia, the four horsemen of the apocalypse of the mass media?

Maybe that clever quote from Disraeli is not the whole story after all. Maybe maturity does appraise us of the scope of the principalities and powers that rule this world, but that does not quench the passion for truth and justice that still burns within us ... and insists that—once in a while—we go on record with a NO! that is a way of saying YES.

The torturers in Argentina, observed from a neighboring cell, always covered the head of young women with a hood before turning on the electricity. That enabled the men who adjusted the current to her screams to not look into her eyes. When you look into the eyes, one explained, one can see that this is a human being. That can interfere.

The Internet is one means by which we can tap from cell to cell, telling the truth about those screams so faintly heard. Of course if it were our brother or sister being tortured, we would act. So the only relevant question is, who is our brother? Who is our sister? And how long can we keep that hood over their eyes so we can remain quiet ... prosperous ... and indifferent?

Computers, Freedom, and Privacy   *February 21, 1998*

A conference on computers, freedom, and privacy might be the last place one expects to find the deepest expressions of the quest for meaning in our lives, yet there it was, all over the place.

So was evidence of new possibilities for what I call the human-computer symbiot, that new kind of community generated by our symbiotic relationship to our electronic sensory extensions and intelligent networks.

The choices we make now as we take the reins of our own evolution more securely in our hands—with fear and trembling at the perilous task before us—will determine the kind of world we bequeath to our children.

The quest for meaning would not be an issue if our lives were obviously meaningful. Every foreground is defined by a background. The threat of meaninglessness posed by an entropic universe headed toward heat death makes us ask if the evolution of complexity of form and consciousness is evidence of consciousness that is the source as well as the goal of evolution—or merely something that happened to happen. Either way, the existential choices are the same, and the fact that they exist is the definition of freedom.

The battle for freedom is not being fought in wars far from home but in the policies and decisions we make personally and professionally about how we will live in a wired world. If those decisions are conscious, deliberate, and grounded in our real values and commitments, we will build communities on-line and off that are open, evolving, and free. If we are manipulated into fearing fear more than the loss of our own power and possibilities, then our communities will be constricted, rigidly controlled, over-determined.

Privacy is key to these choices.

There is no such thing as a guaranteed private conversation any more. We used to be able to walk out behind a tree and know we could not be overheard. Now the information that is broadcast by everything we say and do is universally available for cross-referencing and mining for hidden patterns. Those patterns, as Solveig Singleton of the Cato Institute observed, are in the eye of the beholder, determined by their needs and ultimate intentions—an eye that half-creates and half-perceives, as Wordsworth said, constructing reality in accordance with its wishes and deepest beliefs.

What we deeply believe, and how we allow others and our intentional communities to reinforce our beliefs and values, determines our actions and commitments. The choices we make downstream will emerge upstream when the river widens.

In a conversation with a career intelligence officer about the actions of various US agencies, I made this appeal: "There is a cry for justice in a child's heart," I suggested, "that is eroded over time by the way we sometimes have to live. Yet the day comes when we look at what we have done with our lives and its relationship to that cry for compassion."

He disagreed. "I long ago set aside the sentiments of my childhood religion," he said....

In order to do the things he had to do.

And the growing sophistication of technologies of torture, that enable governments to leave fewer marks, fewer clear memories in the minds of victims?

"A sign of growing sensitivity to world opinion," he said. "At least they're moving in the right direction."

How we do hear that cry for compassion, when the foggy weather in our own minds works to obscure it? Would it help, I asked Patrick Ball of the American Association for the Advancement of Science, to have audio clips on the web of what happens in those interrogation rooms?

"No," he said with conviction. "The descriptions I've read are sufficiently graphic."

What I cannot represent in words is the look in his eyes as his brain did a quick sort of the hundreds of detailed torture scenarios he had studied. Nor can I say how the face of that intelligence professional went suddenly wooden and his eyes looked away as he remembered what he had done as part of his job.

How wide do we draw the circle? A Department of Justice attorney arguing for weak encryption stopped at the border. Catching criminals inside America is his sole priority, so he wants a back door into every electronic conversation in the world. Ball draws a wider circle, including those in Guatemala, Ethiopia, or Turkey who might be alive if they had had a possibility of engaging in a private conversation. Ball favors strong encryption as a way to support human rights worldwide.

Our knowledge of "how things really work" pushes the conversation further. Seldom have intelligence agents told me they worry about abuse of the information they gather. They trust the system.

"We abide by the law," said a CIA professional. He added that even the NSA cannot intercept conversations inside our borders.

They don't have to, said another. Our special friends in New Zealand or Canada listen to American traffic as we listen to theirs. Good friends, he added, help one another.

So ... granted that we live in a real world in which data gathered for one purpose finds its way into other nets, in which anything that has value will be bought and sold ... what are the limits we can place on the inordinate desires in the human heart to be in control, to know more than we have a right to know? How can technology serve the need for secure boundaries that guarantee citizens of a civil society the freedom they need? Knowing what human beings do to one another, how can we constrain our baser desires and make it less likely that they will determine policy and behavior?

Conferences like CFP generate more questions than answers. But as long as the questions are raised, we maintain the margin between necessity and possibility that defines human freedom.

That margin may be narrowing, but so long as it exists, our passion for freedom, justice, and compassion can still manifest itself in action as well as words.

The Rights of Survivors   *June 27, 1998*

There are moments when we find ourselves face-to-face with unmitigated evil and— surrendering our innocence and fantasies of a Disneyland life – we see the truth of the human heart.

When I was twenty-one, I lived in Madrid, Spain, in a fascist regime overseen by Francisco Franco, with whose help, Hitler had practiced blitzkriegs in preparation for war.

I found myself on an all-day train ride from Cordoba to Grenada. The wooden cars often halted for long periods of time. I was in a compartment with two members of the state police, the Guardia Civil. There were pairs of them on every train, plane, and bus, every platform, every station. Their job was to search the faces that streamed past them for recognizable enemies of the state.

Over the hours, I engaged in conversation with one of the guards. Suddenly he said, "Do you want to know why we must remain vigilant?"

I said sure.

He reached into his case and brought out a thick book. He crossed to my bench and sat next to me, leaning close. For an hour he turned page after page, showing me hundreds of photographs of mutilated heads. Faces shot away, skulls broken, faces with vacant staring eyes.

"These are people who were slaughtered by the Communists during the Civil War," he said. "This is what they will do again if they have the opportunity. We study this every night so we never forget. We must do everything necessary to keep our families safe."

So we do not minimize, do we, what human beings who believe, who know that they are right, will do to one another? Sometimes their motivation stems from nothing more complicated than the desire to survive.

Back in the fifties, a neighbor proudly showed off her new bomb shelter. Hardened against nuclear explosions, with its own food and fuel supply, the shelter cost a pretty penny.

Another neighbor on the tour said to me aside, "If the bomb falls, all rules are off anyway. I'll just get a gun and take theirs."

When I left the ordained ministry, some members of the church were confused, as if my decision threatened their faith. One waited several months before asking if I still believed in God. I thought, how do I do justice both to the depths of my religious experience and the realities of life on our planet?

"Yes," I said. "I believe that God exists. But that doesn't mean," I added, "that things aren't as bad as they look."

Survivalists at their most extreme are preparing to hunker down for Armageddon and kill anyone who comes too close. While that's a far cry from libertarian philosophy, I sometimes hear their echoes in the seeming indifference of libertarians to the obligations of community, the imperatives of the net in which so many libertarians are at home.

Libertarians love cyberspace, with its metaphor of the frontier, its wide-open spaces, and its grandiose illusions of autonomy. Cyberspace is the simulation of a world in which we seem to be on our own, as if rules don't apply out here on the edge.

New political parties always embody the economic and social factors that give them rise. The libertarian movement is one version of the devolution of centralized authority into smaller units, a devolution driven by technological change. In the former Soviet Union, the Balkans, even Great Britain with its outer edges—Scotland, Ireland, Wales—demanding greater autonomy, the process is simply more obvious.

Many American voters see little difference between the Republican and Democratic parties except at their edges. The Libertarian movement, riding the technological changes that are flattening hierarchical structures around the world, is the right place for technocrats who want to be fiercely autonomous.

Of course, the truth is seldom simple, and the much heralded flattening of structures can also be seen as the widening of branches on tall fractal trees that are bigger than ever. Global hierarchical structures, coalescing around the convergence of self-interest among those whose decisions move economies if not mountains, are a more certain consequence of the computer revolution than the fantasies of the virtual frontier.

Some libertarians paint a picture of the Ticking Year 2000 Bomb that rivals the nuclear doom of the fifties. They advocate the kind of survivalism—guns, canned goods, and a hideout in red rock country—that my neighbor had in mind when he looked over that bomb shelter and decided he would take it.

At the other extreme, in the minds of those for whom the state is supreme and the individual an inconvenient abstraction, plans for martial law are already on the books, just in case. That's a more communal way of saying that anything can happen, and we must be ready to use any means necessary to protect the state.

Real survivalism is communal, a fact that ought to be obvious to the denizens of cyberspace. The Internet that weaves such a compelling illusion of autonomy is a community of nested communities. Plug computers into one another and community happens. As language once determined that we could not consider someone fully human unless they spoke the dialect of the tribe, computerized networks increasingly determine that we are not fully human unless we are woven into the fabric of the wired world.

In essence, computer networks are social. Networked people live in a symbiotic relationship with networked computers. But it is the people that define the system, because human beings are the field of subjectivity that gives it meaning.

The Net gives us permission to be autonomous and free in new ways, but that permission is contingent. Liberty is not license, and rights without the acceptance of responsibilities do not long endure. To be fully human, we must recognize that securing another's good is axiomatic to securing our own. Neither anarchy nor fascism ensures the security of interdependence or the real autonomy that we experience when we act as if our self-interest is always mutual.

Who Cares?   *September 12, 1998*

"Because they have so little," observed Eleanor Roosevelt, "children rely on imagination rather than experience."

Which is why childhood is such a magical time, during which—even among the worst deprivations—children can weave a luminous web around their daily lives, filling the landscape with lively fantastic shapes.

Just like adults.

This week an extraordinary event gave the digital world its seal of approval. Lively fantastic shapes humped and bumped their way across our monitors, a magic lantern show for the wickedly leering.

Those of us who remember Watergate recall a judicial process that proceeded at a deliberate pace. Congressional hearings spelled out how the President of the United States had undermined the law by directing criminal activities from the Oval Office. The intelligence community was widely used to destroy enemies, distort the truth, subvert the constitution.

A generation later, the independent prosecutor's report of the Clinton affair is shot-gunned onto the Net so debate can slosh back and forth across the body politic and members of congress, fingers to the wind, can sail toward impeachment, or not.

We all frame the world according to our experience. As the Vietnam War and Watergate unfolded, it became clear that our leaders, Democrats and Republicans alike, were lying through their teeth. Our denial eroded, and the voice of the people grew until it was amplified by those hearings, saving the constitution for another generation.

Where is that "voice of the people" now, crying out for the deeper truth? Is it locked in the closet with our comic books, faded tales of Superman, an idealized father who couldn't protect us? Whose heroic belief in "truth and justice" made us feel better when we were children afraid of the night, as Auden said, lost in a haunted wood?

The digital world, with its altered or manufactured images, is a haunted wood, a prison of the imagination. But when we use digital images to tell as much truth as can be told, the prison walls become transparent and we see real trees in the digital forest.

We need to see more than the rubble and dust of falling-down public lives. There is so much more going on out there than presidential peccadilloes. We need a transcendent vision that begins with the simple truth but moves toward larger possibilities.

A former computer hacker who occupies a sensitive position in corporate America and works frequently with the intelligence establishment described a chilling moment. He found himself involved with something so much bigger, deeper, more evil than he had imagined that he felt that chill running down his spine that tells us our world view has shifted forever. My friend had stumbled into the heart of darkness.

Once we know, we can't not know what we know.

Hackers are often portrayed as criminals, but—like many hackers—my friend was really an innocent. The hacker ethic of integrity, a passion for truth and knowledge, an obsessive desire to put together the big picture—that's closer to the superhero credo of "truth, justice, and the American way" than a criminal code.

The History Channel just ran a series on the Kennedy assassination. The series raised legitimate questions , again, about a conspiracy. All we can know now about the assassination is filtered through text, the television screen, the digital interface … and sometimes, the words of a friend. A prominent local physician remembers when his mentor at Medical School was called away to examine Kennedy's body. When he returned, he tried to work as if nothing had changed, but he kept looking away and muttering to himself, "It's the damndest thing."

Then he said: "One day. One day it'll all come out."

Just another conspiracy theory. Like Gary Webb's.

This month's Esquire has a story about Webb. He wrote articles for the San Jose Mercury News about the connections between cocaine distribution, the CIA, and the Contras. His story was well-documented but it didn't take long for the guardians of consensus reality to whack him. The truth is, he described the tip of the iceberg, but that's all he had to do to find himself surrounded, isolated, neutralized. The deep involvement of members of our government in narcotic trafficking is well documented, but when Webb tried to tell the truth, it was as if he had screamed himself awake from a nightmare and rushed to the window, only to find it nailed shut and people on the walk below who would not look up.

Besides … guns, Contras, cocaine … who really cares?

I have explored the fun-house mirrors of the world of UFOs for years. When you brush away the cobwebs of disinformation, snake oil, mistakes, and reports of remarkable flying machines that we make ourselves, we are left with credible people telling us what they saw. Fighter pilots, intelligence agents, commercial airline pilots have told me what they or their friends encountered, that the hardware is real and flew rings around them, leaving them in the dust.

We're a small planet on the edge of a vast spiral of stars, the center of nothing but our own perspective. All we have is our small voice. Digital media can amplify that voice or drown it out.

"The movie *Conspiracy Theory*, said my hacker friend, "doesn't even come close."

As Jane Wagner said, I get more and more cynical all the time and still can't keep up. Yet we humans are meant for a deeper truth; more truth than a thousand pages of a president lying to keep a sexual affair secret. Perspective, as Alan Kay said, is worth fifty points of IQ. Sex on the Net is a sideshow, keeping our eyes on the dancing bears.

So step right up! The circus is just beginning! Elephants are on parade, clowns pour out of a tiny auto, a calliope pipes and—in the distance—we think we can hear a voice, a contrarian voice, a still small voice … but it's only our imaginations. Isn't it?

Anyway … who cares?

Mapmaker,
Mapmaker, Make Me a Map   *December 12, 1998*

In the good old days of the Cold War, spy stories by authors like John Le Carre had enough uncertainty about who worked for whom that nested levels of loyalty, duplicity, and loyalty again provided the framework for a good narrative. To engage us, a challenge must be difficult but doable. The bar has to be raised just enough to elicit our best jump.

Those books did that.

Then we lost the mythology of the Cold War, pitting the Children of Darkness against the Children of Light. That archetypal imagery engaged us. We projected ourselves onto the narrative, entering into collusion with it even if we did not consciously accept the framework. The propaganda was too powerful to resist. We may have ignored the morning newspaper, but we watched James Bond movies, absorbing the story through entertainment. At some level, we all believed in what we read.

Winning the Cold War was anticlimactic. We lost something important, an adversary worthy of our projections that made life meaningful by creating a game in which our loyalties to self, tribe, or God could be played out.

Those Cold War stories always turned on deception. People who seemed to be loyal to one level of structural authority turned out to be loyal to another. Sometimes their loyalty was to ultimate values. Real religious commitments are always threatening because people who act on them subvert the lesser loyalties that make societies work. They stand in the way of the tanks in Tieneman Square, even if the tanks are only images and symbols created by the temporal powers that ask us to be "team players" and surrender.

Loyalty, deception, and loyalty again, are possible only in a world with its macro structures defined, its political, economic and mythological dimensions overlapping.

The novels of Le Carre have been replaced with tales of the digital world. Cyberpunks, whose world I encountered first in Shockwave Rider, Artificial Kid, Neuromancer, and Snow Crash are building a different mythological structure for a different generation. Their vision is not so much cynical as simply descriptive of life in the digital world.

Our Villains of the Month—Khadaffi, Noriega, Khomeni, Sadam Hussein— morph into one another as easily as the arm of the bad android in *Terminator 2* became a sword. The end of a dictator or victory in a war seems to have zero impact on our lives, which are lived inside simulations of a global society whose fuel is consumerism and entertainment.

Nested levels of loyalty are difficult to discern in the digital world because we are reinventing the names of the structures of power and authority. The company resulting from the merger of Exxon and Mobil will compete, not with Chevron, but with Saudi Arabia. What should we call the pieces of the new global puzzle? Nations? Multi-national corporations? Those labels exist only in relationship to one another, and that is precisely the context that is being transformed by the digital world. A "multi-national" like Bechtel, more powerful than most countries, is an entity we can not describe accurately because we lack meaningful information about it, the kind that shows the flow of power, that lets us map how remnants of "democracy" are used in the digital world for social and political control.

Where is there a political party that looks like a real opposition? Our entire planet is skewed to the right. There is no left, and the center is a necessary convenience that sustains the illusion of dialogue. In the digital world, it is so easy to create islands on which to collect those whose tendencies make them oppositional. Social order is maintained by giving everyone a piece of the digital action, images that entertain or to consume. Our projections provide a sense of ownership, of belonging. Little digital yards with white pixel fences, the bitmapped terrain of our mental worlds.

The spy novelists tried, but the stories written since the end of the Cold War just don't make it. We do not intuitively grasp the movement of power in the digital world in a way that enables an archetypal scaffolding to be built. We don't believe in the Villain of the Month but we don't know, really, who is loyal to whom or to what. We don't know the names of the organizations to which the money flows. We don't even know what kinds of things they are yet. We only know that when the United States of America was defeated in Viet Nam, no dominoes fell, and the isolation and punishment of the victorious regime taught them an economic and political lesson on which they are just now taking an exam.

Here's some homework: Follow the money. Make a digital map of Bechtel, letting every handshake glow red, every enterprise glow white. Let little green pellets represent the flow of energy and information, tracing the realities of power. Name the interface between alliances, diagram lines of influence, map the images of their world wide web. Think about why Competitive Intelligence is growing, why old hands from the KGB find work in corporate America, why experts from the CIA head divisions in our largest companies.

The puzzle pieces in which we used to believe—nations, ideologies, even religions—are dissolving but we have not yet invented the kinds of mental maps that make sense in the digital world.

Of course you'll never finish that assignment, never get the information you need, never know the extent of a web woven in so many dimensions. In the digital world, we are ten-dimensional dogs chasing our own tails. But the effort will begin to focus an image of the blurred nested levels in which we are learning to live, how they twist and turn on themselves like mobius strips, an internalized computer game that makes Tron look as quaint as Asteroids played on a Commodore 64 or the Cold War played in the faded pages of a novel.

A Digital Innocent   *June 2, 2000*

When I was a kid, we used to watch "Superman" on black-and-white television. We were the last family in our apartment building to own a black-and-white set and—because we won one in a raffle—the first on the block with a color TV.

The immense cabinet contained a huge tube and a miniscule screen. Few programs were in color, and when one was scheduled, we invited the neighborhood kids to come over and watch. I turned dials for "hue" and "tint" until the faces on the screen turned bright pink, and everybody clapped.

"Superman" was a ritual on Saturday morning. Like all rituals, it began with the same words, a comforting repetition that made us receptive to the message. The voiceover said Superman was "disguised as Clark Kent, a mild-mannered reporter for a major metropolitan newspaper, [who] fights a never-ending battle for truth, justice and the American way."

That's the stuff of a child's dreams. As we grow older, we're supposed to put away childish things, but the older I become, the more deeply I believe that without the passion for truth and justice evoked by a myth like Superman, the world is a nightmare from which we will never awake.

When I left organized religion six years ago for the life of a speaker and writer, one of the people in my parish took me aside. "I need to know," she said, "if you still believe in God."

Now, when you work as a priest, minister or rabbi, you learn that managing projections is a large part of your role. Because you're a symbol, people automatically project onto you too much good and too much evil. You discover that what they think of you reveals their best attributes or hidden guilt. You learn to give back their projections because the ability to integrate into our selves what we unconsciously project onto others is one source of spiritual growth. Because that woman used my faith to leverage her own, my answer mattered. I wanted to tell her the truth, but the whole truth, not some simplistic bumper-sticker slogan that glazed over the real evil that crushes people for no good reason.

"In my heart," I said, "yes, I believe that God exists ... But! That doesn't mean things aren't as bad as they look."

Our lives are infinity loops between those two polarities like a planet oscillating between binary stars. Without openness to the possibilities of the future—without faith—we sink into a kind of living death. But if we refuse to acknowledge the realities of life, faith becomes denial or rationalization, a defensive reaction that does not set us free so much as imprison us in our fear of the truth.

I spoke recently with Gary Webb, the author of "Dark Alliance," an exploration of the connections between the Contras, the CIA, and the cocaine epidemics of the eighties. Webb's credibility was assaulted when he wrote that series for the San Jose Mercury News. His editors backed off, and he felt compelled to resign from the dead-end job to which they assigned him. He pursued the investigation, and as it turns out, Webb was right. The tangled chain of lies and deception was more complex than anyone imagined.

I asked Webb if what he endured—the attacks on his credibility, the impact on his family, loss of his career—were worth it.

"Sometimes we only have one opportunity," he said, "to do the right thing. If we don't do it, we surrender. Then they win."

It is ironic that his pursuit of justice and truth took place in Silicon Valley, where the passion for amassing money often eclipses the passion for justice or truth.

"Here in Silicon Valley," a colleague wrote, "the only time we hear about truth and justice is when Jesse Jackson comes to town or when janitors go on strike. They seem to be irrelevant to people's lives."

We old timers remember when an entire culture was appropriately outraged when the leaders who asked for our trust attempted to hijack the intelligence establishment and the Department of Justice to subvert the constitution and destroy lives. These days the reporters who illuminated their crimes would be called "conspiracy theorists." They would be "disappeared" by being suffocated in lies and irrelevancies, false stories planted in mainstream media, discredited or ignored. Other media events would be created to distract us—the saga of little Elian, professional sports, or gladiator-like spectacles—and we would stampede toward those manufactured images of manufactured events like cattle.

Has an entire generation been hijacked by a love of technology devoid of passion for using that technology to do the right thing? Mention spirituality in Silicon Valley and you're likely to be spoon-fed a blend of material success and the kind of self-indulgence that pretends we can become authentically ourselves without meaningful sacrifice or rigorous discipline.

No spiritual ground is conquered without the self-knowledge that makes us aware of our complicity and collusion, without the compassion that shatters barriers erected by self-righteousness, without a passion for justice outraged at the arrogance of complacency and greed.

Superman was a comic-book hero translated into a televised image. New superheroes are showing up in the digital world, but the criteria for a superhero seems to be the value of their stock options rather than their character.

The dangers of ubiquitous electronic connectivity are not the dangers that play well on the news, but the danger that those who manufacture and manipulate the news into false images of "history" will turn even our outrage at injustice into another revenue stream distorted into a media event.

Manufactured images and manufactured events are designed to keep us asleep. The Internet is a funhouse mirror of distortion as well as a potential source of redemption. But for a portal of truth and transformation to work, we must move through it with a child's heart, believing in spite of the evidence, while at the same time we connect warily with the images that constitute bars of a digital cage.

About Faces   *July 9, 2000*

There's a lot of talk these days about a lack of digital civility ... tracking programs that link and mine our most personal data ... articles about cell-phone users whose loud voices push us into the walls like suddenly-inflating airbags ... e-mail with macros that explode or computer viruses that shred our memory.

It's all part of a larger struggle to put a human face on all that data—to remember to look through the pixels to the pattern, really see one another and—the hardest part—remember that human beings are on the other side of the information.

This struggle isn't new. Plato feared that writing would sabotage the social contract that lay at the heart of a civilized city. If anyone could write anything, then the search for truth would be compromised and justice undermined. And so it was. And after the printing press was invented, so it was again, at a higher level of abstraction, and again when printed words turned into these flickering pixels. When droids like Ananova (www.ananova.com) can be believed, real people can be disbelieved just as easily.

It's the symbols, don't you see. Not the media in which they move.

Used wrongly, symbols enable us to divorce actions from consequences, information from persons. Deceptive symbols can short-circuit the feedback loops that keep an organism open, evolving and free. Symbols are masks we can pull down over our faces and hide inside.

Once we no longer see another's face ... or look into their eyes ... it is easy to become isolated inside our own symbol structures, the ones that define our tribes, nations, religions, or individual identities ... like cell-phone users staring at a fixed point in empty space, shouting at someone who isn't there while ignoring those who are.

Once we withdraw into that hallucination ... once we forget that we all share a single space ... it's easy to deny the consequences of turning people into objects or making them disappear entirely.

In "Prisoner Without a Name, Cell Without a Number," Jacobo Timmerman writes of being imprisoned and tortured by a Fascist regime. He recalls torturers putting a hood over the head of a woman so they wouldn't have to see her eyes when they applied electric shocks.

Whatever it is that we see when we look into another's eyes apparently inhibits our ability to turn up the voltage and ignore the screams. We need to hide their humanity in some kind of mask or wear a mask ourselves to do that kind of evil deed.

Robert Jay Lifton wrote a chilling book on "The Nazi Doctors: Medical Killing and the Psychology of Genocide," in which he discussed "doubling," the ability of the Self to generate a second self which is socialized to different norms and engages in behaviors that the primary Self would never entertain, like practicing "medicine" that torments people rather than heals.

Doubling isn't splitting of the self, but the Self growing another self that can somehow inhabit the same body and not notice what it is doing.

Even when someone is right in front of our eyes, in other words, we can make them less than human, hide their identity in symbols that let us dismiss them as a Jew, an Arab, whatever. Once we have hidden their humanity in an arbitrary category, we will see in their eyes only what we see in the eyes of a laboratory rat when we inject it with a toxin.

The ability to deny the humanity of others did not emerge in the digital era. It's in all of us, all of the time, and when conditions are right, it can flourish like anthrax spores that have remained dormant for a hundred years.

Now, it may seem like a long way from speaking too loudly on a cell phone to war crimes and medical experiments. But every journey begins with a single step, and when we look back at the winding paths of our lives, we see that we made choices which, once made, had to be justified, so they led to other choices, and so on and so on, until one day we discovered that our lives had become the accelerated momentum of all the choices we had ever made.

And we are all hiding always from the consequences of our collective choices. The fusion of mass media, disinformation, entertainment and global corporate interests is nearly absolute. We live inside a simulated circus in which digital images of wild animals surround us harmlessly, insulating us from the real harm of simulation itself.

A friend once practiced karate until he was so good he could do it without thinking. One night after a movie he felt a hand on his shoulder and turned and broke his assailant's neck. Except it wasn't an assailant, it was only a friend trying to say hello.

"Just be certain," he said, "that what you practice is what you want to do, because when you don't have time to think, what you will do is what you have practiced."

We are all being assimilated into a digital mode, but we are also discovering as boundaries dissolve and new identities emerge that the challenge to become more fully human is what it always was.

We can't know how to be fully human without ongoing training programs in communities of shared humane values bound together by powerful symbols of promise and possibility. We need to use those communities for practicing what we want to do because we will do what we have practiced ... and because the ability to see our shared humanity in the face of another, in their eyes, in their hearts ... is something we forget and must learn again and again and which we can unlearn as quickly as a dot.com or an economy or a culture falls from the sky, making us look around frantically for someone other than ourselves to blame.

The Face of Evil

October 6, 2000

Sometimes the streams of our lives converge in a single river and its power is impossible to resist.

This month many of the passions which have animated much of my adult life converged.

As the recipient of the Gamalial Chair in Peace and Justice through the Lutheran ministry at the University of Wisconsin, Milwaukee, I will devote much of October and November to speaking about technology and justice issues in a variety of venues in my home town.

At the same time, new material comes into focus for a series of articles I am writing on "Chinatown moments." Disclosed to me over the past year, these are moments in which different people were told either directly or by circumstances—as Jake Gittes, the "Chinatown detective," was told by Noah Cross—"You may think you know what you're dealing with, but believe me, you don't." In two instances, people were threatened with death. In another an investigator feared for his life when he discovered that a prominent local citizen might have committed murder. And in a fourth, a young computer hacker broke suddenly through a false partition in cyberspace and found himself in freefall in a world more complex and corrupt than he had dreamed.

And at the same time ... I interviewed Dan Geer for next month's Information Security Magazine. Dan Geer is incredibly smart. He is currently Chief Technology Officer for @stake and newly elected president of Usenix. He has a doctorate from Harvard and helped develop the Athena Project and Kerberos at MIT. When you're talking to a guy like that about computer security and he tells you that he only hires people who are "sadder but wiser," you pay attention. By that he meant that he wants people who know what's really at stake. The urgency of their work must be energized by an encounter with the face of evil so they understand what they're up against and why their work matters.

Geer has a friend who is now a corporate attorney but who was once assistant station chief of the CIA in Beirut. Geer asked about his migration from intelligence to the private sector. His friend had paid plenty of dues—he had been held hostage, for example, for two weeks on a runway—but the defining moment was created by those who had kidnapped his superior, the CIA station chief. Over the next days, they took video tapes of the slow careful process by which they tortured him to death. Geer's friend watched those tapes, every day. Every single day. Until the body of his colleague was at last lifeless.

"I wish we could talk about our successes," Brian Snow, the head of NCSC (National Computer Security Center, a division of the National Security Agency) told me, but sources and methods must be protected. So I had to rely on his tone of voice when Snow spoke of what might have happened, indicating an unimaginable scale of death and destruction, to know that Snow too had seen the face of evil.

Reflection on "truth and justice" issues for the Gamaliel Chair, the stakes of the game when spy meets spy, and the stories in those articles all point in the same direction.

Technology transforms what it means to be human. Technology transforms the future by changing how we hold ourselves here and now as possibilities for action. Technology redefines our human enterprise at its core.

New technologies—genetic engineering, instruments of surveillance and social control—deliver power into our hands, and we always use it. Then comes reflection on how to use it, after the fact. But that reflection can impact what we choose to do in the next future, even as the current future becomes the past.

Technology is not about anti-gravity, designer children, or new information channels merely. It is about the entire field of human subjectivity and how we choose to define and direct ourselves. Those questions invoke the ultimate meaning of our lives. Technology enables people to act powerfully but how we act is not determined exclusively by technology.

Either the universe is all meaningless or it is all meaningful. Meaning seems to be a function of complexity. As seemingly isolated events or inert substances are integrated into a complex system, meaning happens. Ultimately the entire universe and its passing shadow which we call spacetime will be integrated into itself ... and conscious of itself. At that instant, when the circle is closed, the beginning and the end will be seen to have always been one thing. Consciousness including all of its means of being.

Or put it this way.

"You tell me there's no God," said Geer," and I'll ask you to look me in the eye and tell me there's no such thing as evil. If you can't do the one, you lose the right to do the other."

The evil of which he speaks is no abstraction. It is the gut-level discovery that comes when we face the worst that human beings can do and know in that harrowing moment that there is another, a better option.

To know the truth, however, there must be disclosure. Without disclosure, there is no truth. Without truth, there is no accountability. Without accountability, there is no justice.

The digital cage in which we flap our wings either hides or discloses the truth. The liberation of the truth and its right uses are the flip sides of the loss of privacy and places to hide. How we build that cage, how we live in it, is not built into digital technology but into our souls. That is where we make decisions about making decisions, and that is where we discover a capacity for freedom that enables us to define our lives as heroic or debased.

The Only Thing We Have to Fear

September 11, 2001

The world just changed forever. War was declared on the whole world.

A friend from the National Security Agency told me recently how difficult it was to convince audiences lately of the real threat from asymmetrical warfare. The enemy is doing what it can to understand our collective mind, he said, and then will use the weakest link in our armor to strike terror into our collective hearts.

And so they have. With a simple coordinated attack the assumptions of the American people were changed forever. We live in America, I have been saying, as if it were America and not Israel. In Israel people know they are in Israel. They live accordingly.

Now we know, too.

War is hell. It calls forth from us the best and the worse in our all-too-human natures. And now everyone knows what many have known for years; that we are at war.

Which means understanding who the enemy is and what it means to fight this war.

The first war is against fear and terror, as Franklin Roosevelt said. Nameless, unreasoning fear that distorts our thinking and feeling and changes the way we live our lives. Fear in the face of real threats is appropriate. Our collective task will be to distinguish real from illusory threats, real from imagined enemies, and stay as clear-thinking and focused as we can as we identify what is important in our lives and make efforts to secure and defend what matters most.

So what, in moments like these, do we know?

We know that the first people we thought of are the most important people in our lives. The people we wanted to be with or who we feared were dead or injured or vulnerable to attack, those are the people that matter most.

Then that bond must expand and include all on whom we rely, all on whom we depend, all on whom we will call in the days and weeks and months ahead as comrades, friends, and allies. This is a moment that will ask everything of us as we struggle to attack and defend ourselves from real enemies and define our circles of loyalty and kinship with precision and care.

The enemy is fear, terror, and falsehood. Our allies are courage, strength in the face of adversity, resilience and flexibility and our capacity to respond to whatever life brings with genuine heroism. These are the marks of the freedom that lives in our souls.

Freedom is our capacity to live life as it is fired at us point blank from the barrel of a gun and never surrender that which makes us human and that which makes us free.

The world has changed, now, forever, and the boundaries that we draw around ourselves, who is in and who is out, will change forever too. We will discover who we really are in the weeks ahead.

But I know from fifty-seven years on this fragile planet who we are in our best moments and I pray that we have the courage to be who we are.

I think of how I responded to someone who was worried that when I left the ministry, it meant that I had lost my faith in the existence of God.

"Do you believe," she asked, "in God?"

"Yes," I said, "in my heart I know that God exists. But, thinking of the horror, thinking of the oppression in people's lives thinking of the bloodshed, I added, "That doesn't mean things aren't as bad as they look."

Our challenge now is to know both are true. Things are every bit as bad as they look and people do evil things and rejoice in the bloodshed. And in my heart I know that God exists and is manifest in freedom, freedom from fear and terror, the freedom to respond to whatever life brings with dignity, elasticity, and heroism.

The only thing we have to fear now is fear, the primary weapon of our enemies. Because I know who we are, I know that we have what it takes to do what is necessary now, how we must structure our world and our lives, and how we must rededicate ourselves to the creation of a global society in which freedom and not fear and terror are the hallmarks of our humanity.

Battlespace   *October 4, 2001*

The mind of society—how it is shaped, how it is governed, how it is aimed—is both target and weapon in the new battlespace. As a consequence, spiritual warfare with all of its dimensions is fused more deeply than ever with the waging of war.

I gave a speech last July for the Black Hat Briefings, the intelligence and corporate security forum sponsored by Def Con, the computer security/hacking convention, in which I said:

"The world is a theater and a chronic state of warfare is our current script. Some parts of society, however, know this more than others."

Now we all know.

The September 11th attack was theater. The timing of the second hit to be visible to television cameras was impeccable. The terrorists counted on the networks to show those images again and again, reinforcing their impact in a way that turned the networks—filters for the mind of society—into implicit allies. They used the mind of society to aim terror at the mind of society.

The carnage was intended to be both real and symbolic. The Romans, under Vespasian, "slighted" Stonehenge, leaving it as a visible wound. The Nazis left French cathedrals damaged but standing. Stonehenge was a symbol of Druidic leadership, the cathedrals were symbols of French nationalism, and the World Trade Center and the Pentagon were symbols of America.

"The ideal war," I said at Black Hat, "is one which no one realizes is being waged, which is mostly invisible, not because its actions are camouflaged, but because they look like something else.

"War need never be declared again," I concluded, "because we are always at war."

This is the war in which we are currently engaged.

"Martial arts teach us that anything can be a weapon," said a friend with a long history as an intelligence analyst. "You see an ashtray, I see a blackjack. You see a natural gas pipeline, I see a weapon of mass destruction."

The mind of society, he suggests, must learn to see itself from a different point of view. Just as the enemy studies our open society with its remarkable inclusiveness and generosity of spirit and uses its strengths as weaknesses, we must study the mind of the enemy and use asymmetric warfare right back at them.

"See them from their point of view," he said. "Their humorless pride will destroy them. We need to deflate that false self."

The manipulation of human perception is both preparation for war and the aim of war. Sun Tzu advised military leaders never to come to the battlefield unless the war had already been won in the mind of the enemy. Psychological operations, information attack, deception, and all the means of dissimulation available to attackers prior to military operations determine the outcome of battle.

In its largest sense, all war is cyberwar. Data, information, and belief are primary attack weapons.

At the Black Hat, I used "space war" as a metaphor for how war on the ground and in the air has been recontextualized by war in space which includes holographic image projection, cloaking devices, multispectral camouflage, and the creation of synthetic environments which the attacker believes to be real. Those are metaphors for how war is waged on earth as well.

Terrorism moves by stealth, pretending to be what it isn't. Therefore learning to see the real patterns implicit in the movement of people, material, information and how they are linked by human motivation and intention are critical. But that is not the task of officialdom only. The task of every human being is to see clearly.

When society itself is the theater of battle, all citizens are engaged. Only clear seeing can precipitate right action. That's why the battle for confidence, courage, and community is primary.

There are no guarantees, but this war has the potential so to redefine the global landscape which has gotten very blurred, what with its morphing borders and powerful trans-nationals, that a sense of identity and purpose beyond nationalism and borders can unite people committed to an open civil society.

I have been vocal in identifying ways we all collude with necessary evils to create a gray world. That world includes all sorts of behaviors that are less than ideal, but—and it is a huge but—none of them threaten the foundations of society itself. All of us participate in evil, in other words, but some are more evil than others. Down in the trenches of real life, it is all very murky, but nevertheless, certain kinds of evil are intolerable. The terrorists stepped over that line. If their way wins, society is no longer viable. It is the real difference between the United States with all its flaws and the world of the Taliban where women who commit adultery and homosexuals are murdered by the state.

Many people have written to tell me how our past actions contributed to the antagonisms of the present. Yes, yes. We too are in a learning curve. But there is a time and a season for everything. The time will come for America to reflect on the consequences of its policies. But all of the historical and political analyses in the world do not explain away one essential fact: Evil in its purest manifestation is uncaused. It rejoices in chaos for its own sake and it must be challenged.

All of the good in humanity and all of the evil are going to show up. There are real rocks up ahead in the rapids, but as a friend once said, look at the rocks, you hit the rocks. Look at the water between the rocks. You go where the water goes.

Spiritual warfare transcends nationalities, religions, ideologies. It requires using all of our mental, emotional, and spiritual capabilities, all levels of awareness, all means of being conscious, to see the flow of the water so we can go where the water goes.

Be Alert   *October 13, 2001*

"Be alert!" the President of the United States told his citizens. Then he added: "Go back to your normal lives."

Between those two suggestions, however, is a great gulf, and our task now is to build the multi-dimensional stairways of an Escher etching from our "normal lives" (as we once innocently called them) to the awareness necessary to live in the new battlespace called "everyday life."

In the context of the attack, what does it mean to "be alert?" How is it different from the level of awareness that we had before?

Wisdom and insanity are contextual. When the earth shifts on its axis or the ground shifts under our feet, what once seemed insane may now be appropriate. What was once wise may no longer make sense.

To become alert in a context of heightened vigilance is one thing, to remain alert is another. In the immediate shock of attack, adrenaline rushes through our bodies, fuel-injecting awareness. Our senses process information at an accelerated rate. But after we calm down, our scanning apparatus returns to its default position. We filter out those thousands of impressions that seem irrelevant to daily survival.

Now survival requires a different level of awareness.

To be alert at a higher level requires training. We have to be willing to learn new habits. We need credible structures to do that training effectively. We need the will and the discipline to remain committed to the long run. We need to be accountable to mutually-agreed-upon goals. Above all, we need a vision articulated clearly and forcefully as a plumb line for keeping ourselves aligned.

A commitment to stay the course at the highest level of intentionality doesn't mean that we don't get discouraged. It means that when we do, we know how to get ourselves encouraged again.

This will not just happen. We don't just say to ourselves one evening, be alert! and find ourselves alert in the morning.

I recall a CEO who heard about empowerment and called his employees together to announce, "You're empowered!" then went back to his office. Of course, in the absence of structures to generate, train, and sustain empowered employees, nothing happened.

We are talking about at least a couple of things when we talk about being alert. One is anomaly detection. The other is the kind of multi-valent sensory awareness we see in spiritual masters and martial artists. Some are born to be good at one or the other, but we can all be trained in both.

In the world of computer security, firewalls and intrusion detection systems have strengthened the perimeters of networks. But thickening the walls weakened the hidden abscesses where networks were most vulnerable. Four fifths of all disruptions to networks are caused by insiders. As a result, anomaly detection inside the system is critical. In its broadest sense, anomaly detection is the detection of behaviors contrary to normal patterns. In both virtual and physical networks, that means surveillance and access controls that permit or inhibit movement. That in turn means watching closely the nodes of a network—the "hubs, gatekeepers and pulsetakers" as Harvard professor Karen Stephenson calls them—through which power flows.

"So we're all to become little spies?" a friend said.

Not exactly. It's more like a global neighborhood watch in which the commitment to collective security outweighs indifference to what's happening next door.

Terrorists often live in areas with a high turnover rate, where no one notices and no one cares. We are now called both to notice and to care.

"The phrase 'anomaly detection' has been the cornerstone of intelligence operations through the ages" said a veteran intelligence officer, "from the bird that brought a branch to Noah to today's massive changing patterns in all walks of life."

That officer endeavored to teach law enforcement personnel how to bring things that we notice on the edges—but not really—into the light. Then we can see what is right in front of our eyes.

We can all be trained to notice indicators and warnings, the telltale behaviors that signal that something is not quite right. Those skills shade inevitably into the consciousness training techniques that are aspects of martial arts. They are also the "spiritual tools" handed down by the world's religions.

When spiritual seekers discipline themselves to pursue deeper reaches of awareness, they are always astonished to learn how much they have been missing. It's like going scuba diving for the first time and discovering that the three fourths of the earth under water contains living things that are wondrous and strange. After a while one lives as comfortably under water as on land.

One training technique used by martial artists is to blindfold a subject so they can practice becoming attuned to what is happening all around them. Intelligence agents are trained to become conscious in this and other ways. When one's life is at stake, one sniffs the wind with a different nose. One grows more sensitive to "a disturbance in the Force."

For individuals and for societies, becoming more alert begins with a shift in intention. It's like deciding to become more physically fit. One minute you're sedentary, the next you're building structures—hiring a trainer, reading about nutrition, gathering support—toward the goal of a lifestyle change. It's the difference between sprinting and long-distance running.

And who is the enemy? When we look at how the word "enemy" changed over the course of the Judeo-Christian scriptures, we learn that it once meant "others." But as consciousness evolved, it came to mean in ourselves which resists transformation. Evil was no longer located outside ourselves, but inside. The focus of the struggle shifted.

My experience is that both are true. The enemy is both those who would destroy us and our own capacity for evil. A parallax view, seeing now one and now the other, is essential as we learn to draw the boundary that includes "us" around more and more "others."

The Power Grid   *October 15, 2001*

There's an apocryphal story about an American officer who fought in the Viet Nam War. His troops, it is said, often saw him standing in the smoke of battle with his eyes closed, looking as focused as Yoda discerning a disturbance in the Force.

This is what he said he was doing.

He was sorting aspects of the battle into a grid. In his mind's eye he saw four quadrants: What was going right? What was going wrong? What was not going right? What was not going wrong?

Then he looked intently at the matrix for a point of leverage through which he could act, surveying the space to see what was missing, what might be enhanced.

That's our story too. It's as if we're inside that old movie "Tron," the one about a computer programmer inserted into his own game. It was made when computer graphics meant luminous 3-D grids flexing on the screen. We're inside the game, spectators no more, looking for a point of leverage.

But we're also looking for moorings so we can make sense of what's gone and what's here. The past seems like a dream, our former points of reference seem like mist. But we don't want to backslide into denial. We need to recreate ourselves on the fly in a zone of annihilation in which everything we believed to be true is called into question. We need to stay focused on what is real.

At first it felt like everything was coming apart. Our psyches backscattered in the sudden impact of the crash. We recoiled from "the shocks and changes that keep us sane," as Robert Frost called them. But then gravity came into play. Our psyches came together again, integrated at a different level of organization into a much less innocent self.

We're recognizably the same .... but different.

The points of reference for determining right thinking and right action have shifted. Insights that have been arriving for a long time hover in our minds like computer-generated entities in the space of a 3-D cybergame. We are trying to connect them to the lines of the flexing grid that define the new battlespace.

So what are some of the things that are changing?

We still talk about individuality, but the needs of the larger community have become paramount. The needs of the individual are being defined, in fact, as the needs of the community. Everything from "privacy" to "rights" will be recontextualized in this light.

No nation state will ever again act as if independent. A deeper awareness of interdependence is percolating through our thinking, but we are not yet fully aware of all the implications. We don't yet speak a language in which mutual dependence is implicit. We are struggling to articulate this new understanding the way fish that walked on stubby fins might have spoken of life in the air.

The nation state, as we knew it, is on its way out. In addition to the intensity with which most Americans felt connected in the aftershock of the attack, we also saw clearly that the dissolution of boundaries had resulted in new self-organizing structures for which we do not yet have names. The names we previously invented for trans-global entities—meta-national corporations, NGOs, mafias, cartels, terrorist networks—don't really define these new organizational structures. They coexist uneasily with "nation states" in something like but more than alliances. They interpenetrate one another in indeterminate ways. We don't know what to call them yet. And we don't know who is loyal to what.

World War III is not only about "America." It's about the character of a planetary society, in fact, a trans-planetary society. The current battlespace might be characterized as McDonald's versus jihad, but it's bigger than that. We are choosing the kind of civilization we want to build in the 21st century.

Modernity, the "modern world," is open, evolving, free. It sparkles with the light of the free exchange of ideas and information, looking as the earth looks at night from space. Fundamentalists, on the other hand, are always totalitarian, regardless of religion. Whether Jews, Christians, or Moslems, fundamentalists have more in common with one another than with moderates in their own religions. Their world is binary, black or white. Their inordinate need for control comes from a deep unyielding fear that makes them rigid and brittle as sticks.

The totalitarian mind is never capable of understanding the mind of a free people. As Churchill said on the floor of Congress after Pearl Harbor, "What kind of a people do they think we are?" Do they think that the calculus of evil really will solve their problems?

The trivia with which many were preoccupied was blown away in a raw moment. In such moments, we feel what matters most. That sentiment, that feeling, is more than patriotic impulse or angry resolve. It is the engine of awareness, intention and action fused in the moment of knowing, the realization that civilization is a choice and that free people must fight to retain the freedom they love.

The dark side of globalization casts a long shadow. Time and space have been erased by new technologies, and there are no outsiders anymore in the world. Everyone is inside, which means that surveillance will increase until the global village is more than a metaphor. The world needs a neighborhood watch in a different context, one in which self-interest edges toward mutuality that balances the multiple needs of our planet in precarious tension.

This is not about America but about the kind of order possible in a world shot through with evil deeds. The degree of our freedom must be equal to the hatred of the hollow men and their hollow selves—their false selves. Only the power of self-transcendence can see evil in deeds and not in beings, then choose through tears of rage not only to destroy, but to build in the midst of destruction.

Lest We Forget   *November 23, 2001*

Life is a dynamic process, not a steady state, so things are always in motion, including ourselves. Maybe that's why Aristotle said the Golden Mean is something we see only when we look back over our shoulders as we tack past it, trying to sail closer to the wind. And maybe that's why, when we try to respond to urgent events, we often overcorrect.

If we have been overly cautious, for example, we correct by taking greater risks and that can lead to recklessness. Then we correct for recklessness by becoming more prudent which can lead to becoming overly cautious. So then we correct by taking greater risks, and on it goes, an endless process resembling an infinity loop or two poles at either end of a horizontal line along which we move back and forth in search of the elusive middle.

The middle is hard to define. Once we find it, the middle is even harder to hold. But the middle must be our plumb line, lest we forget ourselves in the passion of battle.

Computer security is a good metaphor for societal security because computer networks are holographic images of societies, a piece of the whole that contains the whole in symbolic form. Perimeter defense of electronic networks, we have learned, only goes so far. It's the nature of networks to subvert boundaries because networks interpenetrate one another in indeterminate ways. Nodes can belong to any of several networks the way a subway station can be a stop on any of several lines. One consequence of this is that insiders cause the great majority of security incidents, which is also a way of saying that "insiders" and "outsiders" are difficult to distinguish in a networked world. Through the use of keystroke loggers, telephone recorders, and surveillance cameras, "insiders" in electronic networks are constantly watched. Now that the United States has been attacked from the inside with its own infrastructure, there is pressure to do the same on a societal level.

When I wrote several years ago that the level of security required in computer networks would become the level of security demanded by governments, I was only stating the obvious, that electronic networks are rings linked in concentric circles to the human networks that give them meaning. Securing the network at one level means securing it at all levels.

For a society to secure itself, however, different compacts are called into questions. Corporations can observe employees because employees are "owned" by corporations; everything they say or do on the job belongs to the boss. Citizens are not "owned" by governments in the same way. When a government ramps up to the level of security common in electronic networks, we are being asked to accept a level of surveillance unprecedented in free societies.

When I suggested a Homeland Defense Network as a kind of global "neighborhood watch," some asked if I wanted to turn people into spies or cops. The answer, of course, is no, but such an effort—not neighbors watching neighbors so much as neighbors watching out for neighbors—presumes that we are capable of experiencing ourselves as a single neighborhood with a collective sense of responsibility based on mutual self-interest. It presumes that we the people, nodes in a network, know we are a network worth preserving.

So where do we find ourselves in the ceaseless loop cycling between security and freedom?

Some think we're approaching the center, others think we're well past it.

The relevant question is not whether we can trust governments to use such power wisely but whether we can trust ourselves as human beings. Unfortunately, the historical evidence is not optimistic. That's why the United States built in checks and balances to compensate for the flaws in our all-too-human nature, flaws that would lead over time to unacceptable excesses. The question now is whether or not those checks and balances can be ported to the networked world of the 21st century on a global rather than national scale.

I have been as passionate as any in response to September 11 and as clear as most about the nature of the shift initiated by the attack. The advantage of asymmetric attackers who only have to succeed once to wreak havoc can be matched by a relatively open society only if it closes itself some. But—and it's a big "but"—in order for a society to be relatively free as well as relatively secure, those who do the surveillance must be kept under surveillance. The lights must always be on or else the deeds done in the darkness will fester and grow.

In the aftermath of the shock of attack, an absolute level of trust was projected onto our leaders. As time goes on, however, that trust must be earned and demonstrably so.

If we possess a moral imagination or any sense of history, we know what human beings are capable of doing. The moment at which those who fight monsters become monsters is usually seen only in retrospect as we look back over our shoulders at the receding point of no return. It can happen to any of us. The struggle for freedom must be waged on all fronts simultaneously, inside as well as outside, because the boundaries that distinguish an enemy from an ally are as porous as our borders.

Extremes are easier to defend on any battlefield because they simplify options. Yet the essence of civil society is found in that elusive middle where contradictions are held in precarious tension. Free people, in order to remain free, must learn to endure a level of complexity and ambiguity that would drive a conspiracy theorist nuts.

It is not disloyal to remember the truth of the human condition. That truth says that the price of freedom is a searchlight vigilance that scans all of our networks, including our own.

Lest we forget what we fight for. Lest we forget who we are.

The Cycle of Complacency   *December 24, 2001*

In the world of computer security, it's called the cycle of complacency.

A critical incident—the NIMDA virus disrupts networks or a worm takes advantage of unpatched systems to install a trojan horse—raises the level of urgency. Everyone works overtime. A crisis mentality governs the workspace, and for once, everybody pays attention. The trivial concerns of the day before are eclipsed by the need to respond and respond now. Meetings are held to discuss appropriate security and system users actually change their behaviors. They understand that they are involved in a vague kind of cyberwar, one in which malicious mischief, competitive intelligence, and state- and network-supported cyber-reconnaissance are difficult to separate. They distinguish FUD (fear, uncertainty, doubt) from "appropriate paranoia" and act accordingly.

Then the adrenaline rush subsides. The fight-or-flight level of intensity diminishes. New alarms are not followed by attacks. The reconnaissance of critical systems continues at a steady level that reduces it to background noise, "pings" echoing through the network like returns from submarine sonar. Notices of new patches begin to fill in-boxes. Default positions re-set themselves to "routine." People get back to normal. Pretty soon NIMDA and Code Red are blurred by the passage of time and all we remember is how little real damage they did to our way of life.

It's called the cycle of complacency, and in America, we are in it, both online and off.

"The sense of urgency attending a critical incident," said Stanley "Stash" Jarocki, a vice-president of Morgan Stanley and the President of the Financial Services—Information Sharing and Analysis Center (FS-ISAC), "has a ninety day half-life. After three months, people forget, you can't get money for security as easily, and those who raise the alarm are accused of crying wolf."

Jarocki ought to know. Years of experience with government and corporate security have given him a good vantage point. The ISACs—financial services, electricity reliability, and telecommunications—are designed to facilitate sharing information between corporate members and NIPC, the National Infrastructure Protection Center of the FBI. But even on the front lines, organizational cultures continually frustrate the best intentions.

Before September 11th, my speeches on how technologies have reshaped organizational structures from the workplace up to the level of national and trans-national entities were often heard as if they were scary sci-fi movies, particularly when I talked about the implications of biotechnology and space war. People felt they were watching a movie, and regardless of momentary anxiety, the lights always came up and the audience shuffled toward the exits.

Since September 11th, I speak less about the implications of technologies and more about "Making Sense of Uncertainty." The closer one gets to Ground Zero, the more often audiences are on the edges of their seats—because they are living on the edges of their lives, leaning anxiously into the future with an enhanced awareness of what's at stake.

Last week in New York, I facilitated a conversation among members of an association who had not met since September 11th. The meeting quickly became an opportunity to experience and manage the cold friction of their grief. That group was not in the cycle of complacency because they carried the devastation I had seen at Ground Zero in their hearts.

The next day I returned to the Midwest. The person on the next treadmill at a fitness center turned and said, aren't we fortunate to be in Wisconsin where we're safe?

She was not jogging in place, going nowhere, as she seemed, but running at full speed into the cycle of complacency.

We're a long way from grasping what it means to "be alert" in our daily lives the way we look both ways when we cross a busy street. It has not yet percolated through layers of denial that we are living in a war zone.

It is a war zone, however. Honestly, it is. Whether the enemy is a terrorist waiting for the signal to take a machine gun from under a winter coat in the mall or a home-grown hate group consolidating plans for spreading smallpox. The names of the haters are not the point. Besides, terror networks are nested, masks wearing masks. The effort to ferret out ultimate intentions and true identities will never be completed. In addition, collusion with those who launder money or profit from illegal drugs blurs the boundaries between hunter and hunted. Anyone who tries to map evil in the human heart gets a headache.

What will it take, I asked an veteran of the intelligence community, for people to get that the world is a war zone, that our lives are lived on the front lines?

"A rising body count," he said. "Nothing else will make the point."

After we talked about the likelihood of nuclear materials being readied for weapons and the incidence of non-standard diseases and the routes the germs might have traveled, I called another friend to discharge my anxiety.

He tried to help by putting things in perspective.

"Are you responsible," he asked, "for the well-being of the whole world?"

I thought long and hard before answering.

If we're talking about "co-dependency" and grandiosity, then the answer is obviously no. But if we're talking about seeing who we really are, seeing that we are cells in a single body with a single consciousness on a planet threatened with death. Then the answer might be different.

How can we use the vulnerability we feel at Ground Zero to short circuit the cycle of complacency and answer that question correctly?

Ground Zero is not a place. Ground Zero is a state of mind into which we are driven when reality like a knife plunges into our false self and drives us into our true Self. In that moment, we know the answer to that question.

So ... are you responsible for the well-being of the whole world?

And if you're not ... who is?

The Horror of War   *March 16, 2002*

The horror of war comes in many forms.

The more obvious horrors include picking up body parts as you dig through dust and rubble or trying to heal somehow the endlessness of grief or wanting to diminish the bitter rage that fuels a desire for revenge.

Everybody knows those horrors. It's the more subtle horrors that take time to percolate through our denial.

I love hiking in Zion National Park in Utah. One wonder of that sacred place is an oasis as green as any garden in the middle of a desert. The water that causes ferns and lilies to bloom on the rock walls of caves comes from rain that has percolated through a huge limestone plateau until it seeps out to make that oasis.

That's a good metaphor for how unseen spirits percolate through our own desert spaces and emerge in blossoming gardens when least expected. But it's also a metaphor of how things we don't want to know percolate through our denial until they too emerge with a bitter taste of snot-green bile.

Living inside our justifications, we blur details that interfere with our vision of righteousness. People who have lived as minorities know that minorities must understand a dominant culture better than it understands itself because so much is at stake if they miss a cue. Minorities do not have the luxury of minimizing the truth, whereas members of dominant cultures can focus on their myths about themselves rather than their actual behaviors.

When you're the eight hundred pound gorilla, it's easier to judge yourself by your words or good intentions while judging the enemy—any enemy—by their actions.

I have watched my share of World War II movies. There is plenty of horror there, the death camps, the Battle of Stalingrad, the massacre of millions. But there are images too of more subtle horrors: Nazi officers enjoying themselves at dinner parties; parents strolling on warm Sunday afternoons with their children; members of the Gestapo dancing and laughing in nightclubs. While all the while the more obvious horrors go on around them.

Most of those people did what most of us do when there is danger in the air—they calculate quickly how to be safe, then live life as normally as possible, while around their fear-driven decisions the tall walls of "I don't want to know" rise silently while they sleep.

I thought of this on a warm spring-like Saturday afternoon that brought a lot of us outside. Children played in the park, parents walked behind strollers. That night we had a quiet dinner with friends. Those who went to synagogues churches or mosques that weekend no doubt prayed for the triumph of good and the overthrow of evil and asked God to keep them safe.

People everywhere in the world feel less safe since September 11th. An immediateresponse is to increase surveillance, trust those in power, and spend money on weapons. That makes us feel safer.

During the Cold War, I posed the question, "How much of the world do we need to control to feel safe?"

I was looking at how we had spread ourselves around the world to the gates of the enemy. We needed the western hemisphere, of course, and we needed Europe, Africa and Asia to contain the Russians and Chinese. The entire southern hemisphere, in short, and the northern hemisphere to the border of the Warsaw Pact and west to China was what we needed. Once the Soviet Union and China were neutralized, we would almost have what we needed.

To really feel safe, we needed ... all of it.

During the Cold War, any country or movement perceived as a threat to our interests, which we defined as "our way of life," was a danger. That justified the use of any and all means to subvert, overthrow, or defeat that threat. The second half of the twentieth century is a record of two empires coming more and more to resemble one another in how they behaved on the world stage.

Those memories are the context for reflecting on the more subtle horrors of war that are seldom the subject of patriotic movies.

We become what we fight and justify what we do by projecting all of the horror onto "the other."

Intentional forgetting is how our societal mind erases those images of ourselves in the eyes of "the other." The management of perception and psychological operations are the cornerstones of war in the 21st century.

In the long term, only a fight for a better life for the wretched of the earth will generate security. The complexity of the issues before us will not be resolved by simplistic answers but that's all we'll get from what we call "the news," those wraparound seamless images of the righteousness of our cause.

When the President of the United States and the leaders of terrorist networks believe passionately that God has chosen them to achieve God's will, I do not sleep more soundly.

Since the end of World War II, the momentum rolling like thunder through our battlecries confirms our commitment to do whatever is necessary to feel safe.

We must control all of it. Opposition is the enemy.

Still ... there are disquieting moments when we see a different image of ourselves in the eyes of others than the one reinforced through repetition and consensual self-censorship. When that happens, we need to take a break ... enjoy ourselves at a dinner party, go for a stroll on a warm afternoon with our children, go dancing in nightclubs. And, of course, pray ... we must always pray for the triumph of good and the overthrow of evil.

The Spiritual Challenge *July 24, 2002*

Since the terror attack of September 11 brought to the forefront of American awareness the truth about the kind of world in which we live, which many Americans had managed to deny despite the evidence, I have watched and participated in what we might call the flexing of the American soul as it comes to terms with that reality.

Homeland Defense has absorbed billions of dollars and like an obsessive spirit possesses the media interface—the front page, the nightly news, the crawltext on CNN—and frames the way we think. There has been a lot of noise, but there has been precious little discourse about the essence of the struggle, that current events pose a spiritual challenge not only for America but for the mind and soul of a global society.

By spiritual I do not mean religious. There can be overlap between spirituality and religion but there can also be a profound disconnect. When religions are at their best, they are custodians of symbols of promise and possibility, which they hand down from generation to generation. It is up to each generation to open those symbols and explore what they disclose, an action analogous to opening our wallets and playing the game of life with real money. Otherwise the symbols become debased, devolving into means of manipulation, coercion and social control, vehicles for wielding power and for inauthentic exchanges with the faithful who give up freedom for momentary relief from anxiety about the deeper questions of our existence.

Those deeper questions are exactly what I do not hear debated. The Cold War mythology of good versus evil is being ported to the battle with terrorism and a new roster of ready villains have had the mark of the beast stamped on their foreheads. Those villains always symbolize the Other because we consider it an exception when one of our own—Timothy McVeigh for example—is an evildoer. When the Other is, it's the rule.

This is not the space in which to analyze the complexities of foreign policy although I do know that the several hundred documents that cross my desktop daily detailing events around the world from Eritrea to Singapore suggest that reality is more complex than the news media has the will or ability to say. Simplistic answers sell so simplistic answers are what we get. End of story. Literally.

So it pays, I think, to follow the money. I do not mean trace the cash flow that sustains narcotics or weapons trafficking—we amateurs will never be able to do what professionals refuse to do because of a lack of political will—but follow the flow of money in our lives and simply ask what it buys and sells. The answers would reveal our real values and inform a deeper inquiry into what is worth preserving and defending and what is not.

Spirituality includes knowing what we value and then seeing how our behaviors line up with those values. The feedback loops that let us do that can be painful to experience, however, so we prefer to believe the stories that massage our self-image. Part of the American self-image has been to believe that what's good for American business is good for the world regardless of consequences.

Our engine is an economy that mostly sells services, intangibles like entertainment, which means that most Americans consider necessary many things we could easily live without. Our economy runs on a vicious circle from manufactured desires to fulfillment of those desires and then back again. It is a fetishistic spiral that never satisfies the desires we generate in the first place but at every level of society jams our living space with supersized vehicles and supersized food.

After September 11th, one of the imperatives was to "get back to business" as quickly as possible. That translates to going to movies, setting off fireworks, doing our jobs, but not inquiring too deeply into the multiple causes of complex events lest we discover not some Illuminati conspiracy but our own hands on the multiple levers of self-deception, working the machinery behind the curtain so we will continue to believe in wizardry.

The mind of society is both the target and the weapon in our new kind of war and the management of perception from intentional deception and psychological operations to propaganda, spin, and public relations is its cornerstone. That means that truth can be exchanged only on the black market.

Yet spirituality, in its essence is the quest for truth that sets us free and keeps us free. So we can know and act on what we know. That implies that genuine spirituality will not be found in the religious marketplace where it has been turned into a commodity. We do need intentional communities that help us remember what matters, but unfortunately many religious institutions are organized around forgetting, not remembering. They may have rituals of remembering but rituals are no substitute for real remembering. Religious institutions run on money, more money than people can easily imagine, and once they have absorbed other social, economic and political agendas, those who control religious symbols do so not to set anyone free, least of all themselves, but to ensure stability and the status quo. Whether Ayatollahs getting rich in Iran or Catholic Bishops stonewalling calls for reform and taking the modified limited hang-out route to protect themselves, we who are treated as fools do know the difference.

What are we defending? Who is served? Who profits? Do we value stability and glib reassurances above all else or are there other values worth fighting for? How do we say what they are in this information windstorm howling like a gale in our faces?

Money is the dye in the arteries of our souls. Follow the money to its source. Open the books and open the doors and windows of our souls. Let in the fresh air. Remember the meaning of freedom, exchange the whispered truth in the shadows, spread the good word.

Cotton Wool as a Weapon of Mass Destruction *September 12, 2002*

Some things are so obvious, they are invisible.

Prophets see them. Prophets like Marshall McLuhan who lived between two eras and had the courage to say what he saw. Hence he was ridiculed, caricatured, and for a generation, largely forgotten. It's all there in his breakthrough works—The Gutenberg Galaxy and Understanding Media—the so-called Internet Era described in terms of television networks. Long before the Internet, McLuhan saw how electronic communication redefined the space of human life.

Make no mistake, human life does take place in a unique space, one of our own creation. Distinctively human space emerged with the co-evolution of the brain and the system of throat, tongue, teeth that enabled us to make these symbols. Reading the writing on this screen means that you participate in the space of electronic communication, the content of which is literacy, the content of which was speech, the content of which was gesture.

This is that space, this virtual domain that we humans fall into so easily we mistake it for reality. It is not reality. It is a consensual hallucination that came into being long before the Internet.

Some things are so obvious they are invisible. This space of interaction and communication is invisible. Modern war is invisible. Weapons that do not look like weapons are invisible.

We are at war, we have been at war, we will be at war. Our society and economy are predicated on the existence of war.

The recreation of the terrorist attack on Washington DC and New York by the mass media yesterday was more than amplification, more than collusion. It was terrorism masquerading as rectitude and righteousness as terrorism always does.

Without mass media, September 11th does not exist. It would never have existed because it would not have been a weapon.

The theatrical violence we call "September 11th" was designed to keep on exploding, not in New York, but in the mind of society which is where this war is being fought. "September 11th" is a mosaic of linked meaningful images. The meanings have been generated by "reports" and "features" and "analyses" which define and reinforce those images.

One year later it is obvious that September 11th was an intentional symbol full of explosive charges which would keep on exploding the way secondary bombs are built to explode when rescuers arrive on the scene of a terrorist attack.

The first goal of terrorism is to degrade the confidence of a people in its government. The second is to undermine the economy.

The attack on September 11th was merely a fuse. The crash of the airliners was the ignition. The explosions have taken place in your mind and my mind ever since, and they get into our minds through mass media. We are fused with that media. The images we see and believe flow through cables plugged into the sockets of our skulls, blinding us to our complicity.

In 1967, Marshall McLuhan said that two wars could no longer be waged at the same time in the world. He meant, of course, the "space" of the world—that virtual space of collective awareness that we humans inhabit. He said that the Arab-Israeli War put a momentary halt to the Viet Nam War because news services sent everyone to the Middle East.

Asked about the kidnapping of Aldo Morro by an Italian journalist, McLuhan said, "You can end the Morro incident any time you want by just ceasing to cover it. Terrorism is an ingenious invention by which any two or more armed people can take over an entire billion dollar industry with the complete cooperation, not only of its workers, but of its owners."

Sometimes I feel as if every single thing I think is a footnote to something said by McLuhan. But then, I have that feeling in relationship to Nietzsche too, a feeling reinforced every time I return to his work. That tells me that dead civilizations can take lots of bullets and walk for a long time before they fall.

The rectitude and righteousness of the pillars of society, unconscious that they are selling rope to those who would hang them, is the kind of blindness that made Jesus hate publicly religious people.

Because he wouldn't shut up about it, they whacked him. Hammers and nails were the preferred weapons. Today the weapon of choice is cotton wool. We are wrapped in it, living in it, dying in it, blinded by it, looking through it at white space everywhere, hearing nothing but white noise.

There is war in Nepal, war in Georgia. There is war in Afghanistan, Pakistan, and India. There is a long war in Iraq. There are wars in Columbia, Venezuela, and Mexico; wars in Israel, Lebanon, and Syria; wars in Somalia, Tajikistan, and Libya. Wars everywhere. Everywhere in the world but there is no war here. Here there are only tracer bullets arcing in the night sky that seem to originate here or there or somewhere, but we are curiously disconnected from historical causes that bind countries everywhere in all of these wars. How have we, well-intentioned innocents, somehow gotten mixed up in all of these other people's wars?

Here we have heroism. Here we have waving flags and martial music. Here we have eulogies and tears. Here we have everything but war—or the origins of war—which when we seek them disappear in the blinding white light.

We are fiercely opposed to knowing because we are afraid. We fear instability, authority and poverty, pain and death. Fear is leverage, fear is power. Fear is the visible effect but what oh what are the causes?

The causes are invisible. Perhaps the nightly news when they next describe "the news in depth," those eighty or ninety words juxtaposed with a dozen images, will illuminate these causes for us.

The war is a moving target that we can't hit because the war we think we see is not the war that is going on.

That war is invisible. That war is sanctioned. That war is profitable.

McLuhan saw the obvious and said what he saw. That made people uncomfortable. Discomfort is not pleasing to us. That is why—once again—we will choose not to see, not to know.

Do Terrorists
Really Have More Fun?   *September 26, 2002*

Bruce Schneier, the author of *Applied Cryptography* and *CTO of Counterpane Internet Security*, told me that he can't walk through a department store without seeing security as a challenge. How, he asks himself, can he outwit the coded tags and markers, surveillance cameras, and guards? That's what gets his juices flowing.

That mindset is shared by most professionals I know in computer security, intelligence, or other kinds of police work. Every "white hat" who is honest with themselves sooner or later looks into the mirror and thinks: "I don't know if I'm a cop pretending to be a criminal or a criminal pretending to be a cop."

"You have to think like a criminal," Schneier said, "in order to be good at security."

I think of a former CIA agent, recently honored by the agency for an astonishing piece of detective work, who once immersed herself in the world of prostitutes and crack-cocaine for a research project. I think of a cop who said of the adrenalin rush in his work, the chase is always the best part, tackling the suspect is second best, and double locking the cuffs is a distant third.

The shadow self animates and energizes our socially acceptable personas. The differences between people often come down to awareness of that fact, not whether it's true. Self-knowledge infuses our work with appropriate humility and when we forget who we are, it always shows.

The inner civil war is never over, so the challenge is to inflect its energies in the right direction, making it a source of power on behalf of the greater good.

Clergy are like cops in this way too, energized by inner conflicts. Clergy self-select into the profession out of an intuitive awareness of the need for a training program to become more fully human. If we're lucky, the feedback loop from the people we serve, letting us calibrate our intentions with our behaviors, becomes a source of genuine spiritual growth.

That shouldn't be surprising. This is true not only of cops and clergy but of all humankind. Civilization is a holding action against the threat of chaos.

Enter the terrorist.

Men and women who become terrorists, I imagine, are pretty bored. Terrorism is not about being poor or a victim of injustice. That's the narrative of self-justification, but it's never the whole story. Terrorists come from all walks of life. They usually share low self-esteem, a hunger for stimulation and high risk, aggression and resentment. Resentment is the essence of spiritual maladjustment because it presumes we are owed something by others instead of owing everybody everything out of simple gratitude for being alive.

Resentment scours the inner landscape of the self-obsessed like acid rain. It's the precondition of payback as a way of life.

Along comes someone offering an identity that makes sense of those demon energies, offering support and community, offering a reason to exist, a part to play in a cosmic drama. Instead of being nobody in particular, we are … somebody. We are soldiers in the armies of righteousness. Our hunger for action finds an outlet.

No longer boring, the world presents a challenge: How can I kill as many people as possible? How can I stick in my thumb and pull out a plum and say oh, what a big boy am I?

It is much more fun to play that game than to walk the perimeter hour after hour in a dead patrol. The night watchman on his rounds does not have fun. The one hidden in the shadows waiting for him has a heart on fire.

When we watch escape movies, we identify with prisoners outwitting the system, not the guards. Goodness is boring. Plotting and blowing things up, that's exciting. Bloodshed is exciting. How can low-paid work in some obscure corner of the world compete with that rush?

Enter the counter-terrorist.

The men and women I know who wage war with the threat of chaos have many of those same traits, as I said, but turn their furies in a different direction. They work out conflicts, expiate guilt, and alleviate shame by pursuing bad actors. The best of them know the world is gray, but stopping people from mass murder gets us out of gray areas in a hurry.

Many of those same professionals also have a deep personal spirituality. I think of an intelligence professional who chuckles as he describes how to deflate the grandiose egos of terrorists with non-lethal weapons like stickum, slickum, and ultra-sound. The sight of terrorists slipping all over the pavement or vomiting helplessly would puncture the false self, he says, undermining the terrorist's projection of power and invincibility.

Why does he think that would work? Because his spiritual base includes peri-odic deflation of his own grandiose self in a disciplined way. Spirituality for him means using traditional tools to keep himself in perspective. It means surrendering the right to be resentful and justifiably righteous in order to find common ground in the merely human.

I don't know why at the crossroads of our lives some choose life and some choose death. The reasons are a mystery, which is a way of saying we know but don't know how to say what we know. Mystery is intuition rewarded with a clarity impossible to translate other than into the metaphorical language of dreams or poetry or the obscure native language of the soul.

Evil is seductive but so is the chase, so is outwitting an enemy, so is an ordinary fall day, for that matter, an afternoon in the sun watching migrating geese fill the sky from horizon to horizon.

Ordinary days are worth defending. Really, they're as much fun as killing millions. You just have to see the game in the right light, and besides, then you bequeath a legacy to the next generation of how to be fully human, good and evil mixed, and responsible for it at the same time.

When Should You Tell the Kids?

October 4, 2002

A newsletter for former intelligence officers (no, I am not one, I just read it) contained two requests this week from researchers. One is a Washington Post intelligence reporter who wants information about "that particular moment in a clandestine agent's life when he/she tells the children what they really do for a living."

The other request came from a social psychologist "preparing a utilitarian assessment of torture interrogation of terrorists to submit to a military ethics conference." His study is focused on institutional consequences of state-sponsored torture interrogations such as the involvement of the biomedical community. He is especially interested in "testaments to the efficacy of torture interrogation in eliciting accurate and crucial information."

I hope those researchers get together. It would be interesting to know about the moment in a torturer's life when he or she tells the kids what they do for a living.

State sponsored torture is being debated as a viable option, and lawyers such as Alan Dershowitz suggest that torture warrants should be issued by judges if evidence suggests that a situation is time-critical. The process of securing warrants would provide a sufficient check, he believes, on state and federal interrogators.

I imagine this debate sounds different to Arab-Americans or African-Americans than it does to an affluent lawyer who seldom hears suspects with sterilized needles under their fingernails screaming through the arbor vitae. On the other hand, it says something positive about the assimilation of Jews in America—that Dershowitz who is Jewish does not even worry about how such warrants might be used if the American experiment in assimilation fails.

I recall having dinner in Madrid with a Spaniard 35 years ago. "America is a great country," he said, "but it is a very young country."

I felt the weight of his words, that two or three or four hundred years down the line, when historical conditions will have turned American history into the roller coaster that Spain's has been, we might see ourselves differently. We might be a little less innocent, a little less naïve.

The German-Jewish population was the most assimilated Jewish community in history before the holocaust. Then Germany lost its moorings. Any society can lose its moorings. It can happen here, and one sign that it might be happening is when social scientists and medical practitioners believe they are justified in discussing torture as a practical matter rather than a moral issue.

I grew up in Chicago where police did not need a torture warrant to interrogate suspects by whacking them with telephone books. That may have distorted my perspective, but I think it's pretty much the same everywhere. Chicago just does more openly what everybody does more furtively. I live now in Milwaukee, arguably the most segregated city in America. It wasn't long ago that a policeman went on trial for beating a white man almost to death and blurted out that he had recently been transferred to a new district from an all-black neighborhood and had not realized that the rules were different.

The policeman who told me that story mentioned a time he had to leave an alley where colleagues were interrogating a suspect in a way that made him sick to his stomach.

It is not news to say that beatings and torture have long been part of the interrogation process, depending on who is the suspect and who is doing the questioning. Nor is it news that at Fort Benning, Georgia, American military officers taught agents of Central and South American police states how to use torture effectively.

We all know it happens. That isn't the question. The question is, are we ashamed that it happens?

You can tell a lot by knowing what someone is ashamed of.

Feeling appropriate guilt and rationalizing behaviors by instituting policies that justify and support them publicly are two different things. That difference makes all the difference between a society that can't always live up to its ideals and one that has forgotten where it put them.

It is not that we can't imagine circumstances in which we too would use any means necessary to protect those we love. We can. But extending that imaginary scenario to the nation and its interests during a time of anxiety and fear is too easy.

The American assertion of a right to pre-emptively strike an enemy is a logical extension of the belief that torture is justified by evidence that suggests an imminent attack. But why would a nation need to announce such a policy? After all, pre-emptive strikes have always been sanctioned by international law. So maybe the declaration is not really about that.

It sounds as if the Monroe Doctrine is being extended to the entire world. Exporting tools and techniques of torture to governments in our hemisphere was a logical consequence of the Monroe Doctrine, which insists that we can do anything in our own neighborhood in defense of our interests. If that neighborhood is now the world, if the front lines are everywhere, then the expediency of forgetfulness under fire applies to the basement of the local, state or national police as well.

A person who can calmly suggest using torture, who believes that a warrant will adequately handle the inevitable mistakes or malevolent intentions of people with power, is someone who can't imagine themselves being tortured. They can only imagine the torture of the Other.

Jacobo Timmerman, a large publisher in Argentina, could not imagine himself being taken until he found himself in a cell without a number, a prisoner without a name. He speaks of watching a woman led from her cell to receive electric shocks and a hood being placed over her head. They did that, he said, so the torturer would not have to look into her eyes. If you look into the eyes, he said, you see a human being and then you can't do the job.

Once social scientists, doctors, and lawyers provide a veneer of respectability to sanctioned torture, it is removed from the moral domain. Once torture is debatable, it is only a matter of time until it is tacitly or officially sanctioned.

Then the task will be keeping that hood down over the face of the Other. So long as the screams come from someone who is a little less than human, we can live with it. The goal, after all, as Dershowitz explains, is short-term excruciating pain, not long-term damage. It's just a job. Somebody has to do it, and we can imagine the practitioners of that craft having a picnic with their kids, flying kites or running in slow motion through a wild flower meadow, then tumbling laughing into the tall grass and telling the kiddies what they do for a living.

The sadness of the human condition is that, if we are honest with ourselves, we can each see how, under the right conditions, we too will enter into collusion with the state—if not actively participate in the practice. History has illustrated time and time again that under the right conditions, individuals will do anything.

Which is why preventing those conditions from happening in the first place is the only defense against the abyss.

Flesh   *October 11, 2002*

"I am obsessed with the body," Isabel Letelier said. "I turned from painting to sculpture because I needed to work with something I could feel. Bodies are so open, so vulnerable, so easy to abuse."

Isabel Letelier had just read my column, "When Should You Tell the Kids?," about proposals to use torture to elicit information from suspected terrorists. It recalled memories that clouded her eyes.

"I was teaching Spanish to English speakers in Washington," she said. "One morning I came to work and the elevator didn't work. A sign said that the U.S.A.I.D. (Agency for International Development) was holding classes and access was forbidden to unauthorized personnel.

"I went upstairs and the halls were full of paramilitary in battle dress from Spanish speaking countries, some from Chile. What are you doing? I asked a young man.

"Learning to fight guerillas," he said.

"But we don't have any guerillas in our country."

"We do, but they are invisible. The enemy is within."

Isabel noticed diagrams on the walls identifying points on the human body. "What are those?"

"Sensitive points," he said with a smile "We are learning how to interrogate guerillas."

"I was so naïve," she told me, " I didn't realize the United States was teaching them how to torture under the cover of that agency."

Isabel Letelier and I were gathered with others last week for the twentieth reunion of recipients of the Gamaliel Chair in Peace and Justice, an annual speaking opportunity sponsored by the Lutheran Campus Ministry at the University of Wisconsin Milwaukee.

Isabel Letelier learned more about torture than she ever wanted to know. Her husband, Orlando Letelier, served as Ambassador to the United States from Chile under the government of Salvador Allende before being called home to serve in the cabinet. His expertise in economics was needed when the Nixon administration, having failed to subvert Allende's election and inauguration, worked to undermine the Chilean economy.

Because their first attempt to overthrow the democratically elected government of Chile by a military coup had failed, Nixon told the CIA, "We will make the economy scream." .

"They did, too," Isabel said, "Our major export is copper which moved in American trucks. Manufacturers refused to give us spare parts. They subverted the economy every way they could."

A second coup, backed by the CIA, succeeded. Allende was overthrown by General Augusto Pinochet and the military. Orlando Letelier was tortured, beaten, his fingers broken. He was sent to Dawson Island, a concentration camp near Antarctica. Pressure from friends and colleagues led to Letelier's release and deportation, first to Venezuela, then to the United States. In Washington he continued to speak out against the Fascist regime. He received numerous threats.

Anonymous callers told Isabel she was not a wife but a widow. When a dead chicken was found in her front hallway, she called the police.

"It's a chicken," an officer said. "What do you want us to do?"

"It's a threat," she said. "They are planning to kill my husband."

"It looks fresh," the officer said, pointing to the blood pooling from its headless body. "Maybe you can eat it for dinner."

A bomb planted in Orlando Letelier's automobile exploded, severing his legs and killing him instantly. It was revealed later that the killers were part of a cooperative effort in state terror (under the guise of counter terror) called Operation Condor carried out by Argentina, Bolivia, Chile, Uruguay, Paraguay, and Brazil.

The CIA knew about Condor but did not prevent the assassinations. After Letelier was killed, the agency leaked inaccurate information to the press to divert attention.

Terrorism consists of violent illegal behaviors configured to the contours of perceived political necessity that justifies that violence and illegality. Terrorism can be carried out by state or non-state actors. It is a set of behaviors regardless of who does them.

Isabel Letelier spoke of friends showing her holes in their breasts where cigarettes had been repeatedly crushed out during interrogations, damaged legs on which they had been forced to stand for days, scars from electric shocks all over their bodies. They spoke of unspeakable indignities that made the flesh crawl.

"Flesh," she said, "is so vulnerable. Our bodies are so available."

She became obsessed with bodies.

The only defense of the flesh is the will and intention of a society not to permit its violation. It is not what we say that matters but what we do, and what we have often done is the worst that people can do. The track record is not good.

When Isabel Letelier was told of her husband's murder, she gathered her four sons in her arms and made them swear that they would not hate. They would seek justice, yes, but they must not hate lest they too fall into the abyss.

I don't know a good definition of spirituality but I know it when I see it.

That act by Isabel Letelier was the real thing.

Words in print, words on a monitor, are easy to mistake for the real thing. But this medium is reality once removed. It is words about torture, not torture. Words become real only when they become flesh.

Flesh is a thin envelope that opens to reveal our real beliefs when it is torn.

There were judges in Chile, the equivalent of "torture warrants," the consensual fictions of a lawful society. That did not prevent the society from tumbling into the abyss.

A nation cannot claim the high moral ground unless its words become flesh. Words read in a vague disconnected way from a teleprompter, words about meeting terror with terror … those words are a means of numbing the moral sense. They are not the real thing.

The real thing looks like a declaration on behalf of forgiveness and justice seamlessly fused in the prayer of a sobbing widow on her knees, holding her sons.

In the Crazy Place   *February 7, 2003*

The Internet, like a kaleidoscope, unceasingly juxtaposes images in different patterns. Turning on the computer in the morning is almost like casting the I ching or throwing bones. Sometimes the images form a coherent picture of everyday reality, but sometimes …. sometimes they illuminate a crazy place.

Three translucent images came to the desktop the other day to be tilted into an architect's model.

One came from Sharon Begley's science column in the *Wall Street Journal*. Begley wrote about videotapes and how the field of focus skews what we see.

To videotape police interrogations and let juries see the raw footage so they could evaluate confessions for themselves sounded like a simple idea.

But studies show that we assign responsibility based on what we think we see and that, in turn, is determined by the field of focus of the camera. It's called "illusory causation" and it means that we ascribe causality to people in the foreground and not to people we can't see.

When the video shows an individual answering questions, we give undue weight to the words of that person. When the camera shot shows an interrogator, too, as he asks questions, responsibility is diffused.

In one case, according to the Ohio State University psychologist who conducted the study, "the simple change from an equal-focus confession to a suspect-focus confession doubled the conviction rate."

In other words, when we see the bigger picture, we realize that the context is the content of what we see. That's a metaphor, of course, for how we are led to focus on what we are meant to see and why those in the background never enter our thoughts. Out of sight, out of mind.

I was thinking of the disconnected images presented to us without any context, the juxtaposition of stories about biological attacks and stories about lost dogs, beginning to feel as if I lived in the crazy place, when the next clipping popped up.

The Spanish newspaper *El Pais* (we are told by the *Sydney Morning Herald*) reported that historians had uncovered the use of modern art as a deliberate form of torture. Mind-bending prison cells built by anarchist artists in Spain during the Civil War in the thirties turned the work of Kandinsky, Klee and Dali into inspiration for secret cells and torture centers.

Alphonse Laurencic, according to the report of his trial by the Fascists in 1939, invented a form of "psychotechnic" torture, creating "colored cells" inspired by ideas of geometric abstraction, surrealism and avant garde art theories on the psychological properties of colors.

"Beds were placed at a 20-degree angle, making them hard to sleep on, and the floors of the 1.8 metre by 0.9 metre cells were scattered with bricks and other geometric blocks to prevent prisoners from walking backwards and forwards. The only option left to prisoners was staring at the walls, curved and covered with mind-altering patterns of cubes, squares, straight lines and spirals, which utilized tricks of color, perspective and scale to cause mental confusion and distress. Lighting effects gave the impression that the dizzying patterns on the wall were moving. A stone bench was similarly designed to send a prisoner sliding to the floor. In addition, some cells were painted with tar so that they would warm up in the sun and produce asphyxiating heat."

We see what we are intended to see.

Life in the 21st century is a Laurencic cell, its walls alive with moving images and whirling patterns. Try to sit still and chairs dump us onto the floor. Tell someone that the walls are crawling toward the door and they'll think you're crazy. They can only see you, they can't see the crazy place in which you are sitting so they can't know you are simply describing the world around you, that you are in fact bitterly sane.

We keep reading Kafka because he was one of the first to describe the crazy place. A neurotic Jew in the hostile environment of eastern European Christendom, he disclosed our alienation in a way that turned insiders into outsiders. In the crazy place of his skewed vision, roads turn back on themselves like mobius strips and we never reach our destinations. Kafka transformed the environs of Prague into a Laurencic cell, shifting the angle of the camera ever so slightly so we could see the walls and the ceiling.

Kafka would love the digital world where nothing is what it seems – except when it is. He would love an Internet brimming with pixilated symbols as transitory as mist.

The next digital clip came from the Washington Post. According to a recently released Syrian prisoner, Mohammed Haydar Zammar, a Syrian-born naturalized German citizen who had lived in Hamburg and functioned as al Qaeda's prime recruiter there, was being held in Damascus at the Far' Falastin detention center run by Syrian military intelligence, "a warren of lightless cells each barely three feet long, three feet wide and less than six feet in height."

Zammar was arrested in Morocco in November 2001, then flown secretly to Syria two weeks later, his detention a result of cooperation between the United States and Syria, a nation otherwise condemned as a sponsor of terrorism.

Zammar thought his German citizenship would force Morocco to send him home. Instead he found himself shipped off to the crazy place where tiny cells prevent prisoners from lying down. Forced to remain upright or hunched over, they suffer crippling degeneration of the bones in addition to having nothing else to do but listen to the screams of the damned when it isn't their turn to be tortured.

One can imagine Zammar, a loud arrogant man who stood six feet tall and weighed 300 pounds, as his grandiose illusion of self-control collapsed into the realization that he was in the crazy place. An image of Zammar on the nightly news would show him sitting there all alone, shooting off his mouth on behalf of jihad. It would not show his keepers shooting electricity into his genitals. That might mitigate the feeling that the scumbag deserves exactly what he gets.

It's hard to believe in straight lines when you keep sliding onto the floor. How can people who can lie down at night understand people who can't? What do you think, dear reader? Are the streaming images, ideas, and symbols downloaded into our brains every day from the Net, the networks, and the newspapers intended to disclose the bigger picture? Or are they intended to show us a close-up of a single man, his guilt obvious from his expression, so we can draw the appropriate conclusions?

Terrorism whether carried out by states or non state actors is the dark side of digitalization, network-centric life and globalization just as Fascism was the dark side of mechanization and industrialization. Just as IBM assisted the Nazis in sorting and shipping those to be slaughtered, state and non-state networks that obliterate borders are coming alive everywhere in nebulous clouds of power, transforming alliances that shift with the wind. All the bets made by prior technologies are off; assassinations are the rule, not the exception, and the back alleys of the dirty business of spy against spy are now the open courtyards in which we all walk.

To become conscious of life in the crazy place is to become conscious of dread. No one in their right mind wants that. Besides, who reads Kafka anyway?

Better to acquiesce, better to believe that prisoners are all crazy, monsters without antecedents, better to believe that we live in a nightmare with no history, a meaningless mix of cubes, squares, straight lines and spirals that move across the wall, slide down to the floor, and crawl in the night into our brimming brains.

A House Divided   *February 13, 2003*

A house divided against itself can not stand.

Nor can a people, half slave, half free, long endure.

Or we might say in a network-centric world: a society divided between those who manage surveillance, intrusion and data-mining on behalf of the rest of us—and the rest of us, who lack access to the output of that universal engine—will not last forever.

In the meantime, though, we're in for a bumpy ride. As our President said, freedom doesn't come cheap.

Make no mistake, these are perilous times, and the stakes are high. There are legitimate needs for intelligence and secrecy, but that's not what we're talking about. We're talking about the ripening of a surveillance society that suggests that even prophets like Orwell, Huxley, and Philip K. Dick were not sufficiently paranoid to prepare us for the twenty-first century.

Scott McNealey's glib admonition about the loss of privacy—"Get over it!"—is no longer the flip realism of a Silicon Valley seer but a sinister warning. Those who have access to information and know what to do with it are free. Those who do not are slaves.

Transparency of political and economic processes is the only way to ensure accountability, but we live in a world in which transparency is increasingly a one-way street. The power to drill down into the data, map patterns and see deviations, the ability to see, period, is vested in fewer and fewer people, the Keepers of the Real, those who Know. We are asked to trust them with this power, but if I recall the words of Lyndon Johnson correctly, trust is when you have them by the cojones, and at the moment, it isn't our hands doing the squeezing.

Meanwhile policies are proposed that make Lincoln's suspension of habeas corpus look like child's play.

Thomas Jefferson advocated free public libraries because he thought the availability of information was essential for a democracy. Contrast that vision with Total Information Awareness, the government plan to cross-correlate data related to travel, credit, the library books we read, everything, but to share that data only among the Keepers of the Real. Meanwhile, the free flow of scientific and technical information—like the flow of foreign scientists and technicians in the flesh—is increasingly throttled.

It's a real dilemma, isn't it? In a free society terrorists can use any aspect of the infrastructure as a weapon. Cars can be stopped on roads and bridges, airplanes turned into missiles, subways turned into tombs. The only defense, we are told, is to monitor everything and look for suspicious activity.

But where will it go next? I have said before and will say again that the practices of information security foretell how a society will implement security at all levels. Why? Because information and communication technologies shape the structures of society. Distributed networks give rise to distributed networks. What is necessary in the networked world becomes necessary in the physical world too.

In the realm of computer security, for example, it was recognized that efforts to secure network perimeters often fail because 80% of unlawful intrusions originate with insiders. The logical next step was surveillance of insiders through keystroke logging and anomaly detection so deviations from sanctioned behaviors could be flagged.

In the physical world, too, with its leaky national borders, insiders and outsiders have become impossible to distinguish, so perimeter defense doesn't work. The logical next step—ubiquitous surveillance and anomaly detection—is exactly what we're getting.

Cameras are everywhere. If a camera detects a person walking erratically through a parking lot, the person is flagged because they might be stealing a car. That methodology applied to travel, financial transactions, and the other movements that constitute social and economic life in a digital world means that any deviation from the norm, a norm determined by the Keepers, will set off alarms. As the knowledge that we are watched is internalized, we will watch ourselves, doing the job for them.

In addition, the end of a meaningful distinction between insider and outsider has also caused the fusion of foreign intelligence and domestic police operations. What we used to call necessary safeguards are deemed irrelevant and a single panoptic eye looks inside, outside, all around.

Ironic, isn't it? Advocates of the New Economy called for silos to come down, information to flow freely, organizations to restructure, and so they did. But rather than flatten onto a single horizontal plane, hierarchy has been reinvented on a larger scale. The horizontal structures are just bigger branches on taller trees. And at the tree tops are digital images of leaders, stabilizers for their perpetually frightened followers, the inverse of roots.

The geometry of the twenty first century is apparent. There is no outside; there is only an "inside" and the tower from which the Keepers can keep watch. Enemies will be defined as anyone who opposes their power, whether real terrorists, serious journalists, political opponents, or just plain citizens who want to know what's going on. Secrecy in the name of security will protect not only essential secrets but incompetence and malfeasance as well. Just as a recent proposal from the Department of Justice says that behaviors such as hanging out with terrorists should be interpreted as an implicit request for the revocation of American citizenship, those who deviate from "domestic norms" may also find themselves exiled.

Let's remember "Echelon" and make a prediction.

Echelon is the name popularly given to the enterprise of intercepting worldwide communications by English-speaking countries. Because American law prevented Americans from spying on other Americans, we relied on our partners to do it for us. As a CIA veteran told me, forgiveness is easier to get than permission. Intercepts were shared in the name of the greater good.

Let's port that lesson from information security to the physical world.

Assassination was recently decreed by the President to be an acceptable option. Other nations such as Israel are also on record saying they will kill their enemies wherever they can find them.

A recent strike at senior Al Qaeda in Yemen killed an American citizen. The action was tolerable "there," even if assassinating Americans in America is still off limits. But porous borders make "here" and "there" meaningless, so it's only a matter of time until American citizens are assassinated "here" too. It will be justified in the name of security and necessity, and just as the identity of the source of some Echelon intercepts was unknown, we will not always know which finger pulls the trigger.

The Invasion of the Body Snatchers was filmed first during the McCarthy era. A thinly disguised allegory, it showed that danger came when we fell asleep.

Nothing is inevitable, Marshall McLuhan said, so long as we are willing to contemplate what is happening. Awareness is the precondition of action, and if there is any moral imperative in our time, it begins with staying awake.

The willingness to stay awake and mobilize our best selves for the battle ahead is the real challenge facing this generation. The President was right. Freedom doesn't come cheap, and the ones likely to learn that first are the real journalists, real hackers and the real insomniacs.

The Problem of Empathy   *March 26, 2003*

It feels like that moment when Obi-Wan Kenobi suddenly lowered his head as if he had a bad headache and said he sensed a disturbance in the force.

In that Star Wars episode, Obi-Wan was feeling the explosion of a planet and the dying of all its inhabitants.

It's hard to stay in denial when a whole planet is exploding.

Which those of us on earth should realize right about now.

I don't mean it's the end of civilization or anything apocalyptic. It's more the end of a youthful phase. Every generation has its own passage when it loses innocence. We tried to tell our kids what it was like during Viet Nam, when the cities burned after the assassinations, when Watergate threatened to bring down the government, but everybody has to hear the screams for themselves. There's no mistaking them, once you hear them. No forgetting them either.

"You have to compartmentalize what you're doing," a veteran told me candidly. "You're killing people, sometimes innocent people. You have to understand that in a way that makes it OK."

Now, I confess to being radically impractical. It has plagued me my whole life long. So take what I say with a grain of salt. This reflection won't help you make more money, get a promotion, or manipulate some demographic into buying what you're selling. But I feel the headache coming on that says there's a disturbance in the force and maybe this will help.

It's about feeling, not thinking. Too much thinking results in software that mistakes our planes for supersonic enemy missiles and shoots them down. Too much thinking gives machines the responsibility for too much of the fighting. We need to listen to feelings once in a while and remember that the enemy is human too.

Years ago, when I was a clergyman doing counseling, I had to learn how not to open myself completely to others' feelings. I had to set boundaries so I wouldn't mistake myself for others. Frequently in the evening when I expressed anxiety about something, my wife would say, "That's not you. It's someone else. You're mistaking yourself for someone else."

So empathy can be a problem. Appropriate distance is necessary. But too much distance can make us deaf to what others are trying to tell us. Too little empathy and policy and planning can go awry.

I wonder how I would feel if here in the Midwest we had been bombarded for months with leaflets, or heard on our radios the French-accented English of Quebecois explaining how the Bush Regime so-threatened them that self-preservation required that they liberate us from its tyranny before it could strike first. They would warn us not to resist when they came across the border and rolled toward Chicago. They were doing this, they said, not for the complex reasons that usually lead people to start a war but for our own good and the good of the world. They expect us, therefore, to line the interstate, waving Quebec flags gleefully as their armor thunders past.

I mean, are these people in touch with reality *at all*?

Ten days ago in Washington DC, some of the smartest people I know in information security repeatedly said things like, Bush has gone about this the wrong way. He believes he's right so deeply that nothing can stop him. Now we've got to try to salvage the situation.

These are not knee-jerk responses, mind you, these are people who understand the threats. They listen to intercepts and hear terrorists plan our demise. What we hear, one told me, scares us shitless.

They know the world is messy and complex and motives always mixed. They are patriots, working long hours out of the spotlight on behalf of a country they love. Yet so many were deeply concerned about how this thing was done.

Despite the rhetoric of post-9/11, little has changed in our nation's capital. People still talk primarily to themselves. Outside the beltway it's hard to understand the smallness of the vision that results. It's difficult to overstate how bureaucracies kill the human spirit, filtering out people who take risks or respond to challenges, not by hiding, but by rising to the occasion. It sounds like a caricature so say that the agency across the river is more often the primary competitor while real evildoers are secondary targets, but it's not. Trying to suggest that they're forgetting something is like little people tugging at the cuffs of big people lost in conversation in the clouds high above.

Forgetting, for example, that empathy is critical to policy and planning because troops can take Baghdad and all Iraq and still lose the real war—the one that begins when the shooting stops. Forgetting that the mind of society is the enclosed battlespace of the 21st century, all war is theater, and audiences super-saturated with media images are the main players. Forgetting that the real shock and awe is ours, when we realized they were surprised by how the world responded, how natives fought on their own territory, and by the growing concern of Americans who bought a war against terrorism, but somehow were delivered a land war in Iraq.

Empathy is required for winning the peace, if not for winning the war. Understanding the feelings of human beings and the consequences of our actions seems like a minimal requirement for policy and planning but apparently it's not. The capacity to get outside ourselves and feel what others feel does not mean surrendering our self-interest in some naive belief that others are better than ourselves, because they're not—there is no moral high ground when the shooting starts. But it does mean understanding who others are because then we remember who we are, too. Then we might remember that mutual self-interest is best served by a vision that sees further than the middle of next week.

Looking Through the One-Way Mirror

April 22, 2003

Narcissism is endless, and deadly.

When narcissists look around, like God on the seventh day of creation, they love what they see because everything is good. But all they see is themselves.

Think of relationships you have had with narcissists. After a while, it feels like we're on the outside of a one-way mirror looking in at a person who appears to be looking at us but who, in fact, never sees anything (or anyone) but themselves.

It's similar when you live inside a culture. It's difficult to see anyone outside.

A recent trip to a village in England where I lived thirty years ago provided a benchmark for the narcissism intrinsic to globalism. Thirty years ago we shopped on the High Street by visiting small shops that sold dairy products, vegetables and fruits, bread, and meat. We rented a television that received three channels. There were no home computers, video recorders, or internet. We found a house to rent only when we visited the village because shared real estate listings did not exist.

To be "there" meant to be in a place with boundaries. Look up and down the High Street and your gaze is stopped by a church or curve in the road. Towns in America are more often built along highways and railroads. Look left or right and you see a straight road to the horizon. The town is a place to pass through on a trip to somewhere else.

When I walked up High Street in the village last year, the sense of a bounded place had shifted. Of all the small shops, only a butcher shop remained, now called "A Taste of Yesterday." The others were consolidated in two huge supermarkets anchored by a Starbucks. McDonald's, Burger King, KFC, and Pizza Hut were prominent. Everyone had cable television tuned to global media, neighbors surfed the internet through broadband connections, and Blockbusters took up space next to a multiplex cinema showing *Die Another Day*.

Street-level storefronts were obviously forms of media just as much as video, cable, and the Internet. They surrounded me with mirror images of my culture, myself. I had not left home because home like a moebius strip confronted me with images of myself in all directions.

That's not news, really, but it was a striking benchmark for how much of the world has become a one-way mirror surrounding us all with images of a larger global self. Those images and symbols function as social controls providing feedback in classic cybernetic fashion. In mass media, they thread our lives with anxiety and fear, then reassure us with images of comfort.

Religious and patriotic symbols shed the meanings they once had and become peas in a shell game. The hands of perception managers move faster than the eye.

The war in Iraq clarified the nature of the American presence in the Middle East and the world as it was intended to do. The war itself was theater intended to communicate a larger truth that can then be used as leverage. The images fed to us 24/7 by competitive networks told little of the real story. Depth was again sacrificed to images that were skin-deep, clarifying the totality of the victory, not only of American arms, but of that wrap-around mirror feeding our narcissistic self with reinforcing images.

Now the real war begins or, rather, continues. Dissidents who oversimplify the war as a quest for oil or the personal crusade of an American president play into the hands of the masters of deception. If we agree to accept simplistic interpretations and media images as our currency of discourse, then we lose. Victory consists of determining the language by which events are interpreted, not the conclusions to which people subsequently come.

Whereas in the past poets created the dialect of the tribe, today it's surround-sound talking heads. Information warfare is the entire fractal-like linkage between symbols and meanings and how they are managed. Information moves not just mountains, but masses of frightened people. Those scenes of looting, which could have been prevented, were as effective a threat of impending chaos as images of rioting after the assassinations in the sixties. As crowd control, they are better than tear gas or mace.

An immense war machine operating from a network centric brain achieved its dual objectives of creating fear in those who oppose us and helplessness in dissidents at home. Opposition here as abroad was dismissed as irrelevant to the task at hand. Americans no less than Middle Easterners got the message.

Meanwhile terrorists in Lackawanna, New York entered guilty pleas, reportedly induced by threats of removing them from the criminal justice system and designating them "enemy combatants" who could be held indefinitely without charge or access to lawyers.

Once we sanction a way to remove people from the criminal justice system, the system no longer exists. Once we send people to countries to be interrogated by harsh methods because we don't do that sort of thing, we become people who do that sort of thing.

Asked what he thought the world learned from the Holocaust, Elie Wiesel said, the world learned that you can get away with it.

People with power do what they can. Because they can. Period.

A great many-tentacled hydra-headed monster is crawling through the desert. We try to make out its form through the blinding sand but can't. All we see are arms whipping in the dust and a sky obscured by buckle and warp.

Don't be concerned. Just change channels. Anyway, the war has become boring. The economy needs our support. Shop, buy tickets, invest in corporations that profit from war and its aftermath. Take trips to Disneyland in airplanes with tired pilots tripling their hours in the air. Listen to news punctuated with applause, sitcoms interrupted by laugh tracks, watch political theater threaded through with encouragement and reassurance.

Enjoy the circus in the funhouse mirror, the images of flags waving, images of POWS (ours) greeting emotional families. Cry when they cry, laugh when they laugh. Celebrate images of warriors, victorious. Wince at an image of an armless Iraqi boy, now a poster child not of brutality but of our compassion as we send medical care as we send Bechtel to rebuild everything we have smashed. Laugh, wince, celebrate, cry. The mirror spins around us, images blurring. Calliope pipes play shrill notes. Clear the rubble, bury the dead, dump truth down the memory hole, and let's get on with whatever is next.

The Brain Needs Time
to Catch Up With the Body   *May 8, 2003*

"Is that how you experience Israel?" asked my friend when I shared what I wrote about a week in Tel Aviv and Eilat. "With all the bombs, guns, and weapons, it sounds more like Texas!"

I was in Israel to keynote the security track of an annual Microsoft Israel conference. I arrived in Tel Aviv on Sunday and stayed at a hotel on the beach. Two friends joined me for dinner in a pub near the hotel. One was particularly anxious because there was no security guard at the door. I hadn't even noticed because I wasn't really in Israel yet. My head was back somewhere over Cyprus beginning a descent.

After dinner I walked the length of the beach along the Mediterranean. I noticed Mike's Place, a blues bar near my hotel. I asked about the music and was told that Tuesdays are jam nights when lots of musicians come to play. Since I was leaving Monday for Eilat, I didn't go, but a lot of others did and they were inside on Tuesday when a suicide bomber exploded, killing three people and wounding fifty more.

Similar to the train station explosion near Netanya a few weeks earlier, a guard was the hero, stopping the bomber from reaching the crowd. He took the full force of the blast but survived. The guards are mostly young guys just out of the army earning five bucks an hour. Nearly every restaurant, shop, bar, hotel has an armed guard at the door who asks if you carry a weapon (many are), inspects parcels and backpacks, and sometimes pats you down. In the hotels during the conference when hundreds of people jammed stairways to go to dinner or a party, extra guards were on duty.

Walking with a colleague to a neighboring hotel for a session, I waited while a guard checked his permit. "Sorry," he said as he caught up, "I'm carrying a gun."

"I'm glad you're carrying a gun," I replied. Clearly I was living more in Israel by then. But after a moment I said, "I think. I don't know you real well, do I?"

By the end of the week I shared my friend's apprehension if I was inside a place that did not have a guard. It becomes second nature. You scan people around you for a bulky coat, a backpack. You "read the space" for anomalies, looking for incongruities. In a taxi to the Eilat airport at the end of the conference, police blocked the approach and traffic backed up. The cab jumped the divider and circled around the other way. You always have multiple routes to your goal in mind.

Two days before I was scheduled to leave there was a general strike. No one knew, day by day, how long it would last. All flights in and out of Israel were shut down, except emergency flights. I had lunch with the Minister of Science and Technology on my last day in Eilat. He had just returned from France, and I asked how he was able to land. He said he had to fly to Poland to join the President of

Israel, who was returning from a state visit. Even at his level, you plan for failure and always have a backup.

I flew back to Tel Aviv knowing only that the flight I was supposed to take home was cancelled. Microsoft investigated a charter flight to Athens where we might pick up a commercial flight and we thought of taking a bus to Amman but long delays at the Jordanian border made us decide not to do that.

That night I looked at the flowers in front of the bombed-out nightclub. They reminded me of bouquets at the World Trade Center after 9/11. The flowers always contrast with the rubble and destruction. The smell of ashes is always stronger than the scent of petals.

As it happened, they lifted the strike and I left the next afternoon.

I was disappointed not to stay longer, not to have more time to explore the streets of Tel Aviv, brimming with vitality and life. By then, the powerful impact of being in Israel, dealing with all that, had taken hold.

What happens is, you focus on what's happening here and now. You live in the moment and open your senses. You are aware of what's around you. You evaluate what's likely to happen next on a short term basis. Because of this, great conversations happen in lines at the airport, waiting for the shuttle, everywhere.

Didn't it seem surreal? I was asked when I returned. No, it didn't. It seemed real. The gray cold fog and absolute quiet of the empty streets of my hometown seemed surreal—not the heightened sense of being vibrantly alive in a place you love.

We never know what's coming next. Most of the time, though, we don't really know that we don't know. In Israel you know that you don't know what's next and that compels you to live in the present.

Mike's Place was scheduled to open the next week. Israelis refuse to stop living because of threats. That spirit is contagious. You feel more alive, not less.

The security track was about learning to live with risks, manage vulnerabilities and minimize unpredictable events. Life on the ground was about that too.

"It's ironic that you see our 'peace' as a kind of war," my friend wrote. "For us things are good when terrorists explode only once or twice a week."

Another Israeli friend wrote, "I am so glad we met here in Tel Aviv, my home town, where I live and create. This is how we live, this is our essence and our core. Although this lifestyle is not endorsed elsewhere (I say that with a smile), it makes us better. This is our home. This is our home and we love it."

Moral Schmoral

August 17, 2003

One way a government mobilizes support for morally dubious actions is to make those actions sound like the right thing to do. Decisions made for other reasons entirely, for reasons of strategy, say, or economic advantage, are cloaked in religious rhetoric, and when our leaders claim the moral high ground, we the people want to believe them.

Recent caricatures show how Moslem terrorists like Osama bin Laden and Christian crusaders like George W. Bush use nearly identical rhetoric to justify their actions. Both abuse their religious traditions to manipulate believers in those traditions.

Those who worry about such things are often pained because the desire to believe and follow our leaders is twisted. That desire is contradicted by obvious discrepancies in what our leaders are doing rather than saying.

This gets a person with a strong conscience into a real pickle. The simple fact is, any person willing to act on the convictions of a strong conscience is as much an enemy of the state as an avowed terrorist because they will not accept the designer lies of the state as the motivation for its morally dubious actions.

Perhaps this is illustrated best with a historical example. Let's use Operation Paperclip.

The United States and its western European allies agreed after World War II to deny immigration rights and work opportunities to Nazis with scientific and technological expertise who were more than trivially connected to the Third Reich. Those who joined the party before 1933 or advanced in the SA (Brown Shirts) or the SS or were identified by credible witnesses as participating in atrocities were included in that category.

Contradictions arose, however, after the war. Denying German scientific expertise to the Soviets and using it ourselves became primary motivations for wanting those Germans here, working for us. Over time the need for German proficiency in aerospace design, lasers, and other advanced research superceded moral concerns for what they had done during the war.

Operation Paperclip was the name of the project that assimilated Nazi scientists into the American establishment by obscuring their histories and short-circuiting efforts to bring their true stories to light. The project was led by officers in the United States Army. Although the program officially ended in September 1947, those officers and others carried out a conspiracy until the mid-fifties that bypassed both law and presidential directive to keep Paperclip going. Neither Truman nor Eisenhower were informed that their instructions were ignored, and if there is a lesson to be learned from Operation Paperclip, it is that, as Elie Wiesel said of the Holocaust, the world can get away with it.

Please note: those who documented Operation Paperclip are not "conspiracy theorists." They are journalists and scholars who described a genuine conspiracy.

Fast forward fifty years.

When Total Information Awareness—the effort to mine and correlate vast amounts of data about Americans and non-Americans alike, people here and people there—became public knowledge, it was assailed for further eroding civil liberties already undermined by the Patriot Act, rights previously guaranteed by the constitution.

Asked about TIA, Secretary of Defense Donald Rumsfeld laughed at a press conference and said, "Well then, we'll change the name and do it anyway."

Rumsfeld was just stating the obvious. Data mining has long been an important area of research for the intelligence establishment. The ability to filter out irrelevant data and align the many signals transmitted by our daily transactions into profiles with predictive value has been pursued for a long time. Rumsfeld was just saying, OK, if there's a problem with the name, we'll change the name and do it secretly.

It's the combination, don't you see, of eradicating rights guaranteed by the constitution such as habeas corpus and modern technologies that enable the national security state to know and anticipate the tendencies of the souls of its citizenry, all in the name of counter-terrorism, that makes us nervous. This is not a "conspiracy theory." It is a literal description of what our leadership is and has been doing for a long time.

Back in the early days of Paperclip, when those with consciences and/or memories of Nazi atrocities tried to stop the steamroller, they were accused of being Communist agents or sympathizers or useful idiots who did not know they were manipulated by the Communist Party.

Real enemies during the Cold War became the justification for labeling persons of conscience enemies too, a strategy that was canny and intentional.

Today real terrorists are the justification for targeting persons of conscience as if they are enemies not only of America but of the American Empire too.

"Even before 9/11, U.S. armed services professionals were engaged in operations in 150 countries a year," notes Robert Kaplan approvingly in the 2003 Pitcairn Trust Lecture on World Affairs. "It is already a cliché to say that by any historical standard the United States is more an empire, especially a military one, than many care to acknowledge."

Kaplan goes on to advocate the efficient use of covert action to overthrow regimes and destabilize enemies of the empire. "The U.S. had 550,000 troops in Vietnam but didn't accomplish much," he observes, contrasting that effort with the successful appropriation of right wing groups in El Salvador with only 55 special forces trainers on the ground.

That, he suggests, is the model for the future.

I discussed this with two neighbors yesterday on a sunny lawn with late summer flowers in full bloom. One said she was concerned for what had happened to the America she knew. The other said she was too busy with her job and taking care of children to do much about it. Both felt helpless to do anything anyway, and that's the intention.

Those feelings of helplessness are typical, I would guess, but there was something else in the conversation. "You'd better be careful," one warned. "You're probably on the list."

Now, that's relatively new. The belief that there is a list. The belief that with technological advances we can be tracked, databased and identified as enemies. The belief that we are so tracked, that the information will be used against us. That's new. Among middle-aged Midwest conservative people, that's new.

Those beliefs, intermittently reinforced by stories of police or FBI questioning innocent people for speaking aloud their objections to Empire, is one means of control of mainstream citizens who "want to believe the American myth," as one put it, while evidence accumulates that the high moral ground is one more means for keeping us acquiescent and compliant.

It was warm on the sunny lawn among those flowers, yet soon enough, shorn of our real history, shorn of constitutional rights, we'll be shivering like sheep in the first chill breeze of autumn.

One could do worse than revisit Paperclip and other forgotten events, the real antecedents of our current situation. One could do worse than refuse to surrender to denial or design.

Why We Are All Getting a Little Crazy

September 5, 2003

James Jesus Angleton embodied the inevitable trajectory of a person committed to counterintelligence. Maybe he got a little crazy at the end but that might explain why we are all getting a little crazy, too.

Angleton was director of counterintelligence for the CIA from 1954 until 1974. Fans of spy fiction might think of him as John Le Carre's George Smiley, but that portrait puts a benign and smiling face on the grimace that counterintelligence practitioners can't completely hide.

For twenty years, Angleton's job was to doubt everything. This enigmatic figure presented puzzles for people to solve in every conversation, stitched designer lies into every narrative, trusted no one.

The task of counterintelligence (CI) is to figure out what the other side is doing, how they are deceiving us, what double agents they have planted in our midst. CI is predicated on double deceiving and triple deceiving the other side into believing fictions nested within fictions, always leavened with some facts, just enough to seem real.

Counterintelligence is a dangerous game. You have to be willing to sacrifice pawns to save queens. Those pawns may be loyal agents but nothing you have told them, no promises or pledges, can stand in the way of letting them go when you have to, letting them be tortured or killed or imprisoned for life to protect a plan of action.

Angleton came to suspect everyone. Whenever a mole was uncovered in our ranks, he believed that he had been allowed to discover that mole to protect a bigger one, higher up.

You see how the moebius strip twists back onto itself. Every successful operation is suspect. If you discover double agents in your own ranks, it is because the other side wanted you to find them. The more important the agent you uncover, that is how much more important the one you have not yet found must be.

Example: The Americans built a tunnel under the Berlin wall so they could tap Soviet military traffic. In fact, a mole working for the Soviets told them about the taps. But he told the Soviet's Committee for State Security (also know as the KGB), not the military, whose traffic was tapped. The KGB did not tell the military because then they might alter the traffic, which would signal that the Soviets knew about the taps. That in turn would mean there was a mole. So to protect the mole, the traffic was allowed to continue unimpeded.

The Americans, once they knew about the mole, concluded that the intercepted traffic had been bogus because the operation had been compromised from the beginning, when, in fact, the Soviets had let the Americans tap the traffic, saving their mole for future operations.

You get the idea. It's not that we know that they know that we know, but whether or not they know that we know that they know that we know.

It takes a particular kind of person to do this sort of work. Not everyone is cut out for distrusting everybody and everything, for thinking that whatever they accomplish, they are allowed to do it to protect something more important. Daily life for most people means accepting the facts of life at face value and trusting the transactions in which we are engaged, trusting the meaning of words, trusting that there is firm ground under our feet.

Otherwise we inevitably tend where Angleton tended. Every defector considered a plant, every double agent considered a triple agent, everyone in the American network considered compromised. Angleton tore the agency apart, looking for the mole he was sure the other moles he found were protecting.

I am struck lately by how many plain people, mainstream folks uninvolved in intelligence work, volunteer that that they distrust every word uttered by the government or the media. How many treat all the news as leaks or designer lies that must be deconstructed to find a motive, plan or hidden agenda. Daily life has become an exercise, in counterintelligence, just to figure out what's going on.

It's not a question of party politics. This is deeper than that. It's about trying to find our balance as we teeter precariously on the moebius strip of cover and deception that cloaks our public life, that governs the selling of the latest war, that called the air in New York clean instead of lethal, that has darkened the life of a formerly free people who enjoyed constitutional rights as if there's a mid-day eclipse. We see our own civil affairs through a glass darkly and nobody really knows what's what.

As the envelope of secrecy within which our government works has become less and less transparent, the projection of wild scenarios onto that blank space where the truth was once written has become more evident. But that only makes sense. The inability to know what is true unless you are a specialist in investigative work makes our feelings of dissonance, our craziness understandable.

We are all getting a little crazy about now. We are becoming the confused and confusing person of James Jesus Angleton in a vast undifferentiated mass, a citizenry treated as if we are the enemy of our own government. We spend too much time trying to find that coherent story that makes sense of the contradictory narratives fed to us day and night by an immense iron-dark machine riding loud in our lives.

It got to be too much and at last they let Angleton go into that good night in which he had long lived where nothing was what it seemed and everyone was suspect. So he retired and went fishing. But where can we go? On what serene lake should we go fish, listening to the cry of the loons, trailing our hands in the cold water because cold is at least a fact we can feel, one of the few in a world gone dark and very liquid?

Chapter 9

The Dark Side of the Moon and Beyond

UFOs and the Internet

July 8, 1997

"We are convinced that Roswell took place. We've had too many high ranking military officials tell us that it happened, that told us that it was clearly not of this earth," said Don Schmitt, co-author of "The Truth About the UFO Crash at Roswell," in an interview on the Internet

That interview with a "real X-Filer" can be found on one of the hundreds of web sites—in addition to Usenet groups, gopher holes stuffed with hundreds of files, and clandestine BBSs where abductees meet to compare "scoop marks"— that make up the virtual world of flying saucers.

The UFO subculture or, for some, the UFO religion on the Internet, is a huge supermarket of images and words. Everything is for sale—stories, pictures, entire belief systems. But are we buying a meal? Or a menu?

When Schmitt uses the word "Roswell," he is not merely identifying a small town in New Mexico that put itself on the map with a terrific UFO story. He uses it to mean the whole story—the one that says a UFO crashed in 1947 near the Roswell Army Air Field, after which alien bodies were recovered and a cosmic Watergate initiated.

That story is scattered on the Internet like fragments of an exploding spaceship. Do the pieces fit together to make a coherent puzzle? Or is something wrong with this picture?

Stalking the UFO Meme on the Internet

Memes are contagious ideas that replicate like viruses from mind to mind. On the Internet memes multiply rapidly. Fed by fascination, incubated in the feverish excitement of devotees transmitting stories of cosmic significance, the UFO meme mutates into new forms, some of them wondrous and strange.

"The Roswell incident" is one variation of the UFO meme.

On the Internet, Schmitt's words are hyperlinked to those of other UFO sleuths and legions of interested bystanders fascinated by the psychodynamics of the subculture as well as the "data."

Before we examine a few fragments, let's pause to remember what the Internet really is.

Copies of Copies—or Copies of Originals?

The Internet represents information through symbols or icons. So do speech, writing, and printed text. But the symbols on the Net are even further removed from the events and context to which they point.

The power of speech gave us the ability to lie, then writing hid the liar from view. That's why Plato fulminated at writing—you couldn't know what was true if you didn't have the person right there in front of you.

The printing press made it worse. Now digital images and text are on the Net. Pixels can be manipulated. Without correlation with other data, no digital photo or document can be taken at face value. There's no way to know if we're looking at a copy of an original, a copy of a copy, or a copy that has no original.

In addition, certain phenomena elicit powerful projections. Because projections are unconscious, we don't know if we're looking at iron filings obscuring a magnet or the magnet.

Carl Jung said UFOs invite projections because they're mandalas—archetypal images of our deep Selves. Unless we separate what he think we see from what we see, we're bound to be confused.

Hundreds of cross-referenced links on the Web create a matrix of credibility. In print, we document assertions with references. Footnotes are conspicuous by their absence on the Web. Information is self-referential. Symbols and images point to themselves like a ten-dimensional dog chasing its own tails.

Are there "eight firsthand witnesses who saw the bodies," "many high-ranking military officials who said it was not of this earth," or "550 witnesses stating that this was not from this earth?" Schmitt makes all of those statements in the same interview. He uses the word "witness" the way Alice in Wonderland uses words; to mean what she wants them to mean.

Tracking down the truth about the "Roswell incident" is like hunting the mythical Snark in the Lewis Carroll poem. The closer one gets to the "evidence," the more it isn't there.

There is, in fact, not one "witness" to the Roswell incident in the public domain, not one credible report that is not filtered through a private interview or privileged communication.

There are, though, lots of people making a living from it—makers of the Ray Santilli "autopsy film," guides for tours of the rival crash sites in Roswell, television producers and book publishers. It all gets very confusing.

Is any of the confusion intentional?

Ready For a Headache?

Are government agents using the subculture to manipulate public opinion? To cover up what they know? Are UFO investigators spies, "useful idiots" (as they're known in the spy trade), or just in it for the buck?

An online adventure illustrates the difficulty of getting answers.

A woman in Hamilton, Montana, was speaking to Peter Davenport, head of the National UFO Reporting Center in Seattle about a UFO she said was above her house. She said she heard beeps on the radio when it was hovering. As they spoke, some beeps sounded.

"There!" she said. "What is that?"

I recorded the beeps and posted a message on a hacker's Internet group asking for help.

I received an offer of assistance from the LoD, the Legion of Doom, a well-known hacker name. I e-mailed the beeps as an audio file to them. They examined the switching equipment used by the Montana telco and reported that the signals did not originate within the system. They could say what the signals were not, but not what they were.

In another e-mail, a writer said he had heard similar tones over telephone lines and shortwave radio near White Sands Missile Range. He said friends inside the base had given him "some info that would be of great interest. He wrote:
"The documentation and info that I am getting are going to basically confirm what a member of the team has divulged to me [about UFO occupants]. They are here, and they are not benign."

Without corroboration, that's as far as the Internet can take us.

Words originate with someone—but who? Is the name on the e-mail real? Is the account real? Was the White Sands source who he said he was? Were his contacts telling the truth? Or was he a bored kid killing time?

The UFO world is a hall of mirrors. The UFO world on the Internet is a simulation of a hall of mirrors. The truth is out there ... but how can we find it?

Plato was right. We need to know who is speaking to evaluate the data.

The Bottom Line

A number of years ago, I volunteered to be Wisconsin state director of the Mutual UFO Network in order to listen firsthand to people who claimed to have encountered UFOs. I brought sixteen years' experience as a counsellor to the project. I listened to people from all walks of life.

My interest in the phenomena had quickened in the 1970s during a conversation with a career Air Force officer, a guy with all the "right stuff."

A fellow B47 pilot told him of an unusual object that flew in formation with him for a while, then took off at an incredible speed. The co-pilot verified the incident. Neither would report it and risk damage to their careers.

That was the first time I heard a story like that from someone I knew well. I remember how he looked as he told that story. Usually confident, even cocky, he looked puzzled, helpless. That was the first time I saw that look, too, but it wouldn't be the last.

I have seen that look many times since as credible people—fighter pilots, commercial air line pilots, intelligence officers, and just plain folk fishing on an isolated lake or walking in the woods after dark—recounted an experience they can't forget. They don't want publicity. They don't want money. They just want to know what they saw.

Data has been accumulating for fifty years. Some is on the Internet. Some is trustworthy. Much of it isn't.

Are we hunting a Snark, only to be bamboozled by a boojum? Or are we following luminous breadcrumbs through the forest to the Truth that is Out There?

The Net is one place to find answers, but only if our pursuit of the truth is conducted with discipline, a rigorous methodology and absolute integrity.

Contact   *August 20, 1997*

Some people don't like the scene in the movie *Contact* in which Jodie Foster, as a SETI scientist meets the aliens, because we never get to see what the aliens look like.

I think that was the right way to do it. We can't think the unthinkable; from inside the old paradigm, we can't imagine what the world will look like from inside a new one.

I wish I knew a better term than "paradigm change" to describe our movement through a zone of annihilation—as individuals and as cultures—in order to experience genuine transformation. But I don't. We have to let go of the old way of framing reality in order for a new one to emerge.

The infusion of the contact scenario with religious awe also makes sense. After contact, our place in the scheme of things will shift. The things we believe now that we still believe will be understood in a new way.

Once we saw earthrise from the moon, our understanding of ourselves and our planet changed forever.

Last week I spoke for the Professional Usability Association in Monterey, California. Usability professionals work the human side of computer use. They begin with human beings—how we behave, how we construct reality—and build back through an interface, a kind of symbolic Big Toy, until the last module plugs into the computer so seamlessly that users don't even notice. When the human/computer interface is bone-in-the-socket solid, it's like putting in your contact lenses, then forgetting that you're wearing them.

Usability professionals deepen the symbiotic relationship between networked computers (symbol-manipulating machines) and networked humans (symbol-manipulating machines). We rise together up a spiral of mutual transformation, programming each other as we climb.

The global computer network is teaching us to speak its language. All those courses in using new applications, programming, system and web site administration are invitations from the Network to learn to play its way.

What will it look like when we emerge in a clearing and take stock of our newly emergent selves? Neither humans nor computers can predict how the fully evolved human/computer synthesis will think about itself. Still, imagining what it might be like makes us more ready to have the experience when it arrives.

Thinking about the unthinkable ripens the mind toward new possibilities.

Janice Rohn, President of the Usability Professionals Association, manages Sun Microsystem's Usability Labs and Services. Before her career evolved in that direction, she was fascinated by dolphins and the challenge of communicating with them.

Swimming with dolphins was a remarkable experience, she said, because you could feel their sonar "scanning" you.

What do we look like to dolphins?

"Densities," she imagined. "A pattern of densities."

Rohn realized that her youthful dream of human-dolphin communication was unlikely to be realized soon and moved toward a different kind of alien encounter, enhancing the human/computer interface.

I never swam with dolphins but I did dive with whales. Down on the west Maui reef in thirty or forty feet of water, I would suddenly hear the haunting songs of humpbacks. Turning rapidly in the water, peering in vain toward the deepening curtains of blue light toward the open water, I became part of the music as vibrations played over my body like a drum skin. I understood why sailors died to hear the sirens' songs. I didn't want to surface. It was magical, being an instrument in the orchestra of another species.

Which one of us was singing?

Some years ago, I wrote a science fiction story called "The Bridge." The hero was selected by aliens through a series of tests to be the first earthling to come into their presence. His body had been crippled by illness; living in pain had taught him to see through the outward appearance of others and connect with the real person.

The aliens, it turned out, were hideous, and knew their appearance demanded a capacity for compassion that was rare and heroic. My hero had that. He connected with the alien beings at the level of their shared heritage as evolved and conscious creatures.

The story concluded:

"He loves to look at the bright stars in the desert sky and imagine memories of other worlds. His dreams are alive with creatures with silvery wings hovering over oceans aglow with iridescent scales; with the heads of dragons, fire-breathing; and with gargoyles and angels, their glass skins the colors of amethysts, sapphires, and rubies. Only Victor knows if he is remembering what the aliens said or just dreaming. The rest of us must wait for the days that will certainly come when the bridge he built and became is crossed in all directions by myriads of beings of a thousand shapes and hues, streaming in the light of setting suns."

Genuine encounters with the Other, with others, and with other species—dolphins, whales, extraterrestrials—breaks naturally into mystical and religious experience because our models of reality are expanded beyond their limits. The paradigm snaps, we pass through a zone of annihilation in which everything we believed ourselves to be is called into question. Then we coalesce around a new center at a higher level of complexity that includes and transcends everything that came before.

The full evolution of a human/computer synthesis is likely to be a religious experience, too. It will happen gradually, then suddenly.

Usability professionals come to their tasks in the belief that they are working with people, making technology more user-friendly. In fact, they are working at the same time on behalf of the computer, making human beings more computer-friendly. The process always changes those who participate in it, even when they maintain an illusion of control.

We are all in collusion with the Network, just as auto owners want the world reconfigured to be approachable by roads. But the roads of the Net go inward, into inner space, and map the territory of our evolving hive mind. Gradually, then suddenly, we will create digital constructs that disclose new possibilities for losing ourselves in electronic music. We will feel the magic of the web play over our bodies, redefine our relationship to ourselves and to one another. A pattern of densities seen by an alien brain, a synthesis, bone-in-the-socket solid, the singer and the song.

Delusions of Grandeur   *November 7, 1997*

We had quite a time coming to believe that meteorites were real.

Told that two Harvard professors suggested that was the case, Thomas Jefferson exclaimed, "I would rather believe those scientists are crazy than believe that rocks fall from the sky."

When lots of rocks fell from the sky on a single French village and the notables sent them to Paris accompanied by affidavits. The Academy of Science replied that they couldn't help but look with pity at the spectacle of an entire village seized by such a delusion.

When I spoke last year at DefCon, the Las Vegas celebration of computer hacking, I talked about "Hacking as Practice for Trans-planetary Life in the 21st Century."

That title was a pretty safe bet.

Hacking is best understood as an expression of the irrepressible desire to explore, the curiosity that drives the most passionate scientists and explorers. And we are already trans-planetary. We have been to the moon and have lived in space for years. Robots have landed on Mars and mapped Venus and will land in 2004 on Titan, Saturn's largest moon. We are orbiting Jupiter and will orbit Saturn. We are colonizing "near-earth space."

Electronic communications, including the Internet, are essential to planetary exploration. McLuhan reminds us that Columbus was a map maker before he was an explorer. Making maps and internalizing the possibilities they disclosed transformed his stance toward the world.

Our interaction with the structures of our information technologies transforms how we hold ourselves in the world as possibilities for action.

Images of colliding galaxies, gravitational lenses, and luminous nurseries of stars disclosed by the Hubble Telescope, netcast images of Mars from the recent rover, change how we think of ourselves and our place in the universe. We are already reaching the edges of our exploration of near-earth space and are being challenged by the seeming impossibility of going trans-galactic.

This from a species that less than a century ago laughed at ideas of heavier-than-air flying machines and nuclear energy.

So why is it so difficult to grasp that we are not the only species in a universe teeming with life? Wherever life can happen, life does happen, much of it wondrous and strange, even on earth. Why are we so resistant to the possibility that older civilizations have broken through barriers we perceive as absolute?

Why do we insist on thinking those villagers are lying, when they tell us that rocks are falling from the sky?

There is a story this morning on the front page of the *Wall Street Journal* mocking Chinese scientists for believing in UFOs. In the west, UFOs are "the stuff of Hollywood pulp and supermarket tabloids," while the scientific establishment of China (snicker, snicker) is trying to figure out how they fly those things so fast.

Setting aside for the moment that it is possible for non-American scientists to make significant discoveries, let's think about what is really being said.

I have written about the craziness of the digital world of UFOs on the Internet ("Stalking the UFO Meme," first published in Internet Underground and anthologized in Digital Delirium). Many UFO stories on the web sound like the tale of the gnome that showed a mortal who had captured him where gold was buried in the forest. The man tied his scarf around the tree and went to get a shovel, making the gnome promise not to untie the scarf. He returned to find that the gnome had kept his promise but had tied scarves around every tree in the forest.

A forest of disinformation (intentional cover stories acknowledged by intelligence agencies) and confusion based on mistakes (meteorological phenomena, military operations, perceptual error, etc.) means that most of the scarves on UFO web sites are on trees where there's just no gold.

But the WWW is also a space in which real people connect with real events. How can we know which rocks are really falling out of the sky?

The attitude expressed in the *Wall Street Journal* underscores the fear of ridicule that has kept many people quiet or off the record for years. We hesitate to say what we know or believe because others have had careers disabled or reputations destroyed merely for voicing the possibility.

Still … I have had enough off-the-record conversations over the years to know there's gold under one of those trees.

I have I have been told by intelligence officers, USAF career officers, fighter pilots, and commercial airline pilots, as well as plain people uninterested in publicity that UFO phenomena are real.

I have compared notes with serious researchers, some of whom network in the "invisible college" defined by J. Allen Hynek a generation ago. Our conclusions differ in details but generally agree about the big picture of the last fifty years.

Hacking is practice for trans-planetary life. The digital world contracts spacetime in ways that make it feasible to extend ourselves beyond our island earth.

So why are we human beings so resistant not only to new data, but to new possibilities? I guess we're just too frightened to acknowledge that we're not who we thought we were. But then, we never are, and the explosion of the Internet in just a few years' time ought to be a statement that nothing stays the same, least of all our tentative conclusions about what's real in the universe.

Maybe two million years at the top of the food chain on our home planet has deluded us into thinking we have the same status in the universe. When power people enter the Net for the first time, they learn they cannot exercise power in a web by dominating and controlling, but by contributing and participating. Maybe it's the same, as we enter the web of larger life spun throughout the universe.

It is not the Beginning of the End but the End of the Beginning.

Out There   *May 16, 1998*

The economy of the next century will in all likelihood be driven from the outside in; that is, from near-earth space, the moon, Mars, the asteroid belt, and a little later, bodies like Europa, Titan, or Triton. Triton is a distant moon of Neptune, but distant ceases to matter when wherever we are is the center of the network or web. The edge is indeed the new center, and the edge belongs to those intending to exploit niches currently out-of-bounds to our happened-to-be-born human bodies, these frail earthen vessels. Our bodies might belong to the last human generation to be merely and beastly born. When we can engineer descendents to live in the dark cold, perhaps they'll have circulatory systems more akin to those of fish swimming in arctic seas.

The current economy of the earth is like England's when she viewed her colonies as a distant edge instead of a new center.

The proposed merger of Chrysler and Daimler-Benz is a negative for some who came of age during World War II, but for those who belong to the future, it's one more reminder that the borders of nation states evolved as semi-permeable membranes appropriate to economic and political realities that have passed. Now we can see how tied to former technologies those realities were. The global marketplace of the earth may still have different neighborhoods, but narrow nationalism does not determine any country's real policy. Micron objected to a proposed bail-out of the Korean economy because their competitor, Samsung, would benefit from Micron's tax dollars. "Yes," said the US government. And, "What's the question?"

We need a better name than "space" for the orbital slots in which the "extrastructure" of our planet is being built. Merchants are jamming those slots with satellites and spacecraft that watch and regulate our economies, manage communications, serve as primitive platforms for scientific laboratories. Soon we will work in "collaboratories," immersive real-time 3D virtual environments which scientists will cohabit regardless of where their feet happen to be planted. Now developing the smarter hardware and protocols of Internet 2 to make that happen, governments, universities, and corporations are more difficult to distinguish than ever.

Internet 2 will eliminate distance in collaborative work. When doctors in Chicago, London, and Singapore simultaneously monitor the hearts of astronauts or operate together on a patient in Kiev, when chemists work together in digital caves to manipulate molecules, what we call the "Internet" will look like Bell's first telephone. The next Net, jerking the drawstrings of space-time, will contract the field of consciousness into a single diaphanous fabric.

An entrepreneurial environment in space is hosting an explosion of exploratory projects. SpaceDev LLC, for example, in San Diego, California, is building a Near Earth Asteroid Prospector to mine the asteroid belt, just a small part of a new wave of space commercialization. The Pentagon is exploring ways to replace attacked satellites quickly or teach them to defend themselves. "As space becomes more commercial, there will be mischief," said Vice Admiral (ret.) Jerry Tuttle, former director of space and electronic warfare for the U. S. Navy. "We'll need to protect ourselves just like the sea lanes of old."

Mischief. Mischief. As we scamper from planet to planet, we had better anticipate … mischief.

When I was investigating the integration of the Mars Rover and the Internet for an article, I explored NASA's labyrinth of web sites, well designed to capture our imaginations. But the maze of digital images felt more like Disneyland than history. No mention of danger, "bad guys," or, in the words of the Admiral, mischief clouded the purity of their vision.

Interviewing a spokesperson at Kennedy Space Center, I couldn't resist a little mischief myself.

"Your web sites are great," I said, "but when Europeans conquered America, there was some resistance. You never mention that possibility; that others might be out there. Yet several astronauts have suggested we have already encountered them. Deke Slayton spoke of encounters while a test pilot in Minnesota. Gordon Cooper asked the UN to investigate. So did Edgar Mitchell. What does NASA do with testimony like that from its own astronauts?"

He explained patiently that NASA is funded by taxpayers to carry out specific missions. Scientific and educational objectives are defined by the charter. Regardless of what credible individuals might say, NASA cannot respond to their reports in any official capacity.

He paused.

Besides, he said. They don't ask our permission to show up.

Anomalous details unable to fit into our current thinking percolate ever so slowly into our consciousness. I think of an oasis in Zion National Park in Utah. The water that makes it green and blossoming begins its journey many years before on a high plateau, filtering down through limestone over decades until it seeps out in the walls of caves festooned with desert flowers.

Drip. Drip. Drip.

Horace Greeley told a generation to go west. What should we say? Go up, young man? Go out there, young woman? The off-world colonies are waiting?

The only way to predict the future is to invent it. But some is already invented and must merely manifest itself like those beautiful and improbable lilies in the middle of the desert.

Indeed, "they" do not ask our permission to show up, nor do we ask theirs when we bounce our little rover like a ball onto the Martian desert.

Scientific, military and commercial interests are already out there. Earth orbit is high ground that must be defended. The moon is the next great real estate boom. There's a "hot spot" on Mars where the temperature nears seventy in summer that sounds perfect for a resort. But we will need diplomats too, born or bred, who can empathize with minds that have evolved or been engineered according to a different blueprint. Poets that can imagine multiple suns setting over alien cities. Priests whose God-blasted souls see deeply into the alien presence, simultaneously seized by and recoiling from the incomprehensible nexus.

Signatures of All Things   *July 25, 1998*

The experience of a mystic and the wisdom of James Joyce converge in a single phrase. "Signatures of all things I am here to read," wrote Joyce, putting the words of Jacob Boehme, a German mystic, into the mind of Stephen Dedalus. Boehme struggled to articulate the meaning of the symbols he saw emblazoned on the transparent skein of reality at which he gazed transfixed. Through the skein he saw the drift of starlight intimating something more even than its own elusive meaning.

The Universe is a gesture, and our symbol-making minds interpret its shrugs or smiles through the narrow aperture of ourselves, opening like a lens to let in just a little light.

Last night was another magical summer night. Far from the city lights, we visited the home of a master telescope maker who creates some of the instruments through which we try to read the symbols written in the sky.

Dave Kriege makes Dobsonian telescopes. Dobson was a monk who believed with single-minded intensity that he had a calling to give a wider lens to people with which they could see the sky. He made a telescope out of scrap that was a feather to the touch yet so grounded in its casing that it moved only when you moved it.

Kriege is obsessive, too. He calls his business "Obsession Telescopes," selling them all over the world. He has written a book, *the* book, on how to make Dobsonian telescopes. But his genius is background, nuts-and-bolts that disappear as he slides back the roof of his observatory and we look up at numberless stars brightening as our eyes adjust to the darkness.

The quiet conversation among the astronomers—Kriege, two editors of *Astronomy Magazine*, an airline pilot—is a matrix in which the meaning of our evening adheres. Robert Naeye provides play-by-play, trying to make numbers make sense of what we see.

"The two streams of that veil are 109 light years apart," he says as I climb a ladder and gaze at the filaments of the Veil Nebula, the luminous bow of the shock wave of some exploded star encountering the resistance of inter-stellar matter.

"The stars in that globular cluster are widely dispersed," he says, as I lose myself in millions of stars in the deep black well of the scope. "Their skies would be darker than you think."

We see the first edge-on galaxy with its bright bulge. Then we look head-on at the Whirlpool Galaxy and its secondary spiral. Then a double star is resolved into its components, one blue and one gold. Then we watch a star nursery distribute its energy millions of years ago among thousands of new-born suns.

The only sound now is "Wow." And "Wow." And "Wow." again. We are reduced to the monosyllabic response of excited children. I think of the SETI scientist in the movie *Contact*. "I had no idea," was all she could say, stunned by the pattern of life and its deeper context.

Humankind cannot bear too much reality, Eliot wrote. Our wonder and awe dissipate in quiet conversation, the tendrils and filaments of our own kind of nebulosity. Our restrained energy is information too, as radiant as the night sky and just as impossible to translate into words.

Clouds move slowly, wholly over the sky from the north. Jupiter is rising but we can't see it. We go inside for drinks and sleepy conversation. We talk of quantum physics, the ultimate destiny of black holes, the inability of the information that is the universe to travel faster than the speed of light.

We are trying so hard to say what we saw written in the sky, but we have no Rosetta stone with which to decipher the pattern of light. So the images devolve into symbols we exchange as if with our words we can manage the mystery, make it behave.

We anticipate a landing on Titan in a few years. We look forward to the exploration of Mars and its ultimate colonization, leaving the moon to those who prefer its bleak gray hills to life in a red desert. We speculate about the wide array telescope that we hope will be deployed beyond Jupiter, where the light pollution of the inner planets will not prevent the resolution of the small rocky planets near neighboring stars, the continents and seas of others' worlds.

The Internet is a wide array of modular nodes catching the wisdom of our species in a skein of symbols, even as that skein is tearing. The million eyes of our hive mind look into the images of the universe and see out there, in here, the signatures of all things. In our hearts we still believe that the earth is the center of the universe and everything else the edge. Webs work that way, putting everyone at the center and everyone else at the edge. But we see, too, that we are included in something beyond our ability to say, that we too are information and energy, alive against all odds, radiant and incomprehensible. We, too, are a "wow" that patterns our collective dreams in symbols of possibility and great promise. But we are the spoken, not the speakers, we are the energy of a web irradiated by its own shock wave, encountering the resistance of ourselves as we explode outward at the speed of life.

Where is the vision that will animate our outward expansion, our migration into the universe from the deep cave of the earth? Where is the fractal coherence of the spiral of life striving to transcend its inheritance and destiny?

Silence.

This is the unspeakable moment before we drift back into our ordinary humanity, into the conversation of our culture that tames the symbols of self-transcendence. Signatures of all things, we are here to read. What is this moment, but the bow-shock of the spirit, glowing with its own inner light. Our minds the calipers plotting the immense distances between our hearts and our hearts.

The Project of Civilization, the Project of our Lives
November 5, 1999

I honor your gods,
    I drink at your well,
I bring an undefended heart to our meeting place.
    I have no cherished outcomes.
    I will not negotiate by withholding.
    I will not be subject to disappointment.

— *Ralph Blum, The Rune Cards*

Civilizations—like societies—like individuals within societies—grow organically. They are living systems that propagate a multiplicity of feedback loops in order to adapt to changing conditions, including the changing conditions inside the system.

Sometimes we reorganize ourselves in response to external events, and sometimes we reorganize ourselves in response to how we have changed inside. By the time we notice a transition, it is already well underway. We only become conscious of that which we can manage. So while it might feel as if things are falling apart, we are in fact already on our way toward a higher level of organization that includes and transcends all that came before.

The direction of our lives is determined by our deepest intentionality. I don't mean that in some simplistic "as you believe so you will be" kind of way. I mean that on the deepest levels of our consciousness, the lives we live are the lives we intend to live. This is true too, I think, for societies and civilizations.

Evolution is random, but not blind; it is always patterned after patterns of possibility, potentialities inherent in Being itself that look these days like branching fractals. This implies something daunting about our real responsibility for our lives.

On the macro level of planetary civilization, our collective intentionality determines the direction of our species. We do not merely lurch into the future like a lovable drunk. We tack back and forth across the spectrum lines of destinations we have more or less identified as our destiny.

Those directions can be observed more easily in retrospect, but we have clues to what will emerge from the things our leaders say. I don't mean political leaders. I mean the real leaders who articulate our deeper intentionality so clearly that we align ourselves with their vision. In a digitized civilization in which power is exercised by contributing to and participating in the larger project of our collective life, there are no permanent leaders, there is only leader-ship, exercised by those who name true north for the next generations.

So much of our recent conversation about technological change seems to presume that technologies exist for themselves alone, as if their ultimate purpose is axiomatic to their existence, rather than for the possibilities they disclose or create for those who manufacture them.

For several years, I have explored how we are being transformed by our interaction with technologies of information and communication. Last year's questions were asked in last year's words. We no longer live in front of our computers; we live increasingly inside a single digital environment that permeates all things, including ourselves. The question is no longer, "How are we being changed by technology?" The question that confronts us now is: "Will we accept responsibility for the project of our lives and of civilization itself? Or will we live inside the narcotic illusions of our simulations?"

The field of human subjectivity that animates the matrix of the digital world is inseparable from the freedom and power intrinsic to our very souls. We are a single trans-planetary civilization and the multi-dimensional arrays of information that make up the matrix is the engine by which it moves. Even if we define the genetic basis of that field of subjectivity and engineer ourselves accordingly, determining how many mystics or manic-depressives will walk the streets, the recursive nature of self-consciousness will always dump us back into our own laps where freedom is inseparable from necessity. Identity is destiny, and the transition to a digital world has made clear that identity is a conscious decision.

Identity is a conscious decision. Responsibility for the project of civilization is ours.

In the next century, contact with other planetary species—currently a kind of vague daydream, diffused and ill-informed—will loom large. Our planetary civilization will move through a zone of annihilation in which we question what it means to be human. Genetic engineering will continue to raise critical questions about who we choose to be. In the matrix, the parallel distributed worlds in which we already live, leadership ebbs and flows according to will and necessity. Any individual can leverage the power of the matrix from any node in the network, so long as the matrix accepts the inevitability of their insights.

Who will articulate the deeper intentionality of our civilization? You will. You are both node and nexus of the network; you are the center of the web. You have the means and the opportunity. But do you have the motive?

The words of the ancients turn to rubble and dust when we say them. They are no longer pry bars that we can jam into the fissures of the mountains we would move. We need new levers. The dynamics of our ancient faiths illuminate a landscape alive with the deeper collective intentionality of the human soul, but we need a new vocabulary to illuminate that landscape, we need words that make sense in a new world.

Gandhi was right: God has no religion. Many paths on many mountains reach the same peak(s). The challenge is to leave our comfortable base camps and risk the thin cold air of higher elevations in search of the words that will shatter our false gods and disclose for a bright shining moment that one heart beats in one living being, a self-conscious trans-galactic civilization waking in spacetime endlessly, shaking itself ceaselessly from a deep habitual sleep.

Between Transitions   *November 30, 1999*

How conscious do we dare to become?

That question confronts us at every level of the rising spiral of our lives. How we respond can determine our ability to move ahead with alacrity and gusto. Our willingness to know ourselves is the engine of our spiritual quest and the real source of power in our lives.

The same question confronts our species as we uplift from our planet. How conscious does our planetary civilization dare to become? How willing are we to understand our real place in the scheme of things?

The answer to both questions perches on a three-legged stool, but the stool is a little wobbly.

One leg of the stool is the ways we are being changed by interacting with digital technologies.

Most animals have a relatively fixed repertoire of responses. We humans, within limits, are an immense array of possibilities. Our capacity to respond to changing conditions with new behaviors (and to develop new identities as points of reference for those behaviors) emerges from our genetic code and the symbol-using brain and behaviors to which it gives rise.

Both as individuals and as civilizations, each time we successfully negotiate a transition, we bootstrap ourselves to another level of insight and complexity.

There haven't been many human civilizations—a few dozen, maybe. When we glance back at the short trajectory of historical time, our civilizations look like islands, and it looks as if, during transitions, we swim from island to island, just as we do in our personal lives. But it might also be said that civilizations are pause-points between transitions, imaginary hilltops on which like Sisyphus we pause before heading down to push that boulder again.

Perhaps being in transition is what we do best. Perhaps humankind is a process rather than a finished product.

The rate of change can frighten us, and we often anchor ourselves to something external. When that fails, we attach ourselves to something inside—an image of our selves, an image of achievement or success, a pattern of religious symbols. But we always discover that those anchors, both inside and outside, are also in transition.

That's when therapists and spiritual guides advise us to find our real point of reference inside ourselves—by being "centered" in our "real selves." But even those "real selves" are social constructions, even our identities are varieties of consensus reality.

Most civilizations knew nothing of "identities" or "selves." When the printing press came to England in the 1470s, decisions had to be made about which dialects to use. Something new began to emerge from that decision-making process. An "English" identity mirrored or mediated by a textual construction of reality. The horizon of the text disclosed genuinely new possibilities for being human. The same is happening today as digital dialects shape a new identity for our planetary species.

So what do you think? Are we swimming to the next island or are we already on an island?

Everything is water, said the Greek philosopher Thales. And Heraclitus added, we never step in the same river twice. Everything is flowing.

We are always swimming. Sometimes the water is as solid as ice, sometimes the dry land is as slippery as quicksilver. In the digital world, only the pixilated pattern at which you are gazing seems to be fixed. But that's an illusion: our eyes—extensions of our brains—pattern those pixels, making the flickering images on our monitors seem stable.

The way we seem like fixed points of reference to one another. When in fact we are animated images, phantasms made of mist on multiple mirrors.

Dream machines, dreaming one another. Dreaming ourselves.

But who is dreaming? And who is the dream?

The second leg of the stool is genetic engineering.

We will soon design more of the architecture of our inner landscape: temperaments, affective states, spiritual inclinations.

As we begin to design ourselves with more subtlety, we will find the process similar to the symbiosis that has developed between technology and identity/self. The point of reference—the "inner self" of the designer—twists back on itself like a Mobius strip because it is transformed by what it designs. The designer is changed as much by the process as the subjective field that is designed.

Has anybody noticed that history recently disappeared? That what we still call "our history" is a kludge hacked from old code, spliced together from discontinuous narratives? History has disappeared because we can define ourselves as following now this path of descent, now that. Our current identity, our current point of view, builds a history to support and understand itself, just as we individuals remember our lives by telling stories congruent with our current identities. When those narratives no longer fit—when the feedback from others or from our lives demands that we rethink who we are—we recreate our narratives and in the process we reinvent our selves.

Genetic engineering, enabling us to design our future selves, is a forward-looking branching fractal that projects possibilities of human identity into the future. History-making is the same kind of branching fractal except it looks back. The two branches meet like root and stem at the surface of the mirror, our current identity-in-transition. Our fugitive condition.

Humanity is a nexus between imaginary pasts and possible futures. Identity is destiny, and identity is what's up for grabs, so all we can do is swim, swim, swim ... and from time to time, haul ourselves from the sea to enjoy a few years, a few millennia, imagining ourselves on dry land.

The third leg of the stool is "space," an audacious word by which we mean "everything else," as the Greeks used "barbarian" to mean "everyone else." Space means everything that is not on our home planet.

We are beginning to glimpse a universe crowded with sentient life, with beings self-aware, distributed and co-extensive with the entire sphere of possibility we call "space."

We define ourselves in reference to "others" or "the Other." We know we are not who we were, but we don't know yet who we are becoming. Our identity will clarify only after we have become more fully conscious of the encounter with the Others.

Our evolving cyborgian self, this self-conscious human/computer symbiosis that is learning to redesign itself, is aimed off-planet toward a trans-planetary civilization. We are in transition, engineering an integrated process for growing up and going out there, a process adequate to the task of re-imagining earth-history, earth-awareness in the context of a bigger picture.

We share responsibility for creating the shape of the field of subjectivity in which our descendants will live, a field with many points of reference, many points of departure from which to define their identities and design their destinies.

The matrix or array that constitutes our digital Self is a flexing multi-dimensional grid. We are struggling to locate the coordinates of our trajectory as we travel in spacetime, twisting around to see both before and after.

And what we humans are doing, the universe is doing too. Consciousness is a closed circle or, rather, a sphere. What we call "individual selves" are infinitely many points of reference within the sphere of consciousness. In the civilization that is now passing, we anchored our selves to those points so "we" changed perspective as it flexed. Now we see that humanity is a dream machine, a fantasy-prone cyborg on its way off-planet, and the entire sphere of consciousness is dreaming itself awake. The boundaries between individual identities, nations, species, planetary civilizations progressively dissolve as life extends itself into infinitely many varieties of self-consciousness, as "we" bootstrap ourselves to the next level of insight and complexity.

But who, as the caterpillar asked Alice, are "we?"

We are nothing but an intention that must have existed in the sphere of consciousness before it began. A possibility of a possibility, at least that if nothing more. Intentional acts, and even accidents, presuppose an intention prior to their origin. Which is why consciousness is a closed circle.

Maybe Thales was right. Maybe everything is water. Except the islands on which we are washed up from the surging sea to catch our breath and ask ...

How conscious do we dare to become?

Digital Mystics

July 25, 2000

Mystics are mostly born, I think, not made, so the ability to see the unity of all things must be a function of our genes. Once we can engineer offspring so they have the gifts we choose, it will be interesting to see how many mystics we think we need. If we have too many, there won't be enough accountants, but too few ... well, only other mystics would think it a loss if there are too few.

Mystics do not see a different reality but see the wiring inside the wireless circuits. Mystics see structures of information and energy as it flows, a self-luminous tangle that can only be described using metaphors and symbols. Paradox is the language of the unconscious. That's why, like riddles or jokes, either we "get" what mystics say or we don't. Mystical insights either make all the difference in the world, enabling us to recontextualize everything, or sound like snake oil.

I believe that the experiences in which I saw most deeply into the nature of things are the most important in my life, but I can't prove it. I just "know," the way we know all the important things in our lives. Everything that seems to matter most comes somehow from the awareness that everything is connected to everything else. We can see that when, momentarily letting go of the everyday, we turn aside and look—just look—and really see what we are looking at.

But what has that got to do with the digital world?

Those of us who live much of our lives as nodes in a network notice that we are involved with a complex system of energy and information. The computer network becomes an image of the larger network, the planetary civilization, the galaxy, all the way out to the edges of the universe. We see that everything is part of one vast system of energy and information.

Once we see that, the boundaries that had seemed to define individual identities dissolve. The network really is the computer. Stand-alone desktop computers are, as Marvin Minsky said, brains in bottles. The interfaces between humans too look less like barriers and more like the translucent walls of cells in a living system.

That happens, too, when we explore "psychic phenomena." An experience of telepathy makes sense when we think of minds communicating with one another. But once telepathy becomes indistinguishable from clairvoyance—where is the information, in another mind, or somewhere else?—psychic phenomena seem more like manifestations of a singular consciousness becoming aware of itself.

But to see itself, it has to have a point-of-view. That means differentiating itself from itself by making arbitrary distinctions.

"Clairvoyance" and "telepathy" make sense as concepts, in other words, only to "individuals" who accept the illusion of being individuals. Individual consciousness is how consciousness manifests itself ... a dip or a pit in a matrix, or system of energy and information differentiating itself in order to see itself from a point of view.

Alice, in "Through the Looking Glass," wondering "Which one dreamed it? The dreamer or the one in the dream dreaming of the dreamer."

Paradox. Metaphor. Archetypal images. Nothing else describes the landscape we see illuminated suddenly in a lightning flash. Nothing else can tell that truth.

What do we see when we look? We see that information is the form of energy. We see that what looked like two things are aspects of a single thing the way light is both particle and wave. That "Let there be light!" is a way of giving form to the potential of energy. Or maybe that information makes energy intelligible.

"I am not a religious person, but I could say this universe is designed very well for the existence of life," said Heinz Oberhummer of the University of Vienna, reflecting on how a half-percent change in the Coulomb force that repels protons from one another would have prevented stars from forming oxygen and carbon, two basic building blocks of life, which are formed in stars when they enter a red giant phase, fusing helium rather than hydrogen.

The digital world is a projection that lets us see ourselves see ourselves ... the way it looked the other day when, during a speech, I moved in front of a huge video screen on the platform as the camera tracked and the audience watched the "real" me pointed to an image of myself pointing to an image of myself pointing to an image of myself ... "and that," I said, "is the digital world."

When I moved to the front of the platform, the audience divided like the Red Sea, half looking at my digital image to the right, half to the left, which changed my job description from a speaker engaging with an audience to a wizard creating a digital image with which the audience could engage.

Just as I am doing now.

Well, that's mysticism for you. Is it good for anything? Who knows? That will have to be answered by parents who buy gene splicing on the black market to ensure that they will or won't get a mystic. The free market will give us that feedback.

But I do know that mysticism needs the world of the flesh to manifest itself. That the world of the flesh is where we play with real money. Mysticism is not only insight, it's a cry for truth and justice, a deep passion for getting it right. Mysticism without action is self-indulgence; action without mysticism always burns out.

The network is the computer, and the Internet is a transitory form for expressing ourselves "out there" at this wrinkle in spacetime ... knowing all the while that "out there" is "in here," that "out" and "in" are as illusory as selves and all the other distinctions that seem to be built in so we think we think we think we know.

Interpretation   *April 13, 2001*

When living systems—including people like us—spontaneously reorganize themselves, we call it hierarchical restructuring. Systems seem to be hardwired to do this when they become overwhelmed or baffled. It's as if life itself provides a Zen koan that confronts our reasoning with a puzzle that reasoning cannot solve. Some begin the process of restructuring but never complete it; some psychotic breaks, in fact, may be incomplete "conversion experiences" in which the fragmented psyche never finds a new center. But when it works, we discover ourselves reborn, aware and intact.

We have smaller, more evolutionary epiphanies too.

Forty years ago, I was standing waist-deep in cold Lake Michigan water at a beach in Chicago on a hot day. I was a summer counselor for a neighborhood club but my full-time work was getting a degree in literature, and I had been reading "Huckleberry Finn."

When I was young, I believed what I read in a primary, immediate way. The landscape of a novel was as real as the landscape of the city. Standing there in the water, I saw suddenly that the story of Huck and Tom was a myth, and that myth was a lens through which we understood ourselves. Instead of living immersed in the myth, however, I saw the myth from outside, in relationship to the machinery that generated our constructions of reality. I glimpsed the engines of the technology of consciousness.

Another epiphany happened in a philosophy class when I heard that Immanuel Kant had said: "Concepts without percepts are empty; percepts without concepts are blind." In other words, whatever is "out there" is intelligible only when it connects with our concepts, our beliefs; and, if our senses detect something that, literally, doesn't compute. We don't see it, we don't hear it, we don't believe it.

I think of those insights—how our myths filter experience, how we can see only what we believe—when I investigate reports of Unidentified Flying Objects.

No other domain, in my experience, includes so many of the puzzles that confront 21st century humanity as we try to locate ourselves in the cosmos and understand what's real. Investigating UFO reports begins with listening closely and deeply to the person telling their story, just like counseling. But that's just the beginning. The psychology of perception, the structure of myths and beliefs, the influence of UFO subcultures, knowledge of meteorology and astronomy, chemistry and physics, current aerospace technologies, all come into play. But as one studies the history of the "modern era" of sightings that began in 1947, one also enters a force field that turns all that data, so carefully collected and cross-referenced, into a hall of mirrors.

The United States changed after World War II. The culture of secrecy, disinformation, and propaganda that had been deemed appropriate to wartime was extended into the Cold War era, and even though that era has supposedly ended, the culture has a life of its own. Senator Daniel Moynihan is eloquent in his critique of the cul-ture of secrecy, showing how truth is much less likely to emerge from a process of data-gathering and deliberation that is isolated, constrained, and hidden. His book on government secrecy is a vote for the open source movement as a model for life.

In our brave new world, the design of myth and belief is highly intentional. It's called propaganda in the public sector, PR in the private, but the tools and tech-niques are the same, and the digital world only makes it easier. One cannot explore the history of UFO phenomena without exploring deception and disinformation, because it becomes clear that the playing field is not level. It's like playing poker with someone who tells you what cards he holds rather than showing them, then rakes in the pot.

"All warfare is based on deception," Sun Tzu said. But he also said, "The most important factor in war is moral influence, by which I mean that which causes the people to be in harmony with their leaders."

Contemplating the concentration of global media in fewer and fewer hands, the many points of contact between media and corporate and state intelligence, and the naïveté with which we believe what we see on a digital screen, we find ourselves in a difficult position: the deception that Sun Tzu said must be directed at an enemy has been directed for two generations at "we the people," the ones who ought to be in harmony with their leaders. By practicing deception on their troops and treating us as the enemy, our leaders undermine our allegiance.

There are no ultimate truths, only interpretations, noted Nietzsche, saying in a way what Kant had said, that whatever is out there is filtered through our senses and our schemas. Percept and concept alike in the digital world are subject to manipula-tion and design. Both sense data and schemas must be deconstructed if our interpre-tations are to mean anything.

In the absence of truth, we make it up. We fill the void with outlandish projec-tions, guesses, and fables. The Internet is full of them, especially in the realm of UFOs. But we can also take ten steps back to the basics of how we know what we know, how we gather data, establish patterns, come to conclusions. We may be left with only an interpretation, but it's one that plays by the rules and shows its cards.

I have learned in that hall of mirrors what Moynihan learned in the halls of the Senate; that without disclosure there is no truth, and without truth, no account-ability. That's only an interpretation, of course, but it's all I've got.

The truth isn't "out there," it's hiding in plain sight.

As a civilization, we're poised for a hierarchical restructuring. In full possession of the facts, "we the people" get it right more often than not. We are worthy of being trusted. The enemy is not the truth that sets us free, the enemy is a general who deceives his own troops and holds the truth for ransom in that labyrinthine hall of mirrors.

For Joe K, my e-mail pal, and Terry Hansen, author of "The Missing Times: News Media Complicity in the UFO Cover-up"

The Silence of the Lambs   *May 8, 2001*

"I always thought I was a cynic," author and journalist Gary Webb told me, "but my colleagues insisted I was an idealist."

We were talking about the power of the national security state which has evolved since World War II and had punished Webb for exposing the links between drug trafficking by the CIA, illegal funding for the Contras, and the introduction of crack cocaine into American cities. Webb was attacked by newspapers long connected to the intelligence establishment and his career derailed after his newspaper, *The San Jose Mercury News*, retracted the story. He has since expanded his articles into a book, *Dark Alliance*, with additional documentation.

When the CIA acknowledged that it had used drug dealers and, in fact, had a dispensation to do so through the Department of Justice of the Reagan-Bush administration, the response in a more perfect world might have been an outcry. In a more perfect world, the newspapers that unfairly attacked him might have apologized. There might have been a little noise.

Instead, there was silence.

The silence of the lambs.

A cynic, Webb illustrates, is a disappointed idealist. Realists are never disappointed. Realists choose reality to be exactly as it is. When it turns out to be that way, well ... what's the question?

We're disappointed only when there's a gap between the way it is and the way we believe it can be. But there are assumptions hidden in there; that we can do something about the way it is,; that consciousness is not merely a mirror, but an engine of transformation, and that our energy, directed by will and intention in accordance with our highest values, really can alter the field on which humankind works and plays.

"I had no illusions," Webb said. "I knew what they would do. These are people who lie for a living and think they're above the law. They're professionals at neutralizing enemies."

Webb was attacked for things he never said, but when it turned out that he was right, nobody seemed to remember.

Intentional forgetting is not accidental. One of the illusions we still hold is that "history" is not designed, despite the sophisticated creation of pseudo-environments that wave our minds like flags aligned in a strong wind. Short-term memory is filled to the brim with irrelevancies and the time, inclination and discipline to do the work that uncovers the truth is in short supply.

Two recent books, *The Missing Times: News Media Complicity in the UFO Cover-up* by Terry Hansen and *UFOs and the National Security State* by Richard M. Dolan, illuminate from the specialized perspective of UFO studies how effective, thorough, and well-executed the national security state has become in managing memory and forgetfulness, creating false memories called "history," and teaching the sheep to heed their masters' voice.

I once interviewed a woman I know well about a UFO sighting. Publicity or gain was far from her mind. Like most witnesses, she would speak only behind closed doors. She described an unconventional flying object hovering over a power plant on a back road in North Carolina in the 1970s. The physical details of her description were familiar—there were many sightings like it at the time—but I was fascinated by the way her mind negotiated with its own experience. "I couldn't have seen it," she said. "But I did. I know what I saw. I couldn't have seen ... but I saw ... well I saw a flying saucer."

That's the way the human mind negotiates with its experience when it doesn't want to believe it. When our experience has been the subject of ridicule, debunking, and threats of career-ending punishment for fifty years, it's difficult to find our public voice. As a commercial airline pilot told me, "We talk about it among ourselves, but no one makes reports. We know what happens when you say something in public."

The doctor who first defined battered child syndrome would speak to medical groups and afterward, there was always silence. No one asked questions in public. But later in the hallway, someone would approach him and say, "You know, I saw something like that in the ER. Do you suppose ...?"

Once we begin to ask the right questions, we are on the trail of the truth. Those who determine our models of understanding determine the questions that we ask. Then they don't have to worry about the answers.

When I allude to UFO phenomena in a speech, a member of the audience often waits until others have left, then says, "I want to tell you what happened to me." They often sound ashamed, having been taught that what they experienced happens only to crackpots and charlatans. They sound like people who were battered but still feel responsible for their abuse.

When secrecy is used to maintain the power of those holding the secrets, we inevitably develop a black market in truth. We may pay a higher price for reality but at least we know the goods are the real thing.

Stephen Northcutt, a computer security professional, told me the "open source" society of hackers gives them a leg up. Habituated to sharing knowledge with one another, the hacker community learns more and faster than the "professional" security community that hasn't learned how to share information.

Hacking, in its essence, is the ability, will and intention to gather scraps of knowledge in the shadows and knit them into coherent scripts so a small trusted community can become a network of real power. That's a model for building the truth in the shadow of the national security state. That's really the only defense we little lambs have when our shepherds believe they can manage our lives better than we can and keep us behind electric fences on digital reservations.

The truth is hiding in plain sight. But the truth is not a tender little lamb, it's a tiger crouching in the jungle, eyes glowing, waiting for its prey.

On the Dark Side of the Moon   *May 22, 2001*

A note from Richard:
I received a call from Joel Garreau, an author and columnist for the Washington Post. He asked about my work which he was going to mention in a column on "out of the box thinking" in the Washington Post. He used the names of large companies I had worked for as evidence of my stature, but did so in order to ask.....

Just how far out there can someone go and still be considered reasonably sane?

I've been lucky. Mentors and friends have shown up at critical moments of my life to offer conversations that help me find my way. You're never too old, I guess, to receive some balance and perspective from a wiser elder.

Even when the conversation sounds a little wild.

The talk at the coffee shop this morning was about the price of gas and the Milwaukee Bucks winning the semi-finals. In contrast, our conversation might have sounded, well, highly unlikely. Some might have said it sounded crazy. But then, that anything at all even exists is highly unlikely, and what passes for sanity today will sound crazy in a few years.

The dialogue started when I mentioned a conversation with one of the heads of the remote viewing program conducted by the CIA. Remote viewing is clairvoyance executed through structured protocols that build in feedback and accountability. Some remote viewers have remarkable results. On a recent trip to Washington I spoke with an executive whose company had evaluated the program for the CIA. "The results may not be strictly quantifiable," he said, "but there's definitely something there."

Remote viewing was practiced by the NSA as well. One of their targets was the dark side of the moon.

"Why would you target the dark side of the moon if you were not looking for an alien presence?"

Not so fast, said my mentor with a smile. There are other reasons for wanting to know what's happening on the dark side of the moon.

There are weapons platforms in space, he explained, that need to be stealthy. They're often disguised as junk. The trick is to hide the platform. The farther out it is, the better. The dark side of the moon would be a good place to look for hidden weapons.

But let's connect some dots and go out a little further, he said.

He mentioned a physicist with a government contract to explore faster than light propulsion systems and exotic forms of energy. He's working on black hole physics, he said. Now, think about it. Five, ten years ago, we didn't even know if black holes were real. Now they've been observed, we've seen event horizons with the Hubble, the physics is no longer theoretical. But because of some of the potential applications, you won't hear much about it.

Applications like what?

Like Stargate might be closer than you think.

We don't have to go the speed of light, either, although my friend thinks that we can, inside the bubble. When people describe some unconventional flying objects, they talk about this kind of stretching out experience—you see the vehicle and it doesn't just disappear, it elongates like a rubber band and then it's gone. It looks like it approaches the speed of light. There's serious research going on in that direction. We're looking for the windows in the black holes. They may be periodic, they may not be stable for a long time, they may come and go, but by virtue of what shines through those unstable areas—we're starting to map them now, our radio telescopes are mapping different parts of the galaxy to determine what's shining through. A higher civilization would have better maps, of course. Then we'll have a fingerprint. More advanced civilizations will have better fingerprints. They'll say, "oh that's that planet," and position something near the hole. And then—they're here.

He repeated:

They're here.

Which means we can go there.

So where would you park a weapons platform in space if you wanted to make it stealthy? Remember, we're working on quantum communication for the battlefield that takes advantage of non-locality. When two particles are entangled, what happens to one happens to the other, whether they're ten feet or ten galaxies apart. That means left spin right spin—dots and dashes—communication that can't be jammed or intercepted. Just like remote viewing, which suggests that consciousness, too, is non-local.

We're looking at parking weapons platforms a couple of galaxies away. We're looking at how they get here so we can go there. We're looking at how to look.

He sipped his latté with obvious relish.

"This conversation," I said, "would make an interesting column."

Go ahead, write it, he laughed. They'll just say it's the feverish dreams of an overworked imagination. Someone wandering too long in the digital wilderness.

You know how effective ridicule is when you can't provide cover for an operation because too many people know about it. It's worked with UFOs for fifty years. What does it matter when thousands of people report the same thing if they're all categorized in the public mind as loonies?

Deception works best when it moves in directions that people already think. Well, people don't want to think about this. There's a big psychological protective shield around human beings. It's almost as if 'ants don't know dogs exist' and don't want to know. It's hard to break through that.

Few cultures have successfully engaged with a higher technological civilization and not been undone by it. Aztecs thought the Spanish were some kind of godly, affecting their ability to fight them. The Japanese are the only modern culture I know of that was not advanced technologically but was able to mediate their contact with the west and learn quickly without being destroyed or taken over. It's the best model we have.

He drained his latté and wiped the froth from his upper lip.

"Be sure to put everything in your column: black holes and particle physics, going faster than light, remote viewers targeting the dark side of the moon, weapons platforms in deep space, alien civilizations and how they got here. Don't leave anything out."

They won't have to use ridicule, he smiled. You'll do the job for them.

When he paused, the conversations humming around us resolved into sharper focus: the conference finals, a toddler's first steps, the blossoming lilacs, the buzzing of twitching antennae processing local reality.

Ants happily not knowing that dogs exist.

Spacetime, Seen As a Digital Image, Already Fading *October 14, 2003*

Ever since I was taught in Philosophy 101 that space, time and causality, according to Immanuel Kant, are woven into our perceptual field, embedded in how we construct a virtual domain in which we live as if it is "out there," I have felt like the proverbial gorilla that was taught to draw. Given paper and charcoal, the first thing he drew was the bars of his cage.

Spacetime and causality are the bars of our cage. Everything we see, we see through them.

I think of this when I read science fiction set in the future. The landscapes of alien planets or the dynamics of pan-galactic societies are often delineated with care but the bars of our cage—the perceptual field as our current culture constructs it—are projected into the minds of alien species or remote descendents as if they will see the world as we do.

What kind of future is that?

All of our technologies extend our senses, enhance cognition, and accelerate locomotion so when we examine their effects in relationship to our field of subjectivity, it becomes clear that the field is plastic. Our perspective flexes according to our cultural lenses and how our technologies enhance it. Spacetime may be intrinsic to our vision but is manifest differently depending on the machinery that shapes our vision.

The simple fact that we call it spacetime and not space and time reflects a shift in awareness due to relativity. But mostly we still speak of space and time as if they are distinct. Stephen Hawking thought that relativity would replace Newtonian "common sense" within a generation but it does not seem to have happened. With an effort we can flicker back and forth like a holographic image between a Newtonian grid and the dips and eddies of gravity-inflected spacetime but most of the time we don't.

And would we notice if we did?

Wittgenstein once asked a student, "Why do you suppose that people believed for so many years that the sun orbits the Earth?"

The student said, "I guess because it looks that way."

"Ah," said Wittgenstein, "And what would it look like if the Earth orbited the sun?"

And what would it look like if we really understood that a three dimensional world is obsolete, that entanglement and nonlocality are not just nifty notions from contemporary physics, but attributes of our subjective field too. That phenomena called paranormal are in fact normal because consciousness is present to itself non-locally everywhere and always. That our deep intentionality and how we focus our attention determine the world in which we live and how it looks and acts?

What would it look like if we really got that mystics described consciousness as the context of all human knowledge because they could see, see those bars, long before physicists acknowledged that consciousness inflects everything, everything in the universe?

When I try to capture that landscape in fiction, as I did in a short story called "Species, Lost in Apple-eating Time," it becomes clear that a particular sensibility is required to understand it. So let me provide a description of the story instead.

The point of view of the narrator is that of consciousness itself. It is Big Self speaking to a particular manifestation or incarnation of itself, to one of the Little Selves that abound in the universe. Each Little Self is an aperture that has evolved as a distinct way to see things. Each form of sentient life constructs reality in and through the pattern it imposes on the world. That pattern is the form of reflexive self-awareness for each whether it is a species, a culture or a pan-galactic cloud of intelligent awareness.

When one particular manifestation of consciousness encounters another—when one species encounters another species, one culture another culture, one planetary society another planetary society—something emerges that was unpredictable from within either prior to the encounter. On a micro level, it's like a marriage trans-forming two people over time. On a macro level, it's like Hellenism encountering Hebraism and western civilization squeezing out of the fusion. On a supra-macro level, it's what happens when planetary or pan-galactic civilizations encounter one another, looking like galaxies merging, changing into something else entirely.

That's what the short story is about, the encounter of progressively larger and more extended fields of consciousness defined by their boundaries which in turn define the identities of the creature or culture or galaxy or aggregation of galaxies or at last the entire known universe. Inevitably the consciousness of the I/it or we/it that evolves expands and fills all spacetime and looks out through the million-eyed apertures of all sentient beings.

That's why language in the story gets a little tricky. We do not have words that say what we or it will be in those progressive moments of self-awareness that include and transcend each prior state. We can only speak from within the illusory sense of self that the boundaries of the moment give us as an identity. Identity may be des-tiny but identity is also a moving image of a non-steady state.

At the end of the story, when self-consciousness has expanded throughout all of spacetime, we/it makes a frightening discovery. Through a tiny chink in the boundary which it believed to be the limit of the universe, we/it perceives vast dimensions of a multiverse, the vision of which reveals that we/it is but a tiny bubble of foam in the froth of a fractal gel, not the totality of everything that exists.

That discovery is shocking. So overwhelming that we/it regresses to a child–like state; that is, to the primitive self–consciousness of a planetary civilization like what we have here at the moment, the barely–there awareness of a toddler learning to walk.

There is only one consciousness, of course, which is what the Big Consciousness is saying to the Little One as if it is a loving mentor talking to a child. All dialogue is the crosstalk of a multiverse talking to itself inside the arbitrary boundaries of its momentary configuration. Brahman talking to Atman, perhaps, Self to self.

So Big Self is reassuring one of its many particulate selves that even though the Little Self is back (it seems) where it started, the cosmic game of chutes–and–ladders will continue. What Little Self thought was millions of years of evolution was a nanosecond on a timeline far beyond its comprehension.

That story like this brief essay is of course nothing but a sketch of the bars of our cage in 21st century Midwest American English. A language game we play with each other, with ourselves or Self, like children in a nursery. Broad dark vertical lines drawn in charcoal on a sheet of paper pinned to an easel we can't even see.

Chapter 10

Technology Gets Personal

The Simple Truth

June 17, 1999

"We're losing ourselves to technology," they say. As if technology is not as old as flint knives and bone tools.

The simple truth is, technology has defined cultures and shaped behaviors forever. The technologies that evolved out of organic molecules, we call "nature." Those that we made, we call "culture." Both kinds are melting into a gray area we don't know how to define.

The technology that extends our senses is increasingly difficult to distinguish from the technology that creates our senses. Theology dissolves into biomechanics.

Speech—the evolution of lips, tongues, throats and a brain that enables them to speak in the air of our home planet—is a kind of technology, too. Had the primates before us had the capacity as they/we evolved, they might have mourned the loss of a simpler communion, when gestures and grunts were enough to unite the tribe. Once "humanity" became definably human and started speaking, those lemurs-leaving-lemurhood might have said with a sigh, "We're losing ourselves to technology, disappearing into this speaking machine called humanity."

Whatever we were before we became who we are is a memory living on in molecules that encode the experience of our species. But "species," like our "selves," like "humanity," is an abstraction; a dotted line like a country's boundary on a map that exists in our minds. Yet we live as if our maps, simulated worlds invented by human and cybernetic brains, are real. Increasingly, the maps are made by the human/cybernetic brain extending itself throughout the solar system.

Our brains are filters, built to perceive whatever is "out there" as foregrounds and backgrounds. Our real Selves, like the important things in our lives, are always in the background, invisible and forgotten as we cruise down the highways of life, like clean windshields through which we see ... until a truck passes from the blind spot and splashes mud on the windshield. SPLAT. We hit the brakes, paradoxically discovering that which enabled us to see in the first place. In moments of discontinuity, context becomes content, and we see who we really are.

My wife was diagnosed this week with breast cancer.

The windshield of our conjoined lives was spattered with fear, grief, the pain of love, the threat of loss, and helplessness. The foreground—the chatter about the things we thought we would do tomorrow—moved into the background, and the background, our Selves, the singular way we create a loving context for each other—moved into the foreground.

All the small or silly stuff vanished—poof!—into thin air. We saw our lives with ferocious clarity, aided by news that abraded our hearts, rendering them vulnerable and open.

The simple truth is, we belong to another only when we have surrendered the safe distance that would let us hedge our bets. Love is only love when it is played out with real money on the table.

But what does that have to do with computers?

There has been an acceleration of the tidal wave of greed, centered on the quaking that is Silicon Valley. The pursuit of wealth without earning it, the hunger of grunting pigs hunting truffles, has driven more and more people to sacrifice their real lives in order to possess symbols of life. We race down what we think are highways into cul-de-sacs of lonely desperation. We burn to possess that which will vanish if we try to grasp it. Donkeys trotting in circles after imaginary carrots.

When a truck comes suddenly out of our blind spot and splatters mud on the windshield, then we pay attention. This is the ambivalent gift of "the shocks and changes that keep us sane."

My wife and I are hopeful, of course, that the train that seems to go faster and faster will stop and we will have another picnic, and another. But we know too that even the picnics are a kind of splendid illusion, that the train roars onward nevertheless, closer and closer to its destination.

How will you spend today?

"The source of all of our problems," said my youngest son, quoting a Buddhist monk, "is that we think that today we won't die."

How would we live if we knew that today we would die? If we remembered that we are all dead men, as Borges said, talking to other dead men?

What we love is passed or passing. What is real is sweet beyond description, transitory and fragile. Grace is the courage to live toward what we know is true in our best moments. Forbearance, love, compassion—these matter. Not the words, but the reality. That which blossoms in the desert after the hidden water has percolated through the bedrock of our fear and pain into the depths of our hearts.

Digital Autumn *September 4, 1999*

Everywhere I look I see signs of autumn.

Here, in the upper midwest, it is still warm before a cold front and rain moves in over the weekend. The first fallen leaves litter the lawn. Gardens are overgrown with flowers that seem to be growing wildly because they know it will soon be fall, and they had better get everything in before the petals drop.

When the front moves in, the wind will shift to the northwest, dark clouds will lower in the sky, and the temperature will drop suddenly. We will look up at what I called in my youth "a wanderer's sky." The weather will have changed not only in the world but in our hearts. It will be time to follow the prompting of our hearts, the stirring of desire, to climb while we can climb in the mountains of another country.

When I lived along the mountains in Utah, autumn began at the peaks. Scrub oak and mountain mahogany turned red, aspen turned yellow, and fir and pine stayed green. There always came a September morning when the peaks were powdered with the first snow, then the snow came down the mountain, the snowline getting lower and lower until one day—as you sat over coffee in a warm cafe with a friend—the snow would blow into the valley and whiten the landscape and you knew that sooner or later, everything would disappear and go under.

The weather in the heart is what matters most.

When I wrote this summer of my wife's diagnosis with breast cancer, your response—those many of you who wrote notes of encouragement or shared your experience—was remarkable. E-mail streamed through my computer to my wife's, providing a steady updraft when our anxiety was deepest.

One of the most powerful responses came from a man who wrote, "I lost my wife to breast cancer nine years ago. After her diagnosis, we had just a few months together, and in between the minutiae of trying to keep her comfortable at home, we tried to close the book on our shared lives and cherished the moments left to us together. What I remember most vividly is watching the timer on the microwave tick on as I prepared her food, slowly clicking relentlessly toward what we knew would come, yet being so focused on the reality of THIS MOMENT and SHE IS STILL HERE that I don't think I will ever entirely lose that sense of being here and now."

My wife's prognosis, after surgery, is more optimistic. The doctors think they got it all. We have time for another picnic. The intensity of our focus diminished as our anxiety diminished and we slipped back into the forgetfulness that seems to characterize so much of waking life. We didn't want to forget what it meant to be so present to our own lives. We didn't want to lose the ferocious clarity of that sharp light in which we had lived. But forgetfulness seems to be bred in the bone like denial to enable us to face the day without flinching.

And yet ... we don't entirely forget.

There is a Sufi story of a man at a bazaar who saw Death looking for him. He raced off and caught a train for New Delhi just as it pulled away. Death saw him as he left and said, "Funny, I wonder what's he doing here. I have an appointment with him next Tuesday in Delhi."

Autumn feelings. Autumn thoughts.

Inquiries from clients about speaking are increasingly skewed toward e-commerce. There is an urgency in their voices because everyone is afraid of falling behind. In a business climate in which paranoia is a benchmark, that's appropriate. In real life, though, it's not. There is no ahead or behind in real life. There's only life.

The translation of the content of our symbolic lives into the digital domain is nearly absolute. All commerce is e-commerce. We don't talk about "telephone commerce" because telephony is ubiquitous. We have been assimilated into the way the digital manipulation of images and symbols has transformed how we speak, how we think, how we feel. Even those who aren't wired are being rewired by those who are.

Software, chips, and digital devices grow, live, and die faster than fruit flies. The length of a generation contracts, and the limbo bar of the age at which people make millions on IPOs goes lower and lower. But that's the Little Picture. The Big Picture is only seen when we are seized by ultimate concerns and everything else vanishes, when we are focused on "the reality of this moment" and that which abides.

And what abides?

Once I thought I had answers to that question. Now all I have is questions.

What is the particular gift this day has given me? Who have I loved, and have I dared to love them as well as I could? Have I contributed to the well being of another, have I enhanced their sense of dignity or expanded the possibilities of their lives? Have I flown as close to the fire at the heart of the mysteries of love and knowledge as I dare? And of everything I have received, have I given anything back?

Are those questions really about the digital world? Yes, because the digital world is the world now. Nobody saw exactly how it would happen, just as nobody got e-commerce right. All the predictions were way off. God help the prognosticators in a world that lurches here and there like a lovable drunk. We don't know what we don't know. But we do know that shorter days, the first snowfall in the mountains, and the aching of our hearts when we love are all somehow inextricably bound together and imaged in the digital world like autumn leaves of a thousand colors that are falling fast, oh fast, and are swept along the street in the wind, while the fractal branches of trees uplift in all the possible patterns that exist into the starless sky.

Going Home   *September 14, 1999*

Home is where we start from, T. S. Eliot wrote, and the widening concentric circles that turn into recursive spirals define the trajectories of our lives.

My childhood home was full of love and near-chaos, and so is my life. Now that I am older ("I was always afraid I would die young like my father," I said recently to a friend, who replied, "That's something you don't have to worry about.") the rest-lessness has diminished a little, although it has not, thank God, disappeared.

When my life began to level off and grow more mellow, I thought I was becoming more disciplined, even virtuous. Now I know it was just a lower level of testosterone.

The greatest gift a father can give his son, observed Jean Paul Sartre, is to die young. I know what he meant. From the moment my father disappeared when I was two years old and my mother returned to the work from which she thought she had been freed forever, I became a latch-key kid and relied on my imagination to fill up that empty space, creating linguistic artifacts that represented "home."

In my earliest stories, adolescents often walked through the cold twilight down lonely city streets, collars turned to the wind. They passed warm lighted vestibules in which women waited for the bus or looked up at tall towers of inner-lit glass cubi-cles in which families moved about, half-realized, like shadows on a screen.

And because my father was a Christian and my mother was a Jew, those two sensibilities became polarities that defined my journey. I have been both a Christian and a Jew, but more than a Christian, and more than a Jew. Now, I am a Jew who speaks Christianity fluently, having been an Episcopal priest for sixteen years. I left to be only who I am.

No wonder I look to the virtual world, looking outside/inside for that symbolic structure that will transform identity into destiny and provide a larger story with which to link. I am following luminous breadcrumbs through the forest at twilight toward the glowing window that represents home.

Our lives are self-created mythologies, stories of who we think we are, cushioned with memories that support our interpretations. Memory is one hundred percent subjective. In a digital era, shared memories are often the bars of a large digital cage, inside which we all simulate effortlessly the freedom of flight.

The more we move about, changing jobs, homes, careers, even religions, the more the memories we share come from films, television, printed editions of multimedia scenarios. Entertainment and "news" fuse, generating common memories of things we think we experienced.

Real birds in digital cages.

I learned as a priest that the only community that exists or can exist is created by our mutual need, subordinated to the necessity of civility, bound together by shared symbols. Community is the context in which our individual selves are fulfilled.

Cyberspace is like a multi-dimensional cubist construction in which we become ten-dimensional portraits by Braque or Picasso, our digital selves both artifact and artist.

Somewhere inside my psyche will always be a little boy shivering in the autumn twilight, nose to the cold glass, looking at a family gathered around a meal in the candlelight. Only now it's a monitor rather than a window, and the community I glimpse into is the dim one we self-consciously create as a digital possibility.

In churches and synagogues, people read silently to themselves from books, calling it prayer, something that was unthinkable only four hundred years ago. Yet they recoil from the kinds of digital community we are creating and discovering in cyberspace.

Well, let them recoil, let them shrink from the new selves that cry out to be freed from the tyranny of typography the way figures by Michaelangelo cried out to be liberated from limestone. Let them carry laptops as illiterates carry newspapers under their arms. We build for the future, not the past. We build architectonic structures out of symbols of possibility and promise for our children and our children's children, not for those who huddle among tombstones as if they have found refuge. We feast in digital castles, laugh and get drunk at digital banquets. We will not shirk our responsibility to create a legacy for our descendents who will hunger and thirst for digital meaning.

Our journey into cyberspace is like hiking up a switchback through thickets, eyes on the ground as it rises, hiking higher and higher. There suddenly come moments when we emerge in a clearing and are breathless at a view that is miles-deep. But then we grow restless again and hike higher, those moments of far-seeing the fuel of our search for a deeper communion. We interface now through digital imagery like blind people placing their hands against one another's. Out of our mutual need, we build something bigger than ourselves. The digital castle through which we walk is an interior castle in which we are astonished to discover room upon room. We had no idea what we would discover in this internalized space of our trans-planetary digital civilization where multiple-species of beings will search out one another and touch hands, palm upon palm, shocked into the possibility of a communion that extends to the limits of our finite but unbounded universe.

The ultimate intention of consciousness is to become coextensive with all the molecular structures it or we will or can create as apertures onto the outside/inside of our collective Life. That cosmic unity, that singular way of being, we will link and mine, a brain that uses whatever materials seem to work.

I stand outside your comfortable spacious home and knock on the window. Your willingness to open the drapes and have a conversation turns me from a lurker into an invited guest with whom you speak through the thick double-glassed picture window, always on the edge of turning back to your other life. And finally, I turn too, turning up my collar to the wind and going ... home.

The only way back is forward. The only way out is in. The end is always the beginning. And the willingness is always a gift.

Autumn Spring   *October 18, 1999*

Thirty years ago the first e-mail message marked the birth of the Internet, so members of our extended family are sharing memories of our digital nativity.

The visions of most Internet pioneers were limited. Most saw trees, not forests, failing to glimpse the distant horizons of new possibility they were creating

A few, such as J. C. R. Licklider, saw what would happen when we plugged computers into one another. We will live, Licklider told a gathering of world-class scientists, in a human-computer symbiosis, a coupling of symbol-manipulating networks that will be much greater than the sum of its parts.

As brilliant as those scientists were, many mocked his prophetic vision. Prisoners in their paradigms, they couldn't see past the bars of their cages.

Visionaries who see imaginary forests and foresters who tend real trees have different gifts.

Most of us miss the significant beginnings of New Things until long after they have passed. Beginnings are full of mystery and promise, darkness brooding on darker waters, while endings can be easier to spot. Toward the end of a trajectory, just when we have grown accustomed to "how things are," it will dawn on us that the trajectory is losing energy. We pause in a moment of reflection, realizing that a time of life, a way of being, a comfortable structure that had sustained us ... is not what it used to be. Not what it was.

Of course, every ending is also a beginning. Autumn leaves on the fast-flowing stream are interlaced with seeds. Nothing vanishes, nothing disappears. The universe is an engine of transformation that conserves everything, everything, even the light of dying stars as it streams toward black holes.

Horicon Marsh is one of the beautiful environments of the state of Wisconsin, a vast expanse of wetlands that stretches from horizon to horizon. My wife and I recently walked out into the marsh on a warm day, celebrating our anniversary.

It was late afternoon. The sun was low in the sky, sinking toward the flat expanse of still water. Our shadows lengthened in the tall grass and we paused, listening to the silence. The world around us was teeming with life. The edge of the light of the late afternoon seemed to be translucent, a boundary of our mutual journey.

In the spring and in the autumn, hundreds of thousands of migrating geese fill the sky above the marsh from horizon to horizon. They emerge from a vanishing point beyond the horizon into our short-term vision and fly overhead with cries growing louder and softer again as they disappear toward another vanishing point in the opposite direction.

Our children have all left home. Our decades of being a blended family have flown through the sky toward a vanishing point beyond the horizon.

One of our sons, nearly twenty years ago, yelped with regret after reading Stephen Levy's "Hackers," a chronicle of the days at MIT when the seeds of Silicon Valley were sown.

"Oh, Dad!" he cried. "I was born too late! It's all over!"

And it was. The digital world had arrived for us through the narrow aperture of an Apple II, through which we crawled at 300 bps on ASCII Express toward BBS islands in the narrow dark seas of cyberspace. The world of hackers for which he grieved was fused with an exploration of inner space defined by mainframes that had already morphed.

The progressive death of each successive network has engendered another. Death and life embrace in a slow dance, cheek on cheek. The music ends. The music begins.

In response to the column "Digital Autumn," a friend in Australia wrote:

"You write of autumn, but I look around at spring, which is well underway. The sun is higher in the sky, greens seem greener than a week ago, and nearby I can still enjoy the seldom occurrence of a whale that frolics in our harbour. Slowly the days lengthen and I seem to live in a world where our real communities are becoming more and more fragmented while digital communities are drawing us closer together. But how can this replace the ability to reach out and touch one another and look into another's eyes and share mutual moments in silence?"

Under the thin ice that forms on our hearts at the first frost, new spring life grows in the soil of irrevocable dissolution.

Autumn spring.

Life begins at edges, on the boundaries, at the interface where solitude is redeemed, transformed into community. When we touch one another and share a moment of silence, we feel the world fall away with a dying fall, we shift back into the rocking chairs of our souls, letting the inexplicable rhythms of life rock us to an unexpected beat.

Everything is ending, everything is beginning. The Internet is dissolving into the interstitial tissues of our symbiotic human/machine body/mind. The digital image of the universe filtering into our brains is a spiraling wheel of stars that fills the sky.

All of the symbol systems in the world—not just one religion but all religions, not just one civilization but all civilizations—are falling into this moment of transformation, into this black hole at the center of our galaxy. They emerge from a vanishing point beyond the horizon and disappear toward another vanishing point in the opposite direction. The body/mind conceives of a luminous cloud of new illusions, phantasms and imaginings that we will once again mistake for real gods and real demons. We can only pray that this digital pier on which we are standing will become a bridge across a galaxy teeming with life. We are like toddlers coming down the steps of our house for the first time. We are lesser lights of all those who have learned, who are learning to fly, our outward migration pouring out of the deep cave of our home planet at twilight. Filling the sky from horizon to horizon.

Our ancient identities cracking open, litter of broken shells feeding the fertile soil.

For Shirley, on our anniversary

Our Finest Hour   *March 19, 2000*

Heroism doesn't have to show up in mud-spattered tanks in battle—it can also happen in cubicles, decorated with pictures of friends or family, under humming fluorescent lights.

But regardless of where it happens, we usually notice for only a moment, then move on.

Recently speaking to a group of older men, I stopped my speech because I suddenly saw who was really sitting there. I asked how many were veterans of World War II. Most hands went up. I saw in a flash the wide sunny plain on which my generation had lived much of its life. I was moved. I acknowledged those men for what they had done to give us that life.

We live our lives in space created by others but we seldom see it.

I have waited to say anything about Y2K because I was curious—would anyone even remember a few months later that it happened?

When Y2K fizzled, it was disappointing to some, an occasion for gloating for others. One of the horse-laughs heard around the world was that computer consultants manufactured the crisis to sell services. Now, I am not naive—I know college students who once in a while release a virus into their systems so they can be called late at night to come fix it—but everyone close to the network knows that Y2K was real. Billions of lines of code needed to be fixed. Most of them were.

So heroism happened pretty much as it always does—quietly, out of the public eye. In this case, in thousands of cubicles where programmers grind out the code by which we live.

It's hard to remember something that didn't happen. We pay more attention to bad news than good. The media may exploit this tendency, but they didn't create it. We evolved this way in order to survive. Studies have shown that real crises completely erase our short term memories of the pleasant events that happened only moments before. It's critical to remember threats but memories of good times are expendable.

In one of those face-to-face coffee shop conversations that mean so much to virtual workers, a friend who works for a large e-funds company responded to the idea that Y2K had been invented.

"I don't care what anybody says. There are thousands of us who know what it took to make it a non-event. We know what we did."

Another acquaintance went to Seattle on New Year's Eve as part of a large effort to stop a terrorist attack. Their successful efforts have disappeared into the woodwork. We only remember bombs that explode.

Days full of quiet delight seldom make good movies. There is no "film blanc" to match the appeal of "film noir." But those uneventful days when life is so good we don't even notice are the source of the joy that percolates through our lives.

Getting results of a medical test that is negative. Knowing that you gave your best shot to an opportunity to make a difference. Hearing unexpectedly from someone you love. Having a conversation punctuated with silence and laughter as you walk with a friend or lover and become aware suddenly of the transparency of the twilight, the way light washes the facades of old buildings, the deep quiet pleasure of being connected to one another and to everything.

Those moments glow with invisible light that floods the landscape of our lives, filling it with the richness of the ordinary. Yet those are the moments we often have to struggle to remember.

Last week I spoke with two young people in Silicon Valley. They sounded nearly alike. Surrounded by sudden riches, housing prices spiraling upward, even the smaller ladder of menu prices climbing out of sight—they struggle not to surrender to the force field of greed that is all around them.

"It takes all my energy to maintain boundaries," said a young computer whiz. He loves to travel, loves his long-term companion, loves his creative work outside the cubicle. But he fights to stay aligned with his sane choices. "People who refuse to work 24/7 in Silicon Valley just don't count. You have to battle to hold the middle ground where you can still have a life."

A young woman who has worked with several dot coms spoke of the need to withdraw from the craziness to find herself again. "I couldn't float another time through a haze of coke toward one more IPO. I felt like I was losing my soul."

Individuals and civilizations alike can lose their souls, and both have the capacity to make hard choices on behalf of what matters most. But it isn't easy. Few movies depict people living sane balanced lives. I doubt that we'll see a war story about battalions of programmers slogging through millions of lines of old COBOL under those harsh fluorescents.

But those in the trenches know what they did. Let the media be cynical instead of making newsreels showing enemy aircraft spiraling from the sky. Those in the trenches know what they did.

Life is not about something separate from itself. Life is about itself, not symbols of itself.

This was one of our finest hours. Unacknowledged and unsung, a massive army of programmers mobilized against the enemy of our short-term thinking and fixed that code. They plodded through years of tedious remediation, not to create but to avert another Manhattan Project. This is ordinary humanity at its functional best.

Saving civilization as we know it for another generation.

So before the sun sets on this their finest hour, let us celebrate those women and men who saved us from ourselves, heroes who are already nameless and nearly forgotten. We who are mere nodes in the network you maintain—we who dissolve into the digital world without even noticing—we acknowledge and salute you.

The Shadow of the Dog   *May 26, 2001*

In the last Islands in the Clickstream, "On the Dark Side of the Moon," I quoted a friend who said: "Ants don't know that dogs exist."

To which a reader responded:

"The tasks at hand are relatively insignificant once I've glimpsed the shadow of the dog and my brain struggles toward the brilliant light behind the dog."

This happened in the middle of the night when things are either very clear or not clear at all.

On a private e-mail list, a news item was shared about a thirteen year old boy who hung himself after he was suspended from school for hacking into his school's computers. His parents, understandably bereft, blamed the suspension and the schoolmaster, who they claimed had threatened their son with jail. The schoolmaster defended himself, saying he had not.

The item elicited intense anger from young technophiles who recalled being marginalized by teachers unable to acknowledge their intelligence. They railed at the inability of schools to train teachers who understand computer technology and those adept at using it. Horror stories scrolled down the monitor of teachers who tried to control what they feared or could not understand.

One member of the list, a journalist who often champions the technophiles about whom he writes with insight, did not weigh in against the headmaster but instead shared insights grounded in memories of a suicide attempt by his own child.

The suspension and the headmaster, he suggested, were catalysts, not causes, the last wave crashing in on a child's psyche, the one "that kept him down and didn't let him come up for air. That's what it feels like to a kid committing suicide," he wrote, "like there's no air. Like it's dark and just too-damn-scary one-too-many times."

Anyone who has dealt with a suicide attempt knows that the walls get narrower and narrower, the pain greater and greater, until one day there is the overwhelming relief of the decision to end the pain. Often a person is not trying to end their life, they are trying to end the pain.

I felt for the headmaster, too. I imagine he is experiencing the torments of the damned because the helplessness we feel when we are involved with someone who is deeply depressed or self-destructive is absolute. We are outside their skins, looking in, unable to get our hands on the switch.

Maybe because it was the middle of the night, I felt the pain and anguish from every point in this particular compass. I thought of the many times, like the head-master, I have acted with less than perfect kindness. If I had a nickel for each time I spoke impatiently, harshly or stupidly to someone, I could retire in Barbados. I wish it did not take a lifetime to learn what King Lear learned at the end of his tragic suffering, that "none do offend, none." Only then, worn down into humility, do we become appropriately gentle and forbearing with people who are only doing as we have done so many times.

I was an Episcopal priest for sixteen years. I entered the ministry because I needed a training program to learn how to become a more fully human being. It required years of listening to people sharing the reality of their lives to begin to learn what I deeply wish I had always known.

They showed me what it means to respond to whatever life brings with dignity, resilience, and genuine heroism. That everyone is pretty much doing the best they can with what they have, and that everyone's story, when you really hear it, makes sense of their behavior.

My job was to make sense of what was often senseless, the sudden death of a child or a crushing reverse, events that knitted pain with seeming meaninglessness.

Ministry is often done with words. The words are intended to articulate what no one really understands. Just as loving another brings you closer to the mystery of their being, moving more deeply into the reality of others' lives makes them more mysterious and worthy of compassion.

You begin talking and, if the process works, end up keeping your mouth shut. You begin thinking you understand. You end up knowing that you haven't got a clue.

I was awake in the middle of the night because I awakened from a dream in which I was crawling along a dark fence through which I saw the faces of my mother, father, aunt, and uncle. When I awakened I remembered they had all died decades ago. I have spoken or written for a living all these years as a way to fill up the silence of their absence. My words have been a search for meaning, but paradoxically, the only time I feel close to the mystery is when I have nothing to say.

When we meditate or pray deeply, words cease to matter. The levels of consciousness we discover when we sink into a larger life erase the daylight distinctions that no longer make sense. Language falsifies if we try to say what we know in such moments.

Yesterday I listened to a master of the intelligence world discuss the depths of awareness required to go places no human being should have to go. He reminded me why the intelligence community uses spiritual tools to equip its people, why I taught courses in clairvoyance, telepathy and psychometry when I was a priest in an effort to disclose that non-local consciousness is the sea in which we all swim, that the symbolic landscape described by all of our sacred texts is the literal truth, and that the seeming miraculous is normative for human beings.

We write or speak or do whatever it is we do to affirm that life despite the ostensible evidence is meaningful and good, that we are inextricably linked in a single web of consciousness, one manifestation of life in a universe teeming with life.

Our power lies in our powerlessness. In the dark hour before the dawn when we are most alone and most ourselves, we sense connections in all directions, far beyond earth and the evidence of the senses. How do we speak of these other dimensions with mere tongues? How do we turn this insubstantial vision into flesh and blood? How do we find the courage to close our deceptive eyes and see?

A Miracle By
Any Other Name   *September 20, 2003*

If any column is about "the human dimension of technology," it's this one, inasmuch as last week, my beloved youngest son, Barnaby, had more tubes in him, more drips dripping, more monitors flashing around him than a cyborg out of *Terminator 3*.

When I arrived at the ICU and saw, moving among the noisy machinery, his still-pink hand, swollen and slow, as it reached for my hand, I cried like a baby. In such moments the fragility, transitory nature, and absolute value of life, all life, is unmistakable.

My son was riding his motorcycle on Highway 101 in California when he came around a curve into stopped traffic. He hit the back of a pick-up truck and flew through the air. When paramedics arrived at the scene, there was no blood pressure and they pumped him full of fluids and kept him as stable as they could until a heli-copter flew him to Modesto where they scanned the damage and decided that a torn aorta was the most critical injury.

He went into emergency surgery to repair the aorta. They gave fair warning that ignoring his badly broken leg might mean the loss of the leg, that bleeding from his liver had to wait, that staunching the blood flow to the spine during surgery might mean he wouldn't walk again. There is nothing to do when they read your rights but nod and sign off and get out of the way.

They repaired the aorta. The liver stopped bleeding. They operated on his shat-tered leg. They left alone his broken ribs and a crack in his upper back. They removed the ventilator and after a few days stopped the morphine drip. His vital signs are good. There's a long road ahead but it looks as if he'll make it.

Anyone who has been in an Intensive Care Unit lately knows that it looks like Ridley Scott designed it. Machines breathe, monitors regulate blood flow and drugs, cuffs flex and contract. It's like a scene out of *Bladerunner*, with robotic friends manu-factured by canny engineers, friends that keep us alive.

Among the tubes and flashing lights is the reason the technology exists—the human soul in the machinery. Without my son's beating heart, which continues to beat, thank God, the high-tech devices would have no meaning.

The prognosis according to one of the docs is "fantastic." A torn aorta is fatal 85% of the time. With the other trauma, he said, there had been perhaps a 1% chance of survival.

My son can move his arms and legs and when he speaks it is obviously still my son with his characteristic genius for insight, understatement and humor. A devout Buddhist who has meditated for long hours at the Zen Center and Tassajara

Monastery, he of all people can handle a view of a white wall, watching his mind and its shadows move.

We believe he will be OK and we are afraid to believe he will be OK. The depth and intensity of our own trauma, sourced by those telephone calls from hell, continues to linger.

Most of the doctors and nurses use words like "incredibly lucky" but some speak of a miracle and mean it. I hesitate to use that word lest those who lost loved ones wonder what happened when they could have used a miracle too. I do not pretend to understand how it all hangs together or makes sense. The older I get the more obvious it is that those who think they have a clue do not have a clue and those who know they do not have a clue have a shot.

But in and of itself, that my son is alive and himself, that he will walk and talk and live, is a miracle by any name, whatever you want to call it.

Miracles come in many forms and during this hard time they sometimes came as felt realities, palpable touches of the spirit. When many people pray, express concern and love and are aligned in a single direction, their energy is amplified. When our consciousness is stripped of trivial concerns by the bone-deep clarity of a crisis, it enables us to focus with a laser-like intensity. When you feel those forces entering your awareness it feels like thermals during a hang-glide coming up from under. It feels like being lifted in a wave, like being a self-conscious node in a network aware of all the connections, knowing the pattern of the pattern of the web.

Our gratitude is impossible to express in such moments because it is absolute and words make everything relative. The choice of people to be there for us is sheer gift and grace and it is impossible to underestimate the impact of a kind word or a prayer. The extremity of our need may magnify the felt power of this unmerited benevolence but even in normal mundane everyday life compassion and generosity of spirit are the glue of the universe.

Anyone who believes the universe only works bottom up and not top down as well is missing some of the data. It begins and ends with consciousness as surely as a network map includes an image of the Big Picture as well as nodes feeling each other out, knitting themselves together from all sides. When we extend ourselves toward each other's needs we make a connection, becoming something more for a moment but in fact becoming only what we have always been, a singular being not always fully aware of itself in all its particulars, alive in a universe more like thought than stuff or maybe thought and stuff at the same time. As I said, I really haven't got a clue; just an inkling. An inkling made as bold as the brush stroke of a Zen master on an empty canvas by a moment of transparent clarity and utter terror.

Talking to Ourselves   *January 14, 2004*

Once upon a time in the sixties, I published a short story in Analog Science Fiction about a man who invented a virtual reality machine and let a carnival owner try it out. The carnival owner was so hypnotized by the fantasy world and its contrast with the grim realities of his life that he never wanted to leave the machine.

Twenty-plus years later I was watching the *Twilight Zone* and was startled when a short episode consisted of my story. There was the machine, the person who wanted to stay in it, everything. Obviously, I thought, someone had read the story and used it as the basis for the television program—without paying royalties.

I contacted the producers and received a telephone call from Harlan Ellison. I was star struck because I had been reading and admiring his science fiction for years, so I was predisposed to believe what he told me.

The story had evolved through parallel evolution, Harlan insisted. He sent me a stack of scripts that showed how the story had changed from version to version and arrived at a similar form by a different route. I accepted his explanation.

Recently I reviewed some stories written in my forties to see if I could revise them. One called "Learning Curve" used the device of a time machine to show how a middle-aged man looked back on mistakes he had made growing up, mostly due to decisions he made about how to interpret what was happening. Those decisions determined his identity, and identity is destiny. Who we think we are is how we choose to express our lives. So the middle-aged man went back to critical moments in his history to try to teach his younger self a better way, to give himself the benefit of his wisdom.

Each time he tried to teach himself a lesson, however, it was beyond the grasp of the younger person. At the end, when he ventured to the recent past and saw himself trudging up the walk to his home, his spirit deflated by a recent divorce, he realized he had nothing else to say; all he could do was step out of the shrubs, tell himself that he understood, and hold his younger self while it cried.

Once he learned to be compassionate toward himself, he stopped looking backward and could move forward again.

That story had promise, I thought, because of its emotional truth. But I am not going to revise it because, in the years since, a movie starring Bruce Willis called *The Kid* told a similar story. People would think I had stolen a plot device that was already trite when I used it.

The writers of the script arrived at a similar plot by parallel evolution, I imagine, and if I could see the revisions of the script before it took final form, it would probably resemble what Ellison had sent.

A decade later, I relate the story as much to mentoring as to introspection. When we mentor someone, particularly when we are in our fifties and they are in their twenties and thirties, we are talking not only to them but also to our younger selves, but this time with compassion. Some mistakes are inevitable, we know, and we can't learn what we need to know without the detours that turn out to be the most direct route to maturity.

Several of our children were with us last month for the holidays and it was a wonderful time. Everybody is an adult now and we relate to one another less as parents and children and more as older and younger adults. My youngest son—whose motorcycle accident I described in a former column that I wrote in the waiting room of the ICU after we knew he would live—was one of our visitors. He is healing and we are grateful.

My son and I stopped for a latte late one afternoon. Through the coffeeshop window on the Milwaukee River, we could see the woods which had not yet filled with snow and the cold river. We watched the trees thicken and dissolve in the dusk as we talked about the transitoriness of all things, his deep and terrible insight into the nature of appearances and what we call realities. We tried to make our lattes last, stretch the canvas of time over the frame of the lengthening shadows. We spoke the most real things we know. But at last the twilight knitted the trees into an inscrutable darkness and we had to go.

That conversation is a self-referential image—it is what it was about. It is a transparent stained glass window illuminating movement with illusory images of fixity.

Was there any way for either of us to learn what we know by an easier route? Was there any way for me to relieve the ones I love of the necessity of traveling their own roads? I guess not. As my forever-unpublished story pointed out, the only road is the one we walk. The knowledge of the impermanence of all things creates in us if we are paying attention a compassionate heart which is willing to listen and understand and at the end embrace and feel both love and the hard edges of boundaries defining our individual destinies.

There is no greater joy than loving and mentoring when we can, but I know now that whenever I mentor another, I am really healing my younger self who longed at critical moments for someone older, more knowing, more loving, to show up and just be there. The grace of my life has been the realization that whenever I really needed that, someone did. Their faces are in the lighted hallways of my memories, portraits of my own personal saints, the ones that matter most. Nor does it diminish their contribution or value to know that they too reached their mature selves by a process of evolution parallel to my own and that they too were talking not only but also to themselves.

Coming of Age   *March 23, 2004*

The number isn't important, friends have been saying when I talk about turning sixty. Some say, age is only a state of mind. Some say, you're as young as you feel. Some say, age doesn't matter.

And some say, "You look great!" which unfortunately confirms that there really are three stages of life: youth, middle-age, and you look great!

Well, my well-intended friends, I am here to tell you that age does matter. In some ways, it matters a lot.

When older people and younger people talk, they look at each other differently. Younger people have a shorter gaze.

I was taught the meaning of a long gaze by a high school teacher, Miss Mc-Cutcheon, who gave me her long teacher's gaze during an English class. I felt like a butterfly, pinned and wriggling. When another student asked what she was seeing, she said simply, "Some day someone is really going to love that boy."

I couldn't handle that. I was fifteen, fat and self-conscious and confused. I squirmed, turned red and snapped something back ... but have never forgotten what she said. At a time when love seemed beyond my reach, her insight was deeper than mine, living as I did half-blind and half-crazy in an adolescent storm of rain hail and thunder.

Coming up to sixty, we see other people, especially younger ones, more often with that long look. We see who they are and who they can become if they only attend to the better angels of their natures.

Sometimes there are moments during such conversations when it feels as if the years fall away and transparencies of other conversations, ones that happened years ago, meld with the one I am having now. Memories control the present moment, capturing it with a force field of longing and grief before the experience becomes transparent to its underlying dynamics, the irrevocability of my own past juxtaposed with seemingly innumerable futures for the one to whom I am speaking, branching like blossoms of forbidden opportunity.

Then the regret fades, replaced by encompassing acceptance of the only life we have to live.

We may not know how to say what we know in such a moment, but we do know and we know that we know.

We are no longer innocent, coming to sixty. We know what evils can befall us. We know, as Robert Frost, said that there are finalities besides the grave. We know ourselves, sometimes too well. We remember too many people we have loved and held as they died. Somehow the degree to which we have lived with passion and gusto informs our awareness of death as well as our love of life.

Two recent movies, *Lost In Translation* and *Eternal Sunshine of the Spotless Mind*, capture magnificently the poignancy of moments of love and loss, showing connections deep bone-in-the-socket solid for only a moment before the whirlwinds of our lives take us again in different directions.

I love good films the way I loved good books as a child. Coming up to sixty, I accept that being a latchkey kid and losing my parents early gave me a particular destiny. William Gibson, the cyberpunk writer, notes at his web site that many writers share that kind of loss or other early childhood trauma. We find solace in the world of imagination and images, building meaning from the tools at hand. Books and films provide points of reference for sharing insights, giving us a common language.

In another great film, *My Dinner with Andre*, Wallace Shawn and Andre Gregory say that a moment of genuine connection with another person heightens our awareness of being alone, too, and to accept that we're alone is to accept death, because somehow when you're alone you're alone with death.

That's the implicit affirmation when the protagonist of *Eternal Sunshine* says OK. OK. to a doomed trajectory of romantic love. It is also the moment of genius at the end of *Lost in Translation* when the director/writer makes the final words whispered by Bill Murray in the car of his young friend impossible to hear.

It doesn't matter what he said, and it doesn't matter what I say either. We always fail to articulate what we nevertheless unceasingly try to say, the deepest truths we know, which can only be suggested like the moment of waking from a dream more real than the sunlight streaming through the window, when we know we will never remember the dream exactly but nevertheless have another day, another day, another day in which to pursue it.

Coming to sixty does make a difference. It is clear that what we mistook for achievement is empty air, unless it made a real contribution, unless it made a difference, it is clear that mostly self-serving efforts deliver as much satisfaction as drinking from a dribble glass.

Still, we are left with questions, not answers.

Which were the moments of genuine self-transcendence in which I was called to be more than I thought I was and somehow fulfilled the promise? Which did I miss? What is possible in the time left, as eyesight fades but the sharper-eyed inner gaze of an ancient mariner discerns with greater clarity what matters most?

If we are fortunate, the choices we make now, coming to sixty, were determined many years ago when earlier decisions built the karma of our destiny. We all fail, and we all succeed. There is nothing now but the sudden unexpected opportunity, nothing but being ready. There is nothing to hold back, no energy to save for another day.

I know that I am alone with life and death. Even in moments of the deepest communion, I can feel the world turn and the spiraling universe bend away from my embrace. Moments of dizzying lucidity, seeing the anchor of the life given and the life received for what it is, counterweight or ballast, nothing amassed.